RUTHLESS CRITICISM

RUTHLESS CRITICISM

New Perspectives
in U.S. Communication
History

William S. Solomon

Robert W. McChesney

editors

University of Minnesota Press
Minneapolis
London

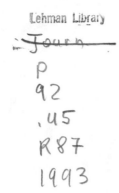

Published by the University of Minnesota Press
2037 University Avenue Southeast, Minneapolis, MN 55455-3092
Printed in the United States of America on acid-free paper

Library of Congress Cataloging-in-Publication Data

Ruthless criticism : new perspectives in U.S. communication history /
    William S. Solomon, Robert W. McChesney.
        p.   cm.
    Includes bibliographical references and index.
    ISBN 0-8166-2169-1 (alk. paper).—ISBN 0-8166-2170-5 (pbk. :
alk. paper)
    1. Communication—United States—History. 2. Mass media—United
States—History. I. Solomon, William Samuel. II. McChesney,
Robert Waterman, 1952–   .
P92.U5R87   1993
302.23'0973—dc20   92-36571
                                                               CIP

The University of Minnesota is an
equal-opportunity educator and employer.

To our parents

Leonard and Gertrude Solomon
Meg and Parker McChesney

CONTENTS

Acknowledgments

Most kinds of work, as sociologist Howard Becker notes, are collective behavior. Accordingly, we would like to thank those who have supported this project. At Rutgers University, encouragement came from all the journalism faculty and staff, notably Professor Richard Hixson, and from Dean Richard Budd. Dr. Dania Stager-Snow, director of computer services, provided invaluable help. At the University of Wisconsin, thanks to Professors James L. Baughman and Stephen Vaughn, and at the University of Washington, to Pat Dinning. Finally, Janaki Bakhle, our editor at the University of Minnesota Press, has been excellent, as has her assistant Robert Mosimann.

Chapter 1

The Contours of Media History
William S. Solomon

We realize all the more clearly what we have to accomplish in the present—I am
speaking of ruthless criticism of everything existing, *ruthless in two senses: The*
criticism must not be afraid of its own conclusions, nor of conflict with the powers
that be.

Karl Marx, letter to Arnold Ruge, September 1843

Both past and present are matters of interpretation, because different
meanings may be given to the same event. For example, the second
Persian Gulf War was debated, variously, as a noble attempt by the
United States to dethrone a tyrant and as a cynical attempt by a U.S.
president to boost his popularity by appealing to patriotism. Further,
the meaning attached to an event can influence how other events are
interpreted.[1] Thus, the above two interpretations of a U.S. foreign
policy suggest quite different views of the U.S. political system and
of the news media that cover it. As with current events, so with the
past: there is "an inevitable taking of sides which comes from selection and emphasis in history."[2] Thus, one's view of the past depends
in good part on one's view of the present — and vice versa.

In the United States today, the public sphere is sharply curtailed
by the corporate sector's increasingly concentrated ownership of the
mass media: "23 corporations control most of the business in daily
newspapers, magazines, television, books, and motion pictures."[3]
Given capitalist pressures to maximize profits, media conglomerates
treat public service as lip service. In the words of an ABC executive,
"The network is paying affiliates to carry network commercials,
not programs. What we are is a distribution system for Procter &
Gamble."[4] Clearly, commercial broadcasting is neither primarily a
tool for education nor an expression of the public interest. "Public"
broadcasting also is dependent on funds from the corporate sector,

1

as rightist political forces have cut back its federal funding. There are no alternative broadcast or cable TV networks. Mainstream print media vastly overshadow alternative media.

Barring dramatic political change, corporate acquisitions and mergers of "media properties" will continue. The media themselves report such activities simply as stock market intrigues — they do not mention the impact on control of public information and mass culture. The democratic potential of new communication technologies will not offset this trend, as these technologies will develop within the same political economy that fosters the mergers and acquisitions.[5]

How did we get to this point? Traditional histories, as John C. Nerone explains in chapter 3 of this volume, paint the mass media as pluralistic agents of progress, maturing and improving as U.S. society evolves toward a more egalitarian form. Such images are consonant with those in grammar school textbooks, yet they do little to explain contemporary society. To reconcile an intensely centralized media with an image of society as democratic and pluralist, the traditional view cites professional ethics, new technologies, and "market forces" as being sufficiently dynamic and/or unpredictable as to make largely irrelevant the issue of media ownership. Thus, capitalism and democracy are compatible, if not interdependent.

This book challenges that premise. The diversity of media voices in the nineteenth century did not lead to a richer and more diverse array of media voices today, to a public sphere where all voices have equal loudness. Rather, U.S. capitalism's development in the nineteenth century and its transition, starting late in the century, from a "proprietary" phase to a "corporate" phase brought the rise of a culture industry that now dominates the public discourse.[6]

Accounting for a culture industry requires different histories than would account for a pluralistic and democratic media system. Happily, recent scholarship has begun to redress the imbalance in journalism and mass communication historiography. This book provides a critical component of this effort to redefine the contours of media history. It offers alternative approaches to the study of such history, examines lesser-studied media, and reexamines dominant media. In chapter 2, Michael Warner uses critical theory and deconstruction to explain the meaning of print during the colonial era. He argues that this should be understood in terms of a basic transformation in social structure, and not "an ahistoric point of reference, such as the intrinsic nature of individuals, reason, or technology."

John C. Nerone notes that "a medium is a set of relationships within a social and cultural ecology." He argues for a more inclusive view than that taken by traditional histories of the media, in terms of the kinds of media studied and their social context. His chapter is a case study of a community and its media: the antebellum press in Cincinnati.

In her chapter on the suffrage press, Linda Steiner uses the concept of community in terms of culture rather than geography. As the suffrage movement sought to articulate new images of women, from the antebellum period to beyond the turn of the century, it experienced much hostility from the general-circulation press and much internal debate. Perhaps as a result of these interactions, the suffrage press developed a different model of journalism than was used by the general-circulation press.

The latter's model, as Gerald J. Baldasty documents for the post-Civil War era, focused on constantly improving the marketability and profitability of its product. News was not treated as a means of telling the public about what it ought to know, regardless of the consequences for circulation figures or advertising revenues. Baldasty lays to rest any notion of the pre-media conglomerate press as being concerned primarily with providing a public service. Here the values of today's culture industry can be seen quite clearly: a 1992 study of the U.S. mass media documents advertisers' pressures on media content.[7]

Yet the latter half of the nineteenth century did have many kinds of media, including a vibrant labor press. In chapter 6, Holly Allen explores conflicting images of gender within the Knights of Labor, as shown through its newspapers. While challenging the growth of corporate capitalism, this movement remained more traditional in its thinking about gender, empowering women only up to a point.

Jon Bekken outlines the diversity of political views within the working-class community at the turn of the century. He illustrates the economic difficulties that labor papers faced in operating within a capitalist society. But the culture industry did not become dominant solely because of "market forces" — government repression played a key role.

Albert Kreiling examines the development of a commercial press in the black community, through a study of the Chicago *Defender*. He emphasizes the cultural and political factions that advocated different models of journalism.

A powerful aspect of the culture industry was the advent of radio, which brought "the outside world into the individual home."[8] The commercial broadcast system needed a basis for pricing its transactions between broadcasters and advertisers. The ratings system, as Eileen R. Meehan shows, embraced sexist assumptions that persist, in varied forms, to the present.

In his chapter, Robert W. McChesney refutes some long-held myths about U.S. broadcasting. Although many countries have chosen government-sponsored broadcast systems, the scholarly and popular consensus in the United States has been that this system always has been a commercial one. McChesney documents a vital step in the building of a culture industry and the curtailing of a public sphere: the replacing of educational, labor, and religious broadcasters with commercial ones, and the subsequent erasure of nonprofit broadcasters' pioneering role from the record of the broadcast system's origins.

Television's advent was far more than a chance for the broadcast networks to increase their profits: Lynn Spigel shows that television in its formative years was contested terrain for society's images of childhood.

The television networks' political timidity during their formative years underlines the powerful links between the federal government and the culture industry.[9] Nancy E. Bernhard documents the networks' almost slavish attempts to curry favor with the government. The latter often determined program content or supplied programming, thus shaping the public discourse on public policy.

Accompanying the culture industry's rise in the twentieth century was the development of mass communication research. This field's close cooperation with commercial interests has received study.[10] Christopher Simpson documents what is perhaps a still more basic influence — that of the military. He examines the U.S. government's key role in creating and developing this field: essentially, the government financed it and determined its foci, from World War I through the post-Vietnam era.

Finally, actions may have unintended consequences.[11] Examining popular culture from 1960 through 1968, Susan J. Douglas shows that it contained mixed messages on female sexuality and social roles. The culture industry sought only the purchasing power of teenage girls. Yet its television shows, films, and popular music suggested empowerment as well as traditional values, in time affecting the political consciousness of millions of women.

This book, then, offers critical scholarship of our past, distant and recent. Each chapter represents current, original work not previously published. Each was commissioned specifically for this volume. The chapters employ diverse approaches, but they are united by their authors' conviction that, rather than strive to be value-free and purely objective, "it is the social responsibility of the historian to do work that will be useful in solving the critical human problems of our time."[12]

Notes

1. This argument is based on Harvey Molotch and Marilyn Lester, "News as Purposive Behavior: On the Strategic Use of Routine Events, Accidents, and Scandals," *American Sociological Review* (February 1974): 101–12.

2. Howard Zinn, *A People's History of the United States* (New York: Harper & Row, 1980), 10.

3. *The Media Monopoly* 3d ed. (Boston: Beacon, 1990), 4. I use Jürgen Habermas's concept, the public sphere, as developed in his 1962 work, *The Structural Transformation of the Public Sphere* (Cambridge: MIT Press, 1989). For an explanation of this concept, see the first part of Michael Warner's essay in this volume.

4. Cited in Ronald K. L. Collins, *Dictating Content: How Advertising Pressure Can Corrupt a Free Press* (Washington, D.C.: Center for the Study of Commericalism, 1992), back cover.

5. For discussions of the power of the U.S. corporate sector, see Thomas Ferguson and Joel Rogers, *Right Turn: The Decline of the Democrats and the Future of American Politics* (New York: Hill & Wang, 1986); Michael Schwartz, ed., *The Structure of Power in America* (New York: Homes & Meier, 1987); and Maurice Zeitlin, *The Large Corporation and Contemporary Classes* (New Brunswick, N.J.: Rutgers University Press, 1989).

6. Martin J. Sklar, *The Corporate Reconstruction of American Capitalism, 1890–1916* (New York: Cambridge University Press, 1988). Sklar argues for capitalism's transition; the link to a culture industry is mine. For a discussion of the culture industry, see Max Horkheimer and Theodor W. Adorno, *Dialectic of Enlightenment* (New York: Continuum, 1989 [1944]). For contemporary examinations of the culture industry, see Ian Angus and Sut Jhally, eds. *Cultural Politics in Contemporary America* (New York: Routledge, 1989); Stuart Ewen, *All Consuming Images* (New York: Basic Books, 1988); Donald Lazere, *American Media and Mass Culture* (Berkeley: University of California Press, 1987); Mark Crispin Miller, *Boxed In: The Culture of Television* (Evanston, Ill.: Northwestern University Press, 1988); and Herbert I. Schiller, *Culture, Inc.* (New York: Oxford University Press, 1989).

7. Collins, *Dictating Content*.

8. Daniel J. Czitrom, *Media and the American Mind* (Chapel Hill: University of North Carolina Press, 1982), 60.

9. Erik Barnouw, *Tube of Plenty* (New York: Oxford University Press, 1975).

10. Todd Gitlin, "Media Sociology: The Dominant Paradigm," *Theory and Society* 6 (July 1978).

11. This point was made by sociologist Michael Schwartz in a March 25, 1992, talk at Rutgers University.

12. Howard Zinn, *The Politics of History* (Urbana: University of Illinois Press, 1990 [1970]), xi.

Chapter 2

The Public Sphere and the Cultural Mediation of Print
Michael Warner

The West treasures few moments in its history the way it treasures the story of the democratization of print. In the century preceding the American and French revolutions, men of letters commonly linked the spread of letters to the growth of knowledge. From an early date they linked it to the democratization of power as well. In their eyes, the citizen's reading took on a mythic significance that it has never lost, even to the present. In this respect, if in no other, we still regard the actors in the Enlightenment roughly as they thought of themselves: as members of a republic of letters. Few still have unqualified faith in the period's claims to reason and progress, but almost all consider it to have been a period that brought about the styles of rationalization and progressive thinking that we call modernity. And almost all would consider the letters of the republic to have played a role in the emergence of that modernity.

But this idea of a revolution in the reading of citizens raises some of the deepest problems in the self-image of Western modernity. Are we to think of the spread of print discourse as ensuring the triumph of the individual and the empowerment of the people? If so, one problem is that "individual" and "people" emerge from a historical change that they themselves could not have brought about. If printing helped give these entities their distinctively modern nature — citizen-individual and national people — then the change in print cannot be explained as the expression of the individual and the people. Instead, it would signal a broad change in social and cultural systems, in which individual and people would be local outcomes rather than origins. Nor can we take for granted the timeless value of peoples and individualisms that have such a specific and recent history. Shall we, on the other hand, attribute the power of print discourse to the intrinsic logic of print technology? If so, nothing necessarily warrants the implication of progress, reason, and freedom. Modern uses of print might illustrate either a systemic sociocultural change or the determining force of technology, but neither of these need be very reassuring ways of telling our own history. Either way, the narrative poses a problem for such uncontested terms of value as *individual, people, reason,* and *democracy.*

In *The Structural Transformation of the Public Sphere* (1962), Jürgen Habermas makes a powerful argument that printing led to a change in the political life of the West.[1] He describes a set of institutions that he calls the bourgeois public sphere, developed in the West beginning late in the seventeenth century. In this new public sphere political discourse could be separated both from the state and from civil society, the realm of private life (including economic life). It could therefore regulate or criticize both. Because of this autonomy, this space that allowed critical regulation, the bourgeois public sphere played a key role in bringing about both the democratic revolutions of the eighteenth century and the modern nation-states that followed. Habermas argues that the independence of the public sphere has since eroded; the media of publicity, in his view, have become increasingly colonized and have lost their critical relation to both the state and civil society. From the beginning, however, reading holds the key place in his narrative. Habermas tells the story of an increasing differentiation of a public sphere from state and civil society as primarily a story about new uses of texts. Newspapers, literary salons, coffeehouses, novels, art criticism, and magazines all play important roles in his account of how the fundamental structure of politics changed.

How did reading come to be so important? One of the great virtues of *Structural Transformation* is that it treats the reading practices of the late seventeenth and early eighteenth centuries not just as more reading, but as a new kind of institution. Reading was relevant in a new way because print discourse was now systematically differentiated from the activities of the state and from civil society. That is why the transformation Habermas describes is fundamentally structural, as his title implies. This perceptive analysis raises the question of how the citizen's reading acquired its new structurally relevant difference from other institutions. And on this score, Habermas follows the traditional premises of the story: he describes a growing tendency of individuals to assert autonomy and citizenship by virtue of their reading and publishing. He sees the dissemination of print quite simply as creating new opportunities for individuals to make public use of their reason. This capacity of individuals to make public use of their reason is supposed as a constant potential. It may be brought into play by historical contingencies, but it does not itself vary locally or historically.

How can we describe the history of the transformation without holding constant the value terms of modernity? There is no doubt that an important transformation took place. And there is no doubt that this transformation was fundamentally one of social structure, linked to the dominant institutions of our world: bureaucratic states, regulated economies, representational democracy, public media, and the like. The problem is to analyze the historical transformation in print discourse as fully historical — to analyze it without attributing its significance to an ahistoric point of reference, such as the intrinsic nature of individuals, reason, or technology.

One of my theses here is that print discourse was a cultural matrix in which the definitions of *individual, print, public,* and *reason* were readjusted in a new set of ground rules for discourse. The politics of printed texts in republican America lay as much in the cultural meaning of their printedness as in their objectified nature or the content of their arguments. The force of the technology and the act of reading performed by the individual citizen were redetermined in the course of this social transformation. What I am calling the cultural meaning of printedness can easily remain invisible. Yet printed objects — which we would commonsensically call "publications" — are intelligible only under very special conditions. To think of them as publications, we must make certain assumptions about texts, speakers, addressees, and the "public." The assumptions that make printed works intelligible as publications also help determine how the political arena operates. They are the basis for deciding who speaks, to whom, with what constraints, and with what legitimacy. Such power-laden but silent decisions could be called the metapolitics of speech. They are always linked to whatever passes for common sense about the medium in use.

Enlightenment intellectuals often expressed strong views about the medium of print. In 1765, for example, in the early stages of an imperial crisis and of his career as a lawyer, John Adams wrote a brief retrospect of the political and legal history of the West. The essay, which appeared unsigned and untitled in four installments in the *Boston Gazette*, depicts the history of power as a history of knowledge.[2] It tells modern history as a story of human self-determination rising through reflection. Much of the power of such a narrative for Adams, as later for D'Alembert and others, was that it offered him a

political self-understanding. But Adams's history offers a more particular self-understanding in two main respects: its history of self-
determination yields a protonationalist consciousness of America,
and its history of reflection takes the form of a history of letters. Writing at the very moment when America was emerging as a symbolic
entity, Adams perfected a story of America's history. It is a history of
literature, and its telos is emancipation.

This is how it works. According to Adams, the papal and feudal
political systems of Europe rested in the last analysis on what might
be called a hegemony of letters: "All these opinions, they [the clergy
and the feudal lords] were enabled to spread and rivet among the
people, by reducing their minds to a state of sordid ignorance and
staring timidity; and by infusing into them a *religious* horror of letters
and knowledge" (1:112). Because the entire political system of feudal
Europe depends on such a relation of populace and letters, a history
of letters can be a history of emancipation. For the same reason, the
emancipation for which the world has longed can be realized in
America. Adams writes:

> From the time of the reformation, to the first settlement of *America*,
> knowledge gradually spread in Europe, but especially in *England*; and in
> proportion as *that* increased and spread among the people, *ecclesiastical* and
> *civil* tyranny, which I use as synonimous expressions, for the *cannon* and
> *feudal* laws, seem to have lost their strength and weight. The people grew
> more and more sensible of the wrong that was done them, by these
> systems; more and more impatient under it; and determined at all hazards
> to rid themselves of it. . . . It was this great struggle, that peopled America.
> (1:113)

The Puritan colonists emerge as the heroes in a political history of
enlightenment.

Adams is aware that the civic humanist terms of such a history
conflict with the terms of American Protestantism's self-understanding.
Yet he presses his point by arguing that the reason for the Puritans'
emigration "was not religion *alone,* as is commonly supposed."
Rather, he claims, it was that they "had become intelligent in general,
and many of them learned"; "to many of them, the historians, ora-
tors, poets and philosophers of *Greece* and *Rome* were quite familiar:
and some of them have left libraries that are still in being, consisting
chiefly of volumes, in which the wisdom of the most enlightened ages
and nations is deposited" (1:113–14). We are perhaps unaccustomed
to seeing the Puritans described as republican classicists in this way.

And the history of racial and sectarian conflict in New England has taught us to be skeptical of Adams's claim that they committed "no other crime than their knowledge, and their freedom of enquiry and examination" (1:114). But the story is a powerful one. Treating enlightenment republicanism as the latent meaning of Puritan history, and employing terms that are simultaneously world historical and national, Adams's revisionist history became a pillar of American nationalism, and has remained so to the present. The success of Adams's narrative depends on his ability to revise the meaning of the Puritans' relation to letters. Rather than simply arguing that they developed a critique of the canon and feudal laws, he argues that they bought libraries.

With respect to the Bible, Adams's history is not far from the Puritans' self-understanding. John Foxe, for example, had famously claimed that "the Lord began to work for his Church not with sword and target to subdue His exalted adversary, but with printing, writing and reading. . . . How many printing presses there be in the world, so many blockhouses there be against the high castle of St Angelo, so that either the pope must abolish knowledge and printing or printing at length will root him out."[3] Adams obviously draws on this rhetorical tradition in Protestantism, but there is a crucial difference between his version and Foxe's. Foxe was able to claim world-historical importance for printing only because of a very determinate assumption about *what* would be printed against the pope. As Stephen Greenblatt has argued in a chapter titled "The Word of God in the Age of Mechanical Reproduction," Protestant reading reinforces the authority of the sacred text even as it translates authority to the private register:

> When Tyndale writes of arming oneself with the syllables of Scripture, or Bainham speaks of his fear that this word of God—pointing to the book in his hand—would damn him, we must take them at very close to the literal meaning: the printed English New Testament is, above all, a form of power. It is invested with the ability to control, guide, discipline, console, exalt, and punish that the Church had arrogated to itself for centuries.[4]

Protestant printing did not take self-reflection as an independent goal; its absolute goal was divine truth, which could provide a basis for social organization because it was assumed to be fixed and knowable independent from, and as a limit to, the rational pursuit of self-interest. Ignoring this organizing and disciplinary force of sacred exegesis, Adams must see the Puritans' literacy as self-reflection for its own sake, and thus as emancipatory in character, if he is to regard their westward migration as the beginning of a national history of enlightenment.

Between Puritanism and Adams's history of Puritanism, the cultural meaning of letters has begun to change, as has their relation to power. No longer a technology of privacy underwritten by divine authority, letters have become a technology of publicity whose meaning in the last analysis is civic and emancipatory. It will be recalled that the struggles leading to the colonial revolution were largely undertaken by writers. At the same time that colonists were engaging in violent crowd actions, organized lawbreaking, and boycotts, they also engineered a newspaper and pamphlet war in a way that was arguably more integral to the American resistance than to any other revolution. Those who organized the revolutionary struggle and were placed in power by it were men of letters. Their paper war articulated and helped to mobilize an intercolonial and protonational public — a public that remained a public of readers. And it was through the texts of that paper war that the democratic revolution in the colonies had such far-reaching impact both on the continent and in the New World. The transformation of letters that lies behind Adams's history was no mean affair.

For Adams, too, the republican destiny of letters takes on a national importance in the context of a global revolution. And indeed, the rising sense in the colonies of letters' importance had important transatlantic parallels. After 1695, printers had rapidly moved out into English towns such as Manchester, Birmingham, Liverpool, Bristol, and Canterbury. Just at the moment when colonists were setting up shop and establishing weekly newspapers, their counterparts in the English provinces were doing the same, and London printers were beginning to produce dailies. The appearance of the press in such places as Annapolis, New York, and Charleston, therefore, figures in narratives that involve the British empire as well as Europe and its empires. The growth of the trade, for one thing, was clearly supported by the financial revolution of the 1690s, with its new methods of capitalization. And the new forms of print discourse sutured emergent forms of political and social organization. Printers were simultaneously products of the transformation of the West and agents in the creation of the West's self-identification, producing the universalizing discourses of the Enlightenment and of the democratic revolutions. American colonists such as Adams made major contributions to those discourses, so the historical horizon of modernity must be made visible in any account of the printing activities of the North American English creoles.

What, then, was the relation between republican enlightenment and printing? Adams implicitly poses the question by arguing that they are identical. In this sense his history is also a theory of print: insofar as his narrative has a plot, the unity and progress of that plot stem from the nature of print. For, while he argues that learning and the press bring about changes in the political world, Adams assumes that printing's purposes, uses, and meaning do not themselves undergo change. The press is a powerful instrument for enlightenment precisely because its nature is *not* contingent. If it were variable in its nature, it might in some circumstances support despotism rather than liberty, and the history of enlightenment would lack a propulsive logic. It would have been hard, for example, for Adams to argue for the democratically enlightening character of print and yet account for the ancient use of printing among the Chinese and the Uighur Turks — who represent, for eighteenth-century thinkers such as himself, the very types of Oriental despotism. In order to pose our question with regard to Adams's rhetoric — to ask, in other words, what was the relation between printing and the Enlightenment, or between printing and republicanism — we have to assume that the purposes, uses, and meaning of print *do* change. The rhetoric of Adams's history would thus be seen as a part of a transformation in the character of print, although his history presupposes the contrary. The establishment of newspapers, the rise of empiricism, capitalism, the Enlightenment, the novel, the democratic revolutions, the rise of a bureaucratic state — all these bear important relations to print; but they might entail transformations *of* print, not just social changes affected by a medium with its own unchanging logic.

The point is worth stressing. Most of the historians who work in the burgeoning field of the history of the book, and most people who speculate on the place of print in history, assume quite the opposite. At some level they suppose printing to be a nonsymbolic form of material reality. Printing, in this view, is naturally distinct both from rhetoric, such as the rhetoric of republicanism, and from forms of subjectivity, such as the enlightenment of citizens. It is mere technology, a medium itself unmediated. There are two main advantages to this set of premises: first, it guarantees that there will be a single object of study, despite vast and frequent changes in the world of culture; and second, it allows one to trace the effects of print within culture by bracketing cultural history itself, since it guarantees that the effects of printing will have a progressive teleology. The history of print, conceptualized by means of these assumptions, was formed by Harold Innis and others in the years after World War II; it often has taken a McLuhanite cast, especially in the work of Elizabeth Eisenstein, Walter Ong, and those who are influenced by them.[5] Print technology is seen as having a logic internal to itself, a logic that exerts causative force in human affairs. The invention of printing, for example, is said to have encouraged rationalization and democratization. And on this model of print history both the right and the left agree. It provides the basis for Ong's nostalgic and rather theological speculations as well as the critical Marxism of his colleague Alvin Gouldner. Gouldner summarizes baldly:

> What the revolution in printing technology did was to democratize the culture of writing. It was consequential, though scarcely alone in this, for a quantitative increase in public discourse and also, for qualitative changes in its character. Like writing, printing and printed objects decontextualized speech and tended to reduce the modalities of communication.[6]

This kind of assertion has gone so unchallenged that it is now common even in the popular histories offered by the mass media. And it cannot go without remark that such a statement bears a striking resemblance to Adams's Whig history.

The assumptions behind the Whig-McLuhanite model of print history operate on a very deep level. Many of those who rely on the model would concede the argument that printing's force depends on its context. Eisenstein in particular regards her work as studying the character of print within the religious and scientific cultures of early modern Europe. Yet the appeal to the agency of print upon culture tends to reintroduce a privilege for technology, for the model of causation presupposes that printing and culture are discrete entities. At the very moment when historians draw their conclusions about the historical effects of printing, they bracket the political and symbolic constitution of print. Just after Eisenstein acknowledges that the consequences of early printing depended on its institutional context, for instance, she goes on to say:

> Yet the fact remains that once presses were established in numerous European towns, the transforming powers of print did begin to take effect. . . . Intellectual and spiritual life, far from remaining unaffected, were profoundly transformed by the multiplication of new tools for duplicating books in fifteenth-century Europe. The communications shift altered the way Western Christians viewed their sacred book and the

natural world. It made the words of God appear more multiform and His handiwork more uniform. The printing press laid the basis for both literal fundamentalism and for modern science.[7]

Politics and human agency disappear from this narrative, whether the agency be individual or collective, and culture receives an impact generated outside itself. Religion, science, capitalism, republicanism, and the like appear insofar as they are affected by printing, not for the way they have entered into the constitution and meaning of print in the first place. The result is that enlightenment and democratization, instead of being seen as politically contested aspects of social organization, now appear as the exfoliation of material technology. Despite the best intentions, print history tends toward Jack Goody's technodeterminism, which sees literate elites as rising with writing and falling with printing—an exchange that appears to have taken place independent of contingent social relations, actions, and representations. In some cases the model of analysis behind this picture is actually less sophisticated than John Adams's, for while he saw printing as having the same progressive effects, he did not fantasize a history of those effects that would bypass the domain of politics and rhetoric.

By attributing social changes of great scale partly to printing, the McLuhanite historians follow a model in which the logic of the technology is seen to "press on and impress both on social activity and human consciousness."[8] This kind of technological determinism must suppose, therefore, that a technology could come about, already equipped with its "logic," *before* it impinged on human consciousness and *before* it became a symbolic action. Otherwise, the object of inquiry would not lie outside the field of collective action and the symbolic order, but would be a contingent part of that field. The technology would no longer appear to have determining power of its own, independent from the collective purposes, social organization, symbolic structure, and practical labor in which it would be constituted. This fundamental premise—that technology has an ontological status prior to culture—must be rejected at the outset if we are to pose the question of printing's relation to republican enlightenment, or to anything else.

To begin with, there is a logical problem for those who wish to see printing as a hard technology outside of the political symbolic order, since it is not clear how print could even be identified on the basis of that assumption. Not all printing is done with a press, nor with ink, nor on paper, nor with movable type, nor even by the method of impression. No hard fact of technology dictates what counts as printing. We know what we mean when we talk about printing, but we know that because we are in a tradition; we have a historical vocabulary of purposes and concepts that gives identity to printing, and meaningfully distinguishes for us between books that have been impressed with types and those that have been impressed with pens.

That tradition has undergone some important changes. In Western culture a growing number of things have come to count as printing, as the technique of impression has become less determinant in its definition: laser printing, jet printing, xerography, and so on. In recognizing such practices as forms of printing, we use the unspoken but increasingly important criterion of a negative relation to the hand. That is why we do not count some other tools of duplication as examples of printing, even though some of them *do* make use of impression. We exclude them from the category of printing because their metonymic link to the hand is too strong. Thomas Jefferson invented a machine for duplicating letters; a pen guided by the hand could by a series of levers be made to guide a second pen in an identical fashion. In Eisenstein's phrase, it was a tool for duplicating. But it would not therefore be regarded as a tool for printing, primarily because it is designed to record its metonymy with the hand. The typewriter is another good example; copies duplicated on a typewriter, perhaps even carbon copies, we do not recognize as printed. But the same copies run through a mimeograph machine could be counted as a kind of printing. They would have been relieved of the pressure of the hand.

In some important ways, this cultural meaning for the hand, which by contrast defines what counts as printing, has developed since the establishment of the printing trade.[9] Early printers, for instance, in no way distinguished their work from hand-produced documents. From a modern perspective, that seems to show how little they understood the latent "logic" of their medium. But that interpretation of the meaning of print is governed from the outset by a presupposed modern ideological definition of print. Along a related line, although printing was initially another way of reproducing in quantity books that were already being reproduced in quantity, at a certain point printing came to be specially defined as publication, now *in opposition to* manuscript circulation. Later, I have argued, publication in the new sense would take on a special political meaning involving a new way of defining the public. These changes were not dictated by any feature of the technology, but they did change our fundamental perceptions of the technology. It is because publication is a political condition of utterance that we meaningfully distinguish between books impressed by types and those impressed by pens, where we do not make the same kind of distinction between those impressed by plates and those sprayed by lasers. The history of printing, in short, cannot even define its subject properly without asking about the history of the public and other political conditions of discourse. What did it mean to publish, and what did it mean to identify printing *as* publishing? These are not questions about the empirical effects of printing; they are questions about the historical constitution of printing.

In addition to the logical difficulty of saying what will count as printing, a second and more serious problem results from the assumption that printing has an ontological status prior to culture. When media and technologies receive this kind of transcendental status, their social investments and rhetorical meaning disappear from the field of analysis, only to return in mystified form, disguised as the previously latent logic of the technology. Let us take the example, already cited, of the uniform mass production that was a feature of late medieval scriptoria before the invention of printing. Persons who already occupied the role of wholesale bookseller were sometimes able to place orders with the scriptoria for two hundred or even four hundred copies of a single work at once.[10] For several decades after the development of the press, editions were not typically larger than this, and were often much smaller. Moreover, because scriptoria had elaborate procedures designed to eliminate variants, and because printers often made changes in the middle of press runs, printed books were not necessarily distinguished for uniformity any more than they were for numbers.

This is not to deny that uniformity and quantity came to be the distinctive characteristics of printing, but to reframe the question of how and why that happened. A practice of specialized duplication had been in place from the outset to motivate the Mainz entrepreneurs in their experiments with printing, so the effects of regularization and multiplication represent not so much the consequences of printing as the tasks, desiderata, and perceptual categories by which printing was defined and made possible. From its first appearance in the West, printing was already organized by purposes that can be described as early capitalism. That is one reason it was developed by goldsmiths, who by casting type were using not only their metallurgical skill but also their unique ability to deploy capital. In cultures where the practices of capitalism did not organize the emergence of printing, as among the Chinese or the Uighur Turks, printing took on different defining features and had different "consequences." Yet the implication of print historians — as well as of foundationalist Marxists such as Walter Benjamin — is that the technology of printing, once "discovered," yielded the result of standardized mass production, with its cultural symptoms.[11] The assumption that technology is prior to culture results in a kind of retrodetermination whereby the political history of a technology is converted into the unfolding nature of that technology. Everything that has been ascribed to the agency of printing — from formal characteristics such as abstraction, uniformity, and visualization to broad social changes such as rationalization and democratization — has been retrodetermined in this way. What have historically become the characteristics of printing have been projected backward as its natural, essential logic. Meanwhile, its historical determinations have not been analyzed, for historians have learned to consider the realm of politics and culture only as the secondary field of technology's presumed effects.

How was printing defined as a technology of publicity, having an essentially civic and emancipatory character? How was the relation between subject and letters altered? What was the relation between the socially determined character of the medium and the texts produced in it? These questions are united by the premise that the cultural constitution of a medium (in this case printing) is a set of political conditions of discourse. Those conditions include the practices and structured labors that we call technology. But I shall suppose that the latter have no ontological privilege over and at no point can be distinguished from their political meaning; that the practices of technology, in other words, are always structured, and that their meaningful structure is the dimension of culture.

Although this way of organizing a study in print history runs counter to the prevailing model, it is not unprecedented. Max Weber, for one, noted a close relation between printing and a systemic social rationalization of the West.[12] Yet, unlike those who have followed, he did not think of these in any way as cause and effect. Rather, he took the observed relation as the occasion to ask why printing had a rationalizing character in the modern West, when elsewhere it did not. In particular, he noted that only in the West did printing result in works planned for markets and publics. He concluded that the rationalizing results of printing, like those of the market and bureaucratic law, presuppose a transformation in subjective orientation.

Hence Weber's culturally oriented study of capitalism. Despite the long and illustrious controversies that have followed, two features of Weber's project should be preserved: first, the insight that the nature of modernity can be derived only from a history of subjectivity and practice, rather than from a realm (such as "society" or technology) assumed to be extraneous to culture; second, that, however much culture might be irreducibly local, it has in the case of the West produced a systemic rationalization, the horizon of which is transcultural. It remains difficult to explain the second of these ideas without abandoning the first. Attempts to account for societal transformation — whether expressly functionalist or not — typically reduce culture, politics, and rhetoric to epiphenomena. And hermeneutic attempts to account for culture, politics, and rhetoric typically obliterate societal rationalization from view or presuppose it as background. Without attempting a full-scale theorization of such problems, I wish to keep the complex relation between the two subjects in view. Any analysis of printing, even were it to begin with the Mainz goldsmiths, would have to begin in the middle.

In early eighteenth-century American society, many different uses for and perceptions of print were already established. Some were regional, others were typical of the imperial periphery, and still others belonged to the tradition of writing in the West. What was printing for, and what was it like? What did it mean to buy a book, to read a newspaper, or to nail up a broadside in the American colonies? The answers to such questions will vary from context to context.

Imagine a career for what could only provisionally be called "a" book. Printed in Philadelphia, let us say, from materials mostly imported, it likely would consist of a text composed by various hands both in and out of the printer's shop. It might be copied largely from a text printed elsewhere, obtained by a publisher who saw an opportunity for a local edition. The composition of the type and printing of the sheets would be done by one or more crews, not all of whose members would even be literate. So the text, before it has even attained the minimally objectified identity that would allow it to be sent to booksellers, customers, and binders, already would have a very different existence and meaning for those who would be said to be producing it. We can further imagine both a customer who, by chance perhaps, is familiar with the title, and a customer whose only familiarity with such titles comes from the local booksellers. We can imagine another life for the object among the carters or mariners who transport a small quantity of the printer's commodities along with other goods to another town. We can imagine yet other meanings for it as it is encountered variously by the printer's wife, his neighbor's slave, the purchaser's child, an Indian trader in the market, or a schoolmaster. Which of these objectifications do we have in mind when speaking of "print"? For it is only by a convention that we could group these different instances as having an identical object, while we exclude other instances, such as the sale of another edition (or state) of a text that is, as it were, more or less the same. More to the point, what are the salient differences among these different possible relations to printed goods — differences that are glossed over when we speak of the "logic" of "the" technology?

Even in its local discourse, print did not and could not have had a universal character or an undifferentiated audience. Both print and writing could only be alien to the entirely or even partially illiterate, including almost all Native Americans and the enslaved blacks. And saying that letters were "alien" to the illiterate is more than a tautology, since it is to these groups that writing and print may have appeared most clearly as technologies of power. For obvious reasons, historians know little about what colonial blacks thought about print. The texts of Jupiter Hammon and Phyllis Wheatley are the exceptions that prove the rule, since they define their public voices as white, even if only proleptically. They understand their literacy to prefigure their celestial assimilation. The slave narrative of Olaudah Equiano, however, gives a vivid record of a nonliterate black's perception of books as a technology of power. Equiano, who was brought to America and the Western world of letters in the late 1750s, writes:

> I had often seen my master and Dick employed in reading; and I had a great curiosity to talk to the books, as I thought they did; and so to learn how all things had a beginning: for that purpose I have often taken up a book, and have talked to it, and then put my ears to it, when alone, in hopes it would answer me; and I have been very much concerned when I found it remained silent.[13]

This account can be a useful piece of defamiliarization for us in several ways. First, because Equiano's master and his white companion, Dick, clearly have been reading aloud, and because Equiano has from the first been engaged in reading the visible world before him, in perceiving the technology of the book he does not initially attach importance to a distinction between reading and speaking. His early perception of writing is that of a mode of practical knowledge and authority — like English, or horseback riding. Second, his account belies the Enlightenment claim that print allows any person to communicate his thoughts to the public. Reading, he saw, was one of the distinguishing marks of white society; like horseback riding or sailing, it was one of the ways that society made itself different, singular. What Equiano registered, in other words, was the way in which writing had a meaning precisely in the limits of its communication. This does not imply that any other form of communication lacks such a meaningful limit, only that one of the meaningful limits of legibility was race. The two whites in Equiano's story recognize the book primarily as communication rather than power.

Today we may find it difficult to see the medium simultaneously as communication and as a structure of power, partly because our idea of communication contains a norm of universality. It is also because we are accustomed to a negative perspective on socially structured illiteracy; we regard illiteracy as the exclusion of some groups from an otherwise emancipatory discourse. Yet we can take a different perspective on the problem by seeing that the boundaries of any communicative context have a positive social character. This means not only that participation in a medium constitutes membership in a community — since to say that would leave a false impression that a medium could actually define a universal community — but also that the positive features of the medium implicitly differentiate the assumed collectivity. Equiano encounters letters from the outside in a context where to encounter letters from the inside would require socialization into white Western colonial capitalism. Race in particular was made one of the social meanings of the difference between writing and speech by racial division in the reproduction of literacy, and by the consequent overlap between determinate features of the medium and traits of race. Black illiteracy was more than a negation of literacy for blacks; it was the condition of a positive character of written discourse for whites. By extension, printing constituted and distinguished a specifically white community; in this sense it was more than a neutral medium that whites simply managed to monopolize.

Printing was allowed to fill this function by the way its material conditions were arranged. These included the system of ownership that made printed artifacts available in the form of property and thus inappropriate to blacks and Indians; its coidentity with educational institutions that socialized whites into the community of learning whereby their status as civilized Christians was defined; and its content, which referred of course to issues in the white world. Just as important, the use of print was understood to entail the authoritative disposition of character that was the personal value of letters, a disposition that was understood as a racial trait and could find expression in a wide range of preferences and abilities under such headings as perspicuity, equanimity, temperance, and judgment. Just as the white community would not have been the same community without its opposition to other groups and its constitution through writing and printing, so also written media would not have entailed the same dispositions of character — and would not have had the same identity — had participation in them not entailed membership in that community.

White colonists early learned to think of themselves as inhabiting the pure language of writing and to think of blacks as inhabiting a dialect, a particularized speech, that expressed their racial nature. In the early 1740s the Maryland doctor Alexander Hamilton, arriving near New York City with his black slave, Dromo, recorded in his journal an encounter between Dromo and a Dutch-speaking black woman:

> Dromo, being about 20 paces before me, stopped att a house where, when I came up, I found him discoursing a negroe girl who spoke Dutch to him. "Dis de way to York?" says Dromo. "Yaw, dat is Yarikee," said the wench, pointing to the steeples. "What devil you say?" replys Dromo. "Yaw, mynheer," said the wench. "Damme, you, what you say?" said Dromo again. "Yaw, yaw," said the girl. "You a damn black bitch," said Dromo and so rid on.[14]

In this drama of unregistered violence the one principle of intelligibility is Hamilton's external relation to the scene. That distance establishes his registration of the scene and produces his pleasure in it. Part of Hamilton's pleasure is that the slaves' difficulty with each other's language dramatizes what he doubtless perceives as their lack of mastery in their own languages (or what he would no doubt consider "their own" languages). "Lack of mastery" in both senses: dialect is perceived by Hamilton as a natural sign of the condition of servitude. Equally important is that his position of recorder, from which he produces simulacra of multiple incomplete dialects within a seamless narrative, matches mastery and writing against inferiority and illiterate speech. The meaning of the scene for Hamilton was established by his ability to scribble an account of it in his room at the New York inn. His comic perception of the two blacks' speech as dialects depends on a norm of written language, and this distinction between written language and the racialized particularities of dialect is clearly an invidious one.

Yet what is invidious about it is not mere personal prejudice on Hamilton's part—a lapse from liberal tolerance—for he had only to record the scene for the valence of the linguistic media to appear. In that cultural context a difference between inclusive universality and blind particularity was immanent to the difference between the (non)dialect of writing and the spoken dialect. Dromo, speaking, identifies himself; Hamilton, transcribing Dromo's phonemic particularity, transcends the racialized identity of Dromo's speech. At the same time, Hamilton's pleasure in transcription testifies, even in the private context of his journal, to a sense of collectivity. To do reading was a way of being white.

Not all whites were literate. The best literacy studies estimate that, of the free white males of seventeenth-century New England, roughly a third could not sign their names. After a long period of little improvement, New England white men achieved nearly complete literacy in the middle of the eighteenth century. Among white women, on the other hand, only a third could sign their names before 1670, and even by the end of the eighteenth century that fraction had not risen to more than half. South of New England, even white males do not seem to have attained more than two-thirds literacy in the same period.[15]

Despite these differentials in the technology, print could represent the white community to itself, partly because more people could read than the statistics suggest. Ordinary patterns of education involved instruction in reading, especially reading of the Bible, for several years before instruction in writing was undertaken, and many students interrupted their educational careers before the second stage. Literacy statistics, which are based almost invariably on signatures of wills, marriage licenses, and other official records, give no indication of those who participated in the written without themselves being able to write. Many groups who do poorly in literacy figures—especially women—probably were able to read. For this reason the historian David Hall has argued that those who were able to read in some degree constituted the vast majority of white colonists, and that the print market was potentially very broad. To illustrate that point, Hall has shown that some popular forms of print, especially devotional and sensational literatures, were extraordinarily common despite severe material limitations on the print market.[16]

Nevertheless, although women were reading printed goods in

colonial America, very few of those goods were written by women. Nor is it the case that the gender barrier in letters dissolved when women took up pens to write. The important question is not access to writing, as a certain liberal humanism would lead us to expect, but rather the meaning of writing. Insofar as written contexts entailed dispositions of character that interpellated their subject as male, women could write only with a certain cognitive dissonance. Female farm children learning to spell out and recite the sacred text of the Bible were not performing the same act as male merchants glancing at the latest commodity prices. Writing was a specialized skill primarily employed in the male-dominated realms of commerce and law; it was especially common for women to be taught reading but not writing. The case of Dinah Nuthead probably was not exceptional in this regard. The wife of a printer in late seventeenth-century Maryland, she could not sign her name but was able to set type and run the press after her husband died. The personnel teaching the different skills of literacy, moreover, were divided in the same way as their pupils. Increase Mather, remembering his education, recorded: "I learned to read of my mother. I learned to write of Father."[17] His experience was typical; to the very end of the eighteenth century, colonists distinguished between "woman schools" that taught children to read and "masters' schools" that taught them to write. Here the terminology speaks, as it were, volumes.

Linguistic technologies also were saturated with class and social status, as can be seen in modern statistical reconstruction. Mid-eighteenth-century Virginia men with personal estates of £200 had a literacy rate twice that of men with estates of £100. Men in the clergy and the professions had a literacy rate of 90 percent or higher, and this figure decreases as one moves down the social scale from gentry to merchants, artisans, laborers, and farmers. No one had a relation to linguistic technologies — speaking, reading, writing, and printing — unmediated by such forms of domination as race, gender, and status. Every printed artifact came saturated with the distinctive qualities of communities, including regional communities.

Printers and readers were more numerous in New England than elsewhere. As Kenneth Lockridge has argued, however, high literacy in early New England did not result in the modernizing orientation toward letters.[18] Printing seems to have been put to conservative uses. Certainly the special tradition of Puritan culture conferred its own features on print and writing. Books that were read in the devotional tradition had a strong public value in the New England towns, where in fact it was not uncommon for committees to inspect each home to make sure that it had a Bible. The reading of these works was a technology of the self. Cotton Mather, for example, records in his diary the uses of the German pietists' writings: "I would endeavour as in Reading their Books, I find the Passages of a raised and noble Piety occurring, to pant and strive after a lively Impression thereof, on my own Mind. And in this Way I would seek a particular praeparation for Services which I may do, in the coming on of the Kingdom of God."[19] The ideal that Mather articulates here contains a norm for subjectivity: reading, ideally, is a way of internalizing that is simultaneously a feature of literacy and a feature of the sacred order. He takes it as a moral imperative for himself but also for the community: "In visits to credible Families, I will bespeak little Studies and Bookshelves for the little Sons that are capable of conversing with such things; and begin to furnish their Libraries and perswade them to the Religion of the Closet."[20]

The religion of the closet prescribes not only that books will be useful, but that their utility will lie in a practice of internalization. In the official text of the Massachusetts laws the colony's citizens were reminded, "When Laws may be read in men's lives, they appear more beautiful than in the fairest Print, and promise a longer duration, than engraven in Marble."[21] On the basis of the same perception, one minister could write, "The life of Reading, is in the performance of our duty in what we learn. Words are but empty sounds, except we draw them forth in our lives. Printed Books will do little good, except Gods Spirit print them in our hearts."[22] Implicit here are assumptions about printing technology that differ radically from those underlying John Adams's history of enlightenment. Sacred internalization renders the nature of print in such a way that the publication of broadsides or newspapers could be seen only as inferior uses accidental to the godly effort to "print" the divinely ordained laws "in our hearts." In this case we do not see individuals emancipated by print; instead, it is the individual who is printed from an authoritative stamp. In the diary entry just quoted, Mather uses the same figure to connect the nature of print with its normative effects: he speaks punningly of the "Impression" that reading should make on his mind.

I want to make a strong claim about this metaphor as an indicator of the meaning of print in Puritan culture. At the very least, the idea of an authoritative stamp — as opposed to far-flung distribution, let us say — is the standard metaphoric use that Puritan rhetoric makes of printing. Such metaphors cannot be sharply distinguished from the objective facts of printing, for there are any number of ways in which printing might be distinguished from other technologies, and to describe it as a definitive impression has as much validity as any. The rhetoric of impression names the literal and defining features of the print medium in a way that already defines the social value of print. Here the emphasis is on the perfect reception by the copy of a master original. Puritan typography and Puritan typology, in other words, could be mutually reinforcing. Insofar as print is construed, valued, and used according to the perception of a relation between type and antitype — a relation that obtains between copy and original as well as between text and animated reading — it expresses the character of authority. Constituted in the context of this symbolic logic, print seems eminently suited to the devotional text. One would not construe the distinctive features of the medium in the same way if the object were a shipping report.

It has often been claimed that New England was an oral society. In an important sense this is true, although not in the way that is usually meant. The conventional distinction between oral and literate societies, in which *oral* means preliterate and innocent of the exploitation that comes through writing, I would reject as sentimental and ideological. It conceals norms not only about language, but about personhood and social relations. New Englanders, far from being ignorant of letters, used them with an intensity equaled by very few other cultures in the world at the time. Yet in an important ideological way it was an oral society. New Englanders accorded a disciplinary privilege to speech, and in most contexts insisted on seeing writing as a form of speaking. Cotton Mather once remarked that his sermons would be more powerful if "Preached a Second Time in the way of the Press." And although he tells us that he gave away his books by the score, he also notes that when giving a book away he liked to instruct the recipient: "Remember, that I am speaking to you, all the while you have this Book before you!"[23]

In 1722, as a new set of print practices was only just emerging, the Reverend Thomas Symmes published a sermon that included a preface commenting extensively on the scene of print in New England society. The chief advantage of the "Art of Printing," he explains, is that by its means, "as many of the eminent Servants of God being dead, yet speak unto us; so many other worthy Persons, and especially . . . the Ministers of the Gospel are still blest with Opportunities of rendring their Usefulness more extensive and durable."[24] The attributes of extension and durability are the classically distinctive features of writing, and print's superiority to script is seen as lying mainly in its greater extension. Extension and durability determine print as a derivative of speech that introduces to the immediacy of speech the dimensions of space and time. In other forms of print discourse, writing's dimensions of space and time appear as exoticism and antiquarianism; here Symmes's terms for those dimensions — extension and durability — bear connotations less of curiosity than of ministerial power. Symmes encourages his fellow clergy to make more use of print. In a revealing moment he explains that the reason they do not is that they hope to "escape the scourge of the tongue."

If the scourge of the oral is the restraint on the press, it is also the validation of the press. Symmes argues that no one need fear superfluous or bad publications, for such works "we are under no obligation in the World to patronize, admit under our roof, or touch with one of our Fingers." Because New England culture structured print in this way, print discourse had not become the basis for the community's self-representation — as it would be for John Adams and his contemporaries — except in its covert identification with the community of white males. The typological and ministerial virtues of print were only one symbolic context for understanding print. I have indicated already that the world of seaport commerce gave printing a set of features that could hardly be incorporated with those picked out by Symmes, Mather, and their fellow clergy. And since the way print was construed always had consequences for imagining society and its norms, there were stakes of power in these symbolic differences.

The New England printing trade and its cultural settings were anything but monolithic; the trade, for example, displayed a much greater specialization than in the southern colonies. As early as 1700 a book buyer in Boston would have had a choice among nineteen booksellers and seven printers. Unlike Virginia, where book owning remained a sign of wealth and distinction, New England had some kind of printed artifact for almost all white families. As David Hall points out, in the same period in which the *Virginia Almanac* was printed in press runs of 5,000 copies (and even this figure is much larger than that of the average press run), New Englanders were buying 60,000 copies of a single almanac and supporting several others.[25]

We like to associate print with general distribution, but the same popular press that put almanacs in the hands of so many New England farmers was also decentralized and heterogeneous. Widely circulated titles were published by means of loose agreements among a number of printers and booksellers, none of whom alone would have had the kind of commercial network of transportation and marketing that is taken for granted by our more modern notion of a publisher. Because almanacs were produced on a schedule, and because their audience included many people who would not have bought any other book, they represent the peak of the book trade's organization. Uniformity was not at a high premium for other kinds of books. Some of the most widely dispersed titles, for example, were what Hall calls "steady sellers" — books usually of a devotional character that remained in print year after year and could be found in households of very little wealth. But these texts had little stability from edition to edition, since each printing was worked up cheaply by a small-time printer trying to reach a local market and would vary depending on what sources the printer had on hand and what tastes he anticipated in his customers. The localism of the decentralized book trade meant that many texts circulated in a more or less "popular" fashion, meaning that the book market was capable of articulating a counterpublic print discourse in broadsides and cheap pamphlets. Those in position to represent the order of colonial society — especially ministers — occasionally expressed some anxiety about this counterpublic potential. Cotton Mather wrote in his diary in 1713 that "the Minds and Manners of many People about the Countrey are much corrupted, by foolish Songs and Ballads, which the Hawkers and Peddlars carry into all parts of the Countrey."[26]

Unfortunately, we know relatively little about this literature — how much of it there was, what all of it was like, who made it, and how it was perceived and read by those who bought it. The counterpublic literature of broadside ballads, devotional books, and sensational pamphlets never articulated a public threat, depending as it did on an invisible worthlessness for its very existence. Not only did it have to be cheap in order to be hawked in the countryside, but in order to be counterpublic (and thus "corrupting") it had to be "foolish," that is, without status and without public reference. Yet it was precisely this extraneous relation to claims of public value that Mather found disturbing. Accordingly, he spent a considerable part of his writing and publishing career in an effort to match the public discourse of theodicy with the reading tastes of the sensational literature, striving for a seamless representation of the world in printed discourse.

South of New England, where the press developed more slowly, it took on a different set of characteristics. Printing appeared in Philadelphia in 1685, and at the same time in Maryland, although in the latter it would continue only intermittently. For the first three decades of the eighteenth century there was no press in Virginia or the more southern colonies, and consequently no newspapers or magazines. What print there was in these colonies was imported. Not until 1730 did Virginians persuade the Annapolis printer William Parks to establish a press and bookstore in Williamsburg. Books still were inaccessible to most people, literate or not. Even as late as 1760, Smollett's *History of England* would have cost a Williamsburg resident the equivalent of thirty hogs.

In this setting, the extension and durability that defined print for Americans decidedly took on the character of the exotic and the antique. Book buying was the province of the wealthy, because imported printed goods were costly, and the great libraries of the southern colonies were, almost without exception, those of the landed gentry, not the clergy — although smaller collections were common enough among ministers and lawyers. The necessity of importing the books for these libraries no doubt contributed to their function as a social distinction, since social distinction took the form of visible luxury rather than intensive pious reflection. Library building, like tea drinking, was part of a symbolic culture of regulated luxury. While Mather's library of 7,000 volumes or so probably lay in stacks and in chests, William Byrd II housed his 3,625 tomes in twenty-four black walnut bookcases.

Despite the scarcity of print, there were many different possible relations to print and writing for colonial southerners, as has recently been emphasized by Rhys Isaac's history of Virginia.[27] Letters could have a prominent role even in the lives of the illiterate and semiliterate. The extreme case was that of slaves, since a slave was required to carry a letter written by his owner simply in order to travel. For whites who could read falteringly, but could not write, books provided enough of a glimpse into other ways of thinking and living as to be a reminder of the distinction between the two domains. Laws were still read aloud at the courthouse to the assembled citizens. In the Anglican liturgy, as well as in the traditions of recitation and spoken commentary surrounding the Bible and common-law judgments, the text was both tied to oral performance settings and employed to underwrite the authority of those settings. Letters thus appeared in intermediary connections between the high culture of learning and the other traditions of the community. Had letters been confined to the silent reading and writing of gentlemen such as George Wythe, they would have been easy to avoid.

As in New England, society in the South was organized by a performative order of speech. The meanings of speech and its privilege, however, were different in the South, chiefly because of the deferential order of status in which the gentry played a pivotal role. As Charles Sydnor so vividly pictures in *Gentlemen Freeholders*, the gentry relied for much of their authority on exemplary speech, emphasizing their local interests by means of an agonistic self-representation. In common parlance, a man "carried his election," and the phrase meant more than mere success. "There was an implication," as Sydnor puts it, "that success was deserved and earned by energy, force of character, ready information, manly presence, and courage."[28] Campaigning for office in such an environment was not a matter of oratorical eloquence, and speech making seems to have been rare during election campaigns. If eighteenth-century Virginia was not oratorical, however, that was not because it was script dominated but because its orality presided over the most mundane levels of interaction. Campaigning meant going among residents, inquiring about wives and children, simulating the immediate, conversational relation of a neighbor. On the other hand, as Rhys Isaac demonstrates, the gentry's authority within the general community had as much to do with script and print as did their authority among professionals and tradesmen. The local allegiance of the freeholder was vouched for in the extensive oral performances by means of which the gentleman familiarized himself with the less wealthy. A more substantial familiarity, however, could compromise the claim to disinterested independence and concerns particular to the broader commonwealth. The social position of the Virginia gentry — not unlike that of their English counterparts — was a complex mediation of orality, writing, and print — a mediation that took place under the categories of familiarity and liberality and that further required certain traits to be seen as natural to letters. In this context, print inevitably had a different use and social meaning than it did in New England.

Few groups in colonial society, North or South, successfully incorporated the use of letters as part of their constitutive self-understanding: chief among these were the clergy, the southern gentry, and the seaport merchants. Yet even for these groups, although the use of printed goods distinguished them advantageously from other colonial groups, the same goods could continually represent their marginal relation to other communities of the empire. For instance, unlike later periods, in which print acquired the ideological character of local and everyday phenomena, print in the early eighteenth century was distinguished for the fact of its distant origins, its ability to cross space and time in a way that made it represent the exotic. So the same Philadelphia merchant who distinguished himself from his wife and his clerks by his familiarity with letters would in turn find himself inscribed in the imperial periphery by a print discourse that everywhere recorded its emanation from distant parts. This second-hand authority of the provinces was reproduced by the colonists themselves. Most early colonial newspapers devoted their prime space to imperial and foreign intelligence (often of military character) rather than to domestic affairs. News from Muscovy and Hungary often occupied the front pages, while the tiny amount of local news generally was relegated to small type just before the advertisements. Local news could be had through hearsay faster than the weekly newspaper could print it, and until the colonists developed an ideological preference for seeing it in the paper rather than hearing it on the street, they turned to print mainly for advices from abroad.

Crossing space in a perceptibly alien way could thus be taken as natural to print. The early papers were not divided by sizable headlines, and it seems likely that they were read through rather than glanced at for selective reading. Moreover, the early presses, like other capitalized trades of the period, were almost always in the seaports, and printers had a very special relationship with merchants and ship captains. The normal errands of maritime commerce were the only channels for transoceanic news, and papers announced ship arrivals more regularly than any other kind of local news. The exotic reference of print came about in a commercial context, and newspapers were a kind of metacommodity — objects of trade that described trade itself. Reading the foreign advices, one would have recognized that print discourse derived its authority and material from the shipping trade. Built into the difference between printed news and street speech was a phenomenological topography of the seaport world that could be thematized as foreign reports.

There was only one kind of printed artifact that could have been regarded as an everyday secular object, a piece of the standard routine of early eighteenth-century society. That was the legal form. Some colonies had passed laws at the turn of the century requiring the use of printed forms in all official transactions (Maryland, for example, did so in 1700). Soon they were available in an astonishing variety: summonses, writs of attachment, deeds of transfer, apprentice indentures, customs receipts, surveyors' certificates, tax assessment forms, land grants, powers of attorney, military supply requisitions, returns, executors' warrants, vouchers, bills of exchange, bonds, debentures, election decrees, jury summonses, petitions for military discharge, complaints for suits in equity, recognizance appeals, commissions civil and military, post-rider oaths, special warrants, bills obligatory, mortgages for slaves, bills of lading, oaths of allegiance, and more. The most prestigious legal forms might be engraved in London, but one of the clearest advantages for the colonists in having domestic printers was the ability to have the simple forms cheaply available. At a time when legal affairs usually were transacted without professional lawyers, printed forms were thought useful insofar as the common-law tradition had developed a set of formulas, the exact following of which had legal value. Accordingly, printers advertised their forms as the "correctest," and legal forms as a genre remained very stable throughout the century. Because most of these forms required the manual insertion only of a name, or perhaps also an amount, their use did not require a high degree of literacy. It may have been largely through legal forms that nearly illiterate artisans and tradesmen in the seaport towns began to regard the use of printed objects as natural to their own legal and economic world. What is more, the printed forms metonymically represented the arena of imperial administration. The handling of these forms constructed for the colonists their relation to networks of power uniting the colonies and deriving from the English courts.

In none of these regional contexts did the use and meaning of print correspond to John Adams's vision before the 1720s. I have sketched these contrasting contexts for print not to give a thorough history of printing in America, which would be another sort of project altogether, but to show that Adams's Whig history of print could hardly be called an adequate summary of the varieties of print culture. It is not even clear that we could define such an entity as "print culture," but it is clear that the use and meaning of print varied too much from one context to another to draw conclusions about its logic and latent politics. Neither in New England nor in the South, among clergy or gentry, men or women, whites or blacks, urban or rural, was print routinely opposed to authority, identified in its nature with popular struggle or with emancipatory reflection, or seen as forming the basis of a protonationalist consciousness. Adams's essay, in short, indicates not the intrinsic nature of print discourse, but a new development — a new culture of print in the decades immediately before 1765.

The colonial printing trade had been around for a long time by the early eighteenth century; the oldest colonial press had been in operation since 1639. But the colonial presses had been relatively inactive. Most seventeenth-century colonists were quite content—insofar as we can tell—to do without a press. On several occasions when printing was introduced it was immediately discouraged, sometimes by royal governors, but also by elected assemblies. The early artisans printed no newspapers or magazines. They seldom concentrated their capital or developed broad enough markets to produce big editions or large volumes. By 1765, however, print had come to be seen as indispensable to political life, and could appear to men such as Adams to be the primary agent of world emancipation. What makes this transformation of the press particularly remarkable is that, unlike the press explosion of the nineteenth century, it involved virtually no technological improvements in the trade. To the end of the eighteenth century, printers were using a wooden flatbed hand press that had scarcely changed since the German presses of the fifteenth century. The material constraints on the press—such as the scarcity of paper or the lack of the skill to cast type domestically—remained in force until the end of the eighteenth century. Nevertheless, printing changed both in character and in volume, after 1720 growing much faster even than the population.

It was in the context of the seaports, their markets, and the networks of imperial administration that American colonists began developing the understanding of print that would find expression in Adams's essay. They began elaborating a new use of print and a bourgeois public sphere simultaneously, incorporating an awareness of a potentially limitless audience *in their perceptions of printed objects*. The audience for print therefore came to be seen as categorically different from a mere crowd. Print discourse became routinized as a feature of the political world because it was seen as impersonal in a way that was now normal and normative. All these shifts in perceptions of print were, as I have argued elsewhere, at the same time shifts in the way political discourse was conducted, as well as shifts in the conventions of individual rhetoric and self-perception.

These transformations were cultural rather than technological; they came about as the language of republicanism was extended to print contexts as a structuring metalanguage. In the culture of republicanism—with its categories of disinterested virtue and civic supervision—a rhetoric of impersonal discourse became authoritative, a way of understanding the publicness of publication. As an example of these discourse conventions, consider the following passage in the voice of the Spectator — a character whose very name makes him the embodiment of disinterested civic supervision:

> It is much more difficult to converse with the World in a real than a personated Character. That might pass for Humour, in the *Spectator*, which would look like Arrogance in a Writer who sets his Name to his Work. The Fictitious Person might contemn those who disapproved him, and extoll his own Performances, without giving Offence. He might assume a Mock-Authority; without being looked upon as vain and conceited. The Praises or Censures of himself fall only upon the Creature of his Imagination, and if any one finds fault with him, the Author may reply with the Philosopher of old, *Thou dost but beat the Case of* Anaxarchus.[29]

Where earlier writers typically had seen the context of print as a means of personal extension, Steele here regards it as an authoritative mediation. He treats the impersonality of the speaking voice in print as an advantage rather than a disadvantage. In the bourgeois public sphere, which was brought into being by publications such as the *Spectator*, a principle of negativity was axiomatic: the validity of what you say in public bears a negative relation to your person. What you say will carry force not because of who you are but despite who you are. Surrendering one's utterance to an audience that was by definition indefinite ceased to be a personal hazard, and became a way of claiming a public disposition.

The public sphere's conventions of print thus entailed a special posture for the individual. The last line of the passage above refers to the fact that Anaxarchus was pummeled to death with iron pestles after offending a despotic ruler. In the ventriloquistic act of taking up his speech, therefore, Steele both imagines an intimate violation of his person and provides himself with a kind of prophylaxis against violation. He has begun to imagine himself as possessing a disembodied public person, separate from but corresponding to his body (he writes, after all, not under the name of Steele, but as the Spectator; and it became the rule for serial essays to be pseudonymous in just this way). The privilege that he obtains over his body in this way does not in fact reduce to the simple body/soul distinction that Anaxarchus's speech invokes. It allows him to think of his public discourse as a routine form of self-abstraction, quite unlike the ascetic self-integration of Anaxarchus. When Steele impersonates the philosopher to have the Spectator (or someone) say, "Thou dost but beat the case of Anaxarchus," he appropriates an intimate subjective benefit of publicity's self-abstraction.

The Spectator also expects, even seems to invite, criticism — whether pummeling or not. The anonymity that makes the character of the Spectator valuable allows the Spectator to be a critic with impunity, and protects Richard Steele in turn from criticism of the Spectator. The idea of civic supervision has become attached to the notion of anonymity in print, now regarded as a good thing. Criticism — in principle open-ended criticism dedicated both to changing opinion and to opposing authority — thus became an organizing principle of Western culture in large part by means of special cultural conventions about print. If anything about print has been democratizing, it is this norm of critical discourse. It has been possible to see that norm as the expression of the nature of print because it has come so deeply to govern our fundamental perceptions of the medium.

Americans learned these conventions in some measure from their counterparts in the imperial metropolis — Benjamin Franklin, for example, was especially influenced by the *Spectator*. But what John Adams was trying to argue in 1765 was that Americans were willing to take those conventions, and the resulting principle of a politics founded on criticism, further than anyone had imagined. The achievements of the democratic revolution had much to do with the development of a print public sphere. But because that public sphere is founded in culture rather than in the inherent tendencies of history, technology, or the market, it is fragile. In an age increasingly dominated by consensus politics, opinion polls, "community standards," content restrictions, and other limitations on the role of public criticism, that may be more important to remember than ever.

Notes

This essay contains, in revised and abridged form, material from *The Letters of the Republic: Publication and the Public Sphere in Eighteenth-Century America* (Cambridge: Harvard University Press, 1990), and from "The Mass Public and the Mass Subject," in *Habermas and the Public Sphere*, ed. Craig Calhoun (Cambridge: MIT Press, 1991), 377–401. Readers interested in further historical detail and scholarly notes should consult the versions found there.

1. *The Structural Transformation of the Public Sphere*, trans. Thomas Burger (Cambridge: MIT Press, 1989).

2. John Adams, "A Dissertation on the Canon and the Feudal Law," in *Papers*

of John Adams, ed. Robert J. Taylor et al. (Cambridge: Harvard University Press, 1977–   ), 1:103–28. Further references to this text will be made parenthetically.

3. John Foxe, *Acts and Monuments*, quoted in Stephen Greenblatt, *Renaissance Self-Fashioning* (Chicago: University of Chicago Press, 1980), 98–99.

4. Greenblatt, *Renaissance Self-Fashioning*, 97.

5. Elizabeth Eisenstein, *The Printing Press as an Agent of Change* (Cambridge: Cambridge University Press, 1979); Walter J. Ong, *Interfaces of the Word* (Ithaca, N.Y.: Cornell University Press, 1977), and *Orality and Literacy* (London: Methuen, 1982); Jack Goody, *The Domestication of the Savage Mind* (Cambridge: Cambridge University Press, 1977). A recent example of this school in literary studies, albeit one that carries its premises to ludicrous extremes, is Alvin Kernan, *Printing Technology, Letters, and Samuel Johnson* (Princeton, N.J.: Princeton University Press, 1987). For an early and incisive critique of the McLuhanite assumptions adopted by this school, see Kenneth Burke, "Medium as 'Message,' " in *Language as Symbolic Action* (Berkeley: University of California Press, 1966), 410–18.

6. Alvin Gouldner, *The Dialectic of Ideology and Technology* (New York: Oxford University Press, 1982 [1976]), 40–41.

7. Eisenstein, *The Printing Press*, 703–4.

8. Kernan, *Printing Technology*, 49.

9. See Jonathan Goldberg, *Writing Matter: From the Hands of the English Renaissance* (Stanford, Calif.: Stanford University Press, 1990), especially the last chapter.

10. Lucien Febvre and Henri Martin, *The Coming of the Book*, trans. David Gerard (London: Verso, 1976), 28.

11. Walter Benjamin, "The Work of Art in the Age of Mechanical Reproduction," in *Illuminations* (New York: Harcourt, Brace & World, 1969), 217–52.

12. Max Weber, *The Protestant Ethic and the Spirit of Capitalism*, trans. Talcott Parsons (London: Unwin, 1985), 15.

13. Olaudah Equiano, *The Interesting Narrative of the Life of Olaudah Equiano* (1789; quoted from the first American edition; New York, 1791, 1:75). There are similar stories about the perspective of North American Indians. See James Axtell, "The Power of Print in the Eastern Woodlands," *William and Mary Quarterly* 44 (1987): 300–309.

14. Alexander Hamilton, *Itinerarium*, ed. by Carl Bridenbaugh as *Gentleman's Progress* (Chapel Hill: University of North Carolina Press, 1948), 40–41.

15. Kenneth Lockridge, *Literacy in Colonial New England* (New York: Norton, 1974). See also William Gilmore, "Elementary Literacy on the Eve of the Industrial Revolution: Trends in Rural New England, 1760–1830," *Proceedings of the American Antiquarian Society* 92 (1982): 87–178.

16. David Hall, "The Uses of Literacy in New England, 1600–1850," in *Printing and Society in Early America*, ed. William Joyce et al. (Worcester, Mass.: American Antiquarian Society, 1983), 1–47.

17. "The Autobiography of Increase Mather," quoted in Hall "The Uses of Literacy," 25.

18. Lockridge, *Literacy in Colonial New England*.

19. Cotton Mather, *Diary of Cotton Mather*, 2 vols. (New York: Ungar, 1957), 2:193 (March 18, 1713).

20. Mather, *Diary*, 2:538 (June 1718).

21. Preface, *The Book of the General Lawes and Libertyes* (Cambridge, 1660).

22. Samuel Whiting, *Abraham's Humble Intercession for Sodom* (Cambridge, 1666), v.

23. Quoted in Kenneth Silverman, *Life and Times of Cotton Mather* (New York: Columbia University Press, 1985), 198.

24. Thomas Symmes, *Discourse Concerning Prejudice*, (1722), ii.

25. Hall, "The Uses of Literacy," 27–28.

26. Mather, *Diary*, 2:242 (September 27, 1713).

27. Rhys Isaac, *The Transformation of Virginia 1740–1790* (Chapel Hill: University of North Carolina Press, 1982).

28. Charles Sydnor, *Gentlemen Freeholders* (Chapel Hill: University of North Carolina Press, 1952), 116.

29. [Richard Steele], *The Spectator* no. 555, in *Selections from the Tatler and the Spectator*, ed. Angus Ross (New York: Penguin, 1982), 213.

Chapter 3

A Local History of the Early U.S. Press:
Cincinnati, 1793–1848
John C. Nerone

This essay is intended as an example of an approach to writing media history. It focuses on a very specific place and period, but the approach has broader implications, both for the early national period of U.S. history and for other nations and eras.

The arguments or assumptions of this approach are, simply put, that the media are creatures in a social and cultural ecology, and that the media are networks of social and cultural relationships. Changes in the media are properly understood, therefore, in terms of the broadest possible focus on social change.[1]

Writing on the media in the early national period of U.S. history has tended to concentrate on journalism, especially as embodied in daily newspapers in major cities. While not exclusive of a broader perspective, "journalism history" does argue by implication that journalism is a thing in itself, a professional practice evolving according to an internal dynamic that creates its own culture and ideology. Journalism is seen as an actor on the stage of history. This is a result of the constraints of the genre (journalism history) and not the specific or conscious contention of any particular scholar. It is a point of view embodied in standard U.S. journalism histories,[2] which have added material on social and economic history in recent editions, but have tended to retain their basic approach, which remains centered on the rise of journalism and the deeds of heroic journalists and editors. Some of the scenery has changed, but the plot remains the same; some characters have been added (representatives of minorities, women, and nonmainstream movements), but the augmented cast reenacts the same basic drama.

Journalism history thus written suffers from three main weaknesses. First is present-mindedness. Scholars are interested primarily in finding the ancestors of the contemporary media in the past. This focus on the present in the past has hampered broad study of the cultural significance of the press in the past. Weekly papers, for example, are generally ignored because they have no modern counterpart, although the vast majority of pre-Civil War U.S. papers were weeklies.

A second weakness, resulting from present-mindedness, is whiggishness. Scholars emphasize successful innovation, and disproportionate attention is paid to newspapers and periodicals notorious for their longevity. Much of the best work in early journalism has been in the form of newspaper biographies or biographies of famous editors. But the overwhelming majority of early journals were failures, without famous personnel, and these have no place in standard journalism histories, despite their evident significance for understanding the culture of their own time.

A final weakness, related to the first two, is topical compartmentalization. Newspapers are studied apart from periodicals; literary and religious, scientific, and reform publications are all given separate treatment. Yet the development of the press in all these areas is more aptly treated as a single historical phenomenon.

The common feature of all these weaknesses is a failure to recognize that, rather than being a thing unto itself, a medium is exactly what the word suggests: something in between other things. A medium is a set of relationships within a social and cultural ecology. The history of the media cannot be understood apart from the history of the social and cultural contexts within which media developments occurred; the proper unit of study is not the individual medium, but the whole set of media within a particular ecology. Put simply, the history of the media should be written as social history: as the history of societies.

Weaknesses in journalism histories have not gone unnoticed,[3] and in recent years a number of "social histories" of journalism have appeared.[4] These works have been more concerned with locating the development of journalism within broader social and cultural movements, but have been criticized nonetheless for failing to displace the basic paradigm of journalism history.

From the point of view of this chapter, this failure can be attributed to an implicit adoption of the parameters of journalism history. Social histories have tended to agree that the object to be studied is journalism as practiced by daily newspapers, and have thus adopted the "factual record" of older journalism histories while explicitly rejecting the conclusions earlier scholars had drawn from these facts. Thus, in the early national period of U.S. history, standard journalism history has identified a "dark age" of partisan journalism,[5] extending from the Revolution to the 1830s, which was succeeded by a more modern commercial journalism in the 1830s, to be succeeded in turn by "independent journalism" later in the century. Social historians of the press have accepted this narrative of a political press giving way to a commercial press, although they have assigned different interpretations and meanings to this record.[6]

This record contains a fair amount of truth, yet it is something else entirely from the kind of record we need in order to understand the development of media as sets of relationships in social and cultural ecologies. The standard history tells us a story about the most important newspapers and generalizes downward, while we want to tell the story bottom-up; the standard history gives us the life of the medium from the editor's desk outward, while we want also to know about the life of the medium from the outside in. To tell these other stories, we must study the media in their complex entirety, keeping alert to their interactions, and we must study them in their social and cultural contexts. Isolating the leading daily newspapers and generalizing thence to national trends is not sufficient.

Instead, the optimum beginning point in constructing such a history is the level of the local study. By focusing on a particular locality, one may examine all relevant media — daily and nondaily, news and nonnews, notorious and commonplace. One may also remain sensitive to interactions with local populations and institutions, ideas, and movements.

What follows is a local study of the press in Cincinnati, 1793–1848. This study suggests that the standard plot of journalism history is misleading in several ways: it miscasts the development of political discourse in the press by obscuring it under the monolithic label of partisan journalism, it attributes too much dynamism to the introduction of the telegraph and penny press, and it errs in portraying partisanism and commercialism as hostile to one another. In addition, it fails to connect developments in "journalism" with developments in related media, such as scientific, religious, and literary publications.

Cincinnati is a suitable focus for such a study. In the years covered here, Cincinnati grew from a frontier village with a single weekly newspaper to the nation's fourth-largest publishing center, surpassed only by New York, Philadelphia, and Boston.[7] The city's development telescopes into a relatively brief time a set of national developments that stretched from the end of the eighteenth century into the beginning of the twentieth. Cincinnati also occupied a central point in the nineteenth-century history of the nation: as regional metropolis of the old Northwest and the new West; as commercial entrepôt for the internal river trade; as a center for regional political movements, Jeffersonian, Jacksonian, Whig, and Republican; and as a focal point of antislavery activism. I will not argue for Cincinnati's "typicality," since no locality in this era can claim to be typical—least of all the most studied (New York, Philadelphia, Baltimore, Boston). But Cincinnati's experience is a good lens through which to re-view key trends.

The essay begins with a discussion of press ideology as it emerged out of the republicanism of the Revolutionary era. This ideology had its origins both outside the press, in the cultural and political currents that flowed from Revolutionary experience, and inside the press, in the material conditions of press production and consumption. This "republican" press began to change rapidly with the expansion and diversification of the 1820s. By the end of that decade, both Cincinnati and its press had come to display permanent political and social divisions that were reflected in an increasingly competitive and commercialized press establishment. Ideologically, the press came to be described as an open marketplace. At the same time, however, limits were imposed—often through direct violence—on entry into the marketplace. Meanwhile, the press expanded into other formats and areas with the appearance of literary, religious, medical, and other professional journals. At first these journals were shaped by a republican hope for the popularization of enlightenment, but practicality and the interests of supporting organizations fostered periodicals tied to institutionalized groups, while "popular" periodicals aimed at entertainment and instruction rather than enlightenment. The essay concludes with a discussion of the implications of this narrative as an alternative to the story told by other "journalism histories."

Early Press Ideology

The starting point for any history of the press in the early Republic is ideology.[8] The way that people envisioned and discussed the issues, events, and institutions of the new nation, and therefore the way they made their history, was deeply inflected by the ideology (or family of ideologies) that historians have identified as republicanism. Republicanism is a protean ideology, and was deployed differently by different groups, but all of its incarnations share a similar vocabulary. In republican thought, liberty is always endangered by power, which seeks to extend itself by corruption. Liberty, and hence the health of the republic, may be maintained only by an alert, virtuous, and independent citizenry. Should the citizenry become licentious — lapse from civic virtue and seek selfish interests inimical to the public good — liberty will quickly yield to tyranny.[9]

The ideology of the early American press was molded by the vocabulary of republicanism and forged in the experience of the Revolution. The role of the press in the Revolution is well known:[10] insofar as the independence movement relied on mobilizing and informing public opinion, its success hinged on effective use of the press. There is an aptness to the fact that the characteristic figure of the American Enlightenment, Benjamin Franklin, was a printer, and that Thomas Jefferson, the author of the Declaration of Independence, was also America's foremost apologist for freedom of the press.

Jefferson asserted that, in a republic, newspapers are more important than government itself, as the basis for such a polity is "the opinion of the people." He believed that face-to-face communities "enjoy in their mass an infinitely greater degree of happiness than those who live under the European governments" because in "the former, public opinion is in the place of law." Jefferson hoped that a free and responsible press could endow modern society with the pristine republicanism of primitive communities. But to do so, the press must function as an extended town meeting. It should feature total access and it should be in itself passive and transparent. For the newspaper to allow public opinion to form naturally, it must be conducted by impartial craftsmen who would keep it open to all parties.[11]

It was this ideology of press significance that fueled the spread of presses and newspapers in the early Republic. The increase in printing was dramatic: the number of newspapers in print increased from around 45 at the time of the Revolution to 200 by 1800 and 1,200 by 1835; the number of newspapers started was far higher. By the 1830s, the United States had more newspapers and a larger aggregate circulation than any nation in the world.[12]

The impetus behind press expansion was largely ideological. The upturn in print production outstripped available markets — that was why so many failed — and predated the inducements of established political parties. Expansion can be best explained by the firm hold on the imagination of an ideal of democratic communication, a newspaper fantasy. Jefferson was only the most eloquent articulator of this fantasy; any newspaper's prospectus and masthead bore some icon of this dream of democratic communication.

This newspaper fantasy did not match reality. The newspapers of the early Republic were small, haphazardly composed, slenderly circulated (albeit more widely read), frequently short-lived craftsmen's products, not mighty engines of democracy. But to say the fantasy did not match reality is not to deny the force and effectiveness of it. A fantasy is not necessarily a mystification — it can also be an ideal that people strive to achieve. Such a fantasy generates rules of conduct, and we find such rules in both occupational and popular attitudes in the period following the Revolution. Popular attitudes labeled the Revolution an epoch-making event. It had ushered in an age "portentous beyond any parallel to be found in the history of Mankind, . . . the most enlightened and scientific Epoch known within the pale of human knowledge." Such an age demanded broad popular access to knowledge of all sorts, hence "the multiplication of periodical publications."[13]

Ideology and attitudes linked the creation of the Republic with the expansion of the press. This press was to assume great responsibilities as a public servant: it would be the "daily TEACHER" and "the prime minister" of public opinion.[14] Federal authorities acknowledged the significance of the press in the life of the Republic by granting postal privileges to newspapers and contracting with newspapers to publish laws and acts of Congress.[15]

The role of the press as public servant carried with it certain restrictions on press behavior. Guidelines on press conduct were based on two ideals: impartiality and impersonality. Both ideals would be invoked routinely in the prospectus of any given newspaper.[16]

John W. Browne, editor of the *Liberty Hall*, in his 1804 prospectus, pledged to be impartial. He promised "to set *Truth*, in its simple dress, before his readers" for them "to exercise their reason thereon"; he pledged that "he will never become the dupe of any party," and promised that "LIBERTY HALL will be open for the reception of any communications, from any and every party."[17] Disavowals of partisanism or partiality were standard before the 1820s, even in newspapers that were tied to political factions. William Maxwell, who established Cincinnati's first newspaper, the *Centinel of the North-Western Territory*, in 1793, adopted as his motto a common formulation of this ideal: "Open to All Parties, but Influenced by None."

Impersonality was the second ideal of the early press ideology. The prospectus of the *Inquisitor and Cincinnati Advertiser* in 1818, for example, pledged to "be ever slow to enter into personal controversy or to engage in violent or passionate discussion," since such personalities would be prohibitive of "a rational and deliberate examination of public affairs."[18] A rational populace required information on which to base its opinions, and it was the task of the press to provide that information. Partisan and personal intrusions prevented the proper fulfillment of that task.

In line with this philosophy, political controversy in Cincinnati papers before 1820 was impartial and impersonal. Contributions were printed under pseudonyms,[19] or as articles copied out of other papers. Individual papers printed opinions from both sides of a controversy. The editor's voice was heard, but in his role as reporter, not as advocate. The bulk of printed material consisted of verbatim transcripts of minutes or acts of legislatures and items copied from other papers.

Newspapers in Cincinnati did not become partisan instruments until after 1820. The political violence of the 1790s, which inflamed the press of the eastern seaboard,[20] was hardly visible in Cincinnati papers. But even in the East, pseudonyms and copy from other papers dominated newspapers' content, and overt editorial comment and partisan promotion was limited, especially compared with the scope it would attain in the Jacksonian era. Repeated invocations of impartiality and impersonality attested to their persistence as significant ideals in press ideology and attitudes toward the press.

Early Press Production and Consumption

The press ideology of the early Republic was mirrored in the craft culture of the print shop. Impartiality and impersonality were not just prescriptions for public discourse, they were also useful strategies for printer-craftsmen and expressive of a self-image as "honest mechanics." The culture of the shop supported republican conceptions of the press. But in the 1820s and 1830s, both craft structure and press ideology were to come under attack.

Cincinnati's first newspapers were conducted by independent printers. William Maxwell, proprietor of the *Centinel*, was a skilled craftsman who composed, printed, and distributed his own paper. His "printing establishment" consisted of a wooden handpress, much like the one Franklin had used decades earlier, and a few cases of type, altogether no more than a man could move in one load with a wheelbarrow. His "employees" were his wife, the former Nancy

Robins, and an apprentice named Benjamin Stokes, who ran away in 1795.[21] Such a printer, operating at peak efficiency, could turn out seventy-five impressions per hour.[22]

Cincinnati's press establishment before 1820 was small, harmonious, and stable. There were only a few weekly papers in publication at any given time; more frequent publication would not become practical until after 1820. Existing newspapers did not vigorously compete for advertising[23] or circulation, nor did they espouse competing political philosophies. And newspaper starts were rare, so that a few successful papers dominated the press establishment throughout most of the period.

Although circulation of early papers was limited by price and printing capacity, availability and readership of newspapers were still relatively high. Mrs. Trollope commented on the amount of time the average American spent reading newspapers, to the sad neglect of other pursuits, and to the great profit of the liquor stores and coffeehouses that subscribed to such papers for the perusal of their patrons.[24] Papers were also available at libraries and reading rooms, and subscribers frequently complained that their nonsubscribing neighbors enjoyed fuller use of their papers.[25] All impressionistic evidence suggests that multiple readership was the rule, especially in an age of weekly papers, when the latest news stayed fresh for seven days. There is no evidence to suggest that readership was limited to a social or economic elite, although modern scholars assume that the content and style of these papers were not suited to the "common man." On the contrary, the assumption of printers' aspirations and press ideology is that all citizens would read these papers — citizens understood to be white males.

This small, stable, uniform, and harmonious press establishment would grow and change rapidly after 1820. Different sorts of periodicals would evolve, and the debate among press products would grow continually more raucous. In turn, the ideology that informed the press and public attitudes toward it would be stretched to the breaking point.

Expansion and Diversification

The early western newspaper was much more than a newspaper. Mrs. Trollope, who (for good or ill) based many of her opinions concerning American society on her experiences in Cincinnati, considered "the universal reading of newspapers" the only exception to an otherwise complete absence of popular literary culture. It was because of its lonely status, she inferred, "that every *American newspaper* is more or less a magazine."[26]

Until the development of specialized periodicals in the 1820s, Cincinnati's newspapers were its only regular outlet for creative literature. Obligingly, most newspapers carried columns of poetry and *belles lettres*, often with pretentious titles such as "Parnassiad" or "Seat of the Muses." The surprising frequency with which stuff presented as serious literature is found in these papers attests to their perceived significance as literary organs.[27]

After 1820, periodicals devoted to all sorts of interests evolved rapidly from the weekly paper. In 1821, Cincinnati's first literary paper appeared. It was followed the next year by the Queen City's first religious and medical journals and its first gossip sheet. In 1826 the first agricultural and German-language papers appeared.[28] This was both a topical and a functional expansion of the press. It coincided with the expansion and coming to maturity of Cincinnati as a regional metropolis and urban center.

As early as 1830, Cincinnati had taken the lead in midwestern economic life. Eight times larger than any other midwestern city, it controlled the meat-packing industry and was the marketplace for much of the agricultural produce of the Ohio Valley. By 1850, the "porkshop of the Union" would also be the world's largest distilling center.[29]

Cincinnati's population was young, energetic, and diverse. There were relatively few older citizens, as most were newcomers to the rapidly growing city. As late as 1840, less than half of the residents of Cincinnati had lived there as long as ten years. In that same year, less than 10 percent of the adult males listed their state of birth as Ohio: surely fewer than one in ten was a native Cincinnatian. More than half in that year were foreign-born; 28 percent were German-born, up from 2.5 percent in 1825; and 33 percent came from eastern states, down from 58 percent in 1825.[30]

As the population grew and diversified, discrete social and occupational classes appeared. Social cleavages along economic lines had long been apparent in associational activities, but in the 1820s an elite class of merchants and professionals emerged. This was a distinctively urban class, alien to the surrounding agricultural region. The elite was mirrored by other distinctly urban classes, particularly propertyless craft and clerical workers, who by 1840 constituted a majority of Cincinnati's householders. There was a tightening of social lines.

In particular, as new productive enterprises substituted wage labor for the traditional craft structure, artisans felt their opportunities constricting. As the village became a city, it lost a sense of community that had been implicit in the republican ideology of the Revolutionary generation. As the polity divided more and more into self-interested groups, there were new tensions between groups and new reasons for associational activities within each group. These developments would all affect the press.[31]

The context of urban change was explosive urban growth. Cincinnati's population doubled in virtually every decade before 1850.[32] Population growth was matched by economic growth, slowed only by the Panics of 1819 and 1837 and a constant shortage of sound currency.

Demographic and economic growth was matched by growth in printing. In 1826, Cincinnati boasted two daily, three semiweekly, and two weekly papers, in addition to a weekly literary paper and a professional journal that appeared twice a month. At the beginning of 1845, there were twelve daily papers, many of which had subsidiary weeklies, along with fourteen weeklies devoted to religion, business, or reform and another fourteen technical, religious, or literary monthlies. Economically, nine printing plants grossed $52,000 and employed 23 hands in 1826, compared with twenty-five plants employing 362 and grossing $518,500 in 1840.[33] From 1815 to 1850, the office of the *Liberty Hall and Gazette* increased in value from $1,000 to $100,000, its employees increased from six to ninety, and the number of copies issued per year rose from 21,190 to 2,475,200.[34]

As the print industry matured, the people involved in producing papers found specialized roles in the workplace. The independent printer gave way to a combination of entrepreneurial publisher, political editor, and wage-earning workers. New technologies were introduced, resulting in rising costs for proprietors; large shops started squeezing out smaller shops. At the same time, surviving print shops sought more secure specialized markets, concentrating on book publishing or job printing, whereas previously the anchor of a shop's success had been a weekly paper. In Cincinnati, the first print shop to specialize in book and job printing was opened in 1828 by Ephraim Morgan and John Sanxay.[35] The rising cost of maintaining a successful print shop forced proprietors to resort to new financial arrangements, including mortgages, joint stock ownership, and sponsorship.[36]

Workers were even more troubled than owners by market and

technological change. Traditionally organized as a craft enterprise, the print shop had taken in youths as apprentices and graduated them as journeymen with marketable skills and some expectation of economic security. Proprietors had themselves worked through the ranks and shared their workers' craft culture. The 1820s and 1830s saw the work of the print shop transformed, however. New presses made physically demanding presswork obsolete. In 1826, Cincinnati's *Liberty Hall and Gazette* bought an iron press, the first one used in the West, capable of turning out 250 impressions an hour.[37] The *Gazette* tripled its per hour output eight years later when it bought an Adams power press, and again tripled its printing capacity in 1843 with the purchase of a Hoe cylinder press.[38] Proprietors began hiring unskilled labor at low wages to do much of the work that had previously required skilled and physically mature journeymen; the journeymen then were left to compete for proportionally fewer skilled positions. In Cincinnati, the first proprietors to recognize the new division of labor and to hire lower-paid workers to do unskilled work were Stephen L'Hommedieu and Charles Starbuck in or around 1830. In 1835, L'Hommedieu bought the city's first steam press, over the objections of his journeymen. As the shop thus became a factory, workers increasingly turned to unions.[39]

The expansion of the press was characterized by an extension of the early "republican" ideology of the press to areas outside the realm of the general newspaper. Early periodicals in fields such as religion, literature, and science were informed by the same sort of devotion to informing the public and conducting rational public investigation that the general newspaper professed. The Universalist *Star in the West*, for example, promised to promote "*free* enquiry," to be a "medium of communication for the *free* exchange of ideas and opinions," and urged "that all liberal minded souls, who love to see LIGHT, knowledge, and noble principles increase, will lend their influence and kind patronage, to support a work, the sole object of which is to support free enquiry, religious freedom, and Christian knowledge."[40] The rationale for journalism espoused here is a religious analogue to the ideology of public service and popular enlightenment that informed the early general newspaper.

Early periodical ventures expressed a genuine belief in the popularization of knowledge rendered arcane not by nature and reason but by society and superstition. Magazinist James Hall stated this belief thus:

The sciences and useful arts, which may be ably supported by popular
disquisition; and many branches of that knowledge, which are now buried
in ponderous volumes, or concealed in the jargon of foreign idioms, may be
emphatically made to be, *knowledge for the people*.[41]

A free rational populace was considered capable of being enlightened
by a free, rational press.

The same philosophy is evident in some medical journals. Although the earliest scientific journals were devoted to orthodox
Baconian inductive investigation by learned practitioners, medical
heresies appeared, with their own journals, espousing a belief that
everyone could become one's own physician. Alva Curtis of the
Thomsonian *Botanico-Medical Recorder*, for example, encouraged "each
and every person to acquaint himself thoroughly with all our simple
articles as well as their compounds."[42] Unlike the more ponderous
orthodox medical journals, the *Recorder* was brief, cheap, and issued frequently. It took pride in claiming that its circulation "far
exceeds the subscription to any other Medical Journal in the United
States."[43]

The republican ideology of the press was extended to include religious, literary, and scientific periodicals. As these periodicals multiplied to encompass a universe of jarring doctrines and disciplines,
however, the ideology that had suited a small, stable press establishment so well would become increasingly obsolete. The ideology of
rational inquiry that informed both early general newspapers and
early literary, religious, and scientific periodicals assumed a unitary
public. Their readerships were not conceived of as groups, organized
and discrete from the general public, with interests that would distinguish them from other citizen/readers. But as competition rather
than monopoly or oligopoly became the rule in culture and politics as
well as in the press, this image of a unitary public would become
problematic.[44]

The expansion of the press into new domains coincided with a
steady speeding up of long-distance communication. The latter process began in the 1790s with the establishment of regular postal
routes, and advanced at fairly regular intervals with the introduction of the steamboat, the building of the National Road, construction of canals, the introduction of express riders, and finally the
construction of a telegraph line to Cincinnati in 1847. The regular
and efficient transmission of information, together with the sophis-

tication of printing equipment and the growth of a sizable local audience, made possible an increase in frequency of publication. Cincinnati's first daily paper appeared in 1825, and its first successful daily in 1827.

The 1820s also saw the rise of mass politics in Cincinnati and elsewhere in the nation. Spurred by the expansion of the electorate and unprecedented high levels of voter participation, political operators constructed party machines that differed significantly from earlier ones in their national organization, their deemphasis of issues in the pursuit of electoral victory, their pragmatic coalition building, their aggressive outreach to voters, and their acceptance of the idea that permanent opposition is a healthy thing for a republic, an idea that in effect incorporated a notion of the political arena as a marketplace.[45] With the rise of the second party system, new papers were started and existing papers co-opted by the new party organizations, which linked them into systems of information diffusion and opinion formation that were national in scope. We might call this process the politicization of the press.

Daily publication coincided with the rise of the second party system to emphasize the position of the editor. Putting out a daily paper required the full-time attention of an editor, and the incessant electioneering of Jacksonian politics also demanded that editors have full-time involvement in partisan organizing and propaganda. One result was the articulation of functions within the press establishment. The composition of the paper became a function discrete from its production or finance or distribution. As the editor became more responsible and independent, he (or, very rarely, she) became more political and active. Editorial opinion became more common, and the editor's voice acquired more authority. The first campaign papers in Cincinnati appeared in 1828, and were conducted by the editors of the city's leading dailies: Moses Dawson of the Jacksonian *Advertiser* and Charles Hammond of the National Republican *Gazette*.

As the newspaper's content became more political, its format, production, and finance became more commercial. Matching politicization was an equally strong and complementary process of commercialization. The commercialization of the press can be seen in a new emphasis on advertising revenue and a new concern with economic information as news content. Commercialization accelerated in the 1830s with the introduction of the cash system of distribution.

Early newspapers relied on many sources for income, including government patronage, partisan subsidies, and retail trade in

Table 3.1
Comparison of advertising and subscription income for
Liberty Hall and Gazette, *1815–41*

Year	Subscription ($)	Advertising ($)	Advertising as percentage of income
1815	3,500	1,560	31
1841	14,800	21,190	59
Net change	11,300	19,630	
Percentage change	323	1,258	

Source: *Liberty Hall*, 1815, and *Cincinnati Daily Gazette, Tri-Weekly, Cincinnati Gazette,* and *Weekly Liberty Hall and Cincinnati Gazette,* 1841. A subjective element is involved in estimating the number of new and repeat insertions of advertisements, which were priced differently.

books, magazines, and patent medicines. But the primary determinants of a newspaper's success became subscription and advertising revenues. As time passed, advertising came to be the more important factor.

Table 3.1 shows estimates of the corresponding increases in subscription and advertising income for the office of Cincinnati's *Liberty Hall.* The increasing importance of advertising revenue indicates a new reliance on the marketplace. The press became a business, selling a service to other businesses by printing prices current and bank note exchange rates, and offering a product to a public now conceived of as consumers. It is in the context of market expansion that we should interpret the expansion of the press after 1820.

Advertising, as a business, was kept separate from the news and opinions offered in the press. Competing papers quickly learned not to let philosophical differences interfere with money-making, and agreed on uniform prices for advertising as early as 1814.[46] Similar agreements appeared from time to time. It is clear that, after 1814, lowering advertising rates was seen as unfair competition, a violation of accepted procedures attempted only by such upstarts as Joseph Buchanan's *Literary Cadet,* which offered rates *"twenty percent cheaper* than the customary prices." The *Literary Cadet* quickly failed.

As newspapers became more reliant on advertising revenue, they also tended to present a larger share of news geared toward economic interests. Content analysis of Cincinnati papers at ten-year intervals from 1795 to 1845 shows a steady increase in the percentage of

Table 3.2

Content analysis of Cincinnati newspapers, 1795–1845

Category	Percentage of Total Items by Category					
	1795	1805	1815	1825	1835	1845
Political/judicial	33	24	22	32	25	25
Military/diplomatic	21	21	32	9	10	6
Indian/slave	6	2	4	2	2	1
Minutes/laws	31	17	14	7	6	3
Commercial/economic	2	8	9	15	17	18
News	—	6	5	10	17	23
Filler	7	17	7	19	16	18
Scientific/agricultural	—	5	7	6	7	6

Note: These figures were drawn from a sampling of two newspapers for each year, except 1795, when only one was published, and 1845, when three were consulted. Papers used were the *Centinel of the North-Western Territory* (1795); the *Western Spy* and *Liberty Hall* (1815); the *National Republican* and *Cincinnati Advertiser* (1825—both biweekly); the *Daily Gazette* and *Daily Republican* (1835); and the *Daily Commercial, Daily Enquirer,* and *Weekly Liberty Hall and Cincinnati Gazette* (1845). Samplings were designed to be representative of the entire conventional newspaper establishment in each year. Samplings covered the entire year, thus accounting for seasonal variations. The basic sampling unit was one item, with additional weight for lengthy items. Percentages for individual newspapers for each year were averaged, then rounded off to whole numbers to yield the figures presented. Content analysis here does not include advertising material. "Minutes/laws" refers to verbatim or condensed digests; "news" includes reports of deaths and weddings, fires, crimes, and other events that fall outside the areas of affairs of state or the markets; "filler" material includes religious and moral essays, poetry, reviews of literature and performances, and anecdotes and short stories.

newspapers' content devoted to commercial and economic information. Statistics on newspaper content are presented in Table 3.2.

The newspaper innovations of the period also had commercial implications. The earliest conductors of daily papers in Cincinnati appealed directly to the "disposition always manifested by the mercantile and trading classes to foster the undertaking of such objects as are calculated to promote their interests." These papers proposed "to promote the interests of COMMERCE and MANUFACTURES" by giving prices current and currency exchange rates for New York, Philadelphia, Boston, Baltimore, and New Orleans, announcing steamboat arrivals and departures, and giving accounts of exports, imports, and the foreign markets.[47]

Cincinnati's first daily was printed in 1825, but its first truly successful daily, the *Daily Cincinnati Gazette*, was not established until

1827. The *Gazette* was also clearly aimed at mercantile interests. Its original subscription list numbered 164, and almost all of the addresses on it were on the lower side of town, in the business district.[48]

The most dramatic innovation of the age was the penny paper. Penny dailies were circulated cheaply and on the "cash system," which meant cash sales to distributors (often newsboys), who sold in turn to readers and subscribers. While it is not certain that this would mean increased reliance on single-issue sales as opposed to subscriptions, still it seems clear that with the cash system of distribution the newspaper became more entwined in the marketplace.[49]

Penny papers were considered disposable products. This can be inferred from the fact that only a few of the thirty-odd penny papers published in Cincinnati between 1836 and 1848 are represented by more than scattered extant issues today. These papers, like conventional dailies of their day, featured a large share of economic information and relied heavily — perhaps even more than conventional papers — on advertising revenue. And the cash system of distribution, which was eventually adopted by conventional papers also, implied increased attention to the needs of the newspaper reader as consumer. Together, the emphasis on advertising plus circulation meant another step in a process that had begun earlier, the commodification of readerships. Readers became not just citizens or voters, but a marketable product to be sold to advertisers. The commodification of readerships thus mirrored a similar part of the politicization process, in which readerships were objectified as armies of voters to be "sold" to party operatives and candidates.

Newspapers became commercial products produced by factorylike establishments competing for public support in the marketplace. But ideology and attitudes still endowed the press with the aura of public servant, and allowed it the single function of transmitting truth in its simple dress. Ideology and attitudes did not envision a welter of competing journals and their competing truths. Dissonance among ideology, attitudes, and social fact generated violence.

Limits on the Arena of Discourse

The newspaper fantasy of the early Republic rested on the image of the extended town meeting. In an extended polity, citizens could not engage directly in face-to-face political debate, but the newspaper (imagined as a completely transparent medium) would permit interaction of an indirect but essentially similar nature. The town meeting could be national in scope, and public opinion would stand in the place of law.

In this newspaper fantasy, however, individual papers must be passive. They must not channel or color the raw information they bear; they must not close their columns to responsible citizens; and they must not indulge styles of debate designed to mislead reason or to exploit irrational passions. Freedom requires virtue.

Politicization and commercialization in the press stretched press ideology. The promotion of political and economic self-interest by individual papers defied the values and expectations of an older generation of citizens and press conductors — it seemed wrong. So editors of partisan and commercial papers began looking for an ideologically comfortable justification for their new behavior. The resolution was the adoption of a model based on an analogy to the marketplace.[50] Parties, values, and newspapers competed in a marketplace, and the market, as though by an invisible hand, regulated conduct in such a fashion that the outcome of the pursuit of private interest in political discourse and in the press would be the common good.

Still, faith in the self-righting market took hold slowly, and in the meantime certain types of press conduct remained impermissible and popular attitudes held certain ideas intolerable. In such cases, direct action — a very visible hand — regulated the marketplace.

Mob action greeted journals perceived as inimical to the common good in Cincinnati in the 1830s. In 1832, a gossip sheet titled the *True Blue and Castigator* began publishing personal material. Finally it offended a local worthy so seriously that he rushed to the printing office and gave Nimrod Wildfire, the paper's pseudonymous editor, a sound thrashing. That evening a mob attacked the *Castigator's* office and threw the printing press into the Ohio River. The paper did not resume publication.[51]

Of greater importance was antiabolitionist violence. Abolitionism seemed to pose a special threat. It seemed to many a foreign import, financed by British and eastern capital, designed to subvert the economic well-being and racial purity of the nation. It threatened to divide and destroy the peaceful system of majoritarian politics that had been established in the wake of Andrew Jackson's electoral victories of 1828 and 1832. And it seemed to expand by a massive propaganda campaign. In the minds of antiabolitionists, the movement to end slavery sparked multiple fears: of foreign subversion, of social revolution, of the demonic potential of novel technologies (especially the steam press). And partisan leaders, who had an interest in seeing that antislavery's sectional appeal was prevented from rupturing the party system, encouraged these hyperbolic fears. The result was a wave of antiabolitionist violence in the 1830s and beyond.[52]

Cincinnati was a center for abolitionist activism. It was the site of the Lane Seminary debates, which are frequently credited with starting the abolitionist movement; it was the home in the 1830s and 1840s of such antislavery stalwarts as James G. Birney, two-time presidential candidate of the Liberty party, and Harriet Beecher Stowe, author of *Uncle Tom's Cabin*.

Cincinnati was also the site of antiabolitionist activity. In 1836, the antislavery *Philanthropist* became a victim of mob violence — its printing press also was thrown into the Ohio River. Comment in the daily papers indicated that the mob action was widely condoned as a defense of the common good against a licentious abuse of liberty of the press.[53] The *Philanthropist* resumed publication; it was mobbed again in 1842.

The German-language press also was perceived as in violation of the principles of the press as an agent of the common good, especially by Whigs and Protestants, since it isolated a linguistic group from participation in the general arena of public opinion. As late as 1844, the Whig *Gazette* attributed defeat at the polls to a papal conspiracy involving the German-language press.[54] The violent controversy over nativism and anti-Catholicism in Cincinnati was intimately linked with the crisis over free discussion, minority opinion, and the common good in press attitudes and ideology.

The violence of the 1830s yielded to an accommodation in the 1840s. Direct action was employed less frequently; market forces were seen as usually sufficient agencies of control; and a stable mainstream matrix of publications associated with commercial, political, professional, and religious organizations served to occupy a secured center. Still, violent suppression of nonmainstream periodicals would recur, especially in periods of perceived instability.[55]

From Popular Enlightenment to Organized Knowledge and Commercial Entertainment

The sporadic violence of the 1830s coincided with several congruent processes. In politics, as noted, there was a shift from a consensus-centered ideology of republican impartiality and impersonality to a competition-driven endorsement of partisan activity. Likewise, in religion, science, education, and literature, early journals devoted to the popularization of enlightenment were replaced by professional organs or by broadly circulated sentimental and commercial publications, the purpose of which was to entertain, and not to enlighten. In all these cases, the utopian ideal of an active citizenry engaged in rational democracy grew more remote.

The religious press became the exclusive domain of denominational publications. The most important example in Cincinnati was the Western Methodist Book Concern, which by 1854 published five journals with an aggregate circulation of 85,000.[56] Religious publications became a big business — in 1851, the Book Concern published $125,000 worth of books and periodicals.[57]

Literary periodicals also became commercial. Early local literary papers had sought to promote serious western literature and had scorned "the sickly sentimentality so common in periodicals of a literary nature,"[58] referring to the popular eastern papers. But these idealistic ventures failed rather quickly. Instead, two formulas for success were discovered. The first was the appeal to sentiment, embodied most effectively in the *Ladies' Repository and Gatherings of the West* (1841–76), a publication of the Western Methodist Book Concern, combining piety and polite literature. The second formula involved cheap, sensational western fiction, and is typified by the weekly *Great West*, founded in 1848, which by 1856 had attained a circulation of 15,000.[59]

A similar move from idealism to commercial reality is evident in the history of educational journalism in Cincinnati. Early journalistic promoters of education had contended that the common schools would have far-reaching social effects: "To the bigoted [sic] and the aristocratic we cannot conceive of anything more disagreeable."[60] The first specifically educational journals were founded in the same spirit. They were aimed at the general public, they pledged to cover matters of general interest, and they were colored by a hopeful expectation that education would be a means for a true popularization of enlightenment. But by the 1840s, educational journalism had become preoccupied with the interests of professional educators and commercial publishing houses. Distributed free to teachers and administrators, these papers were little more than advertising circulars for schoolbooks and other school supplies.

Conventional medical journals had always sought to facilitate "professional intercourse and conversation."[61] The most important figure here, Dr. Daniel Drake of the *Western Journal of the Medical and Physical Sciences*, sought contributions primarily from professional physicians for a readership composed of professional physicians.[62] These journals campaigned actively on behalf of a self-regulating state-licensed medical profession and consonant medical education.[63]

Heterodox medical journals and practitioners originally had appealed to the people to depose this privileged medical establishment, but by the late 1840s, they promoted instead equal *privileges* for "every enlightened, educated, and honest physician, . . . no matter what doctrine he may deem it his duty to adopt."[64] Competing medical sects would thus accord each other equal respectability, modeling themselves on religious sects. But the ideal of popularization was lost in the pursuit of equality of privilege. Heterodox medical journals no longer sought wide circulation, but a professional audience; they no longer sought to make each man his own doctor.

Cincinnati's experience describes a pattern of press development. The ideology of the press was originally broadly utopian. It envisioned the creation of a radically novel republican polity and the broad popularization of all sorts of knowledge. It envisioned the discovery of fundamental truths through publicly conducted rational investigation.

Popular attitudes endorsed this ideology. The public expected the press to educate, and hence credited the press with immense power in informing public opinion. This popular acceptance of the idea of the power of the press and its consequent responsibilities was itself an essential underlying cause of instances of antipress violence in the 1830s.

The expansion of the press led to the obsolescence of this utopian ideology and the popular attitudes associated with it. Competing truths and schools of thought found free expression in a marketplace of ideas. But truth itself became relative or irrelevant, and genuine knowledge became the privileged domain of occupational or professional elites. The press itself, as a social instrument, became subtly conservative.

Implications

This essay represents an attempt to examine the development of the press from an ecological point of view. Press development has been presented as a creature of changing ideologies, political processes, social structures, and commercial activities. The driving force behind the early expansion of the U.S. press was a fantasy that saw popular enlightenment and political involvement through the press as central to the legacy of the Revolution. This fantasy also generated rules of conduct appropriate to monopoly journals published to inform a unitary public of rational citizens. But developments in the 1820s and 1830s — both in Cincinnati and nationally — challenged this set of ideas. The rise of the second party system produced a journalism of partisan self-interest; the expansion of the city and the separation of its population into social, ethnic, and occupational groups produced an increase in the number of specialized periodicals; the rise of a market for certain kinds of print entertainment prompted new kinds of literary journals and some changes in newspaper content and conduct; religious denominationalism changed religious periodicals from public journals based on political models to organs of particular churches; and the resulting confusion over the governing principles of press conduct led to violence, directed especially at nonmainstream groups. The resolution of all these changes was a press and a press ideology patterned on market notions thriving in an expanding market society.

These findings suggest an alternative to currently dominant characterizations of press development in the early Republic. Standard histories, treating journalism as a distinct entity and considering media as things in themselves, have considered the main story in press history to be the liberation of journalism as truth seeking from a number of constraints, the two most important in the early Republic being partisan control and technological inadequacies — especially in the realm of transmitting information over distances. The newspaper is said to have freed itself from partisan control by cultivating support in the marketplace. And the telegraph is said to have annihilated time and space effectively.

On an abstract level, these characterizations are suspect. The marketplace supported newspapers, but fierce market competition made partisan support more important for the survival of commercial papers than it had been to monopoly or oligopoly papers in the earliest decades of the nineteenth century. Surely partisanism in the press did not decrease in the 1830s and 1840s, no matter what conclusions scholars have drawn from the New York penny papers. Likewise, technological innovations such as the telegraph may have contributed to crucial changes, but surely the uses to which the technologies were put were more important than the technologies themselves, and these uses were determined by attitudes and practices already established. In particular, the telegraph did not eliminate informational inequalities or make news transmission instant and automatic; its most important effect was to make news a salable commodity by allowing news organizations such as the Associated Press (eventually) to claim it as property.

If we maintain our definition of a medium as a network of relationships, it is clear that these developments do not constitute the liberation of journalism from constraining forces. Rather, they mark adjustments to changing environments (like the growth of urban markets) that also accomplish changes in the matrix of relationships that constitutes a medium.

These abstract arguments are borne out in the concrete study presented here. In Cincinnati's experience, neither the penny press nor the telegraph prompted revolutionary change in the press. Rather, each marked an incremental step in the direction of previous change, respectively in the processes of commercialization and the speeding up of long-distance communication. The characterization of such change as revolutionary obscures the more important long-term processes at work.

Change in the press establishment was characterized by expansion, by commercialization, and by professionalization and institutional involvement. The press became more pervasive and diverse, and an entire popular culture became available in print. But as the press as a whole became more powerful, the influence of any single newspaper was diminished. The power of the press may have increased, but the power of any single idea or opinion conveyed by the press declined.

Press conductors, especially reformers, continued to invoke the ideology of the press as public servant. They believed that the spread of enlightenment through the press could bring about sweeping changes in society. This strain of thought had the force of tradition in press rhetoric, but it was a tradition that did not match the reality of the commercial press.

Far from being revolutionary, press innovations and the print culture created in early America tended to be conservative in social impact. Because of these innovations, printing became a major industry, and the press developed an economic presence of considerable importance. At the same time, newspapers and periodicals developed a new significance as commercial products.

Rather than being instruments of public enlightenment, however, newspapers and periodicals came to serve political, religious, and professional organizations. Rather than being tools of rational liberty, newspapers and periodicals sought to manipulate public opinion through judicious handling of images and rhetoric. Rather than presenting the truth to public scrutiny, the press deluged a consumer public with contradictory truths competing in a marketplace of ideas.

Notes

1. This is not a novel perspective. Among others calling for a similar approach, see Robert Ezra Park, "The Natural History of the Newspaper," *American Journal of Sociology* (1923): 80–98; Alfred McClung Lee, *The Daily Newspaper in America: The Evolution of a Social Instrument* (New York: Macmillan, 1937); James W. Carey, "The Problem of Journalism History," *Journalism History* 1 (1974): 3–5, 27; Joseph McKerns, "The Limits of Progressive Journalism History," *Journalism History* 4 (1977): 88–92; and Hazel Dicken Garcia's chapters in Hazel Dicken Garcia and John D. Stevens, *Communication History* (Beverly Hills: Sage, 1980).

2. Journalism history has traditionally fallen into several common genres, the two most important being comprehensive histories and biographical studies. Comprehensive histories have been composed primarily for use as texts in courses on newspaper history in journalism school curricula. The most important are Frederic Hudson, *Journalism in the United States: From 1690 to 1872* (New York: Harper, 1873); Willard G. Bleyer, *Main Currents in the History of American Journalism* (Boston: Houghton Mifflin, 1927); Frank Luther Mott, *American Journalism: A History of Newspapers in the United States*, rev. ed. (New York: Macmillan, 1950); and Edwin Emery and Michael B. Emery, *The Press in America: An Interpretive History of the Mass Media*, 5th ed. (Englewood Cliffs, N.J.: Prentice-Hall, 1984). Biographical studies are the most common sort of detailed studies, and focus on either a single newspaper or a particularly noteworthy editor or journalist. Their tone is usually positive, emphasizing the quality and influence of their subjects. Good examples are James L. Crouthamel, "James Gordon Bennett, the New York *Herald*, and the Development of Newspaper Sensationalism," *New York History* 54 (1974), 294–316; and William E. Ames, *A History of the National Intelligencer* (Chapel Hill: University of North Carolina Press, 1972). In the past two decades, increasing attention has been paid to social history in both comprehensive and biographical studies. See, for example, Michael Schudson, *Discovering the News: A Social History of American Newspapers* (New York: Basic Books, 1978); Thomas C. Leonard, *The Power of the Press: The Birth of American Political Reporting* (New York: Oxford University Press, 1986); and Jean Folkerts and Dwight Teeter, *Voices of a Nation* (New York: Macmillan, 1988).

3. Criticism of journalism history's inadequacies became common in the 1970s. The most important critiques are Carey, "The Problem of Journalism History"; McKerns, "The Limits of Progressive Journalism History"; and Dicken Garcia and Stevens, *Communication History*.

4. See especially Schudson, *Discovering the News*; Daniel Schiller, *Objectivity and the News: The Public and the Rise of Commercial Journalism* (Philadelphia: University of Pennsylvania Press, 1981); and Leonard, *The Power of the Press*.

5. The phrase is taken from the table of contents of Mott's *American Journalism*.

6. Most prominent among these historians are Schudson, *Discovering the*

News; Leonard, *The Power of the Press*; and Arthur Kaul and Joseph McKerns, "The Dialectic Ecology of the Newspaper," *Critical Studies in Mass Communication* 2 (1985), 217–33.

7. Walter Sutton, *The Western Book Trade: Cincinnati as a Nineteenth-Century Publishing and Book Trade Center* (Columbus: Ohio State University Press, 1961), 67; Frank Luther Mott, *A History of American Magazines*, 5 vols. (Cambridge: Harvard University Press, 1930), 1:*1741–1850*, 375n.

8. By *ideology*, I mean a shared, relatively unexamined language that includes a normative dimension. In any situation, such a language will structure what people perceive and what they may communicate about matters of common interest.

9. The classic works setting forth the republican ideology are Bernard Bailyn, *The Ideological Origins of the American Revolution* (Cambridge: Harvard University Press, 1967); Gordon Wood, *The Creation of the American Republic, 1776–1787* (Chapel Hill: University of North Carolina Press, 1969); and J. G. A. Pocock, *Politics, Language, and Time: Essays on Political Thought and History* (New York: Atheneum, 1971). The salience of republicanism has been challenged by scholars emphasizing the centrality of Lockean liberalism in the Revolutionary era: see, for example, John Patrick Diggins, "Comrades and Citizens: New Mythologies in American Historiography," *American Historical Review* 90 (1985): 614–38; Thomas Pangle, *The Spirit of Modern Republicanism: The Moral Vision of the American Founders and the Philosophy of Locke* (Chicago: University of Chicago Press, 1988). For a useful summary of the significance of the literature on republicanism, see Joyce Appleby's introduction to a special issue of *American Quarterly* on the topic, "Introduction: Republicanism and Ideology," *American Quarterly* 37 (1985): 461–73; see also the other articles in that issue.

10. The role of the press in the Revolution is discussed in Arthur M. Schlesinger, *Prelude to Independence: The Newspaper War on Britain, 1764–1776* (New York: Knopf, 1958); Philip Davidson, *Propaganda and the American Revolution, 1763–1783* (Chapel Hill: University of North Carolina Press, 1941); Bernard Bailyn and John B. Hench, eds., *The Press and the American Revolution* (Worcester: American Antiquarian Society, 1980); Thomas C. Leonard, "News for a Revolution: The Exposé in America, 1768–1773," *Journal of American History* 67 (1980): 26–40.

11. Thomas Jefferson to Col. Edward Carrington, January 16, 1787, in Andrew A. Lipscomb, ed., *The Writings of Thomas Jefferson*, 20 vols. (Washington, D.C.: Thomas Jefferson Memorial Association, 1905), VI:57–58. For extended treatment of the ideology of impartiality and its relationship to republican ideology, see John C. Nerone, *The Culture of the Press in the Early Republic: Cincinnati, 1793–1848* (New York: Garland, 1989), ch. 3; Michael Warner, *The Letters of the Republic: Publication and the Public Sphere in Eighteenth-Century America* (Cambridge: Harvard University Press, 1990); and Stephen Botein, "Printers and the American Revolution," in *The Press and the American Revolution*, ed. Bernard Bailyn and John B. Hench (Boston: Northeastern University Press, 1981); for a treatment that emphasizes the libertarianism of early printers, see Jeffery A. Smith, *Printers and Press Freedom: The Ideology of Early American Journalism* (New York: Oxford University Press, 1988).

12. Mott, *American Journalism*, 167–68.

13. Prospectus of the *Miami Gazette*, published in the Cincinnati *Western Spy*, April 17, 1813.

14. Culver Smith, *The Press, Politics, and Patronage: The American Government's Use of Newspapers, 1789–1875* (Athens: University of Georgia Press, 1977), 4; G. D.

Abbott, in the *Weekly Liberty Hall and Cincinnati Gazette*, December 5, 1844; *Cincinnati Literary Cadet*, March 9, 1820.

15. For discussion of the quasi-governmental nature of the early press, see Julian P. Bretz, "Some Aspects of Postal Expansion into the West," *Annual Report of the American Historical Association, 1909* (Washington, 1911): 141–49; Smith, *The Press, Politics, and Patronage*.

16. This notion of impartiality was prevalent among American printers throughout the colonial period. See Stephen Botein, " 'Meer Mechanics' and an Open Press: The Business and Political Strategies of Colonial Printers," *Perspectives in American History* 9 (1975): 127–225.

17. *Liberty Hall*, December 4, 1804.

18. *Inquisitor and Cincinnati Advertiser*, June 23, 1818.

19. See, for example, the early controversy over taxation among Manlius, Plebius, Vitruvius, Dorastus, et al., *Centinel of the North-Western Territory*, November 12, 19, 1793; April 4, September 20, 27, October 18, 1794; and a later controversy over the propriety of a public theater in Cincinnati among the Rev. Joshua Lacy Wilson, Theatricus, Philanthropos, and Y., *Western Spy*, January 1815; *Liberty Hall*, January 11, 23, February 18, 1815.

20. The involvement of the press in the political violence of the 1790s is treated in Donald H. Stewart, *The Opposition Press of the Federalist Period* (Albany: State University of New York Press, 1969); Walter Francis Brown, "John Adams and the American Press, 1797–1801: The First Full-Scale Confrontation between the Executive and the Media," doctoral dissertation, University of Notre Dame, 1974; and David Hackett Fischer, *The Revolution of American Conservatism: The Federalist Party in the Era of Jeffersonian Democracy* (New York: Harper, 1965).

21. William C. Robinson, "The Pioneer Printer in the United States," *Journal of Library History* 4 (July 1969): 207–12; Osman Castle Hooper, *History of Ohio Journalism, 1793–1933* (Columbus: Spahr & Glenn, 1933), 4; Charles B. Galbreath, "The First Newspaper in the Northwest Territory (The Editor and his Wife)," *Ohio Archeological and Historical Society Publications* 13 (1904): 332, 345; Maxwell offered a reward of ten cents for his runaway apprentice, a satirically low figure, perhaps attesting to the worthlessness of an apprentice in a firm so small: *Centinel*, June 27, 1795.

22. Hooper, *Ohio Journalism*, 3; Reuben Gold Thwaites, "The Ohio Valley Press before the War of 1812–1815," *Proceedings of the American Antiquarian Society* 19 (1909): 351.

23. Agreements on advertising rates were routine by 1814. "Terms of Advertising in Cincinnati Newspapers," *Liberty Hall*, December 13, 1814.

24. Frances Trollope, *Domestic Manners of the Americans*, ed. Donald Smalley (New York: Knopf, 1949 [1832]), 102–3.

25. See, for example, the letter of Fair Play in the Cincinnati *Independent Press and Freedom's Advocate*, April 11, 1822.

26. Trollope, *Domestic Manners*, 92–93.

27. William H. Venable, *Beginnings of Literary Culture in the Ohio Valley: Historical and Biographical Sketches* (New York: Peter Smith, 1949 [1891]).

28. These papers are, in order, the *Olio* (literary), 1821; the *Cincinnati Remembrancer* (religious), the *Western Quarterly Reporter of Medical, Surgical, and Natural Science* (medical), and the *Thistle* (gossip), 1822; and the *Western Tiller* (agricultural) and *Ohio Chronik* (German language), 1826.

29. Frederick Marryat, *A Diary in America, with Remarks on Its Institutions*, ed.

Sydney Jackman (New York: Knopf, 1962), 222; Francis P. Weisenburger, "The Urbanization of the Middle West: Town and Village in the Pioneer Period," *Indiana Magazine of History* 41 (March 1945): 29–30.

30. Walter Stix Glazer, "Cincinnati in 1840: A Community Profile," doctoral dissertation, University of Michigan, 1968, 102, 212, 213; Charles Cist, *Cincinnati in 1841: Its Early Annals and Future Prospects* (Cincinnati: Charles Cist, 1841), 39.

31. On early social class, see Richard C. Wade, *The Urban Frontier: The Rise of Western Cities, 1790–1830* (Cambridge: Harvard University Press, 1959), 105–6; for rural nostalgia and alienation, see *Western Tiller*, December 1, 1826; on urban stratification, see Glazer, "Cincinnati in 1840," 120–23; on early social stratification after 1820, see Wade, *The Urban Frontier*, 204. Scholars have noted the particular development of artisanal workers in early national cities. Most significantly, Wilentz has identified "artisanal republicanism" in the mentality of New York City's artisans; see Sean Wilentz, *Chants Democratic: New York City and the Rise of the American Working Class, 1788–1850* (New York: Oxford University Press, 1984). Wilentz's work has been influential; his counterpart in studying Cincinnati's artisans is Steven J. Ross, whose *Workers on the Edge: Work, Leisure, and Politics in Industrializing Cincinnati, 1788–1890* (New York: Columbia University Press, 1985) more than complements Glazer's "Cincinnati in 1840."

32. Population statistics are available in Charles Cist, "Population of Cincinnati," *Cincinnati Miscellany* 1 (October 1844): 19; and Cist, *Cincinnati in 1841*, 28–38 *et passim*.

33. In the same years, the city's gross product increased from $1,800,000 to $17,432,670. *Mercantile Daily Advertiser*, September 18, 1826; Charles Cist, "Cincinnati Periodical Press," *Cincinnati Miscellany* 1 (January 1845): 107–8; Benjamin Drake and Edward Deering Mansfield, *Cincinnati in 1826* (Cincinnati: Morgan Lodge & Fisher, 1827), 64–66; Cist, *Cincinnati in 1841*, 56, 58.

34. William Turner Coggeshall, "History of the Cincinnati Press and Its Conductors" (Unpublished manuscript, Cincinnati Historical Society, c. 1860), 14.

35. William J. Rorabaugh, *The Craft Apprentice: From Franklin to the Machine Age in America* (New York: Oxford University Press, 1986), 146; Ross, *Workers on the Edge*, 38–39.

36. Dyer has discussed the various financial arrangements employed by Wisconsin printers in the same period; see Carolyn Dyer, "Economic Dependence and Concentration of Ownership among Antebellum Wisconsin Newspapers," *Journalism History* 7 (1980): 42–46. Her research implies that printers were not financially independent, instead relying on all sorts of individuals and organizations—whether with political, financial, or community interest in supporting a printer or newspaper.

37. *Weekly Liberty Hall and Cincinnati Gazette*, December 12, 1844.

38. Sutton, *The Western Book Trade*, 74; Hooper, *History of Ohio Journalism*, 7; *Weekly Liberty Hall and Cincinnati Gazette*, May 11, 1843, December 12, 1844.

39. On the craft culture of printers, see William S. Pretzer, " 'The British, Duff Green, the Rats and the Devil': Custom, Capital, and Conflict in the Washington Printing Trade, 1834–1836," *Labor History* 27 (1985–86): 5–30, and "The Quest for Autonomy and Discipline: Labor and Technology in the Book Trades," *Proceedings of the American Antiquarian Society* 96 (1986): 85–131. On the transformation of the print shop, see Rorabaugh, *The Craft Apprentice*, 11–14, ch. 4; and Ross, *Workers on the Edge*, 38–39; on print unions, see Lee, *The Daily Newspaper*, 135–39; and Ross, *Workers on the Edge*, 46–48.

40. Jonathon Kidwell, "New Prospectus," *Star in the West* 1 (December 1827): 40. The *Star in the West* moved to Cincinnati from Eaton, Ohio, as the *Sentinel and Star in the West* in 1829.

41. James Hall, "To the Reader," *Western Monthly Magazine* 1 (January 1833): 3–4.

42. Alva Curtis, "Preface," *Botanico-Medical Recorder* 6 (1837): v.

43. Alva Curtis, "Preface," *Botanico-Medical Recorder* 7 (1838): iii. He claimed more than a thousand paid subscriptions.

44. Nationally, the creation of a diverse and pluralistic media environment is the theme of Richard D. Brown's *Knowledge Is Power: The Diffusion of Information in Early America, 1700–1865* (New York: Oxford University Press, 1989).

45. Scholars have disagreed on the extent to which the first party system differed from the second. The argument that the second party system was different is stated best in two classic books: Richard P. McCormick's *The Second American Party System* (Chapel Hill: University of North Carolina Press, 1969); and Richard Hofstadter's *The Idea of a Party System: The Rise of Legitimate Opposition in the United States, 1780–1840* (Berkeley: University of California Press, 1969). See also two essays by Ronald Formisano: "Deferential-Participant Politics: The Early Republic's Political Culture, 1789–1840," *American Political Science Review* 68 (1974): 473–87; and "Federalists and Republicans: Parties, Yes—System, No," in *The Evolution of American Electoral Systems*, ed. Paul Kleppner (Westport, Conn.: Greenwood, 1984).

46. "Terms of Advertising in Cincinnati Newspapers," *Liberty Hall*, December 13, 1814.

47. *Mercantile Daily Advertiser*, September 4, 1826.

48. Hooper, *History of Ohio Journalism*, 71–72; William Turner Coggeshall, *The Newspaper Record, Containing a Complete List of Newspapers and Periodicals . . .* (Philadelphia: Lay & Brother, 1856), 165–66; Robert C. Wheeler, *Ohio Newspapers: A Living Record* (Columbus: Ohio History Press, 1950), 196; *Daily Gazette*, June 25, 1827.

49. The penny press and its historiography are discussed more fully in John C. Nerone, "The Mythology of the Penny Press," *Critical Studies in Mass Communication* 4 (1987): 376–404.

50. It is, I think, anachronistic to describe free press thought in the United States before the Jacksonian era as characterized by a belief in the "marketplace of ideas," a notion most fully developed by Jeffery A. Smith in *Printers and Press Freedom: The Ideology of Early American Journalism* (New York: Oxford University Press, 1987). In prior press ideology, the motivation behind market activity (self-interest) was considered inappropriate—licentious—in both political discourse and press conduct. A more apt characterization than "marketplace" would be a "commonwealth" of ideas.

51. Isaac Appleton Jewett to Joseph Willard, Cincinnati, August 16, 1832, in James Taylor Dunn, ed., "Cincinnati Is a Delightful Place: Letters of a Law Clerk, 1831–4," *Bulletin of the Historical and Philosophical Society of Ohio* 10 (July 1952): 270.

52. On antiabolitionism in general, see Leonard Richards, *Gentlemen of Property and Standing: Anti-Abolition Mobs in Jacksonian America* (New York: Oxford University Press, 1970); Lorman Ratner, *Powder Keg: Northern Opposition to the Antislavery Movement, 1831–1840* (New York: Basic Books, 1968).

53. The events of the riot are recounted in Daniel Aaron, "Cincinnati, 1818–1838: A Study of Attitudes," doctoral dissertation, Harvard University, 1943, 454–

76; Betty Fladeland, *James Gillespie Birney: From Slaveholder to Abolitionist* (Ithaca, N.Y.: Cornell University Press, 1955), 136–42; Patrick Allen Folk, " 'The Queen City of Mobs': Riots and Community Reactions in Cincinnati, 1788–1848," doctoral dissertation, University of Toledo, 1978, 57–147; Richards, *Gentlemen of Property and Standing*, 92–100.

54. Alfred G. Stritch, "Political Nativism in Cincinnati, 1830–1860," *Records of the American Catholic Historical Society of Philadelphia* 48 (1937): 240–49; Joseph M. White, "Religion and Community: Cincinnati Germans, 1814–1870," doctoral dissertation, University of Notre Dame, 1980, 336–38.

55. For more complete treatment of the phenomenon of antipress violence, see John C. Nerone, "Violence against the Press in U.S. History," *Journal of Communication* 40 (Summer 1990): 6–33.

56. Sutton, *The Book Trade*, 160.

57. *Ibid.*, 151–59.

58. *Cincinnati Mirror*, October 1, 1831.

59. Sutton, *The Book Trade*, 191, 197.

60. Moses Dawson, in *Cincinnati Advertiser and Ohio Phoenix*, June 26, 1833.

61. Prospectus, *Western Medical Gazette*, December 15, 1832.

62. Prospectus for volume 6, appended to *Western Journal of the Medical and Physical Sciences* 5 (1832).

63. Daniel Drake, "Essays on Medical Education and the Medical Profession in the United States," *Western Journal of the Medical and Physical Sciences* 5 (1832): 526, 527.

64. "Circular Address to the Medical Profession," quoted in Ralph Taylor, "The Formation of the Eclectic School in Cincinnati," *Ohio State Archaeological and Historical Quarterly* 51 (1942): 281.

Chapter 4

Nineteenth-Century Suffrage Periodicals: Conceptions of Womanhood and the Press
Linda Steiner

In 1861 the editor of the single women's rights organ published during the Civil War argued:

> Let all other available means and avenues for the advocacy of equal rights be made use of, but none of them supply the place of a special advocate to plead the cause of justice for the needy and the oppressed. . . . The Woman's Rights reform needs such an organ, and must have it, unless those who have toiled and hoped and struggled for a more just regulation of human affairs are willing now to give up the warfare and surrender to irretrievable defeat.[1]

Lizzie Bunnell, editor of the *Mayflower*, was one of many suffragists to appreciate the significance of woman's rights papers to sustaining both individuals and the movement as a whole.[2] In the second half of the nineteenth century, suffragists established well over sixty periodicals.[3] As the prosuffrage *Genius of Liberty* put it: "We want a common nervous circulation; . . . we want a general excitement, a common sensibility, and universal will, and a concordant action."[4] Julia Ward Howe repeatedly warned in the *Woman's Journal*, "Our greatest weakness as a class consists of this, that we are segregated, owing each other no allegiance, bearing each other no active goodwill."[5] Periodicals were the means for constructing and maintaining shared sensibility, collective action, and allegiance among women who were, at the least, geographically and socially isolated. Indeed, periodicals provided the arena in which women could come together to experiment with alternative definitions of and for women; they could try on various identities and then advocate those conceptions that offered a sense of significance and value.

When Paulina Wright Davis, an organizer of the first official National Woman's Rights Convention in 1850, requested institutional support for her woman's rights paper, the proposal was rejected as "inexpedient." Instead, suffragists formed a committee to collect and disseminate facts to established periodicals. Davis reported unhappily, "We have striven in vain to convince women that they needed an organ which . . . would be a true and just exponent of our views and principles of actions. . . . no other class of reformers have ever been so unwise."[6]

Nonetheless, suffragists quickly became persuaded that male editors, even reform-minded ones, would only and always ignore, falsify, trivialize, or ridicule their movement. Certainly to the extent that general-interest newspapers covered the movement at all (and many papers engaged in a "conspiracy of silence"), the treatment was consistently hostile. After a group meeting in Seneca Falls in 1848 adopted a Declaration of Sentiment condemning men's tyranny over women, editorials denounced what was essentially the first woman's rights convention as the "most shocking and unnatural incident ever recorded in the history of womanity."[7] Explaining their decision to begin the *Revolution*, perhaps the most famous (or infamous) of the suffrage papers, Elizabeth Cady Stanton and Susan B. Anthony said: "Our three most radical papers — the *Tribune*, the *Independent*, and the *Standard* — were closed against us. . . . Thus ostracized, we tried to establish a paper of our own."[8] The issue was not simply getting enough, or enough favorable, coverage from male editors, or eliminating references to suffragists as "unsexed" and "degraded." Davis explained:

> We have strong objections to monopolies, for we have always found that though the weaker party might have several privileges granted them, still they were held by a very insecure tenure; hence we have doubted the propriety of trusting interests dear and sacred to us even to the *Tribune*. We would prefer a smaller audience . . . looking for the fresh warm thoughts of our contributors . . . to seeing them crowded in out-of-the way corners of political papers.[9]

Establishing and nurturing their own papers for their own sake was important, in part because the movement itself went well beyond (or rather, began well before) enfranchisement. The major task of the movement was to supplant the prevailing conception of woman as pious, submissive, and domestic. Putting this in the affirmative, alternative periodicals were necessary to advocate and celebrate a new way of being that endowed women with a sense of purpose and significance, and to assert that "new woman's" entitlement to status and honor, as marked by the right to vote. Defending the claim that women should be enfranchised could eventually have been accomplished through general-circulation newspapers and magazines. Dramatizing and celebrating how and why these new women talked, thought, worked, and even dressed could not.

The particular contours of the new woman being advocated and defended in the suffrage press changed dramatically between that historic Seneca Falls meeting in 1848, when a controversial resolution calling for woman suffrage passed by a narrow margin, and 1920, when the Nineteenth Amendment enfranchising women was finally ratified by Tennessee, the last state to do so. Women's rights advocates offered competing versions of who or what this new woman should be and therefore why she should be enfranchised and how the battle to win status should be waged. Accordingly, to different degrees and with quite different philosophies, these periodicals took up women's entry into specific professions and occupations and into the work sphere generally, their place in religious institutions, their access to health and education, the advantages of dress reform and physical exercise, and legal reform, including women's rights to inherit, to divorce, and to serve on juries.

Nineteenth-century suffrage editors did more than explain and justify the movement's principles and motives. They helped to articulate a set of principles for and about the press itself. That is, at the same time that these newspapers and magazines managed to construct emotionally and intellectually plausible models of womanhood, they also demonstrated alternative approaches to journalism practice. These editors took seriously their responsibilities and obligations as such, giving thought to what ethical obligations and standards as well as what training were incumbent, to what they as editors owed readers. Their interest was not journalism for its own sake and certainly not for the sake of profit. Nor was their concern professionalism per se, although they admired a professional layout — that is, a basically tidy design that was not unlike the general-circulation papers of the times. To some extent, editors considered their personal reputations. Clara Bewick Colby wrote a sister editor that since she had never before accomplished anything that the public would notice, she was especially determined that her *Woman's Tribune* succeed.[10] More often, however, the honor and prestige of womanhood were at stake. As this essay will show, precisely because they were so passionately dedicated to serving ideological purposes, the women who produced women's suffrage papers were highly self-conscious about their conduct as such.

More and less pointedly, suffrage editors rejected the professional principles and especially the business practices of the nineteenth-century commercial press. For instance, Susan B. Anthony and Elizabeth Cady Stanton's militantly assertive *Revolution* advertised railroads, banks, and Wall Street businesses, as well as woman's rights books, but it adamantly refused to carry advertisements for patent medicines. When the *New York Times* criticized *Revolution*'s "indecency," *Revolution* attacked the *Times*'s insatiable greed, calling the latter's promotion of quack products "a downright affront to all womankind."[11]

The above quote suggests the delight Stanton took in quoting "notices" from other papers, whether negative or positive. Stanton begged exchanges to be argumentative, since "we should like to have some meat on the bone given us to pick."[12] Stanton explained, quite rightly, that her responses to these press reviews would interest future generations.[13] Suffragists were not equally aggressive in confronting male editors, but certainly suffrage papers criticized the "news" and editorial content of various papers, especially the general-circulation dailies and general-interest magazines, and also specialized organs and other reform journals. They urged readers to denounce and complain to callous male editors. When the *New York Tribune* headlined a filler about a drunken woman as "Woman's Rights," Davis bitterly complained, "Although we have never felt that the editors of that paper had any just comprehension of the magnitude and holiness of this work, still we had reason to expect better things of them than this."[14] Some thirty years later, in her valedictory description of "The Ideal Journalist," the *New Era* editor Elizabeth Boynton Harbert pictured herself as a David seeking not to destroy Goliath but to win his allegiance to a noble cause; only the development of self-reliance and self-respect in women, she added, would discourage male reporters from ridiculing or misrepresenting women.[15] Harbert was rare among suffrage editors for her faith in the possibility of general reform. She called for accounts of bravery and heroism instead of crime and misery; she urged journalists to ignore things that never had happened or would happen, when this could be done without sacrificing realism or accuracy.[16] Actually, suffrage editors had no reason to expect better in the short or long term; presumably they harbored little hope of converting professional journalists. But that was not the issue. Their ambition was to do journalism differently. To read the published letters to editors, suffragists' journalism practices were credible and persuasive in readers' opinions, if not in the opinions of professional journalists.

Suffragists' ideas about the press do not constitute a fully worked-out theory. Several questions about ethics and organizational structure were never raised; other problems were addressed but not resolved. Furthermore, suffragists' ideas were often more prescriptive and abstractly idealized than descriptive or pragmatic. In promising to publish "The Organ of each Woman," editors exaggerated both the degree of consensus existing among new women and the possibilities for creating that consensus. As the *Woman's Journal* put it: "This *Journal* is a poor, small link to bind together anything so vast and weighty as the great mass of womankind. Yet this is what we wish it might accomplish."[17]

Suffrage editors did form their own sisterhood. They were mutually inspired by each other's successes. They proudly reported the accomplishments of nonsuffrage women journalists. Honoring the new editor of a more conventional women's magazine, *Lily* claimed, "whenever one woman strikes a blow for the elevation of her sex, it redounds to the interest of the whole; and whenever one fails . . . all feel the calamity and contend against the increased odds in maintaining their individual enterprises. We are bound together."[18] In helping to establish a community of new women, suffrage editors constructed their own spiritual community. Not only did they write for one another's periodicals, they came to each other's aid quite literally; for example, a doctor active in Indiana's suffrage organization substituted for several suffrage editors when they were ill or vacationing.

But the ad hoc and contradictory nature of suffragists' press theory can in part be attributed to the fact that as a practical matter they operated on their own. They rarely met as a group. Even when suffrage editors were able to attend local, regional, or national meetings of suffrage organizations (either to report on them or, more typically, because they served as officers), press conduct per se was not generally an agenda item. Furthermore, the professional women contributing to the suffrage press were often doctors, lawyers, or teachers, but almost never experienced journalists. Many suffragists, including Bloomer, Stone, and Stanton, had written for temperance and abolition papers. A couple of suffrage editors were married to publishers or editors of reform-minded periodicals. Amelia Bloomer was an exception to the pattern, in that she had married the editor of a general-circulation newspaper; she even served as assistant editor for her husband's *Western Home Visitor*, writing weekly columns on suffrage, dress reform, and temperance.[19] For the most part, however, suffragists' sole connection to general interest newspapers was their anger about what those papers reported (or failed to report) about women, the woman's rights movement and its press; while women continued to write on behalf of other reforms, they rarely wrote for general-interest periodicals. Therefore, suffrage publishers and editors necessarily worked out their ideas about how they ought to operate in relative isolation and with few professional resources, support, or training.

Discussions of press theories generally distinguish different nation-states' conceptions of what, or to what extent, newspapers and magazines published within national boundaries owe those nations; that is, they interrogate the rights and obligations of the press with respect to governments. In the United States, these notions are assumed rather than stated. Although ideas of what is ethically necessary or acceptable have varied historically, general-circulation media rarely acknowledge to readers their operating theories. Modern newspapers' staffs prefer merely to reiterate their commitment to collecting and transmitting "the news" or even "all the news" and serving as society's watchdog, openly celebrating their right to maximize profit.

For the most part, the ideas about proper conduct for suffrage papers ran directly counter to the ideals that eventually emerged for modern news media. Irrelevant to suffragists were separation of the business/publishing and editorial departments, staff professionalism, hierarchical and compartmentalized organization. Suffragists did not promise facticity and "objectivity" through the use of apparently neutral, economical prose to transmit facts. The extent of the actual differences should not be exaggerated; nineteenth-century suffrage newspapers resembled their for-profit counterparts in several respects. On the other hand, they advocated experimentation. In doing so, suffragists generated a set of oppositional principles that a century later are still relevant in distinguishing alternative practices from the dominant forms of press practice (i.e., as embodied in those newspapers often regarded as "the" press).

My concern is not particularly to argue that the suffragist press was somehow protofeminist or that twentieth-century feminist media rely directly on these historical antecedents. In fact, twentieth-century feminist mass media reject many practices and principles of their "foremothers," especially the nineteenth-century suffragists' willingness to locate control and authority in the hands of an individual editor, named and titled.[20] They generally prefer a more collectivist, antihierarchical model. Recent feminist mass media usually also exclude male participants, while suffrage periodicals typically favored women and men working together in all sorts of social institutions, including in the movement and on their own staffs. "An anti-woman society cannot be reformed by an anti-male affair," wrote Henry Blackwell, husband of Lucy Stone and frequent contributor and member of the editorial board of the *Woman's Journal*. On the other hand, the nineteenth-century suffrage press provided models useful to the post-1960s feminist press. The "familial" relationship is evident in their shared commitment to expressing clearly a particular political view and to using and developing women's technical and communication skills. They do so even when it entails (and it continues to do so) alienating subscribers, suffering ridicule from unsympathetic press critics and audiences, appearing inaccessible with a dense, crowded design rendered even more forbidding by the lack of fancy (expensive) graphics, relying on and often exceeding the goodwill and resources of volunteer staff members, and narrowly constraining what, if anything, can be advertised.

As a consequence, nineteenth- and twentieth-century feminist media have been destined to die after short, financially unprofitable, if intense, lives. Suffrage periodicals certainly shared a pronounced disinterest in monetary gain. They all charged for subscriptions, presumably setting the lowest fee they thought feasible. Furthermore, with the exception of the ad-free *Genius of Liberty*, they accepted some limited kinds of advertising. But suffragists never found a way to practice their publishing principles while breaking even. The *Woman's Journal*—published by Lucy Stone with the formal support of a national suffrage organization and "stockholders" (essentially patrons), as well as a large circulation base and considerable "appropriate" advertising—managed to survive from 1870 to 1931.[21] Otherwise, of the thirty papers published before the turn of the century that I have studied, only eight survived longer than six years. Financial hardship typically killed off suffrage papers after two or three years. Sometimes women were blamed for this. The *New Era*'s editor bemoaned that women had "failed to rally to the enthusiastic support of the brave journals who have nobly battled for the pure, the good, the true, and also failed to insist that journals whose columns are habitually spiced with ridicule of women and misrepresenting of her work should not be tolerated in the home."[22] On the other hand, whatever the level of impatience or bitterness, suffragists could not overestimate the complexity and enormity of their task; the exhaustion of resources was inevitable.

This essay foregrounds the ideas about journalism articulated in the women's suffrage press. With several of the important themes now briefly introduced, I will elaborate suffragists' press theory as it emerged in seven papers that, in successfully attempting to be national organs, gave serious consideration to the debate and contributed its major terms: the *Lily* (1849–56), the *Una* (1853–55), *Revolution* (1868–70), the *Woman's Journal* (1870–1931), the *New Northwest* (1871–87), the *National Citizen and Ballot Box* (1876–81), and the *Woman's Tribune* (1883–1909). I will mention several lesser known, more regional papers, such as *Genius of Liberty* (1851–53), *Mayflower* (1861–65), and the *Farmer's Wife* (1891–94), if only to show the degree of consensus or overlap on significant issues. This account is roughly chronological, in order to underscore the evolving character of suffragists' press theory and the diversity of sequentially emerging models of womanhood; the nascent conceptions of what I call a "sensible woman," "strong-minded woman," and "responsible woman" operate as a subtext here.[23]

The *Lily* (1849–55)

Many women became suffragists after, or because of, involvement in the temperance and abolition movements. Even if women had not resented their second-class status as participants in those other movements, they often were drawn to suffrage newspapers because they were prevented from communicating their reform ideas by other means, including public speaking. The first suffrage newspaper, the *Lily*, began in 1849 as a temperance organ. As secretary of a newly formed women's temperance organization in Seneca Falls, Amelia Bloomer proposed the *Lily* because local temperance leaders refused to allow women to do much beyond supporting men's activities and attending men's lectures.

As symbolized visually and verbally in its delicate flowery logo, the *Lily* spoke specifically for a "sensible woman," one who was socially and politically conservative, if also intellectually capable and physically active. Nonetheless, the *Lily*'s avowals of purpose turned out to foreshadow many of the commitments and principles of the suffrage press, including its more radical examples. The language of

Bloomer's debut editorial was later echoed by other suffrage editors: "It is WOMAN that speaks through *The Lily*."[24] Bloomer promised that the paper would be "a medium through which woman's thoughts and aspirations might be developed."[25]

As was common for early suffrage papers, the burden of producing *Lily* fell primarily on one individual. Shortly after issuing a prospectus for a paper, the Seneca Falls temperance society abandoned its plans. Bloomer later admitted she feared that if *Lily* failed to appear, "people would say it was 'just like women;' 'what more could you expect of them.' "[26] Therefore, she said, somewhat melodramatically, "to save the credit of our sex and preserve our own honor, we breasted the storm."[27] Her associate editor retired after the second issue.

Bloomer had not attended the Seneca Falls meeting and had not intended to concentrate on women's rights. "But we see and hear so much that is calculated to keep our sex down and impress us with a conviction of our inferiority and helplessness, that we feel compelled to act in the defensive and stand for what we consider our just right."[28] Moral imperative, then, brought Bloomer to thrust *Lily* into the struggle to emancipate women "from the cruel enactment of Unjust Laws by which her rights and inalienable claims to equality have been subverted, from the blighting influence of prejudice by which she has been denied the privilege of being heard in self-defense."[29] Elizabeth Cady Stanton, who had drafted the Seneca Falls Declaration of Sentiment, with its resolution advocating suffrage, first wrote for *Lily* about temperance; but, under the pseudonym Sun Flower, she soon introduced woman's rights. Under her friend's influence, Bloomer extended *Lily*'s realm to politics, the professions, and the public world. By January 1853, its motto professed a commitment to "Emancipation of Woman from Intemperance, Injustice, Prejudice, and Bigotry." Of course, Bloomer herself became best known for her denunciation of the villainous Goddess of French Fashion and her public advocacy of clothing that both allowed and symbolized physical health and activity. *Lily* published instructions for making "trowsers" and advertisements for reform corsets, as well as many articles about women who wore them; it published daguerreotypes of Bloomer wearing the bifurcated clothes that, while not her invention, came to bear her name. The ensuing national attention to dress reform apparently helped *Lily*'s monthly circulation, which rose from 600 in 1849 to 4,000 by 1853.[30]

Bloomer believed in practicing what she preached, conducting the paper on a daily basis in accordance with woman's rights principles. Having defined woman as capable of meaningful paid work, and having committed herself to helping women take responsibility for their own media, Bloomer insisted that women be involved as often and as much as possible in producing the paper. The fact that a woman had engraved the paper's new flag, *Lily* proudly announced, proved that references to "woman's sphere" or "man's business" would soon be irrelevant.[31]

Bloomer's willingness to sacrifice efficiency for the sake of commitment to women employees was tested shortly after she and her husband moved from Seneca Falls to Mt. Vernon, Ohio, where her husband had purchased an interest in a local paper. A showdown began when the male typesetters employed by Dexter Bloomer refused to help *Lily*'s female typesetter, working in the same building. The uncooperative men were immediately fired and replaced by three women and one man. Presumably her husband and other local editors — and certainly editors of large-city papers — would never have tolerated two issues coming out late. But according to Bloomer, such problems were "nothing compared with what has been gained on the side of justice and right."[32]

These claims about justice followed from suffrage politics, not from claims to moral superiority. For two years, *Lily*, like many women's magazines of the time, had decried the evils of tobacco. But in 1851 it dared complain that men regarded smoking as their own exclusive prerogative.

> Yet we contend that if it is right and necessary for man to indulge in such luxuries, it is just as right and necessary that women should do so. The same code of morals should govern both; and there is no reason why men should make beasts of themselves, and then claim to be loved and respected by virtuous and intelligent women.[33]

Again, *Lily* was negotiating an identity for a "sensible" woman, not a saint.

When the Bloomers moved to Council Bluffs, Iowa, Mary Birdsall, secretary of the Indiana Women's Rights Association and former editor of the ladies' department of the *Indiana Farmer*, took over the *Lily*. Bloomer explained that Iowa was "too sparsely settled to make it safe for us to rely on it to support the paper; and the distance is too great and facilities for carrying mail too insufficient for us to calculate on a large eastern circulation."[34] She continued as a "corresponding editor." The paper soon lost its flair, however. Rather than glorifying a style of life centered on exciting issues and significant responsibilities, it offered pedantic moralizing and routine convention reports. Despite acquiring the subscription list of Paulina Wright Davis's *Una*, by late 1856 the *Lily* ceased publication. Years later, Bloomer defended the paper against the accusation that it had died of ridicule (i.e., because of its advocacy of bloomers): "It had done its work, it had scattered seed that had sprung up and borne fruit a thousand fold."[35] Indeed, even more significant than its attempts to fashion a new kind of sensible woman were *Lily*'s efforts to redefine the nature of its work and its relationship to readers.

Genius of Liberty (1851–53)

Genius of Liberty, a Cincinnati paper "Devoted to the Interests of American Women," also sought a new woman, "a natural woman, free and easy in all the powers of her soul and body." Besides women's suffrage, its ambitious program included free coeducational schools offering physical exercise as well as intellectual stimulation for women, dress reform, equal pay for equal work, and women's access to the professions, business, science, and the arts.

Above all committed to the notion of "strength in union," editor Elizabeth A. Aldrich believed the entire country would benefit if and when women worked together. Aldrich assumed, however, that it would be primarily women who would support the cause (and the periodical), because their lives would be more directly improved by it. She told male editors:

> Agents we want from our own sex, all through the country, and from the other sex, too, but we suppose that you have your own papers and interests to sustain and hence we go to the Women especially for co-operation, and we expect to obtain it. Our countrywomen will advance a good work as soon as they feel and know that it subverts nothing but wrong, and erects rights, truth, God, and humanity.[36]

Genius itself voiced diverse positions, including ones opposing Aldrich's. Aldrich adopted a conciliatory tone in addressing not only unsympathetic editors but also antisuffragist women. She encouraged converts to be tolerant of "those who now sleep from the morphine of old customs, habits and prejudice." She refused to modify her platform to attract those "less fortunate" women, however, arguing that the 60,000 women of Cincinnati could support a periodical that would present women's true interests, promote reform, and improve national conditions. Unfortunately, subscribers could not sustain the paper. Ultimately, Aldrich arranged for *Moore's Western Lady's Book* to designate ten pages as a "Genius of Liberty Department."

The *Una* (1853–55)

Una, published in Providence, Rhode Island, was also "A Paper devoted to the Elevation of Women." Considerably more philosophical and less "newsy" than the *Lily*, Paulina Wright Davis's paper celebrated the same "sensible" women that Bloomer had addressed. Financially independent after her first husband's death, Davis explained that she established the paper not because she had personally suffered, but because "in our sympathies we have suffered from every affliction upon the dependent class to which we belong. We bear in our heart of hearts, their sorrows and carry their griefs."[37]

Una's inaugural issue promised "to speak clear earnest words of truth and soberness, in a spirit of kindness."[38] Like the heroine of Spenser's *Fairie Queene*, *Una* was conceived as embarked on a "weary, dangerous pilgrimage through the wilderness of ignorance, error, pride, despair and bigotry."[39] It counseled moderation and patience: "While we do not deprecate the aggressive where truth urgently demands it, we cannot forgo our belief that a victory won by persuasion and argument is more certain of good results than a triumph wrung from weakness or extorted from fear."[40]

Lacking the journalistic experience and technical assistance that Bloomer enjoyed, Davis found herself exhausted after the first year; she even had written articles under different names to give the effect of wider support. Davis apparently faced more than the usual run of difficulties trying to attract women who either were middle-class and therefore controlled little cash of their own or worked but could not afford the subscription price of one dollar. Davis was once even obliged to rebuke gentlemen who apparently dealt with counterfeit money by turning it over to their wives to pay for their reform periodicals.[41] Even after she moved her monthly paper to Boston and secured the assistance of a publisher and coeditor, circulation continued to be problematic. Davis reasoned, "That *The Una* has not been liberally sustained by women does not prove it the less needed. Slaves know no want of freedom till the soul begins its development through the light of truth."[42]

Jane Swisshelm, editor of the (Pittsburgh) *Saturday Visiter*, which was abolitionist but definitely not prosuffrage, blamed Davis's problems on *Una*'s exclusive attention to women: "People do not want a whole meal of one dish without sauce, or a whole paper on one subject."[43] But Davis ignored Swisshelm's advice, reporting on suffrage meetings as well as covering the larger question of women's political activities. *Una* devoted even more space to the importance of mutual respect and equality of relations in marriage, and to women's rights to work, professional education, and coeducation. *Una* often discussed hygiene; it dramatized the special value of women doctors, including several who were themselves passionate activists for women's rights.[44]

Una often complained that when they were not tyrannized, American women were overpraised; characterizing women as angelic was wrong, and it also failed to compensate for material inequality. "We ask for her less flattery, less adulation, and more equity, fewer compliments and more completeness, fewer fair words and more fair treatment," *Una* said.[45] This applied as well to *Una*'s conception of what it owed women, and the extent to which the suffrage press could criticize women or expose their faults. *Una* therefore protested when a woman's poetry was published with a note asking that the poet's unhappiness be a passport to favor. Similarly, coeditor Caroline Healy Dall's series on women of antiquity included references to "ignoble" women: "The Life of Woman has yet to be written, and we should do small justice to her sphere, her accomplishments or her hopes, if we held up to men's eyes only the names of the pure and high-hearted."[46]

Worn out from pleading for advertising, subscriptions, and donations, and with the publisher complaining that he was forced "to live on air," Davis finally abandoned the experiment. Later she wrote, "Thus failed a hope and an agency which should have been the pride of women."[47]

The *Mayflower* and the Civil War

During the Civil War, the one women's rights periodical published was a semimonthly owned and edited by Lizzie Bunnell. Bunnell supplemented advertising revenues with profits from her Indiana farm to finance the paper from 1861 until it ended in 1864 or 1865. At fifty cents a year, the *Mayflower* was one of the cheapest reform organs published at the time.

The *Mayflower* officially defined itself in terms that might seem more congenial to the "true women" of the time: chaste literature,

happy homes, purity. But Bunnell emphasized civic duty and hero-
ized the women who dressed as soldiers and fought alongside men.
One prospectus promised: "During the present war we shall especially aim to inspire in woman a heroism worthy of the days in which
we live, and urge her to deeds of patriotism commensurate with the
mighty interests at issue."[48] Nonetheless, an August 1861 editorial
cynically predicted that women's sacrifices and patriotism would be
quickly forgotten once the war was over:

> The fact is men have rather more than got their hands full with this war,
> and they welcome woman as a powerful and generous ally—the contract
> being, on our part, that we are to do any work they give us; and on their
> part, that when they are done with us, they will turn us over to our former
> occupations and abuse us just as handsomely as ever.

Despite a postwar campaign for simultaneous enfranchisement
of women and African Americans, as Bunnell had expected, many
prominent abolitionists and liberal editors withheld support of wom-
en's suffrage, arguing that the two causes were not equally important. In 1866 Lucy Stone and her husband Henry Blackwell issued a
prospectus for *Universal Suffrage,* to advocate "enfranchisement and
complete recognition of the industrial and social and political equality
of women and Negroes."[49] With Republican-abolitionist friends refusing to help, however, they were unable to raise the $10,000 they
needed. Many woman's rights reformers conceded that "this was the
Negro's hour." Others felt betrayed.

Revolution (1868–70)

While campaigning in Kansas for one of the many unsuccessful state
referenda to enfranchise both women and African Americans, Elizabeth Cady Stanton and Susan B. Anthony (who had become close
friends and coworkers after being introduced by Bloomer) persuaded
George Francis Train, a Democratic financier with a variety of controversial political interests, to subsidize a suffrage weekly. They returned to New York City and on January 8, 1868, *Revolution* appeared
on newsstands with the motto, "Principle, not policy; Justice, not
favors." Train supplied another motto: "Men, Their Rights and Nothing More; Women, Their Rights and Nothing Less." Anthony was
publisher; Stanton and abolitionist Parker Pillsbury were coeditors
until 1869, when Pillsbury's name was dropped.

Revolution was exceptional in many respects, from its conception

of audience and subject to its definition of its own role and responsibility. *Revolution's* new woman was not so much "sensible" as militantly "strong-minded," a term both supporters and critics often
used to describe the willful, determined, contentious women whom
Stanton and Anthony idealized as the new woman. Besides suffrage,
Revolution advocated equal pay for equal work, an eight-hour work-
day, and religious reform. Fond of stating commitments in terms of
dualisms, *Revolution's* social goals included "practical education, not
theoretical; fact, not fiction, virtue not vice; cold water, not alcoholic
drinks or medicines."

No less controversial were the bases and origins of the paper itself.
Liberal Republicans attacked Stanton and Anthony for associating
with Democrats, "the anti-nigger party." The distinguished abolitionist William Lloyd Garrison wondered how Stanton and Anthony
could have "departed so far from true self-respect as to be travelling
companion and associate lecturer with that crack-brained harlequin
and semi-lunatic. . . . [Train] is as destitute of principles as he is of
sense, and is fast gravitating toward a lunatic asylum."[50] Indeed, after
giving them $600, Train left for Ireland, where he immediately was
jailed for a year for Fenian activities; he ended up in a mental asylum.
His friend David Meliss, financial editor of the *New York World*, provided some funding for a while longer, in exchange for space in the
Revolution for his lengthy articles on monetary and trade policy; not
until May 1869 did *Revolution* sever the official connection to Train
and Meliss.

Consistent with her claim that she was entitled to think and judge
for herself, although perhaps contradicting her motto, Stanton told
her critics, "So long as we are enabled to proclaim our principles it
matters not who helps to do it."[51] In a letter she admitted she would
accept money from the devil; her virtue was not like a dress that
could be stained by association.[52] Arguing that the controversy over
Train was merely an excuse to silence suffragists, Stanton inverted
abolitionist mythology and symbols for her own purposes, mocking
the reformers who refused to print her articles. Paulina Wright Davis,
who became *Revolution's* corresponding editor, vehemently attacked
Wendell Phillips for counseling suffragists to bide their time. The
paper's moral responsibility was to enable and represent women as
"bold, resolute, constant, united and vigilant." They would not be
pacified by "half-loaves."

Although this is more reflective of Stanton's ad hoc strategy for
defending herself against attacks than of a fully worked-out ethical

theory, Stanton often defended a cavalier attitude about moral compromise. When reprimanded for plagiarizing a minister's anecdote, Stanton, ever the pragmatist, called the Rev. Collyer a member of a class that had robbed her of civil and political rights; he had probably stolen the anecdote from a woman. White males were "fair game for literary pilfering," she wrote Collyer.[53]

The New York Working Women's Association, which met in the same building housing the *Revolution*, criticized the paper for not being handled entirely by female printers. "We must creep before we can walk. We want a little more money first, and then we can have women altogether," Anthony apologized, promising the printing contract to a cooperative female union if one were formed.[54] Serving and attracting the support of working women were certainly among Anthony's major goals: "We fixed our subscription at two dollars per year, much below a 'fair price' that we might place our paper within the reach of the working people — especially all women who earn their own living."[55] As it turns out, Anthony and other strong-minded suffragists remained frustrated by working women's refusal to be coupled in the public mind "with short hair and bloomers and other vagaries." Across the country, nonprofessional working women continued to disdain women's rights as a white, middle-class movement. In any case, nearly all the ethical tensions that wracked *Revolution* resulted when its office practices contradicted avowed principles; the inconsistencies of its principles or philosophy were rarely blamed.[56]

Revolution immediately attracted press attention. Whether or not the paper actually had 5,000 exchanges, as it claimed, many male editors noticed its "thoroughly Amazonian liking for a fight." In the *Independent*, Theodore Tilton predicted: "The *Revolution*, from the start, will arouse, thrill, edify, amuse, vex, and nonplus its friends. But it will compel attention; it will conquer a hearing."[57] Stanton was no less proud when a *New York Times* critic sneered: "Opposites are so confounded, similarities are so confused and distorted, incongruities are so delightfully jumbled, and there is such a strange mixture of thick and thin."[58] The point is that *Revolution* showed women expressing themselves forcefully on incendiary and even taboo topics. If Revolution insisted that contributors be economical and terse, it was not to imitate commercial press style, but because floweriness was inappropriate in new women. "Give us the facts and experience, in words . . . as hard as cannonballs," Stanton told correspondents.[59] In turn, readers congratulated both *Revolution* and themselves for reading it; it was to their credit to support a paper "so different from the namby-pamby, milk-and-water journals that dare not publish the truth."[60]

Certainly the paper's name was no accident. Suffragists well understood the importance of symbolizing themselves by the names they chose. "The time has passed for *Lilys, Sybils, Unas, Mayflowers, Dewdrops,* etc. and we have come to the *Revolution.*"[61] Stanton told Anthony:

> If all these people who for twenty years have been afraid to call their souls their own begin to prune us and the *Revolution*, we shall become the same galvanized mummies they are. . . . A journal called the *Rosebud* might answer for those who come with kid gloves and perfumes to lay immortal wreathes on the monuments which in sweat and tears others have hewn and built.[62]

Elsewhere, Stanton claimed that Mary Livermore, in calling her Chicago suffrage paper the *Agitator*, had rejected mild, serene names like *Rosebud*, thus demonstrating that her paper would be *Revolution's* twin, "whose mission is to turn everything inside out, upside down, wrong side before."[63] Ironically, Livermore, who organized and then headed the Illinois Woman's Suffrage Association, later repudiated the name *Agitator*, saying she had neither chosen nor liked it.[64]

Explaining opposition, promoting courage, and bolstering otherwise flagging commitments to a new way of life required several other rhetorical devices. *Revolution* often strategically exploited the vocabularies of history, religion, and nature. But military language was *Revolution's* favorite weapon: "An army of able-bodied, strong-nerved women are ready to fall into rank and file, and help carry on the war of the *Revolution*. Already we have smelled powder and shot away out West."[65]

Like its sisters and successors, *Revolution* enthusiastically and regularly reported on reform journals and various papers interested in women's interests, such as the *San Francisco Pioneer*, which was reoriented to women's suffrage by its editor, Emily Pitts Stevens, after December 1869; and the *Chicago Legal News*, edited by Myra Bradwell. Even when they disagreed with *Revolution's* philosophy, articles were reprinted from many other suffrage periodicals. Stanton and Mary Livermore borrowed from and wrote for one another, although their styles were quite different, with Livermore, whose husband then owned and edited a Unitarian paper, planting the *Agitator* explicitly on Christian ground. *Revolution* created a storm of criticism among suffragists by offering compliments to Victoria Woodhull and her sister Tennie C. Claflin, who irregularly published *Woodhull & Claflin's Weekly* in New York (1870–76) in order to advocate women's suffrage as well as rather eccentric economic and religious theories, and to promote Woodhull as a presidential candidate. Such applause was not a matter of unwillingness to criticize women. *Revolution* deplored the racism of a magazine published for southern women, and it mocked "weak-minded" women, both by name and as a "class."

The 1870 treasurer's report for the paper and Stanton's newly formed suffrage organization showed a deficit of only two dollars. But Susan B. Anthony was apparently $10,000 in debt. *Revolution*'s circulation, initially 2,000, peaked at 3,000. In May 1870 Anthony sold the paper for a dollar to a joint stock company led by Laura Curtis Bullard, one of *Revolution*'s foreign correspondents. Stanton was invited to write on "pleasant" topics for Bullard, but was little moved to do so, telling Anthony, "I am not to be bought to write at anybody's dictation."[66] Worse, *Revolution* was hardly revolutionary under Bullard. Gentility replaced anger, sentimental fiction replaced political analyses, and delicate religious language replaced denunciations of clerics. Bullard further alienated Stanton and Anthony by "polluting" the paper with advertisements for quack medicines. In any case, neither sweet talk, a lowered price, quack medicine, nor a second transfer of the paper to the publisher of a Unitarian weekly was sufficient. *Revolution* ceased entirely in 1872.

In 1870 Paulina Wright Davis described *Revolution*'s "great" work: "It has been hated, abused, slandered, misquoted, garbled; nevertheless it has been a terror to evil doers, and a help to those who would do well."[67] According to suffragist historian Eleanor Flexner, "The *Revolution* did more than just carry news, it set a new standard of professionalism for papers edited by and for women. It gave their movement a forum, focus, and direction. It pointed, it led, it fought, with vigor and vehemence."[68] Certainly it dramatized and glorified a new "strong-minded" identity for American middle-class women. While its contribution to professionalism was inconsistent and perhaps even rather minor, *Revolution* raised many significant questions about how and why to publish suffrage papers, debates that still challenge feminist successors.

Revolution's failure, in any case, had more to do with style than with money. Many suffragists were increasingly uncomfortable with, if not hostile toward, the political philosophy represented by Stanton and *Revolution*. The *Woman's Advocate* (then six months old and published in New York by William Tomlinson with the help of Lucy Stone and her husband, brother-in-law, and sister-in-law) had called for a new centralized suffrage organization: "Present unity, future prosperity, the honor of the Cause alike demand it."[69] Stone's followers were even angrier after Stanton and Anthony organized something of a coup; embittered by a resolution adopted by the American Equal Rights Association favoring the Fifteenth Amendment, which enfranchised African-American males, in May 1869 Stanton and Anthony pulled out of the AERA and established the National Woman Suffrage Association (NWSA), which elected Stanton president.

The *Woman's Journal* (1870–1931)

Already geographically and philosophically alienated and now organizationally outmaneuvered, outraged New England suffragists led by Lucy Stone called for a "more comprehensive organization." In November 1869 representatives from twenty-one states met in Cleveland to form the American Woman Suffrage Association (AWSA).[70] Not surprisingly, the group's first concern was a periodical. Within three months, Lucy Stone had raised $10,000 to launch the *Woman's Journal*. The *Journal* hoped to make itself superfluous, it said; when women's disabilities were eliminated, the paper's work would be complete and its name an anachronism. This turned out to be a protracted battle. Indeed, having consolidated with various suffrage papers over time, the Boston-based publication essentially continued until 1931, by which time Alice Paul and the National Woman's Party had already proposed an equal rights amendment.

Officially "Devoted to the Interests of Woman, to her education, industrial, legal, political equality, and especially to her right of Suffrage," the paper ignored controversies that *Revolution* embraced. The "responsible woman" at the heart of the *Woman's Journal* eschewed military or "revolutionary" vocabulary. Citing the untold damage potentially resulting from "dragging in" divorce reform, Henry Blackwell announced in the inaugural issue:

> As advocates of equal rights, we protest against loading the good ship
> "Woman Suffrage" with a cargo of irrelevant opinions. . . . A certain
> narrowness and precision are as essential to practical action as are breadth
> and comprehensiveness to theoretical speculation. . . . In order to
> command the universal support which is essential to political success,
> Woman Suffrage must cease to be treated as a symbol of social
> innovations.[71]

Mary Livermore moved from Chicago to Boston, merging her *Agitator* into the *Journal* and serving as its first editor in chief. In August 1870 the *Journal* also took over the (Dayton, Ohio) *Woman's Advocate*, "Devoted to Woman, Her Emancipation from Religion, Social, Political and Moral Slavery."[72] The *Journal's* original board of contributing editors included Julia Ward Howe, William Garrison (founder of the abolitionist weekly *Liberator*, he was later replaced by Henry Blackwell, who later served as managing editor), and T. W. Higginson (a Union Army colonel who wrote controversial essays fairly regularly until 1885). After two years, Lucy Stone took over as editor in chief.

The general-circulation newspapers and opinion magazines immediately contrasted *Revolution* and the *Woman's Journal*, generally preferring the latter's mild, earnest tone, and neat, dignified layout. *Harper's* recommended the *Journal* to suffragists "who wish to keep the issue clear from entangling alliances with other reforms and the needless host of individual whims and vagaries." This was precisely the impression the *Journal* wanted to give, and it used such praise as house ads.

In truth, even the *Journal* conceded that as crucial as suffrage was, it could not solve all the problems of women or the world. "Nobody claims that Woman Suffrage is to bring about the millennium. It is only one means for the elevation of women . . . the necessary first step, the initial movement."[73] Furthermore, the *Journal* debated several allied reforms, especially dress reform. Writers urged women, especially club women who were less vulnerable to ridicule, to wear clothes "which shall characterize us as working women, which will show our disgust with living like dolls, and our readiness to serve humanity."[74] One contributor objected to hitching dress reform to suffrage "like a tail on a kite," since hideous reform clothing could alienate potential converts.[75] But another asserted that a corseted waist constituted "prima facie evidence of want of brains, rational faculties, self-respect."[76] Unlike *Revolution*, whose ethical debates followed from conflicts between suffrage principles and its publishing practices, the *Journal* agonized over how "purist" the new woman should and could be expected to behave.

The *Journal* quickly amassed support from suffragists; Blackwell claimed the circulation increased in three years from the original 800 to 4,500.[77] Furthermore, although the *Journal* ran at a deficit, it benefited from several revenue-producing strategies, including fundraising festivals and fairs, sales of stock to individuals and suffrage organizations, clubbing offers that offered reduced rates to those jointly subscribing to the *Journal* and designated other family magazines, and premiums for group sales. The *Journal* attracted considerable classified and commercial advertising — first for suffrage and reform literature and specific services for women, and later for appropriate women's products, ranging from sewing and washing machines to dress reform corsets and the "emancipation waist" to rest homes and real estate. Winning these accounts was difficult. In 1877 Lucy Stone privately bemoaned her exhaustion from walking miles to get advertisements for crockery, groceries, books and soap: "I do wish there was some way to carry on *The Woman's Journal* without such a hard constant tug."[78] But no one doubted the struggle was worthwhile; the Blackwell family apparently poured thousands of dollars into the paper.[79]

National Citizen and Ballot Box (1876–1881)

After 1870, the National Woman Suffrage Association had no outlet of its own. NWSA members complained: "Certainly a movement which, like the aggressive advocacy of Woman Suffrage, directly antagonizes the narrow views and senseless prejudices of moss-grown, self-sufficient foggyism, needs a channel through which unremittingly to pour truth into the popular mind."[80] The Toledo chapter of the NWSA therefore established the *Ballot Box*, with Sarah Langdon Williams, former women's page editor of the *Toledo Blade*, as managing editor. After three years, Matilda Joslyn Gage, who had headed NWSA in 1875–76, moved the paper to Syracuse; Stanton, Anthony, and other NWSA members served as corresponding editors. Gage renamed it *National Citizen and Ballot Box*, under the NWSA's controversial and dramatically tested theory that the Constitution already enfranchised all citizens, including women.[81] Influential suffragists praised its radical spirit. A reader said later, "It meets the need, perfectly, of ones like myself, who are rooted and grounded in the faith, but are isolated from the multitude and must do their work alone — deploring the lethargy and stupidity of women about them, wondering if they must wait for emancipation until all these are converted."[82]

Ballot Box was less aggressive than *Revolution* about marriage, child care, and divorce. But it strenuously objected to double standards, especially when legislated: "Until woman is at liberty to indulge in petty vices if she chooses, she will not be free, as man is free; and a virtue which is the result of force or constriction is a mere sham."[83] Echoing the reasoning and rhetorical style of *Revolution*, Anthony defended a woman accused of bribing voters with food to oppose a despicable candidate: "It is a fine point of morals for enslavers and champion thieves to preach honesty and integrity to their victims in their methods of escaping from their despots, or regaining their stolen property."[84] The *Journal*, on the other hand, condemned King as well as Anthony and Gage for supporting her; one horrified *Journal* reader intoned, "Women whose logic is so faulty, whose moral sense is so blunted, ought to be made to quail before the indignant remonstrances of all honest women."[85]

Still another bone of contention between the two factions was the multivolume *History of Woman Suffrage*, an expensive and exhausting project that Gage, Stanton, and Anthony produced and reprinted in the *National Citizen* as it was being written 1879–81. Gage justified printing the history in the newspaper as a way of encouraging readers to feel personally responsible for the book's account and to submit corrections. Lucy Stone, on the other hand, said she was "too busy" to write a history, and she challenged Gage's ability to deal fairly with divergent approaches.

When the *New Orleans Picayune* warned that lack of advertising and the long list of delinquent subscribers would "knock the stuffing out of the *Ballot Box*," Gage replied that she "gaged" her efforts by sense of right, not patronage, adding that once Louisiana women were enfranchised, they would prevent any stuffing of the ballot box. Certainly Gage's paper had a smaller circulation than the *Journal*, then between 3,000 and 4,000. Bravado aside, in October 1881 Gage suspended the paper, transferring its subscription list to the *Alpha*. She implied that the *National Citizen* would reemerge after the second volume of the *History of Woman Suffrage* was completed, but the paper never reappeared.

Regional and State Organs

Even the *Journal* could not speak for everyone around the country. In 1871 the highly enterprising Abigail Duniway began the *New Northwest*, "A Journal for the People, Devoted to the Interests of Humanity, Independent in Politics and Religion. Alive to all live Issues. Thoroughly Radical in Opposing and Exposing the Wrongs of the Masses." Duniway moved her entire family from Salem, Oregon, to Portland to run the paper, three of her six children providing the manual labor.

Duniway emphatically supported Stanton and Anthony's philosophy. Others may have regarded her as on the fringes of the movement, even from the strong-minded view; she saw herself as a pragmatist with a healthy respect for the power of drama. For example, Duniway was reluctant to join others in criticizing Woodhull and Claflin, noting that the beautiful, cunning Victoria Woodhull was "the only woman who can get the ear of the men who have usurped our rights; and women just speak through her until they can get into power."[86] Even when she finally distanced herself from the free-love advocate Woodhull, she noted that male sinners far outnumbered their female equivalents, and that men published hundreds of immoral papers.[87] Duniway did not mince words when it came to ridiculing "men's rights editors" as "slimy," "debauched," "odiferous." After sixteen years she gave up the project; her subsequent suffrage publishing ventures were all shorter-lived.

Balance, published by several Chicago women from 1871 to 1875, disrupted only briefly by the fire of 1873, spoke for "responsible women." Every back page repeated a promise "to weigh measures and men (and women) in a fair and impartial manner, and try to do justice to all; we do not intend to run into any wild extremes but preserve an 'even balance.' " On the other hand, it also vowed, "We shall be fearless and outspoken on every subject that claims the attention of the public." *Balance* may have been launched as a business venture, but it was not a financial success and its circulation reached only 900.

Another midwestern paper consistently combining suffrage and prohibition was *Our Herald*, "Devoted to the Best Interests of Home and Native Land; Freedom and Law Know No Sex." *Our Herald* developed out of the *Temperance Herald*, begun in 1878; in 1881, when Helen Gougar took over as editor, the name and focus changed. Active in Indiana suffrage organizations, Gougar reprinted as much from *Queen Bee* (a Denver suffrage paper), the *Woman's Tribune*, and the *New Northwest* as from temperance organs. In December 1884, Gougar, busy on the lecture circuit, turned the paper over to a frequent contributor, Elizabeth Boynton Harbert. With $500 from her husband and promises of support from friends, Harbert moved the paper to Chicago, where she headed a local suffrage society. She renamed it the *New Era*, "Devoted to Philanthropy and Reform and

Having a Circulation Extending into Every State and Territory in the United States."

In the twelve issues she put out, Harbert worked hard to promote both geographical and spiritual unity. She reported the activities and accomplishments of suffragists and suffrage organizations across the country, especially in the Midwest. The *New Era* also reported programs and services of apolitical groups, including women's clubs. It even redefined so-called antis, explaining, "Next in value to the woman who breaks out of her sphere to demand the ballot is the woman who breaks out of her sphere to oppose it."[88]

Clara Bewick Colby edited and published the *Woman's Tribune* from 1883 to 1909. Although the Nebraska Woman Suffrage Association established the *Woman's Tribune* to take up the slack left by the suspension of the *Western Woman's Journal*, published by a Nebraska state senator who supported the AWSA and *Woman's Journal*, Colby was a vocal fan of Stanton and Anthony, who regularly submitted columns. Colby's densely laid-out, no-nonsense weekly aimed to give not theory but "facts and information as a help to people to do their own thinking and draw their own conclusions."[89] After achieving success in briefly publishing the paper as the daily organ of the International Council of Women, from 1889 to 1892 Colby alternated between publishing in Beatrice, Nebraska, and Washington, D.C. She then kept the paper in the national capital, where her husband worked for the attorney general. From 1904 to 1909, by then divorced, Colby published the *Tribune* from Portland, Oregon, where she engaged in bitter debates with Abigail Duniway, primarily over Duniway's antipathy to temperance.

More than any of her colleagues, Colby hoped to produce a lively paper that would instruct women on everything. She devoted a great deal of space to regional and national suffrage activities, but she also advocated many reforms she believed were important to women, including widening their occupational choices (ranging from journalism to agriculture). She opposed vivisection, licensing of prostitutes, and capital punishment. But she also took up other events of the day, for instance, opposing the annexation of Hawaii. Ironically, it was Susan B. Anthony who criticized such breadth: "Our suffrage women get enough of all that in their ordinary papers, and don't wish to pay a separate woman's paper merely to have that kind of reading."[90]

The *Farmer's Wife*, begun 1891 in Topeka, Kansas, clearly dedicated itself to suffrage and to Populism, with the motto, "Equal Rights to All, Special Privilege to None." It was edited by Emma D. Pack, former editor of *Villa Range: Ladies Home Journal*, and published by her husband Ira Pack, former publisher of the *City and Farm Record*.[91] It also carried articles about the Women's Christian Temperance Union, farming, and education. The Packs published monthly until 1894, when, Democrats having broken with Populists over woman suffrage, Republicans won and the referendum on women's suffrage was defeated.

Advantageous postal rates, improved mail delivery systems, and technological advances in printing also encouraged the emergence of smaller state publications, such as the *Wisconsin Citizen* (1887 to 1917). The *Woman's Standard* was published in Iowa from 1886 to 1911; one of its publishers was a woman who firmly believed that her wealth conferred societal obligations. Even Alice Stone Blackwell admitted that state papers, while they might divert subscriptions from still-struggling national publications, might fill a niche; she praised the *Illinois Suffragist* when it first appeared in 1881 with its "boiled down and skimmed news" from around the state.

Unification in the Movement

Harbert was one of several editors to urge organizational unification within the suffrage movement: "In order to organize for effective work, all personal preference and ambitions must be surrendered, and self-sacrifice be the watchword of the crusade."[92] Many of the younger suffragists, already comfortable with their modern identity, could not understand, much less justify, the split; they simply wanted enfranchisement. Although surviving advocates of the "responsible" style continued to resent Stanton's and Anthony's national prominence, the two factions therefore began a process of rapprochement; they were reunited in 1890 as the National American Woman Suffrage Association (NAWSA).

The merger brought few changes to the *Woman's Journal*. In the interests of modernity and comprehensiveness, however, it added some features and departments; to signal its intention to attract working women, for example, in 1889 the *Journal* inaugurated a column on the Women's Educational and Industrial Union, edited by that organization's founder and president. Still controlled by the Stone-Blackwell family, especially with the help of their daughter Alice, the *Journal* also enjoyed the aid of several former suffrage editors and hosts of correspondents. *Journal* contributors included such authors as Louisa May Alcott, reformer Frances Willard, doctors and lawyers, and many suffrage activists.

The *Woman's Tribune* could publish whatever Colby liked, although it continued to suffer for its reputation as radical, especially when it began to publish excerpts of *The Woman's Bible*, Stanton's strident critique of mainstream religion. The *Journal*, on the other hand, was constrained by two major responsibilities. Even before it was officially adopted by the NAWSA in 1900, it needed to help reconcile the factions. In part it served organizational solidarity by offering itself as a friendly, intimate national "newsletter," reporting on suffrage teas, petition drives, banquets, concerts, lectures, and Yellow Ribbon Teas.[93] Second, it needed to represent both everyone within the movement and those who potentially could be convinced. It described itself as widely read by club women, advocates for various reforms, missionaries, professionals, housewives, and mothers; and it tried actively to serve these specific constituencies. Agnes Ryan, a *Journal* business manager, explained later that even periodicals that aim to make converts, not money, cannot afford to ignore circulation. She added:

> This is no easy matter if one has convictions and wants to run the paper according to high ideals and with certain principles dominant. . . . the paper must, therefore, be so edited and the letters of the departments must be so written as to make every one feel that the Journal is fair to all and that whatever it does is done with no personal animosities, with no biases, and purely for the welfare of the cause and in accordance with the best ideals we have been able to work out.[94]

By the 1890s the movement also turned to general-circulation periodicals. The *Journal* encouraged suffragists to write columns for general newspapers and to distribute its various specialized pamphlets and bulletins; it asked newspapers to let women "take over" their offices for an issue. In 1882 Blackwell had designed a supplement excerpting *Journal* items to mail to hundreds of newspapers to republish; in 1888 this was formalized into a low-cost, four-page weekly, the *Woman's Column*. Edited by Alice Stone Blackwell until 1904, the *Column* emphasized suffrage events and positions and carried little advertising except for the *Journal* and other suffrage tracts. But to attract more conservative middle-class women, it also attended to other social issues; its tightly edited, commonsense articles were intended for outsiders, not converts.

Conclusion

The exigencies of operating relatively small and dramatically under-funded papers on the basis of volunteer help and advocates' submissions account for many of the suffragists' press principles. Suffragists' assertions about how newspapers ought to be operated can often be connected to the difficulties of actual practice and their attempts to transcend, bypass, or at least justify these difficulties. As this overview of the nineteenth-century suffrage press demonstrates, ideals could not always implemented. More important, as the considerable variety in the definitions of the new woman predicts, not all suffrage papers agreed on specific principles for conduct. On the other hand, a nascent theory of the press was explicitly proposed and negotiated by the suffrage editors; it was worked out in the cumulative history of their practices. The main tenets, many of which hold true for the contemporary feminist press, were that the periodicals operate in accordance with the ethical and political principles of the movement itself, and that content serve and represent women.

As suffragists saw it, established general-circulation papers cared nothing about journalism ethics or social good, but only about making a profit and protecting specifically male interests. Existing press principles, to the extent these were adhered to, were at best irrelevant. The notion of specialized beats covered by professional reporters who assiduously maintain their distance from sources, subjects, and audiences, and defined in terms of a strict division of labor, was not viable. The idea of separating editorial and business functions was equally unhelpful, because it presumed that the newspaper had dual functions, distributing information and earning profits. Suffrage editors mocked not only mainstream newspapers' willingness to modify their position to attract subscribers and advertisers, but also their definition of news itself. Suffragists' commitment was not to some mythologized version of the free press, but to an emergent version of the new woman and of communication. Their goal was to bring these women together in a meaningful community and to argue for the new woman's status — as marked by enfranchisement — and her right to "communicate."

While the papers were often in the hands of one or two women, they offered maximum space to readers. Aldrich promised, "[*Genius of Liberty*] is not one's but it belongs to All; every one will be heard in her own style, principle, and want; 'tis the common property of

Woman, ready for the equal insertion of articles of one and all."[95] Her language, typical of early suffrage editors, is remarkably prophetic of the continuing commitment of feminists to let women express themselves in their own ways; feminists in both the movement and the academy still experiment with using their own media to speak up and speak out.

Embedded in the theory of newspapers' responsibilities to readers was a conception of readers' responsibilities to their newspapers: readers owed their papers support, emotional and financial. Of course, these newspapers generally failed for lack of such support. Nonetheless, dialogue among the papers' audiences also suggests that they acknowledged their obligations and appreciated the access. Subscribers accepted suffrage papers as "theirs"; they regarded editors not as distant professionals but as friends. Readers gratefully accepted the invitation to submit their thoughts, responses, and experiences, even their criticisms. One regular *Lily* contributor stopped herself from digressing: "But I am getting sentimental, and that I never wish to be in writing for the *Lily*, because it is such a little paper, and visits us so seldom that we wish to see its leaves only filled with the practical and earnest truths of everyday life."[96]

One respect in which twentieth-century press theory differs markedly from its apparent nineteenth-century "foremothers" involves the specificity of its conception of womanhood. Suffragists felt responsible for recording and incorporating into one global version of the new woman both the pain and the triumphs of women around the world, over history. The name for the *Woman's Journal* was thus justified as "not partial, nor restricted, for what concerns woman concerns the race."[97] But they exaggerated the ability of their movement and their periodicals to represent all humanity. In distinction, the twentieth-century feminist press hesitates to refer to "womanhood." It tends to be more sensitive to both potential and acknowledged differences by race and ethnicity, sexual preference, culture, age and physical ability, and class and professional status. The current segmentation within the feminist press is merely one indication of the challenge to the assumption that women form some singular universal group on the basis of either biology or history. Nonetheless, the suffragist project was a brave attempt not only to redefine womanhood but also to demonstrate the value and viability of alternative approaches to doing journalism, which may in turn suggest alternative approaches to doing journalism history.

Notes

1. *Mayflower*, November 15, 1861, 168.
2. Following their own usage, I use here the terms *woman's rights* (preferred over *women's rights* because it symbolizes a sense of gender unity) and *suffragist* (preferred by Americans over *suffragette*, which is associated with the more confrontational British movement). A somewhat more difficult decision is how to refer to individual women, who typically used their husbands' last names if they married, with Lucy Stone being the prominent exception. In general, I use whatever last names they themselves used at the time (rather than using both their birth and married names), although, following modern usage, I do not use courtesy titles. Lizzie Bunnell, it might be noted, later married and took her husband's name, Read.
3. I have studied about thirty suffrage periodicals, especially the ones for which there are many issues extant. I have found reference to about 40 other papers published in this 1850–1900 period, but I cannot confirm that all of these put the same priority on suffrage. Another twenty or so papers published in the 1900–1920 period of the movement are not examined here.
4. *Genius of Liberty*, November 15, 1852, 12.
5. *Woman's Journal*, January 11, 1873, 12.
6. *Una*, November 1854, 362–63.
7. Miriam Gurko, *The Ladies of Seneca Falls: The Birth of the Woman's Rights Movement* (New York: Macmillan, 1974), 103.
8. *Revolution*, May 14, 1868, 296.
9. *Una*, February 1855, 25.
10. Cited in E. Claire Jerry, "Clara Bewick Colby and the *Woman's Tribune*, 1883–1909: The Free Lance Editor as Movement Leader," in *A Voice of Their Own: The Woman Suffrage Press, 1840–1910*, ed. Martha Solomon (Tuscaloosa: University of Alabama Press, 1991), 110–28.
11. *Revolution*, August 20, 1868, 106.
12. *Revolution*, February 5, 1868, 66.
13. *Revolution*, June 18, 1868, 371.
14. *Una*, December 1854, 376–77.
15. *New Era*, December 1885, 356–61.
16. Ibid.
17. *Woman's Journal*, January 11, 1873, 12.
18. *Lily*, December 15, 1865.
19. In her salutatory article for the *Visitor*, she noted that the *Lily* freed her from having to write anything "obnoxious" on women's rights for the *Visitor*, although she promised to be "an uncompromising opponent of wrong and oppression in every form, and a sustainer of the right and the true." Dexter Bloomer, *Life and Writings of Amelia Bloomer* (New York: Schocken, 1975 [1895]), 150–54.
20. Indeed, although the fact that many heroines of the suffrage movement are editors may bespeak the importance of the suffrage press, it also may reflect the extent to which, in "naming" themselves as editors, those women created themselves as heroines. E. Claire Jerry describes Clara Bewick Colby as trying to use the *Woman's Tribune* to catapult herself into national prominence. I cannot here develop an argument about contemporary feminist media; for an extensive analysis of their organizational structures, see Linda Steiner, "The History and Structure of Alter-

native Women's Media," in *Women Making Meaning: New Feminist Directions in Communication*, ed. Lana Rakow (New York: Routledge, 1992).

21. In 1917, the *Journal* merged with two other periodicals to form the *Woman Citizen*; it was known by that name until 1921, when it resumed the *Woman's Journal* name.

22. *New Era*, December 1885, 356–61.

23. I describe the historical and cultural evolution of these conflicting visions of the new woman in "Finding Community in Nineteenth Century Suffrage Periodicals," *American Journalism* 1 (Summer 1983), and "Evolving Rhetorical Strategies/Evolving Identities," in *A Voice of Their Own: The Woman Suffrage Press, 1840–1910*, ed. Martha Solomon (Tuscaloosa: University of Alabama Press, 1991).

24. *Lily*, January 1849, 4.

25. *Lily*, April 1850, 30.

26. Bloomer, *Life and Writings of Amelia Bloomer*, 42.

27. *Lily*, January 1853, 12.

28. *Lily*, March 1850, 21.

29. *Lily*, December 1851, 93.

30. Gurko, *The Ladies of Seneca Falls*, 57.

31. *Lily*, January 1853, 1. One year later, however, an inside note suggested that the new type and head were set by men.

32. *Lily*, May 1854, 19.

33. *Lily*, April 1851, 30.

34. *Lily*, December 15, 1854, 181.

35. Bloomer, *Life and Writings of Amelia Bloomer*, 187–88.

36. *Genius of Liberty*, October 1852, 1.

37. *Una*, February 1853, 1.

38. Ibid.

39. *Una*, February 1854, 212–13.

40. *Una*, December 1853, 1.

41. *Una*, July 1853, 151.

42. *Una*, January 1855, 1.

43. Quoted in *Una*, February 1855, 25.

44. Davis had little formal education but her adult study of anatomy and physiology enabled her to travel around the country lecturing to women about health.

45. *Una*, June 1855, 72–73.

46. *Una*, February 1855, 26–27.

47. Paulina Wright Davis, *A History of the National Woman's Rights Movement, for Twenty Years, with the Proceedings of the Decade Meetings Held at Apollo Hall, October 20, 1870, from 1850 to 1870* (New York: Kraus Reprint, 1971 [1871]), 20.

48. *Mayflower*, November 15, 1861, 171.

49. Louise R. Noun, *Strong-Minded Women: The Emergence of the Woman Suffrage Movement in Iowa* (Ames: Iowa State University Press, 1969), 79.

50. *Revolution*, January 29, 1868, 49–50.

51. *Revolution*, May 14, 1868, 296.

52. Theodore Stanton and Harriet Stanton Blatch, eds., *Elizabeth Cady Stanton as Revealed in Her Letters, Diary and Reminiscences*, 2 vols. (New York: Harper & Brothers, 1922), 2:119–20.

53. Stanton, *Letters*, 1:167.

54. *Revolution*, October 1, 1868, 96–97.

55. *Revolution*, August 20, 1868, 105. Taking this a step further, some twentieth-century feminist periodicals have discounted rates for working and unemployed women.

56. One such exception to this rule occurred when, having often decried tobacco, *Revolution* recommended the homey setting and excellent pay at a cigar-making factory.

57. *Revolution*, January 22, 1868, 34.

58. *Revolution*, January 15, 1868, 26.

59. *Revolution*, January 6, 1870, 9.

60. *Revolution*, October 29, 1868, 260.

61. *Revolution*, April 30, 1868, 259. *Sybil* was a dress reform paper published 1856–64 in Middleton, New York; *Dewdrops* was published in the 1870s in Chicago. There was no *Rosebud*.

62. Stanton, *Letters*, 1:123–25.

63. *Revolution*, March 18, 1869, 161.

64. Livermore originally opposed women's suffrage, but her experience with various reforms during and after the Civil War convinced her that only enfranchised women could muster the political resources to combat poverty, intemperance, and prostitution.

65. *Revolution*, May 7, 1868, 281.

66. Stanton, *Letters*, 1:126–27.

67. Davis, *A History of the National Woman's Rights Movement*, 23.

68. Eleanor Flexner, *Century of Struggle: The Woman's Rights Movement in the United States* (New York: Atheneum, 1971), 151.

69. *Woman's Advocate*, July 1869, 13–14.

70. Several histories of the suffrage movement—which, incidentally, ignore the periodicals except as occasional sources of data about events and organizations—fully describe the formation of these two groups and other organizational events. Among them are Eleanor Flexner's *Century of Struggle* and Aileen Kraditor's *The Ideas of the Woman Suffrage Movement 1890–1920* (Garden City, N.Y.: Doubleday, 1971). There are also useful biographies and autobiographies of several suffrage heroines who edited or published periodicals, including Susan B. Anthony, Elizabeth Cady Stanton, Amelia Bloomer, and Abigail Duniway.

71. *Woman's Journal*, January 8, 1870, 4.

72. One former *Advocate* editor, A. J. Boyer, briefly helped out on the *Journal*, but eventually began another suffrage monthly called *Nineteenth Century*; his former colleague Miriam Cole, still serving as the *Journal*'s western correspondent, attacked this as issued by "radicals run mad." *Woman's Journal*, April 29, 1871, 136.

73. *Woman's Journal*, March 12, 1870, 76.

74. *Woman's Journal*, July 12, 1873, 219. Whether women actually worked outside the home in jobs requiring practical dress was not at issue; certainly, few Journal readers were working in factories.

75. *Woman's Journal*, October 11, 1873, 324.

76. *Woman's Journal*, January 25, 1873, 26.

77. *Woman's Journal*, February 22, 1873, 60.

78. Quoted in Lois Bannister Merk, *Massachusetts and the Woman Suffrage Movement* (Cambridge: General Microfilm, 1961), 26.

79. Agnes Ryan, *The Torch Bearer: A Look Forward and Back at the Woman's Journal: The Organ of the Woman's Movement* (Boston: Woman's Journal and Suffrage News, 1916).

80. *Ballot Box*, April 1876, 1.

81. Indeed, operating under this theory, Susan Anthony, along with other Rochester women, cast a ballot in the 1872 election; for this she was arrested, convicted, and fined. Gage also tried to vote in 1872. The AWSA and the *Journal*, however, scorned such attempts to vote, saying nobody ever scored a mark by firing a blank; the *Journal* later reported gleefully on women voting where and when it was legal—Wyoming having entered the Union in 1890 as the first state providing full voting rights for women, and Colorado, Utah, and Idaho enfranchising women later in the decade.

82. *Ballot Box*, October 1879, 4.

83. *Ballot Box*, May 1881, 3.

84. *Ballot Box*, August 1880, 1.

85. *Woman's Journal*, August 21, 1880, 232.

86. *New Northwest*, December 1, 1871, 2.

87. *New Northwest*, July 14, 1871, 1.

88. *New Era*, August 1885, 227–31.

89. *Woman's Tribune*, January 1, 1884, 1.

90. Quoted in E. Claire Jerry, "Clara Bewick Colby," 118.

91. Thomas R. Burkholder describes this in "The Farmer's Wife, 1891–1904: Raising a Prairie Consciousness," in *A Voice of Their Own: The Woman Suffrage Press, 1840–1910*, ed. Martha Solomon (Tuscaloosa: University of Alabama Press, 1991), 153–64.

92. *New Era*, September 1885, 282–83.

93. American woman suffragists deserve the credit for inventing the yellow ribbon as a symbol; they tied them where they could, including on trees, and wore yellow armbands during parades.

94. Ryan, *The Torch Bearer*, 28–29.

95. *Genius of Liberty*, October 1852, 1.

96. *Lily*, December 1852, 98.

97. *Woman's Journal*, January 22, 1870, 27.

Chapter 5

The Rise of News as a Commodity: Business Imperatives and the Press in the Nineteenth Century
Gerald J. Baldasty

In Edward Bellamy's 1888 novel, *Looking Backward, 2000–1887*, a man of the nineteenth century awakens to find himself in Boston in the year 2000. This time traveler, Julian West, is amazed to find that Americans have crafted a perfect society, eradicating war, poverty, private property, competition, labor strife, crime, corruption, anxiety, and status and class divisions. In contrast to the tumultuous 1880s, it is Utopia.

West's host in the year 2000 is a Dr. Leete, who patiently introduces him to this new world. Among its many virtues are newspapers that truly serve society and its citizens. As Dr. Leete tells West:

> The newspaper press is organized so as to be a more perfect expression of public opinion than it possibly could be in your day, when *private capital controlled and managed it primarily as a money-making business*, and secondarily only as a mouthpiece for the people.[1]

Looking Backward, vastly popular when it was published, seems like pallid science fiction today. Our vantage point near the year 2000 shows us that Bellamy was not much of a prophet. But part of the book rings true. Although the book is highly polemical, it nonetheless describes many of the taxing problems of late nineteenth-century America. Some of Bellamy's observations may be strained, but many are not. In particular, his view of the press as a "money-making business" is apt — for both late nineteenth- and late twentieth-century America.

That newspapers were businesses was not just the view of novelists such as Bellamy. Only three years after *Looking Backward* appeared, a South Dakota editor exhorted his peers to remember that newspapers were primarily businesses. "All the world and the rest of mankind must be made to understand, at once and forever, that a newspaper office, in country village as well as in city, is a business established by which editors and printers must make a living."[2] In 1892, another editor said:

> The first business of the newspaper is to collect the news of the world and publish it. Its publication is a legitimate business for profit. The newspaper is not a missionary or a charitable institution.[3]

When William Sohier took over the *Boston Journal* in 1894, he stressed, "One thing should be clearly understood, and that is that this property has been bought for business purposes, to be run on business principles. . . . You cannot put that too strongly."[4] Newspapers were like other businesses of that era, one editor noted, in that it was "desirable to make receipts meet expenditures."[5]

The business imperative directed publishers and editors to two goals: first, to keep operating expenses low, and second, to enhance revenues. These two goals, seemingly so simple, had a profound impact on how news was defined. Reflecting business imperatives and publishers' desire for profits, news became a *commodity* — a product shaped and marketed for profit. News was not simply a report of the day's events. Rather, it was a selection of reports that could be produced within a newspaper's business constraints. One editor said that newspapers must present news that "the people want and are willing to buy. No matter how choice your selection, if the people will not buy and read your paper, you may as well leave the business."[6] Another editor advised that "the man who manufactures the newspaper must as surely cater to the public taste as he who manufactures tobacco, or neckties, or candies, or groceries, or any other article of consumption."[7]

This emphasis on the profitability of news was not new in the 1880s and 1890s; an entrepreneurial view of journalism had given birth to the penny press of the 1830s.[8] But the penny press style of journalism was not dominant before the Civil War.[9] Only in the latter decades of the century did news as a commodity come to typify the content of the mainstream press. This is a study of that mainstream press, of daily and weekly newspapers from large cities to small towns that attempted to provide general news and information while maintaining profitability.

This essay analyzes the newspaper industry's emphasis on profits — and the concomitant notion of news as a commodity — in the last two decades of the nineteenth century, and it details how those developments influenced news gathering and processing. In particular, the constant pursuit of profits created working conditions that often sacrificed accuracy and quality for economy, while encouraging fabrication and sensationalism. Newspapers generated a cafeterialike approach to news, serving up a vast assortment of articles daily in the hope of appealing to every potential reader. The effort to please all readers all the time often meant that difficult or divisive issues received little attention. Contests, prizes, and self-congratulation were part of the way newspapers marketed themselves. Commodification of the news also accentuated the importance of advertisers, and newspapers wooed them by catering to upscale readers and by espousing advertisers' commercial and political interests.

Keeping Expenses Low

Publishers and editors faced a variety of financial demands in the production of their newspapers: printing presses, type, newsprint, office buildings and real estate, and workers' salaries all represented major expenditures. Just housing a newspaper could be expensive. In the early 1890s, James Gordon Bennett of the *New York Herald* bought a block of land for $300,000 and spent an additional $600,000 on a building for his paper.[10] In 1891, the new headquarters of the *Chicago Daily News* cost $300,000.[11] At the same time, the new office of the *Chicago Tribune* cost $500,000 — with an additional $250,000 for new presses and machinery.[12]

Expenses were greatest on metropolitan newspapers, where the cost of newsprint alone easily could exceed $100,000 a year.[13] Gathering *local* news totaled $100,000 a year or more for many metropolitan newspapers,[14] and composition costs (setting type, making up the pages) could double these expenses.[15]

Working Conditions and Salaries

Publishers had little or no control over real estate prices, construction costs, or even the costs of printing presses or newsprint. But they could determine their workers' salaries. Given that the supply of reporters exceeded demand in most metropolitan areas,[16] publishers often saw low salaries as one way of keeping operating expenses down.[17]

Reporters' salaries were low, and their hours were long and the work difficult.[18] Reporters often were expected to produce a dozen or more articles a day — and most could not rely on telephones for gathering facts; they went afoot.[19] Many reporters worked for "space," being paid according to the number of columns they wrote.[20] Bonuses or pay raises came for exclusive or sensational stories. One reporter, sent to cover a drowning, discovered that the "victim" had survived. He bemoaned his fate; if she had drowned, he would have received $6 for the story, rather than a paltry $2 deemed appropriate for a near miss.[21] To make matters worse, he had lost the chance of another profitable news story while chasing the drowning story.[22]

Not only were wages low, they were frequently reduced. "Space" pay reporters often saw their wages unilaterally cut by management. If a reporter had earned, for example, $15 for his week's work, he might well receive only $12 or less in actual pay.[23] If a reporter fought this system, he was fired.[24]

Low pay, long hours, and hard work drove all but the young out of the industry. The *Journalist*, a reporter's trade magazine in the 1890s, noted that only reporters without families or other responsibilities could *afford* such low pay. "Gray hairs and men in their prime are at a discount," one observer wrote in 1896.[25] When some journalists proposed building a home for old, retired journalists, one writer argued that it was simply unnecessary because very few stayed until they retired — reporting was a young man's game.[26]

These working conditions — part of publishers' strategies to keep operating costs low — influenced the news. They drove seasoned reporters out of the newspaper industry. Bonuses paid for sensational or exclusive stories created powerful incentives for reporters to get stories without regard to ethics. H. L. Mencken described his experiences in the 1890s, when he worked for the Baltimore *Sun*. He and two rival reporters were covering the docks when a longshoreman drowned. To save time and effort, they headed to a nearby tavern and fabricated a story that all three could share.[27]

Such deceit was not uncommon. John Fox, a young reporter in New York City in the 1880s, found that he simply did not have enough time or energy to write stories that were completely truthful. He often worked fourteen or more hours a day, seven days a week. He found that at its best, space pay encouraged padding of news stories. More often, it led to exaggeration and lies. He did not like this system, but he adopted its methods:

> I find I am falling into the habit of tinging things and of trusting to my imagination. I am frequently forced to this because I have no time and because it is often impossible to make personal investigation. I know that this is dangerous and that one will become so that he is unable to describe things as they really are, that finally he will actually deceive himself without knowing it.[28]

Working conditions distorted the news and encouraged fabrication and sensationalism. The *Brooklyn Weekly* noted that U.S. newspapers "are dressed up and high spiced and all sorts of imaginary conversations and episodes are introduced."[29] One writer in The *Journalist* said that reporters simply did not have the time or incentive to be accurate. "No matter of names misspelled and facts distorted and faked. They must get the story, get it quick and if it is not spicy enough, make it so."[30]

Patent Insides

Reporters' salaries were a major concern in the metropolitan newspapers, where editorial staffs were large. Outside of the big cities, in newspapers with small staffs, publishers sought to economize by filling their papers with news and features purchased cheaply from a few national syndicates.[31]

Some of these syndicates — called newspaper unions[32] — offered a rather creative way for the publishers of small newspapers to fill their papers. The newspaper unions produced what were called "patent insides": four- or eight-page papers with some pages filled (with general news, innocuous editorials, feature articles, and advertisements) and others left blank. These half-full papers were shipped to local editors, who completed the production process by filling the blank pages with local news and more advertisements.[33]

These patent insides were cheap and popular.[34] The newspaper unions operated via economies of scale: they purchased paper in large quantities at a discount, rewrote news that was already published (thus minimizing news-gathering costs), and sold advertising for the pages they produced. Local publishers bought the half-full papers from the newspaper unions at roughly the retail price for blank newsprint. For the price of blank newsprint, the local publisher got a half-printed paper, replete with articles of general interest — without facing the cost of news gathering, composition, or printing on those pages. The newspaper unions profited because they sold their products to thousands of newspapers. Local publishers profited because they could produce their papers cheaply. In all, the newspaper unions serviced about 7,000 (or three-fourths) of the nation's weekly newspapers in the late nineteenth century.[35] (Small dailies also relied on the newspaper unions, although the percentage that did so is not clear.)[36]

The driving force in the use of patent insides was the bottom line; they were popular because they were so cheap. As such, the product — news — was shaped with profit in mind. The results were mixed. Weekly newspapers and small daily newspapers expanded in the late nineteenth century without significant increases in subscription costs.[37] One industry observer praised the patent insides, saying "A vast mine of literary and news matter is opened up for any publisher who desires to buy it; and the cost is so trifling that the richest treasures are within easy reach of the poorest."[38] But that same observer noted that the patent insides could be a curse. "Underneath the pleasant exterior there is an insidious danger which has sent more than one unlucky editor to his doom." Editors had little control over the material they received. One industry observer noted:

> Sometimes entire pages are made up of available and desirable articles; but more frequently, they contain one or more columns that the editor does not want, but which he has to buy in order to get the one or more columns that he does want. And it is herein that the editor begins to find himself between the devil and the deep sea.[39]

The product (news) was shaped to increase its marketability. Given the nature of production, distribution, and marketing, the material in the patent insides was often out of date or so innocuous as to be frivolous. Nathaniel Fowler, Jr., who wrote extensively on newspapers and advertising in that era, faulted the patents for their blandness. To appeal to thousands of newspapers across the country, the patent insides "must be compromising to the extreme."[40] Some editors found that other nearby newspapers had the same stories from the newspaper unions, or that many of their readers had already seen the patent-inside articles in magazines.[41]

Beats and Creating the News

The desire to keep operating expenses low also placed a premium on local news that could be gathered cheaply. Once again, concerns about profits shaped the product. Volunteer correspondents provided a steady supply of news for weeklies across the country.[42] Metropolitan publishers and editors, equally eager for cheap local news, relied on a beat system, sending reporters daily to places where news might be expected (courts, the police station, city hall, or hospitals). Beats were economical in two ways. First, they were predictable: the number of reporters needed and the number of news articles produced would not vary greatly day to day. Second, beat reporters usually collected facts that already had been processed or structured in some way by others. Reporting on trials or getting crime news from the police blotter was cheaper than dealing with the unstructured world.

The beat system emphasized certain kinds of news, for it was essentially coverage by the press of other institutions (the courts, police, hospitals, city hall), and it served to deemphasize news that did not occur on a beat. Beat reporting is not in any fashion inherently bad. Much of the coverage of government institutions stemmed from a strong sense within the newspaper industry that the press should serve as a watchdog on government and public officials. But beat reporting also was an important part of the economic imperatives of the newspaper business, and as such helped determine the shape of news.

Editors could not count on beat stories for the compelling, eye-popping stories that boosted street sales; beat articles often were mundane accounts of arrests, trials, or city council hearings. So editors sent reporters out to create the news. Elizabeth Cochran, who wrote under the pseudonym Nelly Bly for Joseph Pulitzer's *New York World*, won her job by feigning insanity to gain entry into a New York mental hospital. Once there, she exposed its squalid conditions. After that, her career was one creative splash after another. She jumped off ferry boats to test rescuers, posed as an immigrant to expose fraudulent employment agencies, and repeated the fictional Phineas Fogg's route around the world in eighty days (she did it in seventy-two).[43] It all was interesting and eye-catching. It also was news shaped and marketed with an eye to profits.

Nelly was not alone. Other newspapers copied her escapades. The *Chicago Herald* sponsored an expedition to the North Pole and covered it extensively, until ice crushed its ship.[44] Other reporters pursued murderers, inspected asylums, jumped off ferry boats, fainted on city streets to test ambulance services, and broke into city morgues to test security.[45]

Enhancing Revenues

In the late nineteenth century, readers and advertisers were the two sources of newspaper revenue. Consequently, publishers and editors shaped and marketed the news with an eye to its popularity with both groups.

Circulation

Readership has always been the simplest measure of a newspaper's success. Generally, the greater a newspaper's circulation, the greater its profits and perceived influence. In fairly competitive newspaper markets (such as New York City, Chicago, or Boston), the scramble for circulation dictated a fairly careful shaping and marketing of the news.

The first strategy for success in circulation was to offer news so diverse and varied that it would appeal to a vast number of readers. In 1896 one editor said that "no newspaper enterprise can be a financial success unless it appeals to the sentiments of the great masses."[46] Editors attempted to offer something for everyone. In 1898, one Sunday's edition of the *Pittsburgh Leader* provided articles on fashion (including "April wraps: Novelty coats and capes that captivate feminine fancy"), gossip about former President Cleveland and his family, women polar explorers, baking, egg farming, how to eat with chopsticks, identical twins in Michigan, big-game hunting, women fire fighters, travel abroad, species of trees in North America, insects, mining in British Columbia, and a short story.[47]

Newspapers routinely offered content on sports, music, theater, art, fashion, cooking, agriculture, books, religion, stock markets, real estate, children, science, and society, while also covering politics and government, crime, accidents, suicides, and strikes and publishing jokes, poems, short stories, or serialized fiction. The rationale for this was clearly one of marketing the news. As one trade journal writer noted:

> The effect of organization and competition has been to make the modern newspaper like a great hotel. No guest expects to go through the whole bill of fare. Each calls for what he likes best. . . . One reader turns to the stock market, another to politics, another to baseball, another to book reviews, another to musical and theatrical notices, another to a sermon or lecture . . . and so on. . . . A spice of humor is always in order and sometimes a startling turn of a phrase will attract attention.[48]

Table 5.1
Diversity in content of five metropolitan newspapers, 1897 (in percentages)

	Pittsburgh Leader	New York Journal	Chicago Tribune	Boston Globe	San Francisco Chronicle
Politics	9.0	18.2	20.1	15.1	16.0
Crime and courts	6.5	12.4	10.0	6.5	12.8
Accidents	4.8	20.2	7.6	8.1	11.9
Society and women	11.4	9.9	5.0	8.5	6.7
Leisure	34.6	14.0	18.0	25.3	18.5
Business and labor	16.6	7.5	16.4	11.4	21.9
Religion	7.4	1.9	5.5	4.6	4.4
Education and science	5.3	0.5	3.9	2.2	1.6
Comics and jokes	1.3	10.4	2.2	6.3	1.4
Other	3.1	2.8	6.1	11.8	4.9
Column inches	N = 2,835.3	N = 14,294.3	N = 11,274.5	N = 13,592.5	N = 9,709

Note: These newspapers were chosen because they were prominent, large-circula-tion metropolitan newspapers. Each newspaper was coded for the week of October 16–21, 1897; this date was selected by use of a random-number table. Each story was coded for length and subject matter. Most subjects are self-explanatory. "Leisure" included leisure-time activities: sports, reading, theater, music, and general enter-tainment. Two reliability tests were conducted on the content analysis scheme, with an overall reliability of 95 percent.

On Sunday, October 16, 1897, the most prominent story[49] on the front page of the *Boston Globe* dealt with a football game:

HOT WORK ON THE GRIDIRON
Harvard Defeats West Point 10–0 After a
Stubborn Contest

That same day's *Globe* also contained articles on local theaters, a con-test, short stories, comics, and jokes. A content analysis of five met-ropolitan newspapers in 1897 demonstrates that such diversity was common in late nineteenth-century U.S. newspapers (see Table 5.1).

Beyond diversity, editors sought to make their newspapers inter-esting. H. N. Rickey, editor in chief of the Scripps-McRae newspa-pers, stressed that each one of his editors should see "the importance of making his paper as entertaining as possible."[50] Another Scripps manager told the six editors under his command, "I do want to urge that we give at once, more thought and attention and hard work to being amusing and entertaining."[51] A writer in *Newspaperdom*, a newspaper industry trade journal, urged that the newspaper "must be vivid, bright, pyrotechnic enough in its features to force itself into popular attention at every turn."[52] The search for "vivid, bright and pyrotechnic" stories led to coverage of disasters, murder, suicide, love triangles, elopements, gossip, and any truly odd story. And interesting stories should be short and snappy. One journalist advised that "short paragraphs and articles are preferred. Longer ones are looked at despairingly and skipped."[53] H. N. Rickey said in 1909, "The average newspaper reader of today is too busy with his own affairs to waste time wading through column and two column articles in newspapers, unless such articles are of extraordinary importance."[54]

Politics and the Press

Shaping the news with an eye to its popularity meant that editors downplayed their political views lest they offend readers — in sharp contrast to the highly partisan content that characterized the vast majority of U.S. newspapers in the early nineteenth century.[55] The *New York Evening Post* editorialized that partisan newspapers are "apt to have a short life."[56] The editor of the Abbeville, South Carolina, *Press and Banner* warned that partisan papers failed much faster than nonpartisan newspapers.[57] In 1892, the new proprietors of the Harrisburg, Pennsylvania, *Morning Call* cited economics as a reason for avoiding politics. "The experience of former publishers of this paper admonishes us that it is neither pleasant nor profitable for a newspaper to become an organ for the politicians."[58] One industry observer noted in 1893 that more and more readers wanted their politics "straight."[59] The *Cincinnati Tribune*'s editors wrote in 1895 that the most popular newspaper was one that was "not merely partisan in its utterances."[60] In 1910, H. N. Rickey warned that "politics seems to be occupying too great a proportion of both our editorial and news space these days."[61] Rickey worried that "we are going to nauseate our readers and make them all mighty tired of the whole political business." He added, "We must not lose sight of the fact that we are publishing newspapers and not political pamphlets, that one of our chief aims is to interest women and that we must not let our political enthusiasm run away with our sense of proportion."[62]

Partisanship could offend readers; it also could cause ruinous competition. In one-newspaper towns in New York and California in the late 1890s, two-thirds of all newspapers claimed to have no political affiliation whatsoever.[63] A newspaper industry trade journal writer outlined the rationale:

> In a little country town there may be published a paper which is sufficient for the needs of the community as a medium of information and communication, but because its politics is democratic or republican, somebody is constrained to start a paper to represent the opposing party. The result is a division of patronage and a consequent struggle for existence on the part of both papers. . . . The history of journalism is replete with the disastrous careers of such ventures.[64]

Even editors with strong and well-known political views distanced themselves from political parties. The *St. Louis Republic* admitted its Democratic views, but vowed to treat all parties and ideas fairly. "In short, the *Republic* will remain a staunch Democratic newspaper but it will discuss men and measures, parties and principles, in such a spirit of candor and fairness as will prove informing to Democrats and Republicans alike and will repel or offend no good citizen."[65] And one trade journal praised the Clinton, Missouri, *Bugle*, which, although Democratic, "advocates no party, leans to no sect."[66]

Marketing Newspapers

Competition for readers encouraged publishers and editors to claim that their product was somehow different from the standard fare of other newspapers. The *Pittsburgh Leader*, for example, pledged to offer more diverse content than any of its competitors:

> No matter in what you are interested, you will find the subject of your hobby duly exploited. . . . in fact, whatever you most like to read, you will find the "Leader's" departments are the most carefully prepared, the most complete and the most interesting.[67]

The *Pittsburgh Leader* also boasted that its news coverage was far superior to that of its rivals. As part of its coverage of a Knights Templars meeting in Pittsburgh in 1898, the paper ran a long article extolling its own enterprise:

NEWS OF THE CONCLAVE
HOW THE 'LEADER' HANDLED THE GREAT LOCAL EVENT
Rivals Were Not Merely Outclassed; They Were Overwhelmed —
Readers Let Into the Inside Work of Taking Care
of a Great News Item[68]

The article said that the *Leader* was *first* in publishing "the correct information on the great parade. . . . Other afternoon newspapers merely reproduced the formation in the official program, giving a few additions which were mostly inaccuracies." The *Leader* added that boasting was usually inappropriate, but

> it would be an injustice to the readers of the paper if they were not
> informed in some measure of the means which the *Leader* took to
> thoroughly cover the great conclave, while other Pittsburgh newspapers
> were almost helpless before it and made but a pitiful showing in
> comparison with the magnitude of the opportunity presented.[69]

The *Chicago Herald* claimed in October 1894 that its reporting of the previous week was without rival. "THE HERALD reports everything that is of human interest that concerns a respectable number of the people, and does it in a manner that leaves nothing further to be desired."[70]

Contests and prizes also figured in newspaper promotion. The kinds of contests seemed unlimited, as readers were asked to nominate their favorite police officer, street car conductor, clerk, or servant girl. The *St. Louis Star* offered cash prizes for essays on the life of George Washington.[71] The *Cincinnati Tribune* offered a free trip to the 1893 Chicago World's Fair to the "Ten Most Popular Pastors" (and their wives, if they were married).[72] The *Detroit News* held a contest for the best bread, and more than 2,000 entered the contest.[73] The *Chicago Herald* gave away books, geraniums, photographs, and dolls in its flurry of contests in the mid-1890s.[74] The *Syracuse Evening Herald* gave away the *Encyclopedia Britannica* in 1892, and the Elmira, New York, *Star* offered free trips for contest winners.[75]

Advertising Revenues

Advertising represented the other major source of newspaper revenue in the late nineteenth century. *Printers' Ink*, an advertising and publishing trade journal, proclaimed, "In the estimation of the newspaper manager, columns of advertising rank out of sight of news in point of solid value. He well understands where the reliable supports of his business prosperity lie."[76] *Fame*, an advertising journal, contended that newspaper subscriptions "barely pay for the cost of white paper. The chief revenue comes from advertising."[77] Given advertising's value — it constituted two-thirds of all newspaper revenues —

publishers and editors who wanted to increase revenues obviously paid close attention to their advertising columns.

Circulation determined advertising revenues. Indeed, the greatest economic value of circulation was not in the money that subscriptions or street sales generated, but in its ability to raise advertising rates. The marketing calculus for advertisers was twofold. First, advertisers considered the size of a newspaper's circulation; they were willing to pay higher rates to larger newspapers because they wanted to reach as many potential customers as possible.[78] In response, publishers and editors sought large circulation. Second, advertisers analyzed the nature of a newspaper's readership. Advertisers wanted to market their goods to people who had money and who were willing to spend it. In response, publishers and editors aimed their newspapers at key consumer groups in the country — families in general, and women in particular.

The *Oakland Enquirer* promised advertisers that its paper circulated to "the best class of people."[79] The San Francisco *Evening Bulletin* warned advertisers not to be misled "by newspapers of a much inferior grade, but claiming larger circulation, for in reaching the *purchasing class*, the BULLETIN HAS NO COMPETITOR, it is peerless as an advertising medium."[80] And the editor of the weekly *Bucyrus* (Ohio) *Journal* claimed that his paper "includes among its subscribers the wealthiest, the most intelligent and the most enterprising of our citizens."[81]

Serving an upscale market really could influence advertising rates. In the mid-1890s, the *New York Evening Post*, with a circulation of only 25,000, charged twenty cents a line for ads, while the *New York World* — with a circulation *twenty-five* times larger than that of the *Evening Post*, charged only twice as much for ads. As one industry observer noted, "This is accounted for by the fact that the *Post* goes to a distinct class — a moneyed class — and for that reason proves a more profitable medium for advertising the highest class of goods than does the *World*."[82]

Advertisers prized women readers because they were seen as the buyers of the mass-produced goods flooding the U.S. market in the late nineteenth century. One advertising trade journal, *Profitable Advertiser*, said that women were highly attentive to ads, particularly ones for department stores.[83] The *Cincinnati Tribune* estimated that "80 percent of all domestic buying is done by women of the household."[84] The *Dry Goods Economist*, a major department store trade journal, told merchants that "nine-tenths of the money earned by man is spent by woman."[85]

Fowler urged that newspapers fill their columns with "news" that would appeal to families in general and women:

> The daily paper which has succeeded and which continues to succeed is the paper which prints the most matter of interest to women. . . . The great daily, filled with the bright news of the day to whet the appetite of the readers with its children's columns, its women's column, its column of style, its miscellany, is the paper which has the great circulation and the one which pays the advertiser more to the square inch than any other paper can pay to the square foot. . . . There is not a single case on record of any daily paper succeeding . . . which does not arrange its matter, from editorial to its news, so as to be pleasantly absorbed by the women of the day.[86]

Content for women was common by the 1880s. Fashion, cooking, household hints, and society news all figured prominently in late nineteenth-century newspapers. The *Pittsburgh Leader* ran recipes on its editorial page.[87] The *New York Tribune* ran a course in shorthand for women.[88] Fashion news appeared in the *Cincinnati Tribune, Boston Globe, St. Paul Globe,* and *Chicago Herald.*[89] Analysis of five metropolitan newspapers in the late 1890s shows that content for women averaged 8.3 percent of editorial content (see Table 5.1). On Sunday, October 16, 1897, the *Boston Globe* printed articles on society happenings (both in Boston and abroad), a woman's advice column, and fashion news:

FOR WINTER DAYS
Charming Indoor Gowns
For Cold Months
New Styles Avoid All Kinds of
Exaggerated Departures
Smart Skirts Measure Four
and One Half Yards
Small and Modest Bustles
Are Now in Vogue
Trains to Add Grace At Home
Are Only Half Suggested

The *Globe's* Sunday magazine supplement also contained a good deal of material designed to appeal to women: piano music ("Varsity

March") and comics about beleaguered housewives and landladies. That same day, the *Globe*'s "Housekeeper's Column" offered menu suggestions, sixteen recipes (including "Macaroni a la Creme, Apple Suet Pudding and Pop Overs"), as well as advice and patterns on sewing and crocheting. This column appeared daily.[90] The weekday editions of the *Globe* also offered news about society and "frivolous, fanciful, ever-changing fashion."[91]

The business imperative of pleasing advertisers went beyond shaping the news for customers in general and women in particular. Publishers and editors recognized that promoting advertisers in their news columns could keep old business and perhaps entice new advertisers to their columns. Jason Rogers, former editor of the *New York Mercury* and a newspaper industry observer in the 1890s, said that newspapers should promote advertisers in their own columns:

> In cultivating local dry goods advertising, both for purposes of revenue and circulation . . . a publisher should, with a spirit of broad minded liberality, make a regular daily feature of news from the store. Such an article lends great additional value to a woman's page, provided it is not allowed to take too "shoppy" a turn.
>
> If one of the large stores has just received a new consignment of imported goods and yet is not a regular user of the advertising columns of your paper, a well-written news story on the woman's page will convincingly prove the value of the paper as an advertising medium, entirely aside from the display of liberality and fair play involved.[92]

A good deal of news did indeed seem to follow Rogers's advice that newspapers promote their advertisers. The *St. Louis Republic* ran an editorial in 1889 praising one of its advertisers: "Every city has its model advertiser, whose success points its own moral, and no business house in St. Louis is better entitled to that enviable distinction than D.CRAWFORD & CO. No mercantile concern is better known to the people of this city; none has had a more rapid and remarkable growth."[93] The *Detroit News Tribune* published a series of "practical talks" with advertisers and the purchasing public.[94] The *Chicago Herald* called its regular advertisers "solid and substantial."[95] The *Berkshire* (Massachusetts) *County Eagle* reviewed the "opening" of the spring hat season with praise for area merchants:

> The store of J. Muhlfelder never presented a more attractive appearance than it did last evening when the spring opening began. . . . Miss Speigel has the choicest assortment of "loves" of hats and is being congratulated on

her auspicious opening. . . . But these newspaper descriptions of the wonderful creations are, of necessity, very unsatisfactory, and the best thing the ladies can do is to see them for themselves.[96]

The *Dedham* (Massachusetts) *Transcript* sprinkled promotions for its advertisers amid its local news columns. On February 8, 1896, the local items included a testimonial to the fine inventory at the Charles A. Wragg Co., a bicycle shop.[97] On January 23, 1897, the *Transcript* included this item in its local news columns:

Attention is called to the advertisement of Mr. Bewe, the Hyde Park shoe dealer, in another column. He offers his customers full value for their money and keeps a large variety to select from.[98]

Puffs

Shaping the news to please advertisers took two forms. First, editors printed "puffs" for businesses, mentioning them favorably in their news columns. For example, a feature story on Christmas shopping might indicate that a particular store had unusual bargains on high-quality merchandise. Or a review of a concert might praise not only the pianist, but the Steinway piano.

Some advertising agents insisted that puffs were just part of the newspaper business. A writer in the trade journal *Advertising World* contended that puffs were due to advertisers. "A newspaper should mention its advertisers whenever possible in a newsy way. In fact, it should do everything within its power to bring results to those who are using its columns."[99] Publishers and editors complained that advertisers always were hounding them for puffs, but apparently still acquiesced to the demands.[100] Puffs were so common that one company, the Ferguson Telegraphic News Service, *specialized* in them. In its own ads, the firm promised to concoct news stories that would incidentally promote products. The firm claimed that it had successfully placed such puffs in newspapers in St. Louis, Boston, Denver, Chicago, Cincinnati, and Omaha.[101] *Printers' Ink* praised Ferguson, noting that puffs were a common practice and highly beneficial to advertisers.[102]

Blurring News and Ads

The second form of news that was designed to please advertisers consisted of general news stories that profiled businesses or business-people. These articles tended to promote the advertiser and his goods. In 1885, for example, the *New York World* devoted a full page to the opening of a new department store:

THE GRANDEST DRY GOODS STORY IN BROOKLYN
THE GREATEST EVENT IN BROOKLYN'S DRY GOODS ANNALS
An Immense Establishment Surpassing in Beauty Anything Ever
Produced in this Country
The Rise, Progress and Achievements of a Famous House
Illustrating Anew the Time Honored Adage, that "Great Oaks
From Little Acorns Grow."
What the Ladies Will Look For and See There[103]

In 1885, the *Boston Globe* gave similar attention to one of its major advertisers, Jordan, Marsh & Co.

JORDAN, MARSH & CO.
Their Colossal Sale Draws Thousands from Every Section

The article described the merchandise on sale and called readers' attention to the department store's ads in that day's paper:

> Limited space, however, precludes the possibility of our enumerating all the lots offered, and it will thus remain for the readers of THE GLOBE to peruse the advertisements this firm have placed on the fourth, fifth and sixteenth pages of this issue, or better, to call in person at the store of Jordan, Marsh & Co., early Monday morning and inspect in person the remarkable values this popular house is offering.[104]

Two months later, the *Globe* praised the "indefatigable energy and persistent activity" of the firm.[105]

Fame, an advertising trade journal edited by Artemas Ward, contended that major advertisers received special treatment from newspapers. If a runaway horse bolted into Macy's and killed a child, Ward wrote, the ensuing news story would spare Macy's unwanted publicity by referring only generally to "a dry goods store."[106] In the late 1890s, when a major New York City department store faced a lawsuit for falsely accusing a shopper of shoplifting (she was also injured in the ensuing confusion), all but one New York City newspaper suppressed the name of the store.[107]

Newspapers also catered to advertisers by allowing them to run some of their ads disguised as news articles. These "reading notices," as they were called, were essentially the appropriation of the news *form* for advertising purposes. Advertisers liked reading notices because they believed news articles had greater credibility with readers than did ads. The *Newberg* (Oregon) *Graphic* in 1896 ran one advertisement that at first looked like an article about a Civil War veteran:

A WAR REMINISCENCE
Scene at Hatcher's Creek & Peters-
burg Recalled
John B. Scace Speaks to a Reporter
of Stirring Scenes — Escaped with a
Slight Wound, but Like Other
Veterans, Has Suffered Since
— a Story That Reads Like
a Page from History

The first four paragraphs of the "article" dealt with Scace's recollections of the war, his injuries, and his recurrent, war-related health problems. The fifth paragraph noted that only one remedy could cure him — Dr. Williams' Pink Pills for Pale People.[108]

Publishers and editors also catered to advertisers by promoting their business interests. The clearest example of this was in editorial opposition to patent medicine labeling laws. A variety of states proposed such legislation in the late nineteenth century, but patent medicine manufacturers strongly opposed it. They feared that labeling laws would give away their trade secrets, but they also feared that labeling laws would reveal that many so-called medicines contained large amounts of alcohol or small amounts of drugs or poisons.[109]

The patent medicine manufacturers enlisted the help of newspapers in fighting the labeling laws. In 1897, the *Cincinnati Post* condemned a proposed Ohio labeling law as an attempt "to drive proprietary medicines out of the state."[110] Some advertisers insisted upon such editorial material in their advertising contracts with newspapers. J. H. Zeilin & Co. inserted the following clause in its advertising contracts with newspapers in the 1880s: "Nothing shall be published which may be calculated to injure the business of J. H. Zeilin & Co., or by mentioning the same in censure; but will exert ourselves to protect and promote their interest."[111] The *Journalist* condemned New York newspapers' subservience to patent medicine manufacturers. "It is not a pleasing condition of affairs to see the press of a great city array itself on the side of fraud and deliberate swindling, if not worse, bought by a few inches of advertising at cut rates."[112]

Conclusions

In the past few decades, a variety of authors have examined how news is created. They have noted that the definition of "news" is a fairly complex process that reflects not only events that occur in the world, but also the values, interests, and needs of reporters, editors, media organizations, and society itself.[113]

In the late nineteenth century, many things influenced the definition and production of news. Central to that process were the needs of news organizations themselves. These business imperatives — notably the dual needs to keep operating expenses low and to enhance revenues — clearly influenced the definition, selection, and publication of news.

Thus, news was not merely a reflection of what was occurring in the world; it was also a commodity shaped and marketed for profit. "News," then, had at least two functions: to inform and to generate profits. Profits, per se, need not be antithetical to information. But the dual goals of the newspaper industry could clash; the profit-seeking mentality at times clearly overwhelmed the newspaper's informational role. The fabrication and sensationalism engendered by the space system, for example, hardly can be considered informational. The banality of the "patent insides" stemmed from marketing strategies rather than from a desire to inform. "News" articles that flattered or promoted advertisers, too, were essentially profit driven; information in such a setting would be secondary. All were part of the definition of news; all were central to news as a commodity.

Notes

1. Edward Bellamy, *Looking Backward: 2000–1887*, Tower Books ed. (Cleveland: World, 1945), 163, emphasis added. The final chapter of *Looking Backward* reveals that West's visit to that utopian future was just a dream.

2. Address of Col. P. Donan at the 1891 Minnesota Editors and Publishers Association meeting, *Journalist*, May 2, 1891, 7.

3. *Newspaperdom*, July 1892, 3.

4. *Newspaper Maker*, January 1, 1895, 1.

5. *Newspaperdom*, July 1892, 3.

6. Ibid.

7. *Newspaper Maker*, June 24, 1897, 8.

8. James L. Crouthamel, *Bennett's* New York Herald *and the Rise of the Popular Press* (Syracuse, N.Y.: Syracuse University Press, 1989).

9. John C. Nerone, "The Mythology of the Penny Press," *Critical Studies in Mass Communication* 4 (December 1987): 376–404.

10. *Chicago Herald*, December 3, 1893, 29.

11. *Journalist*, March 14, 1891, 6.

12. *Newspaper Maker*, May 2, 1895, 1.

13. *Printers' Ink* estimated the paper costs of major metropolitan newspapers in 1890. The *Boston Globe, Boston Herald,* and *Chicago News* all spent more than $300,000 a year on paper; the *Cincinnati Enquirer, Philadelphia Press,* and *Chicago Herald* spent more than $200,000 a year; and the *San Francisco Call, Philadelphia Times, San Francisco Examiner, Chicago Tribune, St. Louis Republic,* and *Baltimore American* more than $100,000 a year. *Printers' Ink,* May 28, 1890, 869.

14. In 1890, the bills for local news coverage by the New York City daily newspapers ranged from $1,500 to $3,400 a week—$78,000 to $176,000 a year. Ibid., 870.

15. In 1890, *Printers' Ink* estimated annual composition bills on major metropolitan dailies: *Cincinnati Enquirer,* $166,000; *Chicago Herald,* $109,500; *Chicago Tribune,* $130,000; *New York Times,* $156,000; *St. Louis Globe-Democrat,* $104,000; *Boston Globe,* $213,000; *New York World,* $312,000. Ibid.

16. *Journalist*, June 13, 1891, 4.

17. The rapid growth in news staffs in the late nineteenth century made salaries a major expense for many newspapers. The *New York Herald*, for instance, had only seven staff reporters and editors in 1860; by 1890, it had more than a hundred. *Newspaperdom*, July 1892, 12.

18. *Journalist*, February 7, 1891, 4–5.

19. John W. Fox to M. Fible, May 11, 1884, March 14, 1886, September 16, 1886, John Fox Letters, Southern Historical Collection, University of North Carolina; *Fourth Estate*, March 9, 1901, 396; *Journalist*, September 15, 1900, 178; October 20, 1900, 210; Ted Curtis Smythe, "The Reporter, 1880–1900: Working Conditions and Their Influence on the News," *Journalism History* 7 (Winter 1980): 3–5.

20. *Journalist*, June 23, 1900, 75; *Newspaper Maker*, August 23, 1900, 6; *Journalist*, September 1, 1900, 157; Augustus J. Munson, *Making a Country Newspaper* (Chicago: Dominion, 1891); Nathaniel C. Fowler, Jr., *The Handbook of Journalism* (New York: Sully & Kleinteich, 1913), 74–75, 96–99, 114–18, 124–27.

21. *Journalist*, August 14, 1897, 133.

22. Ibid.

23. *Journalist*, August 18, 1900, 139.

24. *Journalist*, January 9, 1892, 8.

25. *Newspaper Maker*, January 9, 1896, 5; also see *Newspaper Maker*, August 2, 1900, 6.

26. *Journalist*, July 14, 1900, 108.

118   Gerald J. Baldasty

27. H. L. Mencken, *Newspaper Days, 1899–1906* (New York: Knopf, 1941), 262–63.

28. John W. Fox to M. Fible, May 11, 1884, John Fox Letters, Southern Historical Collection, University of North Carolina.

29. *Newspaper Maker*, April 2, 1896, 7. Also see *Journalist*, April 4, 1891, 9; April 11, 1891, 4.

30. *Journalist*, September 15, 1900, 178.

31. By 1900, there was a variety of syndicated matter offered to newspapers across the country. The newspaper unions provided one of the most basic services to U.S. weeklies and small dailies. Other syndicates offered short stories and topical features (e.g., stories about Thanksgiving, St. Patrick's Day, or Christmas). See Elmo Scott Watson, *A History of Newspaper Syndicates in the United States, 1865–1935* (Chicago, 1936); Alfred McClung Lee, *The Daily Newspaper in America: The Evolution of a Social Instrument* (New York: Macmillan, 1937), 579–89.

32. The term itself is confusing. They were not unions in the twentieth-century notion of labor unions. Rather, they were businesses that produced a vast amount of news and feature material and distributed it to thousands of U.S. newspapers.

33. Earnest E. Calkins and Ralph Holden, *Modern Advertising* (New York: D. Appleton, 1905), 82–83; *Newspaperdom*, August 1892, 7–9; *Printers' Ink*, January 14, 1891, 97, 100; April 8, 1891, 489; April 22, 1891, 551; January 6, 1892, 27; *Newspaper Maker*, August 29, 1895, 3; Lewis M. Grist, "Use and Abuse of the Plate Service," *Newspaperdom*, March 1892, 6–7.

34. "Patent outsides" were also available. The newspaper unions prepared the outside pages of the paper, leaving inside pages blank.

35. Calkins and Holden, *Modern Advertising*, 82; Grist, "Use and Abuse," 6–7; *Pacific Printer*, April 1880, 5; June 1881, 2–3; *Inland Printer*, February 1900, 681; April 1900, 46–47.

36. *Newspaperdom*, June 1892, 4.

37. Grist, "Use and Abuse," 5; Munson, *Making a Country Newspaper*, 125–26; O. F. Byxbee, "Establishing a Newspaper," *Inland Printer*, February 1900, 681; Calkins and Holden, *Modern Advertising*, 83–84.

38. Grist, "Use and Abuse," 6. Also see *Proceedings of the Eighth Annual Meeting of the Associated Ohio Dailies* (Springfield, Ohio: Hosterman, 1893), 86.

39. Grist, "Use and Abuse," 6.

40. Fowler, *The Handbook of Journalism*, 127.

41. *Pacific Printer*, December 1891, 8.

42. Hugh Wilson, "Country Journalist and Printer," *Newspaperdom*, December 1892, 2; *Observer* (Oakland, Oregon), April 10, 1891, 4.

43. Madelon G. Schilpp and Sharon M. Murphy, *Great Women of the Press* (Carbondale: Southern Illinois University Press, 1983), 133–47; *Printers' Ink*, February 12, 1890, 368.

44. *Chicago Herald*, May 27, 1894, 29; July 15, 1894, 24; August 3, 1894, 1; October 28, 1894, 16.

45. *Pittsburgh Leader*, September 15, 1897, 1; *Newspaper Maker*, July 25, 1895, 4; February 10, 1898, 4; December 6, 1900, 4; *Cincinnati Tribune*, January 13, 1895, 6.

46. *Newspaper Maker*, March 19, 1896, 2.

47. *Pittsburgh Leader*, April 3, 1898.

48. *Newspaperdom*, July 1892, 13.

49. It was the only article with a three-column headline. Moreover, it was at the top of the page.

50. H. N. Rickey to editors of the Scripps-McRae League, October 13, 1909, Series 3.1, Box 30, Folder 11, E. W. Scripps Correspondence, Ohio University.

51. B. H. Canfield to Moriarty, Preciado, Sanders, Smythe, Allen, Sawyer, October 11, 1911, Series 3.1, Box 35, Folder 4, E. W. Scripps Correspondence, Ohio University.

52. *Newspaperdom*, June 1892, 9.

53. *Newspaperdom*, July 1892, 3.

54. H. N. Rickey to editors of the Scripps-McRae League, December 17, 1909, Series 3.1, Box 6, E. W. Scripps Correspondence, Ohio University.

55. William E. Ames, *A History of the* National Intelligencer (Chapel Hill: University of North Carolina Press, 1972); Carolyn Stewart Dyer, "Political Patronage of the Wisconsin Press, 1849–1860: New Perspectives on the Economics of Patronage," *Journalism Monographs* 109 (February 1989); Gerald J. Baldasty, "The Press and Politics in the Age of Jackson," *Journalism Monographs* 89 (August 1984).

56. Quoted in the *Newspaper Maker*, April 4, 1898, 5.

57. Quoted in *Newspaperdom*, December 1892, 1.

58. Quoted in ibid., 35.

59. Ibid., 1.

60. *Cincinnati Tribune*, May 17, 1895, 4.

61. H. N. Rickey to Ohio editors of the Scripps-McRae League, September 30, 1910, Series 3.1., Box 32, Folder 15, E. W. Scripps Correspondence, Ohio University.

62. Ibid.

63. Gerald J. Baldasty and Jeffrey B. Rutenbeck, "Money, Politics and Newspapers: The Business Environment of Press Partisanship in the Late Nineteenth Century," *Journalism History* 15 (Summer–Autumn 1988): 62–63.

64. *Newspaper Maker*, August 4, 1898, 5.

65. *St. Louis Republic*, May 31, 1888, 4.

66. *Journalist*, April 18, 1891, 7.

67. *Pittsburgh Leader*, January 21, 1898, 3.

68. *Pittsburgh Leader*, October 16, 1898, 12.

69. Ibid.

70. *Chicago Herald*, October 12, 1894, 6.

71. *Newspaper Maker*, April 18, 1895, 4.

72. *Cincinnati Tribune*, June 20, 1893, 4.

73. *Newspaper Maker*, March 11, 1897, 2.

74. *Chicago Herald*, December 10, 1893, 43; February 19, 1894, 7; February 14, 1894, 8; January 4, 1895, 8; January 19, 1895, 10.

75. *Fame*, November 1892, 300; April 1898, 323.

76. *Printers' Ink*, October 22, 1890, 405.

77. *Fame*, September 1894, 259. "It is a well known fact that there are scarcely half a dozen newspapers published in the United States that could exist were the advertising patronage cut off entirely. In the case of only a few of them is the subscription price large enough to pay for the publication."

78. For discussions on circulation, see the following advertising trade journals: *Fame*, June 1892, 112; September 1892, 203; May 1896, 222–23; November 1896, 335–36; *Advertising*, May 1897, 53; *Printers' Ink*, January 29, 1890, 321; October 21, 1896, 3–5; December 15, 1899, 189.

79. Lyman D. Morse, *Advertiser's Handy Guide for 1896* (New York: Lyman D. Morse, 1896), 706–7.

80. James H. Bates and Lyman D. Morse, *Advertiser's Handy Guide for 1893* (New York: Bates & Morse, 1893), 637.

81. Flyer, J. Hopley Papers, Box 4, Ohio Historical Society.

82. Addison Archer, *American Journalism from the Practical Side* (New York: Holmes, 1897), 3.

83. *Profitable Advertiser*, February 1892, 297.

84. *Cincinnati Tribune*, April 28, 1894, 4.

85. *Dry Goods Economist*, January 30, 1897, 65.

86. Nathaniel C. Fowler, "Reaching the Men through the Women," *Printers' Ink*, July 22, 1891, 51.

87. *Pittsburgh Leader*, April 23, 1898, 6.

88. *Newspaper Maker*, July 30, 1896, 4.

89. *Cincinnati Tribune*, July 19, 21, 24, 26, 28, September 16, October 19, 23, December 3, 1893; April 22, 29, May 6, 13, 20, 1894; *Boston Globe*, April 5, May 10, 1885; *St. Paul Globe*, May 10, 1885; *Chicago Herald*, June 22, December 25, 1881.

90. *Boston Globe*, October 17, 1897, 8; October 18, 1897, 8; October 19, 1897, 8.

91. *Boston Globe*, October 17, 1897, 4.

92. *Newspaper Maker*, November 19, 1896, 3.

93. *St. Louis Republic*, May 5, 1889, 4.

94. *Newspaper Maker*, January 20, 1898, 4.

95. *Chicago Herald*, January 12, 1895, 9.

96. *Berkshire (Massachusetts) County Eagle*, April 3, 1895, 5.

97. *Dedham (Massachusetts) Transcript*, February 8, 1896, 3.

98. *Dedham (Massachusetts) Transcript*, January 23, 1897, 3.

99. *Advertising World*, December 15, 1898, 18.

100. *Printers' Ink*, January 15, 1890, 262; A. O. Bunnell, comp., *New York Press Association: Authorized History for Fifty Years, 1853–1903* (Dansville, N.Y.: F. A. Owen, 1903), 26; *Ad Sense*, August 1900, 34.

101. *Printers' Ink*, March 12, 1890, 464.

102. Ibid.

103. *New York World*, February 15, 1885, 10.

104. *Boston Globe*, February 8, 1885, 3.

105. *Boston Globe*, April 19, 1885, 2.

106. *Fame*, April 1897, 55–56.

107. *Newspaper Maker*, December 23, 1898, 4.

108. *Newberg (Oregon) Graphic*, November 6, 1896, 4.

109. *Newspaper Maker*, February 17, 1898, 1.

110. *Newspaper Maker*, December 9, 1897, 4.

111. Advertising Contract, J. H. Zeilin & Co., Hopley Papers, Box 3, Ohio Historical Society.

112. *Journalist*, April 9, 1892, 8.

113. Herbert J. Gans, *Deciding What's News* (New York: Pantheon, 1979); Gaye Tuchman, *Making News: A Study in the Construction of Reality* (New York: Free Press, 1978); Michael Parenti, *Inventing Reality: The Politics of the Mass Media* (New York: St. Martin's, 1986).

Chapter 6

Gender, the Movement Press, and the Cultural Politics of the Knights of Labor
Holly Allen

> Within these walls we know no creed
> No nation, sex, or clan
> For "Justice unto all," we plead
> Based on the "Rights of Man"[1]

In these four lines is much that distinguishes the Knights of Labor as host to a broad-based, gender-inclusive labor movement in the Gilded Age. As the poem suggests, the Knights defied divisions based on "nation, sex, or clan" in their expansive plea for "Justice unto all," providing what Leon Fink has described as "a vast umbrella under which practically every variety of worker sought protection."[2] Yet a gendered reading of these lines reveals a partial contradiction: despite the claim that the Knights "know no . . . sex," the author uses clearly gendered language to invoke a republican tradition "Based on the 'Rights of Man.' "

Exemplified in these lines is a tension that runs throughout the Knights between gender-neutral policies and practices on the one hand and clearly gendered rhetoric on the other.[3] Focusing on three newspapers associated with the Knights, the *Journal of United Labor*, *John Swinton's Paper*, and the *Labor Leader*, this essay explores the organization's complex gender dynamics. It shows that Knights newspapers acted as a crucial context for the negotiation of a variety of cultural issues, including gender conflict. These newspapers often disagreed in their interpretation of important cultural issues: By demonstrating the contentious role of these newspapers and their editors, this essay illustrates the centrality of *diversity* and *contestation* to the Knights' movement culture. Only through an appreciation of the diverse and contested accents of that culture can the complexity and variability of its gendered meanings be grasped.

Movement Culture and the Knights of Labor

In his study of nineteenth-century U.S. labor movements, Bruce Laurie describes the Knights as "the most democratic, if not socialist, labor movement of the century and perhaps of American history."[4] The Noble and Holy Order of the Knights of Labor was founded in 1869 as a secretive fraternal organization of Philadelphia garment cutters. Its membership gradually expanded to other trades throughout the 1870s, yet by the time of the great railway strikes in 1877, the organization remained predominantly a Pennsylvania-based group of skilled workers. Knights ideology was extremely inclusive, however, and after that point membership continued to expand nationally. At the same time, the number of unskilled workers and immigrants rose significantly. Propelled by growing conflict between employers and an increasingly industrialized work force, the organization grew steadily throughout the early 1880s, extending membership to women and African Americans and reaching its peak with the labor uprisings of 1884–86. Overall, between two million and three million people were members of the Knights between the early 1870s and the mid-1890s. More than 600,000 new members joined between the summer of 1885 and the spring of 1886, and membership reached its highest point that summer with 750,000 members.[5] The Haymarket affair of 1886 initiated the movement's demise; by 1890, factionalism, misleadership, and employer repression had decimated the movement.

As the newspapers associated with the movement reveal, the phenomenal growth of the 1880s often engendered conflict within the Order. Some Knights, including a significant portion of the leadership, resisted the changes that came with the incorporation of larger and ever more diverse constituencies. Changes in policies and practices concerning gender provoked particular controversy, as this essay will show.

Yet it is precisely the Knights' breadth and dynamism that earned the organization the historical prominence it enjoys. Several scholars have shown that the Knights fostered a vibrant movement culture that fundamentally challenged the dominant U.S. culture of the Gilded Age. Lawrence Goodwyn first used the phrase "movement culture" to describe the rich cultural dimensions of the Populist movement.[6] Goodwyn argues that the Populists effectively mobilized a mass-based democratic movement in opposition to the social and political values of the dominant culture by providing their constituents with an *alternative* culture. Labor intellectuals such as newspaper editors figure prominently in Goodwyn's account as agents of cultural change and as educators within the movement. Indeed, what is perhaps most interesting about the phenomenon of movement culture as Goodwyn describes it is its *prescriptive* character: according to

Goodwyn, an oppositional movement culture is consciously shaped and disseminated by labor intellectuals, who both appropriate and seek to transform elements of a "received" culture.

Historians such as Leon Fink, Gregory Kealey, and Bryan Palmer have found the concept of movement culture particularly apt for describing the Knights of Labor.[7] Following Goodwyn, they argue that the Order was able to mobilize the largest and most representative labor body of its time because it effectively challenged the cultural hegemony of liberalism with a radical *cultural* alternative. Central to the success of that alternative culture, Fink asserts, was its ability to appropriate and transform "residual" cultural elements. Observing that the Knights drew upon the republican tradition that constituted the "vital center" of nineteenth-century political culture, Fink writes: "Engagement and even partial assimilation of the dominant culture by an opposition movement might be a sign of political strength, rather than weakness." He argues that the Knights' involvement with mainstream culture enabled them to "draw on constituencies attached to traditional values."[8]

The Knights also were very involved with a more broadly defined culture of *class*. In their work on the Ontario Knights, Kealey and Palmer describe that involvement as dialectical and prescriptive: "On the one hand, the Knights of Labor developed out of the class culture while, on the other hand, they pushed that culture forward, striking a posture of opposition."[9] In this sense, the movement's success depended not only on its ability to address the received *political culture* of Gilded Age America, including the rhetoric of natural rights, but also on its skill in engaging the everyday *cultural politics* of its predominantly ethnic, working-class membership, including the social practices of gender.[10]

Goodwyn has argued that newspaper editors and other intellectuals play a crucial role in creating a movement culture. This chapter incorporates that insight, but also explores the contested aspects of movement culture as well as its prescriptions. In what follows, I will present discussion of how three different newspapers functioned as a middle ground for the negotiation of class, gender, and cultural issues between the movement leadership and the rank and file. By emphasizing contestation, I will revise the concept of movement culture as it has been applied to U.S. labor movements of the Gilded Age. Challenging the notion that labor editors straightforwardly collaborated with the leadership to enforce specific cultural values upon the membership, I will argue that labor editors often acted as advocates of rank-and-file dissent, and that they frequently were the most articulate and powerful dissenters themselves.

Indeed, labor editors held a unique position within the movement: while their public status gave them considerable influence over the leadership, and some editors held focal positions in the Order, they also were participants in the separate sphere of the labor press, which had its own cultural and political conventions distinct from the Knights.[11] This chapter will consider some of the points of conflict between the leadership of the Knights and the newspapers associated with that organization. I will argue that the Knights of Labor and the labor press should be understood as parallel movements that intersected at important points, not simply as different facets of a single, coherent movement.

Such a perspective implies that any understanding of the gender conventions of the Knights derived from journalistic sources must consider the complex and semiautonomous nature of newspaper publishing vis-à-vis the broader movement. Yet, far from impeding the effectiveness of these sources, it is precisely this *multivalence* that makes a gendered analysis of the movement press valuable: through it we can see the variety of gender images, practices, and prescriptions that shaped the experiences of men and women within the movement.

In addition, labor editors differed from the national leadership on the basis of their greater exposure to the interests and concerns of the rank and file. Letters to the editor were only a small factor in editors' relationships to the membership. More generally, the need to secure reader subscriptions compelled editors to engage daily with rank-and-file concerns.

Also, it is important to consider the *cultural significance* of the labor press within the working-class community. Late nineteenth-century workers viewed the labor press as far more than reading matter. For them, labor newspapers were a crucial component of everyday life. In this way, the labor press was analogous to and overlapped with the immigrant press.[12] At a time when changing work processes, immigration and ethnic diversity, and geographic mobility powerfully challenged community formation, the labor press was an organ of unity and coherence for its membership. It helped workers and their families to make sense of the world around them. Also, because the Knights emphasized the integrity and intellectual acumen of the laborer and the importance of self-improvement, newspapers served an educational purpose as well, providing reading matter and information that working-class readers used to further their collective intellectual aspirations.[13]

Yet, given the gender inclusiveness of the Knights, it is important to consider the different reactions these newspapers might have received from male and female audiences. Indeed, the analogue of the immigrant press has important implications for gender. If the Gilded Age immigrant press can be said to have served as part of a public, ethnic subculture that was dominated by men, to what extent were the Knights' newspapers also directed to a male readership? Given the fact that the majority of Knights were men, how did women engage with the movement press? Based largely on a content analysis of the three papers in question, I will assess in this chapter the accessibility and appeal of movement newspapers to a female readership. I will argue that such papers did include features specifically targeted at women, in addition to covering issues of concern to both sexes. At the same time, however, to greater or lesser degrees, these papers included rhetoric and reportage that marginalized women, or that positioned them in subordinate roles.

Although it is likely that men dominated both the production and consumption of the newspapers associated with the Knights, women nevertheless interacted with these papers in significant ways, and the newspapers attempted to address issues of concern to the entire working-class community. Overall, the newspapers of the Knights furthered the movement's goals of education and solidarity; in addition, they offered workers a sense of community coherence analogous to that of the immigrant press, and they invited rank-and-file perspectives on national policy and practices within the movement. Because of this, the newspapers of the Knights are among the most crucial remaining artifacts of Knights of Labor movement culture. Far more than the ritual guidebook of the Order or the proceedings of District and General Assemblies, these papers get at the heart of everyday life within the movement. They reveal the vibrancy and diversity of the Knights' movement culture. Equally as important, they illuminate the organizational shortcomings and conflicts within the movement, including those of gender.

Viewing the movement culture of the Knights as a process of deliberate cultural transmission from the leadership and its intellectual supporters to the rank and file misreads the complexity of movement culture as well as its vitality and promise. A better understanding of movement culture — and of social change more generally — can be gained from considering what the print media reveal: its complexity, its diversity, and its reliance on the media as a force for cultural co-herence *and* conflict. In the midst of coherence and conflict, the Knights fashioned a gender politics every bit as complex and contra-dictory as the movement itself.

Journal of United Labor

The *Journal of United Labor* was the central newspaper of the Knights. Published in Philadelphia, the *Journal* began in 1877 and lasted well into the 1890s. Unlike *John Swinton's Paper* and the *Labor Leader*, it did not identify with a broad network of labor newspapers. Rather than seeing their work as part of the broader movement of the labor press, the editors of the *Journal* viewed their task as that of communicating with and informing their readership about decisions and events at the national level.[14] Its status as the central organ of the Knights also ex-cused the paper's editors from the acute financial anxieties that plagued the labor press more generally. The hierarchical structure of the Knights allowed for the paper's effective distribution at district and local levels. Its national scope and organizational credentials as-sured a fairly wide readership, although in many locations it com-peted with local labor newspapers, including some that were pub-lished independently by Knights of Labor District Assemblies.[15]

The *Journal of United Labor* also was distinguished from other labor newspapers by its unusual format. While most labor newspapers fol-lowed a four-page format with an average of five columns of small type per page, the *Journal of United Labor* was fourteen pages long, with only three columns per page and larger type. It was folded ver-tically rather than horizontally, so that it opened more like a book or magazine than a newspaper. Subscription cost was one dollar per year, or ten cents per month, and publication occurred "semi-monthly." Overall, the *Journal's* format was less cost-efficient than that of other papers, even including occasional illustrations, such as portraits of the national leaders of the Knights. Because it was sub-sidized by the national organization, the editorial tone was generally magnanimous. While its editors might exhort readers to garner sub-scriptions from among their friends, they were less dependent on income from subscriptions than were most labor newspapers.

The magnanimity of the *Journal's* tone says a great deal about its place within the movement culture of the Knights. It suggests that the division between the ideological concerns of the leadership and the bread-and-butter concerns of the membership was recapitulated within the movement press. The fact that newspapers such as the *Labor Leader* and *John Swinton's Paper* had to depend on subscriptions to maintain financial solvency probably made them more receptive to reader concerns and interests than the *Journal of United Labor*. The *Journal*'s editors were less interested in *catering to* their readership than in *directing* readers down the correct organizational path. Consequently, if the *Journal* were the only remaining document on which to judge the Knights, we might not apprehend the extent of serious conflict within the movement. For example, we might not appreciate the degree of member controversy over such issues as strikes and trade unionism, or women's incorporation into the movement.

As the organ of the national leadership, the *Journal* might have positioned itself as the arbitrator of local and regional disputes, but generally it did not. Instead, it acted as a forum for the elaboration of national policy on a variety of issues, ranging from strikes and trade unionism to suggested readings and leisure-time pursuits for its membership. Comments on temperance, marital life, and self-improvement through literary and other pursuits were only a few of the nonworkplace issues encompassed by the *Journal*. The breadth of the *Journal*'s social and cultural scope reflects the expansiveness of the Knights' movement culture as a whole. The paper's advisory tone reflects the prescriptive accents of that movement culture as well, as it sought to reshape the behaviors and views of members into a single, coherent culture.

The prescriptive tone of the *Journal* with regard to both labor and cultural issues is consistent with the national leadership's sense of its role as a national directorate in all areas of working-class life. This role became increasingly difficult to maintain in the 1880s, when the movement experienced a precipitous rise in membership. In the midst of a rapidly growing, increasingly heterogeneous movement, the national leadership used the *Journal* as a means to instill unity of policy and purpose among its diverse and widely scattered constituents. In addition, it sought to ensure proper observance of the rituals and principles of the Order.[16]

An important feature of every issue of the *Journal* was a statement from the Grand Master Workman, who throughout the period 1880–1887 was Terence V. Powderly. The *Journal* also published poetry and letters from the membership, and it regularly ran a list of newly organized Knights assemblies nationwide. In the period 1884–86, this list generally occupied several columns. Information about the Order's budgetary status also was included.

What clearly was missing, however, was a positive sense of the Knights' vibrancy and diversity in this period. Given the rapid growth of its membership, the national leadership of the Knights perceived that their hold on the organization was increasingly tenuous. Particularly in the period 1883–86, new members were joining far too quickly to be properly steeped in the principles and traditions of the Order. Moreover, in this period, local assemblies increasingly used the Order as a forum for pursuing objectives that ran counter to national policy. For example, many new members in the mid-1880s maintained prior membership in trade unions, thus defying the leadership's sanction against dual unionism. The problem of dual unionism applied specifically to skilled workers who entered the Knights in this period. However, the vast majority of new entrants were unskilled workers, many of them immigrants, and many had been steeped in workplace traditions very different from those envisioned by the Knights leadership. The strike issue became a particular focus of tension between these workers and the leadership. Throughout the 1880s, while the national leadership remained firmly opposed to strikes, advocating boycotts and workers' cooperatives instead, many members of the Order embraced strikes as a practical means of improving work conditions.[17]

Because the *Journal* acted as an organ for the *containment* of rank-and-file militancy, it was not always effective in engaging the rank and file or in meeting its practical needs. Many of the explanations of policy contained in the *Journal* had an almost punitive and certainly controlling tone. In this way, the *Journal* reveals the extent to which the leadership *feared* the energy of the rank and file.[18]

Gender Analysis

The tension between the Knights leadership and its diverse constituents can be seen in the *Journal*'s approach to gender. Of the newspapers discussed here, the *Journal* was most committed to the rhetoric and practices of fraternalism, which were addressed primarily to male members. Because few women achieved national prominence in the Knights and so were less likely to participate in fraternal ritual, their activities received minimal coverage in the *Journal*.[19] However, the *Journal* did address both male and female members through routine discussions of the movement's domestic ideology. Susan Levine has described that ideology as "domestic idealism"; she links it to the Victorian cult of true womanhood. That the *Journal* did promote an image of working-class "true womanhood" can be seen in its vigorous advocacy of temperance, its insistence on the sanctity of the home and of woman's place within it, and its assertion of domesticity as a crucial component of working-class life.[20]

However, as the national organ of the Knights, the *Journal* also played an important role in reshaping the Order's policies and practices to meet its changing social basis. This can be seen in the *Journal*'s efforts to justify revisions to the rhetoric and rituals of fraternalism that were intended to accommodate women's membership in the early 1880s. Yet these efforts conflicted with the *Journal*'s simultaneous promotion of a rhetoric of *manhood*. An examination of that rhetoric reveals that it served a variety of functions. Among other things, it acted to preserve the Order's fraternal traditions and to unite male wage earners across the boundaries of ethnicity and kin.

Women's increasing involvement throughout the 1880s had significant ramifications for the status of fraternal ritual within the movement. The process of revision began in 1880, when the General Assembly passed a resolution that would incorporate women into the Order, and a "committee of five" was appointed to undertake the necessary formal revisions that would accommodate women in the ritual activities of the movement. This action resulted in a much-revised edition of the *Adelphon Kruptos*, the ritual guidebook of the Order.

In the spring of 1882, the *Journal* published statements of controversy and protest ensuing from these revisions. Particularly noteworthy is a letter submitted by Robert Linn, apparently a prominent member of the Order. Linn was torn about the changes in the *Adelphon Kruptos* that were intended to accommodate women. On one hand, Linn wrote, "I am glad that women are eligible for membership." Yet he protested, "but . . . changing the phrase 'Universal Brotherhood,' to 'Universal Organization,' will work injury to our N. & H. O. and the cause of humanity."[21] Linn argued that the Knights' rhetoric of brotherhood and their fraternal rituals distinguished their assemblies from ordinary trade organizations. He protested the leadership's decision to revise the *Adelphon Kruptos*, declaring, "I believe that if the changes had been submitted to the members of the Order all of them would not have been adopted." He lamented, "Oh how much sweeter and ennobling was the old phrase, 'Universal Brotherhood,' to even that of 'Universal Organization.' "

What is remarkable about the *Journal*'s response to Linn is its apparent sympathy with his concerns. Publishing Linn's commentary side by side with a statement of their own position, the *Journal*'s editors responded:

> Some of our most earnest, faithful members are honestly in doubt as to the wisdom of making these changes in the fundamental law of the Order, but we are satisfied that when they fully understand the reasons, they will be satisfied. . . . The words "Universal Brotherhood" were changed to "Universal Organization": not because it was deemed a better, or more expressive term, but solely because the work had to be adopted for women as well as men, otherwise the changes would not have been made.[22]

Significantly, the editors conceded Linn's point that "Universal Brotherhood" was a "much sweeter and ennobling phrase" than "Universal Organization." They remarked, "The terms are synonymous, but we agree with Brother Linn, that we should prefer the original word if the Order was confined to the male sex."

What made the *Journal*'s editors prefer "Universal Brotherhood" to "Universal Organization"? The Order's strategy of elaborating alternative metaphors of family and community to counteract the divisive impact of ethnicity and kin offers one explanation. Here we see that the *Journal* played a focal role in articulating a definition of community and kin that relied significantly on a rhetoric of *manhood*.

That ethnicity and kin posed partial obstacles to the cohesiveness of the Order is indicated by the complexity and variability of immigrant family life in this period. The example of Irish Americans is instructive, because of their high rates of participation in the Order. Mid-nineteenth-century Irish immigrants usually were single and detached from family groups, but by the 1880s Irish-American kinship networks had grown very tight.[23] While the Knights' leadership often worked closely with ethnic organizations such as the Irish Land Leagues, they nevertheless considered strong ethnic identification a hindrance to the movement, because such ties competed with loyalty to the Order and divided the membership.

The leadership's gendered response to this issue included the following statement from Terence Powderly, published in the *Journal* in 1881. Powderly's statement is notable for the way in which it operationalizes the term *man*:

> Toilers of America, will you continue to uphold this relic of bigotry and ignorance? If you do, you may as well relinquish, now and forever, all hope of securing equal rights for all men. . . .
> If you are desirous of doing your duty I say to you, while you may have

your national organizations, while you may cherish a love for your native land, while you should be ever ready to extend a helping hand to your suffering countryman, yet I say that in affairs where a common cause demands, drop the English, Welsh, Irish, German, and Scotch and let the latter part of the word stand, be a MAN.[24]

Within the Knights' newspapers, the metaphor of brotherhood and a noble, solidaristic construction of manhood challenged ethnic and kin allegiances by offering a more expansive notion of kinship, conflating a sense of familial solidarity with working-class community. Part of what is being enacted in the passage above, and in other facets of the movement press, is the Knights' attempt to inculcate an alternative sense of family loyalty and to create a transcendent notion of kinship as a means of unifying the movement. This example suggests that it is very important *not* to view the Knights' gendered rhetoric in straightforwardly dichotomous terms, as signifying perceived divisions between men and women. Rather, the Knights deployed the rhetoric of manhood as a signifier of *class* as well as of gender: it was used to define working-class manhood in opposition to the *unmanly* conduct of tradition-bound, ethnically identified men, of nonproducers, and even of Chinese laborers, whose presence in the West brought out the racist accents of the Knights' manly vision.[25] Viewed in this light, as a signifier of class and not of gender, the Knights' construction of manhood has consequences that are all the more interesting for women's participation in the movement.

The alternative model of kinship put forth by the *Journal*, with its heavy reliance on masculinist rhetoric, likely constrained women's participation in the movement, even as its editors sought to ease women's entry into membership. This contradiction illustrates a tension between *rhetoric* and *practice* that runs throughout the gender politics of the Knights. Yet because the *Journal of United Labor* was largely a compilation of official movement rhetoric, with minimal input from the membership, it provides an unclear picture of how gender operated at the level of everyday, lived experience within the movement.[26] Clearer evidence of this can be gained from *John Swinton's Paper* and the *Labor Leader*.

John Swinton's Paper

John Swinton was a famous reform journalist long before he began the newspaper that bore his name.[27] Previously on the editorial staff of the *New York Sun*, he was nationally known as an outspoken advocate of the working man. For Swinton, leaving the *Sun* to begin *John Swinton's Paper* in 1883 marked the fulfillment of a long-standing dream: As he would later describe it, in 1883 the labor movement appeared to be in profound disarray. The forces of capital were winning the battle against a disorganized and increasingly exploited working class. Strident voices were needed to educate and inspire the masses of working poor and also to facilitate the development of an articulate, organized labor movement. With this recognition, John Swinton began weekly publication of *John Swinton's Paper*, which he termed "the only paper in New York City for all the rights of the whole people."[28]

Unlike the *Journal of United Labor*, *John Swinton's Paper* followed a more conventional weekly format. Pages were large and folded horizontally and each page contained five columns of small type. With the exception of advertisements, there were no illustrations. Advertisements were confined to two columns on the back page; generally these promoted goods and services of particular interest to working people, such as union hall rentals and union label products. Advertisements were too few to add significantly to the income from subscriptions. Subscriptions cost three cents per copy or one dollar per year, and judging from the editor's frequent statements of financial woe, this income was inadequate to cover the cost of publishing the paper.

Financial adversity finally did force *John Swinton's Paper* to fold, during its fourth year of publication. That the paper was not able to make ends meet might indicate its failure to garner a popular readership, but this assumes a one-to-one correspondence between circulation and readership, and does not account for the possibility that individual copies of the paper had multiple readers. Indeed, the influence of the paper should not be underestimated. By the time John Swinton began publishing his paper in 1883, he already was nationally respected as a labor journalist and editor. His paper bridged the gap between national and local issues quite effectively. With features such as "Strikes Here and Elsewhere" and "City and the World — the Latest News," the paper placed local events first and foremost, but it also sought to locate those events within a national context.

Geographic breadth was not the only way in which *John Swinton's Paper* was expansive. Consistent with the vision of the Knights, its principles also were very sweeping. A list of principles was printed in every issue of the paper; they included the following:

1. Boldly upholding the rights of man in the American way.
2. Battling against the accumulating wrongs of society and industry.
3. Striving for the organization and interests of working men, and giving the news of the trades and the unions.
4. Uniting the New Political Forces, searching for a common platform, and against the coming billionaire whose shadow is now looming up.
5. Looking toward better times of fair play and public welfare.[29]

What is noteworthy about these principles is the sense of possibility they imply, not only in the realm of industry, but in politics and society. They suggest the editor's deep engagement not only with questions of unionization, but also with issues of more sweeping social transformation. What they do not suggest, as Bruce Laurie has argued in the case of the Knights, is a thoroughgoing critique of the prevailing economic system.[30] In the fourth principle, it is not a system of productive relations but rather the "coming billionaire" who oppresses workers. The solution posed in point five is therefore not revolutionary change, but rather "fair play and public welfare."

The key to "fair play and public welfare," according to *John Swinton's Paper*, is the natural rights of man embodied in American traditions. Restoring those American traditions, therefore, will usher in a new era of democracy. In an editorial titled "What We Are Here For," Swinton wrote:

It is time to make a struggle for the Declaration of Independence, the self-evident and everlasting truths of which are being overwhelmed by the tides of plutocracy. It is time to proclaim again its true and original purposes, to apply them to institutions and legislation, to enforce them upon all men and every man.[31]

As this statement suggests, the received political traditions of democracy and republicanism exerted a powerful influence over the editor of *John Swinton's Paper*. In striving for social change, Swinton sought to restore a democratic culture that was alleged to have existed previously, not to create something entirely new. In this sense, his vision was limited. Yet at the same time, the paper's willingness to embrace all kinds of issues and causes — from third-party politics to trade unions to the Knights of Labor — expresses an openness and engagement that held considerable promise. Situating the Knights within this broader vision in 1885, Swinton wrote:

> We especially rejoice over the gigantic strides of organization and union in these times. We see them in a thousand unions, and we cannot just now refrain from pointing to the remarkable manifestation of them . . . in the General Assembly of the Knights of Labor. We rejoice that these bodies are taking hold of their proper business, we rejoice that so many men are grappling with the roots of our social evils, and taking their stand on the solid ground of man's natural rights. We rejoice over the growth of that courage without which great conquests are impossible.
>
> Let these things yet go on; let us strive, with might and main, to advance them.[32]

By mid-1885, as the Knights gained astounding momentum, the Order occupied more and more space in the journal, while space accorded to other labor organizations diminished. By this time, Swinton himself had invested many of his personal sympathies in the Knights, as the organization most likely to fulfill his dream of a unified, articulate, well-educated labor movement of the uplifted working classes. Yet, as the above passage reveals, Swinton always positioned himself as an *advocate* rather than a member of labor causes. Throughout the years of his involvement with the Knights, he reserved the right to criticize the Order. Indeed, in 1887 he took frequent exception to the "crude incompetency" of the leadership, as it interfered repeatedly in local labor disputes, to the detriment of its members.[33] As a long-time labor journalist, Swinton's deepest commitment was not to the Knights of Labor per se, but to the masses of working people who flocked to the Order in the mid-1880s.

John Swinton's Paper was very short-lived, lasting only from October 1883 to August 1887. Its demise corresponded to the broader decline of the Knights. However, *John Swinton's Paper* always had financial difficulties, and its demise must be understood in the context of an evolving newspaper business as well. It is possible that, given its editor-intensive approach, *John Swinton's Paper* found it difficult to compete in an era of increasingly professionalized, commercial journalism.[34] Yet *John Swinton's Paper* shared with the official Knights leadership a relative distance from the rank and file. While the paper included considerable coverage of local events and many features designed to appeal to diverse audiences, its aspirations to a national readership and its overbearing editorial tone detracted from its local appeal. Unable to succeed financially, *John Swinton's Paper* folded when its founder's private financial reserves were exhausted.

Gender Analysis

As in the case of the *Journal of United Labor*, the tension between the political agenda of labor intellectuals such as John Swinton and the probable concerns of the membership can be explored through the template of gender. As a document of the Knights' gender politics, *John Swinton's Paper* adds considerably to the evidence contained in *Journal of United Labor*. Three of its features merit particular attention: its rhetoric of manhood, its discussion of workplace activism, and its reportage of public, mixed-gender entertainments.

Related to the rhetoric of fraternalism and the notion of male kinship articulated by the *Journal of United Labor* are the images of brotherhood and manhood that pervade the poetry of the movement. Such poetry abounded in *John Swinton's Paper*.[35] Because poetry often was submitted by the rank and file, it illuminates the membership's own sense of how gendered rhetoric operated in the movement. The following passage from a poem printed in *John Swinton's Paper* exemplifies the masculinist emphasis of movement poetry:

> Man of labor! know thy right,
> Men of labor! know thy might;
> Every wheel must stand still;
> When it is thy strong mind's will.[36]

As this passage suggests, individual and collective strength was central to the Knights' construction of manhood, as were intellectual acuity and determination. That the sense of collectivity implied here was specific to the working class is suggested by the poet's oppositional tone, which assumes the likelihood of a standoff between producers and nonproducers.

Also central to the concept of manhood articulated in *John Swinton's Paper* are the qualities of valor and moral rectitude. These are evident in another poem, titled "Manhood":

> Our manhood free, we dare be strong,
>   To shield the weak and helpless.
> Our motto be: "Protect from wrong,
>   And for the right be fearless!"
>
> True manhood is a moral force,
>   To bid the wrong defiance,
> Gives weaker brothers in their course
>   Its strength as their reliance. . . .

> Our country calls for manhood's might,
>   To stand for honest labor;
> Till all producers get their right,
>   With neither fear nor favor.[37]

Implied in this appeal to manhood is a clear conviction that manliness itself is the key to setting right the socioeconomic, political, and moral order of Gilded Age America. As its author suggests, such manhood will ensure freedom and independence for all producers. Indeed, the association of the gendered rhetoric of the Knights with notions of independence and producers' rights — long defined as male in opposition to the feminine trait of dependency — pervades the literature of the Knights.[38] It is particularly evident in Swinton's invocations of a natural rights tradition, as exemplified by the editorial statements cited above.

In addition to the rhetoric of manhood and producers' rights, *John Swinton's Paper* contains many illustrations of the Knights' gender *practices*. The information it provides about community activities and events, as well as occasional writings from the rank and file, shows how gender operated in the day-to-day activities of the movement. Beginning in 1883, an increasing number of articles appeared that addressed the working conditions and labor activism of women workers. In its description of conditions among New York women workers (which appeared with increasing regularity as more and more women turned to the Knights for guidance in their workplace struggles), *John Swinton's Paper* adopted a dual approach: on one hand, writers bemoaned working women's degradation, casting them as passive victims whose plight called for manly assistance from the Order. This is evident in the following account of women's employment conditions, published in 1884:

> There is no more terrible symptom of the disease which has eaten so deeply into our modern civilization than the degradation of women which it inevitably entails. The spectacle of thousands of our fellow women being subjected to loathsome and laborious tasks peculiarly unfitted for them, or driven to an alternative course of life so awful that many of them choose death rather than endure it, is one no man can contemplate with calmness.[39]

This passage articulates the view that women's very participation in the work force represents a profound and inflammatory injustice in the context of an emerging industrial order. In addition to asserting that women's proper place is in the home, it alludes to prostitution as the most extreme form of gender oppression. In this way, it reflects the Knights' conventional image of women both as homebound "true women" and as thoroughly sexualized beings. In either case, the image impeded the Knights' acceptance of women as active participants in the movement.

Yet not all newspaper reports constructed women in this way. Numerous articles presented a much less conventional view of women's labor activism, welcoming women into the movement as sisters in toil and struggle. These articles reasoned that,

> since women are now drafted into the armies of capital, and subjected to the laws of this cruel war, it is very certain that, in the course of time, they will adopt all the ways of the old troops of the line. They will organize to uphold their claims; they will *strike* in defense of their rights; they will learn to stand up against Pinkerton's thugs, and they may even have to march in procession under the black flag of hunger.[40]

Elsewhere, the paper's editor noted optimistically, "Dress-makers, Shoe-fitters and working women in many other industries are being organized in this city. . . . The movement is spreading." Describing the relatively new phenomenon of female activism in 1885, he remarked, "When they understand the labor question, they are better workers than the men."[41]

The importance of such radically inclusive statements of support for women's labor activism should by no means be underestimated, for they reflect a crucial facet of the Knights' gender politics. Yet as the pages of *John Swinton's Paper* suggest, the Knights found it difficult to define working women's labor activism in relation to the ideal of chivalric, working-class manhood. The nature of this difficulty is encapsulated in articles such as an 1885 piece describing the "heroic" labor militancy of striking Yonkers carpet weavers, significantly titled "Yonkers' Manly Women."[42] That women's labor militancy should be described as "manly" suggests persisting notions about gender in the rhetoric of the movement.

Women's growing participation in the Knights was greeted with enthusiasm, in part because it enhanced the appeal of the movement's cultural activities for male members. As the pages of *John Swinton's Paper* suggest, benefit concerts and similar events were a means of mixing labor politics with heterosocial pleasure in the lives of activist men and women.[43] What was less evident in *John Swinton's Paper* were the activities of *non*-wage-earning women. That the Irish-American women who formed the bulk of the Knights' female membership tended to leave the work force after marriage has been well documented.[44] Yet, in spite of low rates of Irish married women's work force participation, the paper gave little attention to married women's activism. Granted, occasionally a reader would write in about the importance of women's virtue in furthering the interests of the working class. Such letters often contained exhortations to married women to join the struggle, as the following passage from *John Swinton's Paper* exemplifies:

> Come then, fellow countrywomen, assist us in the holy work. You can do much to strengthen us. Let every wife join her husband, and every damsel her sweetheart, brother, or other relative, while to those who stand lonely, I say, take courage and take part with us. . . . Your help, so far from being inconsistent with your sex, is a duty of paramount importance, which will place you on a better, more equal footing with man, rendering you more invaluable, more endearing to those to whom God has given you as his choicest gift.
>
> Woman! To your duty then.[45]

While such appeals elaborate what married women could do for the movement, they are less informative about what the movement could do for married women. Such newspapers did not ignore non-wage-earning women entirely; *John Swinton's Paper* printed occasional domestic advice, as well as articles on temperance and women's suffrage. Levine remarks about *John Swinton's Paper*, "Suggestions for 'Food for Hard Workers' were interspersed with reminders that 'to organize is justly one of women's rights.' "[46] Relative to the attention given the activities of young, wage-earning women, however, *John Swinton's Paper* demonstrates minimal consciousness of married women's specific concerns. More insight into the gender politics of the movement press can be gained from the *Labor Leader*.

Labor Leader

The *Labor Leader* represents a very different facet of the movement press from *John Swinton's Paper*. While *John Swinton's Paper* was deeply committed to the Knights during its years of publication, it also represented the idiosyncracies of its editor and often diverged from strict adherence to Knights policy. Particularly during the early years, it embraced many political and trade union causes in addition to the Knights.

To categorize any labor publication as either outside or inside the

Knights movement culture is extremely problematic, given the heterogeneity, factionalism, and national versus local divisions that characterized the movement. The *Labor Leader* further exemplifies these characteristics. In contrast to *John Swinton's Paper*, the *Labor Leader* was the explicit organ of Knights of Labor District Assembly 30 in Massachusetts.[47] Representing predominantly textile and shoe workers from the towns surrounding Boston, D.A. 30 was one of the largest and most influential assemblies in the Order, and it contained a high percentage of female wage earners.

Like the newspapers of other District Assemblies, the *Labor Leader* followed a format similar to that of *John Swinton's Paper*, but it saw its function within the Knights as extending beyond weekly publication of the paper. It also sponsored a Knights of Labor lecture series, featuring the paper's business manager, George McNeill, as a means of educating its readership. In addition, it fostered other activities of the Order by providing a forum in which local events could be announced, and it encouraged reader participation in these events.

In general, the breadth of topics covered in the *Labor Leader* speaks to the immense vibrancy of the Knights' movement culture at the local level. That culture spilled out into all areas of life and put forward a positive social vision that extended far beyond the local community. The *Labor Leader's* diverse features included news about local and national labor events, as well as "Literary Notes," "Cooperative Notes," serialized fiction, and letters to the editor.

Even though the *Labor Leader* was an explicit organ of the Knights of Labor, its reportage reflected the extent of district and local autonomy within the movement. At the outset of its publication in January 1887, the paper sought to clarify its stand on many debates within the national organization, particularly the conflict between trade unions and the Knights. The *Leader* stated that it did not condemn trade unionism, and that it believed trade unions and Knights assemblies could work in concert within a broadened labor movement. This stand probably reflected the growing strength of trade unionism in Massachusetts in the late 1880s, as well as the weakening of the Knights at that time. That the *Leader* willingly defied the national leadership with regard to trade unionism is illustrated by the following passage, in which McNeill protests one member's expulsion in 1887 for belonging to the cigarmaker's international union. McNeill stated: "We believe his expulsion to be unconstitutional, and the policy that inspired it born of bigotry and nurtured in spite." McNeill accused the Knights' leadership of "demagogery," invoking the rhetoric of natural rights as a means of illustrating the leaders' wrongdoing:

> There are certain natural rights, among them the right to liberty of opinion, which we refuse to surrender to employers or the state. It is too much to expect its surrender, even to an Order professing to desire justice. We know that the rank and file of the KOL do not approve of this—let us call it—mistake.[48]

As this example implies, a tradition of natural rights explains a great deal of the dynamism and contestation that animated the movement throughout the 1880s. Both the editors of the *Leader* and the national leadership employed a discourse of natural rights. So important was that discourse, in fact, that it formed the vocabulary in which disagreements could be articulated, such as that concerning dual unionism. In this way, the natural rights tradition did not simply constrain but also enabled the immense energy and often conflicting activity that made the Knights a vibrant movement culture.

Further evidence of district autonomy that helps to illuminate the concept of movement culture as it pertains to the labor press can be found later in the spring of 1887. In April of that year, a controversy arose nationally over the Order's official endorsement of an exclusive list of newspapers. In their April 9, 1887, issue, the editors of the *Journal of United Labor* provoked immense controversy within the movement press when they published a list of twenty-one labor newspapers that had exclusive endorsement from the Order. Judging from the *Journal of United Labor*, the purpose of this list was to censure certain labor newspapers that were critical of the national leadership. The immediate provocation for this action was a financial scandal involving several members of the Knights' national executive committee. In attempting to diffuse the power of the labor press to generate rank-and-file criticism of the leadership, the list of twenty-one papers was announced.

As a paper that routinely criticized the national leadership, the *Labor Leader*, not surprisingly, was excluded from the official list, as was *John Swinton's Paper*. The *Leader's* business manager, McNeill, responded, "The *Labor Leader* takes no umbrage at the fact that it is forced to struggle on unblessed by official recognition." He added defiantly, "Our motto still stands, and will stand: 'Where truth leads we dare to follow.' And we must, of course, take the consequence."[49]

Further invoking the concept of truth in journalism, McNeill conceded that the editor of the official journal had the right to state his approval or disapproval honestly. He added, "And as a defender of that right . . . I will in future numbers give the names of a few papers that I approve." Pledging to add the names of other papers "as fast as they step into line with those who dare to follow where truth leads," he issued the following list:

All K. of L. papers that teach and practice the principles of the order.

All trades union papers that hold up the courage of the weak and stimulate organization.

All cooperative papers that can cooperate in this grand movement.

All greenback papers that favor covering the bare backs of the poor.

All socialist papers that teach that the social state is the highest development of manhood, womanhood, and childhood.

All papers that seek the good of humanity.[50]

This extremely inclusive list contrasts sharply with the exclusionary and repressive policy of the *Journal of United Labor*. In this way, it reflects an important distinction between the official newspaper of the Order and the "movement press" more broadly conceived. Whereas the official paper sought to instill loyalty to the Order in its readers, the *Labor Leader* and papers like it saw their role as distilling the truth of the labor situation, regardless of the consequences for specific organizations. Part of this commitment to truth was an optimistic belief that in truth resides the answer to all of labor's ills. As agents in the search for truth, labor newspapers collaborated with each other. This can be seen in the Associated Labor Press of which *John Swinton's Paper* was a part;[51] it also can be seen in McNeill's defense of the labor press against the attempted censorship of the *Journal of United Labor*. Indeed, a commitment to truth seems to be the point of entry for most labor newspapers into the Knights movement culture. It is consistent with the Order's overall sense that education is the key to social betterment, and that justice is encompassed by the natural rights tradition.

Gender Analysis

Like the *Journal of United Labor* and *John Swinton's Paper*, the *Leader* endorsed suffrage, but such endorsements occupied minimal space. In what other ways did it engage a female readership? One answer is that, like *John Swinton's Paper*, the *Leader* acknowledged women's important role as initiators and administrators of public, heterosocial events. Indeed, an examination of the *Labor Leader* reinforces the view that balls, musical and literary entertainments, and other fund-raising activities were important events within the Knights movement culture. Yet, as in the case of *John Swinton's Paper*, such events pertained most directly to the experiences of young, wage-earning women. Like *John Swinton's Paper*, the *Leader* demonstrates minimal consciousness of non-wage-earning women's specific concerns.

Yet while newspapers of the Knights were not explicitly attentive to non-wage-earning women's concerns, central among the Order's cultural objectives was reshaping the domestic sphere. In addition to challenging tight kinship bonds by appealing to a more expansive sense of community solidarity, the movement press addressed itself to issues of marriage and family life in ways that probably were calculated to engage a female readership. Serialized fiction was a popular feature of both *John Swinton's Paper* and the *Labor Leader*.[52] The stories often emphasized youthful romance, courtship, and the ideal of companionate marriage. Since marriage was the overdetermining factor in many non-wage-earning women's lives, such fiction was probably successful in reaching a female audience.

Knights stories spoke directly to generational conflict within ethnic and working-class families over the right to choose freely in marriage. Exemplifying this literary theme is the story of "Ella Inness: A Romance of the Big Lockout, or, How the Knight Won the Prize." Serialized in the *Labor Leader*, this story casts efforts at parental control over marital choice in a negative light, while celebrating the autonomous union of a young mechanic and a working girl. Yet freedom of choice in marriage is only one of many morals of this story. Also prominent is a complex statement about modernism, progress, and social change. The story's hero not only removes the heroine from her father's home, he also takes her from the farm to the suburb, setting her up in humble, working-class domesticity as his lifetime companion. In this way, the story addresses the gender implications of a new set of work relationships, as well as of a new set of family relationships. What is called for in these modern times, the story seems to suggest, is a return to a chivalric standard of romance and companionship between men and women. In the story, such a companionate, nuclear family model equips both hero and heroine to take part, free from the shackles of a received culture, in the movement culture of an emerging artisan class. After marrying the hero, the story's heroine emerges as an authentic true woman in the Knights' vision: ensconced in her suburban cottage, she labors on behalf of her husband, her children to be, and her class.

Through its publication of "Ella Inness" and other serialized fiction, the *Labor Leader* illuminated a dual set of role prescriptions for its female readers: the first corresponds to the moment of romantic, youthful autonomy made possible by wage-earning status, and the second corresponds to the much longer period of humble, working-class domesticity and material dependency. Both of the prescribed experiences are consistent with the Knights' central construction of working-class manhood, according to which men are primary agents of the working class and women have agency only insofar as their experiences approximate those of men (as wage earners) or their activities enhance the efforts of their male protectors.

As the Order expanded to encompass women in the 1880s, the rhetoric of manhood and brotherhood subsided in the movement press. This can be seen most clearly in the *Leader*, which did not begin publication until 1887. Yet, even as this rhetoric subsided, it remained implicit in the domestic vision of the Knights. As the *Leader*'s publication of "Ella Inness" suggests, that vision remained strong throughout the 1880s and into the 1890s.[53]

Conclusion

During the 1880s, and particularly in the period 1883–87, the Knights of Labor mobilized vast numbers of working-class men and women in support of its broad-ranging vision for labor reform. Central to the success of the Knights, as several historians have argued, was the organization's ability to provide its constituents with an *alternative* movement culture. At the same time, historians assert, the movement's success hinged on its ability to tap into important elements of a "received" culture. The result is what Kealey and Palmer have described as a dialectic of "residual *and* emergent, class *and* movement."[54]

As the newspapers discussed here reveal, one element of the received culture that the Knights only partially transformed was a gendered construction of working-class experience. Indeed, the Knights' adoption of fraternal ritual and their rhetoric of brotherhood and manhood placed them squarely within a larger, male-dominant tradition of late nineteenth-century labor reform.

On one level, the centrality of constructions of manhood and brotherhood to the rhetoric of the Knights reflected the Order's origins as an all-male fraternal order, replete with secrecy and ritual. As the Order evolved throughout the 1880s, it abandoned much of its gender-specific rhetoric, increasingly addressing its class-conscious exhortations to working women as well as men. In this sense, the movement underwent a fundamental change in the period under investigation, and was remarkable for the extent of its gender inclusiveness before its decline in the late 1880s.

On another level, however, the masculinism of the Knights can be seen as continuous throughout the organization's history, confining women to limited roles within the movement and idealizing their eventual return to a reconstituted domestic sphere. This is evident throughout the movement press, in reportage, fiction, and verse, as well as in letters submitted by the membership.

In examining newspaper reports of the movement's public, cultural forms, the place of heterosociability in the activities of the Knights is both striking and potentially deceptive. No doubt reflecting a larger cultural trend toward increasing heterosociability in Gilded Age America, labor editors hailed women's participation as a valued additive to the received culture of fraternalism. Yet this does not necessarily imply a radically egalitarian stance. That women figured prominently in the public cultural events of the movement in the mid-1880s does not necessarily mean that they would continue to play an important role in the movement after marriage and withdrawal from the work force.

It is true that, in some respects, the Knights' domestic idealism accorded a privileged status to the working-class wife and mother, who shouldered the important task of educating family members. Editorial statements in all three papers examined here promoted the importance of harmonious home life and reverence for motherhood. Furthermore, the movement endorsed woman's suffrage and temperance. Yet in these respects, women's status in the movement merely reflected the bases of women's cultural authority in the broader society. Moreover, issues such as temperance and suffrage were secondary to the Order's primary objective of labor reform.

An examination of the Knights' newspapers reinforces the perception that women occupied limited roles in the movement, but it also affords a partial explanation for that limited status: women's roles within the Order were marginal in part because, as Joan Scott has observed in the case of the Chartists, the rhetoric and formal structures of the movement frequently excluded them.[55] In the case of the Knights, one factor that served to marginalize female participants was the movement's profound preoccupation with constructions of working-class manhood, and with an implicitly masculinist natural rights tradition.

Yet, given this essay's emphasis on the centrality of *diversity* and *contestation* to the Knights movement culture, it would be profoundly inconsistent to suggest that the gender politics of the Knights were characterized by a rigid constellation of clearly definable trends. Rather, the gendered meanings and experiences of the Knights membership were probably *more* variable and complex than even the movement's newspapers are able to reveal. That profound disagreements characterized relationships among producers of the movement press, the leadership, and the rank and file suggests the likelihood that similar disagreements existed throughout the Knights movement culture. Moreover, the multiplicity of cultural forms contained in the newspapers, such as ritual, poetry, fiction, and heterosocial events, further suggests that women had a wide array of options from which to fashion their own relationships to the movement. While an analysis of the movement press suggests that many of these forms inscribed a confining set of dual role prescriptions for women, how women *received* those cultural forms is another question entirely.

The unprecedented extent to which women did participate in the Knights suggests that, in addition to the gender inclusiveness of official movement policy, the simple fact of the movement's vibrancy, diversity, and depth probably destabilized dominant gender categories in ways that created unique openings for women.

Certainly, the relationships among rhetoric, cultural forms, and social practices in the Knights of Labor are extremely complex, frequently contested, and often contradictory. A gendered analysis of the movement's newspapers and their editors offers a new perspective on women's labor activism. That women actually shaped a role for themselves within the movement is indicated in part by their initiation of heterosocial activities, their engagement with fictional narratives, and the many accounts of their workplace struggles that appear in the labor press.

Although these accounts of women's workplace struggles are instructive and inspiring, they represent primarily the experiences of young, wage-earning women. How to get at non-wage-earning women's experience remains a difficulty that the study of movement newspapers only partially overcomes.

Notes

1. *The People* (Providence, Rhode Island), March 20, 1886, cited in Paul Buhle, "The Knights of Labor in Rhode Island," *Radical History Review* 17(Spring 1978): 59.

2. Leon Fink, *Workingman's Democracy* (Urbana: University of Illinois Press, 1983), 13.

3. For a social historical analysis of women's role in the Knights, see Mary Blewett, *Men, Women, and Work: Class, Gender, and Protest in the New England Shoe Industry, 1780–1910* (Urbana: University of Illinois Press, 1988); Buhle, "The Knights of Labor in Rhode Island"; and Susan Levine, *Labor's True Woman: Carpet Weavers, Industrialization, and Labor Reform in the Gilded Age* (Philadelphia: Temple University Press, 1984).

4. Bruce Laurie, *Artisans into Workers: Labor in Nineteenth-Century America* (New York: Farrar, Straus & Giroux, 1989), 11.

5. Ibid, 142.

6. Lawrence Goodwyn, *The Populist Moment: A Short History of the Agrarian Revolt in America* (New York: Oxford University Press, 1978).

7. See Leon Fink, "The New Labor History and the Powers of Historical Pessimism: Consensus, Hegemony, and the Case of the Knights of Labor," *Journal of American History* 75 (June 1988): 115–36; Gregory S. Kealey and Bryan D. Palmer, *Dreaming of What Might Be: The Knights of Labor in Ontario, 1880–1900* (Cambridge: Cambridge University Press, 1982).

8. Fink, "The New Labor History," 128–29. The terms *residual* and *emergent* are taken from Raymond Williams, *Marxism and Literature* (Oxford: Oxford University Press, 1977).

9. Kealey and Palmer, *Dreaming of What Might Be*, 279.

10. In terms of gender, this distinction necessitates a dual analysis: On one hand, it requires that the Knights' engagement with a gendered political rhetoric of natural rights be examined; on the other hand, it demands that their "dialectical and prescriptive" involvement with the lived gender relations of the membership be considered. As this essay will show, newspapers provide a fruitful context in which to explore both the rhetorical and the social questions posed here.

11. In the Gilded Age, labor newspapers often were dominated by single editors or small editorial staffs. They generally could not rely on institutional affiliation for financial support, and most were dependent on reader subscriptions and daily sales for their livelihood. Additionally, while many espoused a primary political cause, most were open to a variety of causes and issues of concern to labor.

The number of causes to which a given newspaper in the Gilded Age might adhere was phenomenal. Newspapers might champion the Greenback-Labor movement, trade unionism, the Irish Land Leagues, or a variety of third-party political ventures, just to name a few. In the mid-1880s, many labor newspapers took up the Knights of Labor as their primary cause. Yet, as this chapter will show, not only were such newspapers generally committed to a variety of other causes as well, they often challenged the national leadership of the Knights.

12. For an interesting discussion of the *Irish World*, edited by Patrick Ford, see Eric Foner, "Class, Ethnicity, and Radicalism in the Gilded Age: The Land League and Irish America," *Marxist Perspectives* 1 (Summer 1978): 6–55. Of the relationship between ethnicity and class, Foner writes: "In the urban centers of Gilded Age America, class and ethnic differences overlapped. The majority of workers were

immigrant, and the majority of middle class, native-born. Thus, many could agree with Terence Powderly that 'the American labor movement, and . . . the Irish land movement' were 'almost identical.' " (p. 44).

13. The centrality of education to culture of the Knights can be found through-out the fiction of the movement, particularly in stories of the young mechanic. See Mary Grimes, *The Knights in Fiction* (Urbana: University of Illinois Press, 1986).

14. During the period 1880–1887, the *Journal of United Labor* had three different editors: Charles H. Litchman, Robert D. Layton, and Frederick Turner. Turner was editor during the most vibrant period of the Knights, 1884–87. While the *Journal* contained leadership and membership submissions, at any given time it had an ed-itorial staff of one.

15. The *Labor Leader* is an example of a district assembly publication that com-peted with the *Journal of United Labor* for a local readership. In addition, members probably were drawn to a variety of other labor publications aside from the *Journal*. It is possible that subscribers to the *Journal* were primarily district and local assem-blies. Members might have read the paper in Knights of Labor reading rooms and labor halls, rather than at home. Because of this, it is all the more likely that the *Journal's* readership consisted primarily of men, who were more likely to frequent such places. Many women, particularly non-wage-earning wives, were more likely to read papers that were brought into the home.

16. For a discussion of nineteenth-century fraternal rituals and manhood, see Mary Ann Clawson, *Constructing Brotherhood* (Princeton, N.J.: Princeton University Press, 1989); Mark C. Carnes, *Secret Ritual and Manhood in Victorian America* (New Haven, Conn.: Yale University Press, 1989). These works primarily address the sig-nificance of fraternalism for *middle-class* culture. Their treatment of working-class fraternal organizations such as the Knights is therefore somewhat incomplete. For another perspective, see Eric J. Hobsbawm, *Primitive Rebels: Studies in Archaic Forms of Social Movements in the 19th and 20th Centuries* (New York: W. W. Norton, 1959).

17. See Laurie, *Artisans into Workers*, 173–75.

18. That the *Journal's* relationship to the membership was characterized by a high degree of insecurity is suggested in part by the occasional editorial remark that Knights members should read the *Journal rather than* any other labor newspaper. As editor Charles Litchman stated in 1880, "The *Journal* is the *only* official organ of the Order. It is *all our own*, and no other paper or publication has any official indorse-ment whatever from the General Assembly. It therefore . . . should cordially be sustained above all others"; *Journal of United Labor*, July 15, 1880. As this statement suggests, from an early point the offical journal felt threatened not only by the vi-brancy and diversity of its membership but also by competition from other newspapers.

19. That women did participate in fraternal rituals is documented in Levine's *Labor's True Woman*, and in the District Assembly proceedings of the Powderly Pa-pers. However, Levine also provides evidence that women created their own rituals in opposition to the received rituals of fraternalism.

20. See Levine, *Labor's True Woman*, 129–53.

21. Robert Linn, "Correspondence," *Journal of United Labor*, March 15, 1882.

22. *Journal of United Labor*, March 15, 1882.

23. See Albert Gibbs Mitchell, Jr., "Irish Family Patterns in Ireland and Lowell, Massachusetts," doctoral dissertation, Boston University, 1976.

24. Terence V. Powderly, *Journal of United Labor*, January 15, 1881.

25. For a fictional example of Knights of Labor anti-Chinese sentiment, see T. Fulton Gantt, "Breaking the Chains: A Story of the Present Industrial Struggle," in *The Knights in Fiction*, ed. Mary Grimes (Urbana: University of Illinois Press, 1986).

26. Mary Blewett makes the argument in *Men, Women, and Work* that it is really at the *local* level that studies of gendered experiences in the Knights become meaningful. She asserts that because the Knights' organization was *so* diverse and multilayered, an analysis of gender that relies primarily on *national* policy and practice will have little to do with actual, lived experience in the movement. See Blewett, chapter 8, "New England Shoe Workers and the Knights of Labor."

27. Not only did the paper bear John Swinton's name; he was also its exclusive editor and primary contributor. The paper had other regular contributors and published reports from a national press bureau under the title "Associated Labor Press," but primarily its voice was that of John Swinton.

28. Statement published in every issue of *John Swinton's Paper*.

29. *John Swinton's Paper*, December 3, 1883. This list was a regular feature of the paper.

30. Laurie, *Artisans into Workers*, 152. Laurie writes: "Knights affirmed the sanctity of private property even as they reviled its excessive accumulation. . . . they were not socialist despite their collectivist language and the recognition of the need for more forceful government . . . reflected in the Reading Platform."

31. *John Swinton's Paper*, December 16, 1883.

32. *John Swinton's Paper*, October 11, 1885, 1.

33. See Laurie, *Artisans into Workers*, 173.

34. Although I acknowledge John C. Nerone's important work in demythologizing the conventional narrative of nineteenth-century journalism history (see Nerone, "The Mythology of the Penny Press," *Critical Studies in Mass Communication* 4 [1987]: 376–404), for the current essay I have derived the analysis of Gilded Age journalism in part from Michael E. McGerr, *The Decline of Popular Politics: The American North, 1865–1928* (New York: Oxford University Press, 1986).

35. The *Journal of United Labor* also contained poetry on a regular basis.

36. *John Swinton's Paper*, 1883 or 1884, no date.

37. *John Swinton's Paper*, November 4, 1883.

38. See Joyce Appleby, "Republicanism in Old and New Contexts," *William and Mary Quarterly* 3rd ser., 43 (1986): 20–34.

39. *John Swinton's Paper*, October 26, 1886.

40. *John Swinton's Paper*, May 3, 1885.

41. *John Swinton's Paper*, April 26, 1885.

42. *John Swinton's Paper*, June 14, 1885.

43. Levine discusses heterosociability in the movement in *Labor's True Woman*:

   Taking the Order's Constitution literally, women shaped their local assemblies into social reform clubs as well as trade union centers. . . . Denver's Labor Assembly No. 1424 carried the order's principles to the dance floor. . . . The local offered twenty-eight dances, each sponsored by a different group. . . . At another ball sponsored by Kansas Lady Knights, the women suggested that none of their brother Knights "walk with a non-union girl in the promenade so long as a union girl was without a partner. Should

any girl violate this rule, all the girls are to step out of the promenade and boycott the entire crowd." (pp. 116–17; *Labor Review*
[Argentine, Kansas] August 1, 1891, courtesy of Leon Fink)

44. On the topic of Irish American married women's work force participation,
see Hasia Diner, *Erin's Daughters in America: Irish Immigrant Women in the Nineteenth
Century* (Baltimore: Johns Hopkins University Press, 1983), 70–105. See also Albert
Gibbs Mitchell, Jr., "Irish Family Patterns in Ireland and Lowell, Massachusetts,"
doctoral dissertation, Boston University Graduate School, 1976.

45. *John Swinton's Paper*, May 10, 1885.

46. Levine, *Labor's True Woman*, 119–20; *John Swinton's Paper*, December 13,
1885.

47. In contrast to both the *Journal of United Labor* and *John Swinton's Paper*, each
of which had a single editor at any given time, the *Labor Leader* had an editorial staff
of two: Frank Foster, managing editor, and George McNeill, whose official title was
business manager. After 1887, McNeill withdrew from the staff, and Foster became
the exclusive editor.

48. *Labor Leader*, January 29, 1887.

49. *Labor Leader*, April 23, 1887.

50. Ibid.

51. A regular feature of *John Swinton's Paper* was something called the "Associated Labor Press," which included excerpts from labor newspapers from around
the nation.

52. "The Order's literary overtures lessened the isolation of women in the
home and brought them into contact with contemporary political and cultural
trends"; Levine, *Labor's True Woman*, 119.

53. Evidence that the Knights' domestic vision persists into the 1890s can be
found in the *Journal of United Labor*. In addition, Levine's findings corroborate this
assessment. See Levine, *Labor's True Woman*, 129–53.

54. Kealey and Palmer, *Dreaming of What Might Be*, 279.

55. Joan Scott, "On Gender, Language, and Working Class History," in *Gender
and the Politics of History* (New York: Columbia University Press, 1988), 53–67.

Chapter 7

The Working-Class Press at the Turn of the Century
Jon Bekken

At the turn of the century, the U.S. labor movement published hundreds of newspapers in dozens of languages, ranging from local and regional dailies issued by working-class political organizations and mutual aid societies to national union weeklies and monthlies.[1] These newspapers practiced a journalism very different from that of the capitalist newspapers (produced and sold as commodities by publishers closely tied to social and economic elites), which, they contended, were poisoning the minds of the public. Labor editors were, for the most part, drawn from the ranks of the movements they served, sharing their linguistic and ethnic diversity, social and economic circumstances, and aspirations. Their newspapers were an integral part of working-class communities, not only reporting the news of the day or week, but offering a venue where readers could debate political, economic, and cultural issues. Readers could follow the activities of working-class institutions in every field and could be mobilized to support efforts to transform economic and political conditions.

This essay introduces the broad contours of this working-class press and illustrates its distinctive character. Although working-class newspapers share important similarities and concerns, there was, and is, no such thing as a "typical" labor newspaper—just as there was no such thing as a "typical" daily newspaper in this or any other era.[2] Labor newspapers ranged from small, irregularly issued sheets to twelve- to sixteen-page dailies that were as large, and in many ways as professional, as many of the capitalist newspapers with which they coexisted. This press was issued in scores of languages, reflecting the country's largely immigrant working class. Some papers were delivered automatically as part of membership in various working-class organizations; others were sold to supporters on news-stands or by subscription. And while most working-class newspapers were financed primarily by the movement itself (either through direct subsidies or through subscriptions and benefits), others relied on advertising revenues for a large share of their income. Nor was the working-class press politically monolothic. Like the labor movement itself, this press spanned the range from a fairly narrow focus on workplace conditions to advocacy of social revolution. Most labor editors espoused a commitment to social reform, but many believed their goals could be accomplished within the framework of the existing political, social, and economic order.

Regardless of political orientation and organizational affiliation, the working-class press addressed issues of class and politics in a manner fundamentally different from that of its capitalist counterparts. Socialist and radical newspapers were dedicated to promoting class struggle on the political field, but they also devoted substantial attention to union struggles and issues. Union organs were more narrowly focused on organizational and trade concerns but addressed political issues as well, and sometimes were explicitly committed to a socialist (or other working-class) political agenda. And foreign-language workers' papers often crossed these lines, simultaneously serving unions, mutual-aid associations, and socialist organizations (which often shared ownership and control) as their official organ.

The working-class press stemmed from an alternative press ideology, one that sought to erase distinctions between newspapers and readers and to involve its supporters in every aspect of the newspaper, from management and editorial decisions to reporting. In doing so, it was forced to deal with the marketplace, the organization of news, and fierce repression. This essay focuses primarily on Chicago, a city that offers a microcosm of the country's diverse, largely immigrant, working class and its press. Chicago anarchists, for example, published eight newspapers (including a German-language daily) in the 1880s. In 1910, Chicago socialists issued daily newspapers in Czech, English, German, and Polish, and (together with unions, mutual aid associations, and other working-class organizations) published two dozen weeklies and monthlies in nearly every language spoken by Chicago's largely immigrant working class.[3] These papers were deeply rooted in their communities, even if they were generally supported by militant minorities. Every major U.S. industrial center supported a similar array of labor organs, and working-class publications could be found anywhere workers were organized to improve their conditions through political or union struggles.

Origins of the Labor Press

American workers had long felt the need to establish their own press and other cultural institutions. In 1797, William Manning proposed a workers' society, the most important function of which would be to publish a monthly magazine and a weekly newspaper. Nothing came of his plans at the time, but at least sixty-eight labor newspapers were founded between 1828 and 1834.[4] Like other alternative media, this early labor press depended upon the health of the labor movements it served for survival, virtually disappearing during periods when workers were under particularly severe attack and could not muster the resources to sustain it. Only in the 1860s did labor movements, and the labor press, become established firmly enough to survive economic downturns and repression. More than 120 labor newspapers were established between 1863 and 1873, including many dailies established as strike papers that often disappeared when the strikes that called them into existence came to an end.[5] Since then, the working-class press has maintained a continuous, substantial presence, albeit one that has declined in recent years.

In the decades surrounding the turn of the century, the United States, and especially its industrial centers, was transformed by rapid urbanization, immigration, and corporatization, and by the growth of mass-production industries employing tens of thousands of often unskilled workers. In 1880, less than 30 percent of the U.S. population lived in urban places (i.e., cities and towns of 2,500 or more inhabitants). By 1920, more than half the population lived in urban places — nearly 30 percent in cities of 100,000 or more. Chicago's population soared from 503,185 in 1880 to 1,698,575 by 1900. By 1919, 90 percent of Chicago wage earners worked for corporations, not individuals, in increasingly large factories.[6]

Workers responded to these developments by organizing and strengthening local and national unions such as the Knights of Labor and the American Federation of Labor. Immigrant workers organized mutual-aid societies to protect themselves in the event of unemployment, illness, and death. Radical workers organized socialist and labor parties, often closely linked to unions and ethnic societies. And these labor unions, political parties, and other working-class

organizations issued their own publications or, when their means
were insufficient, endorsed sympathetic publications in exchange for
space in which to promote their activities and concerns.[7]

Across the United States, nearly half of the members of the labor-
ing population were either foreign-born or the children of immigrants
at the turn of the century. In 1900, 43 percent of Chicago residents
were immigrants, and another 34 percent were born to immigrant
parents. Chicago's working class was thus composed largely of first-
and second-generation immigrants.[8] As a result, the first labor newspaper published in Chicago was *Der Proletarier*, a German-language
weekly begun in 1853.[9] Chicago's immigrant working class sustained
daily newspapers in Czech, German, Lithuanian, Polish, Russian,
Slovak, Slovene, and Yiddish — alongside shorter-lived English-
language dailies issued by the Knights of Labor and the Socialist and
Communist parties. Foreign-language working-class dailies were
more numerous and longer-lived than their English-language counterparts across the country. Nine of the fifteen daily U.S. labor newspapers published in 1925 were foreign-language papers.[10]

Although Chicago's labor movement was relatively well organized,
it faced a hostile press. In the 1870s, Chicago English-language dailies
were uniformly hostile to strikes, picketing, class-based politics, and
labor methods generally, although they were sympathetic toward
educational and cooperative ventures.[11] In the 1880s, these papers
called for the suppression of militant labor tendencies and cheered
the execution of the Haymarket martyrs.[12] In later years, these
general-circulation capitalist dailies generally claimed to champion
the interests of workers, but believed that the interests of labor and
capital were fundamentally the same — and that both were subordinate to the "public interest." They strongly backed arbitration of labor
disputes, opposed sympathy strikes, and called for forcible suppression of strike-related disorder.[13] Competing publishers periodically
did issue English-language dailies catering to working-class readers,
such as the *Daily Labor World*, published from 1898 through 1900, or
the Scripps League's advertising-free *Day Book*, published from 1911
through 1916, but the labor movement found that its views were
largely excluded from the commercial marketplace of ideas.

Convinced that the press mattered, unionists were determined to
contest the battle for public opinion as best they could. Homer Call
edited the *Butcher Workmen's Journal* "at my odd hours, usually after
my day's work is done and when I should be asleep." C. E. Schmidt,
also of the Amalgamated Meat Cutters union, maintained that the

labor press was "the only press that would take the interests of the toiling masses in consideration."[14] In 1948, packinghouse union leaders remained convinced that they could get fair coverage only in their own publications. As their mimeographed *Daily Strike Bulletin* remarked:

> 12,000 UPWA members must have thought they were dreaming yesterday, when they looked for accounts of the giant rally at Strike headquarters Thursday night. In some editions of the daily papers there was no mention of the meeting at all. . . . So if you thought you were at a big meeting the other night, brothers and sisters, just forget it. After all, if the papers didn't report it, it couldn't have taken place.[15]

Functions of the Labor Press

Workers' newspapers were an integral part of the communities and movements they served. The Industrial Workers of the World's newspapers were published in several languages, as well as for particular regions and industries. They played a vital role not only in reaching out to prospective supporters but also in keeping members — who often had little other regular contact with the national organization — informed of internal debates and discussions. The weekly *Industrial Worker* not only served as the IWW's main organ for shaping and disseminating its views, it played a major role in helping the IWW organize the timber industry and maintain contact with its highly transitory membership.[16] One Wobbly organizer argued that the press was the IWW's "most vital part":

> If we have no press we will soon have no organization. . . . We strengthen the organization when we build up the press. It is our chief point of contact with the unorganized, whom we must reach to succeed in our revolutionary task of overthrowing capitalism. As we push the press among the unorganized . . . they will give power to the organization until it shall be invincible.[17]

Other working-class movements placed similar emphasis on their press. The Socialist party published scores of weekly and daily newspapers across the country. While its foreign-language press was the most successful (many surviving the party's demise), Socialists published English-language dailies in Chicago, Milwaukee, New York, Oklahoma City, and Seattle. The Milwaukee *Leader* — longest-lived of these papers — is illustrative. Born in December of 1911 as the English-language daily of Milwaukee's Socialist party, shortly after the party had won several positions in local elections, the *Leader* doubled as the official organ of the Federated Trades Council (AFL) and played a crucial role in enabling socialists to win support outside of their traditional German ethnic base.[18]

The *Leader* played a vital role in promoting and sustaining not only the Socialist party, but also Milwaukee unions. *Leader* pages aired workers' grievances, publicized the activities of Milwaukee's vigorous labor movement, and devoted extensive space to the Socialist party's program and campaigns. Yet the *Leader* strove to be a complete newspaper, with local, national, and world news (heavily spiced with human-interest stories) along with business, sports, and women's pages. These efforts were hampered by insufficient resources, and by the difficulty (especially before the Federated Press was organized) of obtaining timely reports of labor and socialist news. The *Leader*, especially during its early years, was forced to rely on the United Press for the bulk of its news reports — dispatches that often were hostile toward more militant sectors of the labor movement and seemed quite out of place in the *Leader*'s pages. One *Leader* headline informed readers that "tin soldiers" had fired on women and children, while the UP dispatch beneath reported that a mob of strikers had attacked state militia. Despite such difficulties, the Socialist party and the Trades Council struggled for decades to keep the *Leader* afloat despite continuing losses.[19]

Perhaps more typical was the Seattle *Daily Call*, launched in 1917 with just $500 capital. The *Call* was frequently the target of police attention, and its printing plant was vandalized by a mob of sailors on January 5, 1918. Yet the paper continued publication for four more months before closing in favor of the new daily *Seattle Union Record*.[20] The latter was published by the Seattle Central Labor Council, which had previously published a weekly paper of the same name. Launched with $20,000 (the bulk of which was contributed by Boilermakers Local 104, which purchased advance subscriptions for its 5,000 members), the *Record* printed twelve to twenty-four pages daily and quickly reached a circulation of 50,000. But the entire capital went to purchase a press and rent a building, leaving the paper without working capital. "Many unions subscribed to *Record* stock and enabled it to continue, but the big department stores confined themselves to bargain basement advertising while the usual institutional advertising was absent."[21] The *Record* played a major role in building the 1919 Seattle General Strike, but five years later the Labor Council fell under conservative leadership that saw little need for a daily labor newspaper and sold it to its editor.[22]

Organizing the News

Central to maintaining a workers' press is the problem of obtaining news from labor's perspective. To counter what they saw as a strong antilabor bias in the mainstream press, and to secure access to unreported labor news, editors organized a cooperative news-gathering service in November 1919. With the support of labor, socialist, farm-labor, and other papers, Federated Press bureaus in Washington, Chicago, and New York dispatched daily releases, beginning in 1920. Federated Press began with 110 member papers, including 22 dailies and ranging from AFL central council organs to Socialist and Farm-Labor party papers. Although the service was devoted primarily to domestic labor and socialist news, news also was provided by several European socialist newspapers. Since labor newspapers were typically impoverished, the service was available for $1.50 to $15.00 weekly, depending on frequency and circulation.[23]

By 1925, two years after the AFL had denounced Federated Press as a vehicle for communist propaganda, the Federated Press circulated its daily 5,000-word service to 150 papers and a supplemental weekly labor letter to 1,000 subscribers.[24] In addition to breaking labor news, Federated Press provided in-depth articles on industrial and financial trends, wage levels, and corporate profits. The service survived until 1956, when it had 53 member papers and was one of four news services available to working-class newspapers (the other three were tied to the AFL or CIO). But union subscribers canceled the service after the AFL-CIO merger and the resulting purge of left-wing unions, and Federated was forced from the field.[25]

Repression of the Socialist Press

The socialist press was the movement's main vehicle for propaganda and education, reaching its high point in 1912–13 when the party issued more than 300 English- and foreign-language daily, weekly, and monthly publications. These papers combined Socialist muckraking, popular exposition of Marxist theories, and news of the Socialist, labor, and farmers' movements, in an effort to "reach and convert the masses, to bring the message of socialism to the greatest number of people."[26] Total circulation exceeded two million copies before World War I, with the *Appeal to Reason* — far and away the circulation leader — boasting a weekly circulation of 761,747. Sixteen unions with a total of 330,800 members "officially indorsed the socialist programme," and several local and national union papers supported the cause. "Aside from these official organs . . . there are a large number of socialist papers which receive much of their support from trade-unionists. For instance, about 550 local unions have subscribed to the *Appeal to Reason* . . . to be delivered to each of their members."[27]

The *Appeal to Reason* was one of very few socialist papers to pay its own way. It dominated the socialist publishing field, and was the U.S. socialist movement's central weekly for more than twenty-five years, especially in the Southwest. Key to its success was the Appeal Army, which sold subscriptions and organized club subscriptions (several copies shipped to a common address, at a lower rate, for distribution) and formed the basis for Socialist party organizations in rural areas. The *Appeal* and its kindred publications "performed a vital function for the young socialist movement — they were its major means of communication."[28]

Most socialist papers, however, were short-lived and financially precarious even before the hysteria and government repression accompanying the outbreak of World War I:

> Within five months after war had been declared, every leading Socialist publication had been suspended from the mails at least once, and many were barred for weeks at a time. . . . In addition to pressure applied by the federal government, Socialist papers in dozens of small towns and cities faced the wrath of vigilance committees organized by local chambers of commerce and boards of trade.[29]

In Chicago, for example, IWW newspapers and correspondence were barred from the mails, as was the Italian-language *La Parola dei Socialisti* (The Socialists' Voice), after it denounced the war as a slaughterfest in which capitalist jackals fed on proletarian corpses.[30] The editor of the English-language *Chicago Socialist* was one of hundreds of labor militants prosecuted (and convicted) on federal charges of disrupting the war effort.[31]

Only a handful of radical papers survived the war. By 1919 the socialist press was largely confined to the larger cities, where socialist newspapers did not need to rely on the postal service and where movement institutions were better able to withstand the repression.

The once-burgeoning socialist press in the West and Midwest was decimated (although some papers, such as the Oklahoma *Leader*, lingered on into the 1940s). Newspapers published by other radical organizations suffered similar fates.

Repression was not limited to time of war. In 1887, the editors of the *Alarm*, *Chicagoer Arbeiter-Zeitung* (Workers' [daily] Newspaper), and *Die Anarchist* were hanged after they were convicted on charges stemming from speeches they had delivered and articles published in their newspapers.[32] In 1910, Catholics brought an obscenity indictment against the Polish People's Publishing Company for printing a cartoon in their newspaper depicting a priest carrying a nun (both in full clerical garb) over the caption "Porwanie Sabinek" (Abduction of the Sabines).[33] Newspaper publishers pressured local newsstands not to carry the Chicago Federation of Labor's paper, the *New Majority*.[34] And in 1912 newsboys selling the socialists' *Chicago Evening World* were beaten and shot (and some killed) by "circulation agents" hired by other publishers in an effort to drive the *World* off the streets.[35] Working-class newspapers in other cities were subjected to mob violence, destruction of their presses, deportation of their editors, criminal libel and/or indecency prosecutions, and similar actions.[36]

Labor Papers and Working-Class Communities

Its purpose is to safeguard and promote the interests of the worker and to spread socialist teaching among our countrymen. It will work to gather all workers in one association to establish a social order which will grant the worker his rights. It will oppose corruption, rottenness, exploitation and capitalist domination. It will fight against monopoly and the predatory nature of the system and will aim at liberating work from the yoke of capitalism.[37]

By 1890, Chicago was the country's second-most populous city and a major hub for transportation, communications, finance, and agriculture. Many of those working in these industries were recent immigrants who spoke little if any English. Their wages were irregular and often insufficient to support life. Many worked ten- or twelve-hour days in dangerous sweatshops, and they lived in the worst housing the city had to offer. But Chicago workers did not passively accept their lot. Rather, they built a rich array of ethnic, community, workplace, and political organizations that helped them to survive from day to day. Through these institutions, including the labor press, they asserted their human dignity and their intention to take control of their own destinies.

Several Chicago unions sponsored labor newspapers at the turn of the century. The Chicago Trade and Labor Assembly (later the Chicago Federation of Labor) experimented with a succession of official organs, beginning in 1864 with the privately owned *Workingman's Advocate*. Unions often relied upon sympathetic printers to publish newspapers that they then endorsed, and sometimes subscribed to in bulk for their members. Such arrangements protected the movement's meager financial resources, and helped insulate unions (which often had Anarchists, Democrats, Republicans, and Socialists as members) from disputes over what policies the papers should promote. But while union-published organs could be costly (both economically and politically), private publishers could not be relied upon to advocate movement policies consistently. The Trade and Labor Assembly repudiated the *Progressive Age* in 1883 when its editor embraced the temperance movement; the Chicago Federation of Labor denounced its hitherto official organ, the *Union Labor Advocate*, in 1910 when the paper sold its advertising and editorial columns to antilabor firms and political candidates. As official organ, the *Advocate* rented space in the federation's offices and was paid $25 per month to publish the CFL minutes. It also published paid and unpaid articles on union principles and concerns, photographs of union officials, listings of union offices and meeting times, and abundant advertisements from a wide array of businesses and unions.[38] Several union locals later endorsed the *Chicago Labor News*, but it too succumbed to the temptation to increase revenues by taking advertising for strikebreakers and convict-labor goods, while criticizing the Chicago Federation of Labor for propagating socialism.[39]

In the wake of the First World War, the progressive unionists who had long dominated the Chicago Federation of Labor decided that the labor movement needed its own newspaper and political party. The Cook County Labor party was established in December 1918, and the *New Majority* began publication January 4, 1919, as the federation's and party's official weekly organ. The CFL owned the *New Majority* outright, having concluded that private publishers and publishing cooperatives could not adequately ensure movement control and accountability.

The paper was not merely a means for communicating official news to union members, it was a vital part of the CFL's efforts to bring together organized and unorganized workers, farmers, and other productive citizens in a "new majority" that could defeat the monied interests that controlled industry, politics, and the city's newspapers. The *New Majority*'s staff box explained that it was

> dedicated to the hand and brain workers of the United States who have been scattered hopelessly as minorities in miscellaneous groups, but whom when they start to function unitedly in politics, will form a new majority that will sweep all opposition before it and take over the government to be administered thenceforth by the workers.[40]

In 1919 it seemed that this majority's day might be at hand. The socialist vote had increased dramatically, labor and farm-labor parties were being organized across the country, unions were growing stronger and more militant (particularly in the mass-production industries), and revolutionary and labor movements seemed on the verge of political power in much of the world. Despite overwhelming approval in a referendum of CFL locals, however, the Labor party proved quite controversial, especially after it failed to draw significant local support at the polls. Socialists persisted in running their own tickets, Communists insisted that the new party be placed under their leadership, and American Federation of Labor leaders and their local allies demanded that the CFL return to the national AFL policy of rewarding labor's friends and punishing its enemies within the Democratic and Republican parties. In 1924 the CFL capitulated, shutting down its labor party and converting the *New Majority* into the tamer *Federation News* (published to this day). But the Chicago Federation of Labor continued to believe that the labor movement must control its own organs of communications — publishing the *Federation News* and establishing its own radio station, WCFL, which CFL Secretary Ed Nockels described as "the strong right hand of labor" essential to defending labor from the attacks of the monopolists who controlled the airwaves.[41] (For more on broadcast communications, see Robert W. McChesney's chapter in this volume.)

CFL-affiliated unions also issued their own periodicals — usually newsletters devoted to upcoming meetings and social events, although often carrying substantive news as well. The Local 194 *Painters Bulletin*, for example, contained notices of upcoming union meetings and for the local's cooperative store, news of efforts to organize local and national labor parties, detailed union financial reports, officers' reports, and other relevant information.[42] The *Painters Bulletin* was one of more than fifty labor papers published in Chicago in 1920, ranging from the *Commercial Telegraphers Journal* to the Czech-language IWW monthly, *Jedna Velka Unie* (One Big Union).[43] Unions also issued newspapers for special occasions. The Chicago Federation issued a *Daily Labor Bulletin* during the 1905 Teamsters' strike. At least ten issues were produced over a two-week period.[44] Similarly, hotel culinary workers published 5,000 copies of a daily bulletin during a 1920 strike to keep union members posted on the strike's progress.[45]

Immigrant Labor Newspapers

Unions were hardly the only working-class institutions. Chicago workers built vibrant working-class cultures organized along ethnic as well as class lines. Neighborhood bars served as social centers, but also as meeting places for union locals, mutual-aid societies, and political organizations. Several immigrant communities sponsored workers' choirs that not only helped to preserve immigrant language and culture, but also provided entertainment at movement picnics, benefits, and mass meetings. Mutual-aid societies insured workers against illness and death, but also published working-class newspapers, assisted strikers, and sponsored educational programs and cultural events. Chicago Czechs, for example, built a network of associations that "eventually pulled most families into a round of organized life," ranging from dramatic societies to Czech-language branches of the Socialist party. Free-thought schools suffused the city, also serving as meeting places for a wide array of Czech organizations. Ukrainian workers formed mutual-benefit and fraternal societies, and sponsored reading rooms, choirs, drama groups, ethnic schools, and the weekly newspaper *Svoboda* (Freedom). The Ukrainian Workingmen's Association combined ethnicity and class awareness, advocating labor unions in the United States and revolution in the Ukraine.[46]

Polish fraternal associations not only provided insurance and mutual aid (ranging from death benefits to housing loans), they published daily newspapers, operated schools, supported the Polish national cause, and sponsored choirs and other cultural outlets. The socialist *Dziennik Ludowy* (People's Daily), published from 1907 until 1925, was embedded in a dense network of sympathetic unions, singing societies, the Polish People's University, and similar institutions. *Ludowy*, like most working-class dailies, was organized as a joint-stock cooperative. Polish socialists, union locals, and other supporters bought shares in the Polish People's Publishing Company, setting editorial and business policies at annual shareholders' meetings. Readers not only owned the newspaper and provided its operating capital, they sent in the detailed reports of Polish-American activities, working conditions, and strikes that filled much of the paper's twelve pages of local, national, and international news.[47]

While firmly based in the Polish community, *Dziennik Ludowy* was committed to the broader American working-class movement from the start. Polish socialists joined fellow socialists of other nationalities for street meetings, demonstrations, and political campaigns. They addressed their supporters not as Poles who happened to be workers, but as workers who happened to be Poles. They were exploited as workers, and could secure their emancipation only through working-class organization:

> Every time the American citizen who has the misfortune of being a
> proletariat compares that which the present government gives him with that
> which he should get, so many times must he clench his fists and say: "This
> government is my enemy." . . . The police, the courts and the legislature
> are the servants of the Moloch God. . . . Capital and the present
> government are like master and servant.[48]

Chicago's Lithuanian socialist daily, *Naujienos* (News), was owned by local socialists, party organizations, union locals, and other sympathetic organizations. The Society of Blessed Lithuania, a sick and death benefit organization, bought three shares in the publishing company at ten dollars each. When Lithuanian communists attempted to take over, the Society directed its delegates to oppose their efforts to remove the editor and change the paper's political stance.[49] (Communists later established their own weekly, *Vilnis* [The Surge], which became a daily in 1926.) When *Naujienos* held a ball to celebrate its second anniversary, its editor gave a speech proclaiming that the paper belonged to

> the people themselves, the Lithuanian workers. . . . *Naujienos* is a
> progressive and revolutionary newspaper. It does not classify Lithuanians
> by religious creeds, but distinguishes them as workers or capitalists. And
> since practically all Lithuanians are workers, *Naujienos* has the largest field
> in which to thrive.[50]

These structures were not merely formal mechanisms; they exercised real power over newspapers' business and editorial policies. The *Arbeiter-Zeitung* was closely controlled by the Socialistic Publishing Society, which ousted several successive editors as the Society changed its policies from political to a union-centered strategy, and ultimately declared itself anarchist. Between 1874 and 1910, when the *Arbeiter-Zeitung* was reorganized as a Socialist party organ, the average editorial tenure was less than three and a half years, and would have been only two years were it not for editor Max Baginski's thirteen-year term.[51]

Chicago's labor movement was built in solidarity with, not in opposition to, ethnic institutions. Socialist party rallies might include Czech, German,and Yiddish workers' choirs, along with speakers in a half dozen or more languages. Many unions organized ethnically based locals that were deeply rooted in immigrant communities but also linked workers across ethnic lines through district or industrial councils, the Chicago Federation of Labor, and other structures. Nor was this counterculture restricted to immigrant communities, although they were its strongholds. The Chicago Federation of Labor and the Women's Trade Union League joined forces to organize a Chicago Labor College in 1919, and the CFL went on to launch its own political party, newspaper, and radio station.[52]

Ethnically based mutual-aid associations provided a full range of services — from sickness, death, and burial insurance to social functions — through the 1920s. In 1918 the Illinois Health Insurance Commission found that four-fifths of working-class families were insured through such institutions. But as immigrant workers saw their unions smashed, their societies undermined by government regulation, and their wages (when they were able to find work at all) eroded in the postwar years, community resources were strained to the breaking point. Mutual aid societies and other institutions simply were unable to meet their communities' enormous needs, and federal and state governments ultimately stepped into the breach.[53]

Economic Constraints

The tumultuous history of the *Chicago Daily Socialist* illustrates many of the dilemmas facing organizations trying to publish working-class newspapers within the constraints of a capitalist economy. The *Daily Socialist* was launched from the offices of the weekly *Chicago Socialist* with virtually no operating capital in response to the urgent need for an organ to reach English-speaking voters during the 1906 elections.[54] Chicago already was saturated with English-language dailies, several of which collapsed in the next few years. The market was dominated by a handful of publishers, who ensured their success through shared news-gathering and distribution facilities and agreements governing advertising rates and policies, press times, and labor relations. The *Daily Socialist* immediately entered into a desperate campaign to raise operating capital and funds for a printing press. Financial crisis followed financial crisis throughout the *Daily*'s six years.

The paper drew financial support locally and nationally through donations, stock purchases, low-interest bonds (used to finance the *Daily*'s printing plant), and benefits such as an annual fund-raising picnic in Chicago's Riverview Park. In its first year of operation, the paper ran a deficit of $42,000 (some of which went to buy the printing plant). The deficit was reduced to $14,000 annually by 1910, but by that time the paper owed $55,000 in bonds and had $40,000 invested in its stock, on assets of $40,000. Only the fact that this debt was owed almost entirely to party members kept the paper afloat.

The *Daily Socialist* modeled its business practices on the capitalist press, selling for a penny in order to compete for working-class readers with papers such as the *Daily News* and relying upon advertising revenues to support the paper. But the *Daily Socialist* never carried much advertising, even during the 1912 lockout of union pressmen, when it enjoyed a circulation greater than all other English-language Chicago newspapers combined. Ironically, the paper went bankrupt only during the lockout, after it succeeded in increasing circulation from the 30,000 to 40,000 subscribers it held for most of its life to nearly 300,000 copies daily (in morning and evening editions). With the tenfold circulation gain the *Socialist* changed its name to the *World*, expanded from four to twelve pages daily (soon falling back to six to eight pages), purchased new presses, added the morning edition, and increased its staff. The expansion proved disastrous; its capitalist competitors sold newspapers below the cost of production, relying upon advertising revenues to make up the difference, but advertisers spurned the *World*. Chicago department stores, for example, were a mainstay in the *Tribune* and *Daily News* columns, but never advertised in the *World*. Instead, the paper's advertising revenues came from socialist publishers, patent medicine manufacturers, and small businesses dependent upon working-class customers. While Chicago socialists could afford, if sometimes reluctantly, the preexpansion deficits, the paper still lost money on every copy sold — increased circulation served only to magnify the extent of the losses. By December 1912 the *World* owed more than $125,000, excluding the value of its stock, and the Socialist party initiated bankruptcy proceedings rather than allow a local business syndicate to take over the paper.

The economic structure of the newspaper industry that had taken shape by the turn of the century was fundamentally hostile to labor and socialist efforts to launch competing voices. The advertising subsidies that supported their capitalist competitors were, by and large, unavailable. And yet it was difficult to ask working-class readers to pay cover prices higher than those charged by their capitalist competitors. Instead, the inevitable losses (only a handful of labor papers, such as the Yiddish *Daily Forward*, which sold as many copies in Chicago as its three competitors combined, ever turned a profit) were covered by donations, benefits, and organizational subsidies. The socialist daily *Spravedlnost*, for example, relied upon donations from Czech-language union locals, mutual-aid associations (most notably the Bohemian National Cemetery Association), and party branches — in addition to picnics, dances, and book sales — to cover often substantial losses.[55]

Foreign-language labor papers were able to survive in this hostile economic climate precisely because they could operate outside of the dominant capitalist relations of production. They not only did not compete directly with the capitalist press, they could draw upon their communities' institutional networks and resources for news, readers, and support. English-language working-class papers, however, never satisfactorily resolved the dilemmas imposed by the capitalist marketplace. Many labor papers refused to enter the marketplace, relying upon union dues to cover operating expenses. But this discouraged efforts to reach outside unions' ranks to counter antilabor propaganda or to reach out to potential supporters. Publishers of privately owned labor organs tended to combine modest organizational subsidies with advertising, primarily from firms (such as union-label manufacturers) explicitly catering to unionists. But unionists objected to some of these advertisers, while publishers sometimes resorted to misrepresentation or intimidation to obtain advertising from employers, hoping not so much to reach union readers as to ensure labor peace. It was, Chicago Federation of Labor President John Fitzpatrick argued, a short step from taking advertising to full-out racketeering. "*The Unionist* . . . has gone the limit in sandbagging the businessmen of Chicago. . . . Our office has spent considerable time trying to counteract [its] work." By then the CFL had launched its own organ, the *New Majority*. "If our own paper is going to get into that situation by accepting advertising, I say throw it in the waste basket and forget it."[56] But the *New Majority*'s deficits soon outran the CFL's resources, and the paper was compelled to accept advertising.

Every Reader a Reporter

Labor newspapers only rarely were edited by professional journalists. Rather, editors were selected on the basis of their involvement in labor organizations (and replaced if their performance proved unsatisfactory).[57] None of the first five editors of the *Arbeiter-Zeitung*, for example, was a professional journalist: two were typesetters (a traditional background for labor editors) and the other three were a cutler, a mason, and an upholsterer. Ivan Molek, editor of the socialist Slovene National Benefit Society's daily newspaper *Prosveta* (Enlightenment) for fifteen years, worked as a laborer and miner before beginning his career as an editor.[58]

Labor papers typically had small editorial staffs, relying on their readers (and the exchanges) for the bulk of their copy. The *Chicago Daily Socialist* regularly proclaimed that it had the largest staff of any newspaper in the world, its 30,000 volunteer readers/reporters. The editors regularly published suggestions to these contributors about how to prepare their copy, and it promised to print copy submitted by labor unions exactly as written. At times, particularly after the *Socialist* dropped its wire service (from October 1907 until April 1910) in solidarity with a telegraph operators' strike, such copy filled a very substantial portion of the newspaper.[59] Chicago's Croatian communist daily similarly encouraged its readers to submit articles on working conditions, union activities, local communist efforts, and analysis of workers' struggles and their progress:

> News . . . must reveal what the workers think about the giant corporations who direct their lives, about the brutal system which is crushing them more pitilessly than expensive machinery. . . . To get such information you must be a workingman. When you write, you become a workers' correspondent.[60]

Even conservative labor papers encouraged readers to participate in writing their news. Shortly after the *Union Labor Advocate* lost its status as the Chicago Federation of Labor's official organ, it wrote:

> To the 250,000 men and women carrying union cards in Chicago and Cook County, we wish to state that this is YOUR PAPER. . . . Any communication you desire to send to this office touching upon the interests of organized labor will receive careful consideration, and if the cause be benefitted through publication it will appear in our columns.[61]

Thus, the labor press was not established merely to serve the needs of labor readers — in large part it was written, edited, owned, and controlled by the working class, both individually and through organizations. Readers related to the labor press in a manner very different from their relations with the capitalist press (which many also read). While some readers occupied the more passive consumption role typical of the capitalist press, a substantial proportion of labor press readers participated in the process of creating and sustaining their own media institutions.

Conclusion

Labor organs reflected the organizational and ideological diversity of the nation's working-class movements, ranging from nonpolitical organs largely restricted to reports on the progress of one or another labor union to revolutionary journals published by anarchist, socialist, and communist organizations. Whatever languages they spoke, most workers could choose not only between the capitalist and the labor press, but which labor papers, if any, they would support.

In the 1880s and 1890s most labor papers were issued by working-class political organizations, but the number of union organs climbed sharply in later decades, as did the number of working-class publications in general. Only with the onset of the Great Depression did the numbers of labor newspapers begin to decline, in Chicago as across the country — caused by the collapse of the community institutions that supported, and often published, these papers; by the postwar Red Scares; and by tightened restrictions on immigration.

While there are no longer any daily labor newspapers being published in the United States, unless we count the union-owned Wilkes-Barre *Citizens' Voice*, in their day these papers played a key role both in the labor movement and as newspapers in their own right. Thousands of labor newspapers, on-line computer systems, and radio and cable and broadcast television programs attest to the labor movement's continuing emphasis on controlling its own means of communication.[62]

The labor press not only offers a model of communications practice sharply different from the capitalist model that predominates today, it played a vital role in working-class movements, and the broader society, of its day. Even immigrant communities were not insular; they rubbed against the broader society on a daily basis in their communities (several ethnic groups typically lived in the same block, and often in the same buildings) and workplaces.[63] These working-class institutions served not as enclaves, isolated from broader economic and political currents, but rather as bases within which workers could develop their own ideology and strategies, and that could sustain them as they entered into broader economic and political struggles.

Thus, the working-class press was part of a vital alternative public sphere, helping to constitute the community of publics C. Wright Mills insisted is essential to genuinely democratic societies.[64] For a significant minority of the population, labor and ethnic newspapers were the primary source of news. Fifty-five years ago, James Monaghan noted that his contemporaries had only a

> restricted vision of the true life of Chicago. During the presidential campaign it was said that Roosevelt was supported by only one metropolitan daily, the *Times*. As a matter of fact he was supported by at least twenty foreign language papers.[65]

While the labor and radical movements of which these newspapers were a part may have failed in their ultimate objectives, they helped transform the political and economic landscape in important ways. Workers carried the perspectives they developed in their press, and the information they gained, with them as they engaged the larger society. When journalism historians ignore the working-class press (and other alternative presses), we not only fail to take account of a persistent, and at times quite important, oppositional press, we also fail to grapple with such vital questions as press freedom (both political and economic) and the nature of the relationship between the media and the publics they serve.

Notes

1. This chapter draws heavily upon my dissertation, "Working-Class Newspapers, Community and Consciousness in Chicago, 1880–1930," University of Illinois, 1992.

2. See, for example, John C. Nerone, "The Problem of Teaching Journalism History," *Journalism Educator* 45 (Autumn 1990): 20–21. I discuss the variety of journalisms practiced in Chicago between 1880 and 1930 in Chapter III of my dissertation.

3. The *Arbeiter-Zeitung* was published daily from 1878 until 1920 (though as a Socialist party organ after 1910), surviving as a weekly and, finally, fortnightly until 1924. At various periods, Chicago socialists and communists also issued dailies in Croatian, Lithuanian, Russian, Serbian, Slovak, Slovene, and Yiddish. Bruce Nelson, *Beyond the Martyrs: A Social History of Chicago's Anarchists* (New Brunswick, N.J.: Rutgers University Press, 1988), 115–26; Bekken, "Working-Class Newspapers."

4. C. K. McFarland and Robert Thistlethwaite, "20 Years of a Successful Labor Paper: The Working Man's Advocate, 1829–49," *Journalism Quarterly* 60 (Spring 1983): 35–40; Jon Bekken, " 'No Weapon So Powerful': Working-Class Newspapers in the United States," *Journal of Communication Inquiry* 12 (Summer 1988): 104–19.

5. Donald Myers, "Birth and Establishment of the Labor Press in the United States," master's thesis, University of Wisconsin, 1950.

6. *Historical Abstracts of the United States* (Washington, D.C.: U.S. Government Printing Office, 1975), 11–12; *Statistics of the Population of the United States at the Tenth Census* (Washington, D.C.: U.S. Government Printing Office, 1883), 536–37, 538–41; *Twelfth Census of the United States Taken in the Year 1900* (Washington, D.C.: U.S. Government Printing Office, 1902), 796–99, 878–89; Lizabeth Cohen, *Making a New Deal: Industrial Workers in Chicago, 1919–1939* (New York: Cambridge University Press, 1990), 13.

7. Sally Miller, "Different Accents of Labor," *Labor's Heritage* 2, (July 1990): 62–75; Dirk Hoerder, ed., *The Immigrant Labor Press in North America, 1840s–1970s* (Westport, Conn.: Greenwood, 1987).

8. *Twelfth Census of the United States Taken in the Year 1900*, vol. 1 (Washington, D.C.: U.S. Government Printing Office, 1902), 613, 651, 796–99, 878–79.

9. Edward Sheppard, *The Radical and Labor Periodical Press in Chicago* (Champaign, Ill.: Institute of Labor and Industrial Relations, 1949), 12; Anne Spier, "German-Speaking Peoples," in Hoerder, *The Immigrant Labor Press*, vol. 3, 456.

10. Labor Research Department, *American Labor Press Directory* (New York: Rand School of Social Sciences, 1925). Hoerder, *The Immigrant Labor Press*, provides comprehensive bibliographic information through the 1970s.

11. Zonita Jeffrys, "The Attitude of the Chicago Press toward the Local Labor Movement, 1873 to 1879," master's thesis, University of Chicago, 1936.

12. Nathaniel Hong, "They Hang Editors, Don't They? Free Speech and Free Press Issues in the Haymarket Case, 1886" (paper presented at the meeting of the American Journalism Historians Association, Coeur d'Alene, Iowa, 1990). For discussion of Chicago's working-class movements and communities of the day, see Paul Avrich, *The Haymarket Tragedy* (Princeton, N.J.: Princeton University Press, 1984); Nelson, *Beyond the Martyrs*.

13. David Nord, "The Business Values of American Newspapers: The 19th Century Watershed in Chicago," *Journalism Quarterly* 61 (Summer 1984): 265–73. Labor movement criticism of the press was persistent. The *Union Labor Advocate* ("Million Against Million," November 1910, 74) denounced the English-language dailies as "servile slaves" of the employers. The Chicago Federation of Labor maintained that newspaper publishers were financially corrupt and editorially dishonest (e.g., John Fitzpatrick to Elizabeth Drew, January 13, 1919, Fitzpatrick Papers, box 7, folder 54, Chicago Historical Society).

14. Homer Call to Mary McDowell, November 22, 1902; C. E. Schmidt to McDowell, April 2, 1903 (Mary McDowell papers, folder 15A, Chicago Historical Society).

15. "What Rally?" March 27, 1948 (McDowell papers, folder 15B).

16. Thomas McEnroe, "The IWW: Theories, Organizational Problems and Appeals as Revealed Principally in the *Industrial Worker*," doctoral dissertation, University of Minnesota, 1960; Warren Van Tine, "Ben H. Williams, Wobbly Editor," master's thesis, Northern Illinois University, 1967; Salvatore Salerno, *Red November, Black November: Culture and Community in the Industrial Workers of the World* (Albany:

State University of New York Press, 1989); Dione Miles, *Something in Common: An IWW Bibliography* (Detroit: Wayne State University Press, 1986).

17. C. E. Payne, "Our Press," *Industrial Pioneer* 4 (July 1926): 20–21.

18. The *Leader* continued until 1942 (alongside, for much of that time, German- and Polish-language socialist weeklies), maintaining a circulation of 30,000–46,000 copies. The Federated Trades Council then launched the weekly *Labor Press* to partially fill the void. Elmer Beck, "Autopsy of a Labor Daily: The Milwaukee Leader," *Journalism Monographs* 16, (August 1970); Sally Miller, "Of Ethnicity and Labor," in *Socialism and the Cities*, ed. Bruce Stave (Port Washington, N.Y.: Kennikat, 1975); Thomas Gavett, *Development of the Labor Movement in Milwaukee* (Madison: University of Wisconsin Press, 1965).

19. Jon Bekken, "A Socialist Women's Page? The *Milwaukee Leader* and the Woman Question" (paper presented at the meeting of the Union for Democratic Communications, Ottawa, Ont., May 1988).

20. Harvey O'Connor, *Revolution in Seattle* (New York: Monthly Review Press, 1964), 93.

21. Ibid., 114.

22. Roger Friedheim, *The Seattle General Strike* (Seattle: University of Washington Press, 1964), 51, describes the *Union Record* as "the only daily labor-owned newspaper" published in the United States—overlooking the short-lived New York *Daily Leader* and the Unitypo papers. R. Thomas Berner, "Unitypo: The ITU's Editor and Publisher," *American Journalism* 2 (1985): 144–64.

E. B. Ault (a typographer and Socialist party member), elected *Record* editor in 1908, testified before the Commission on Industrial Relations on the weekly edition's operations, and on industrial conditions. *Final Report and Testimony of the Commission on Industrial Relations* (Washington, D.C.: U.S. Government Printing Office, 1916), 4185–4202.

23. Andrew Long, "The Federated Press," *Survey*, October 23, 1920, 126–27; Alfred McClung Lee, *The Daily Newspaper in America: The Evolution of a Social Instrument* (New York: Macmillan, 1937), 541–42; E. N. Costello, Report, January 1921 (Carl Haessler Collection, box 4, folder 1, Archives of Labor and Urban Affairs, Wayne State University).

24. "A.F. of L. Reports on Federated Press," *New Majority*, October 20, 1923, 2; Labor Research Department, *American Labor Press Directory*.

25. "Member Papers as of April 1, 1956," correspondence, Naomi [signature illegible] to Carl Haessler, October 23, 1956, announcing that the *Dispatcher* would not renew, "This . . . seals our fate. . . . Would you do a news story with announcement and FP history background for use in our final service?" FP retained some funds in hopes of reviving the service. See Haessler's letter to Marshall Bloom, Liberation News Service, March 10, 1968: "I am enclosing $100 from what's left of FP's abortive hope that the labor movement would once more have a body of . . . editors independent and strong enough to subscribe to an independent objective news service, which is what FP had been from Jan. 2 1920 till it was effectively smothered by the AFL-CIO bigshots." Haessler went on to describe FP's workings and offer suggestions for improving LNS (Haessler papers, box 4, folder 9).

26. James Weinstein, *The Decline of Socialism in America* (New York: Vintage, 1967), 85.

27. John Kennedy, "Socialistic Tendencies in American Trade Unions," *International Socialist Review* 8 (December 1907): 330–45.

28. Elliott Shore, "Selling Socialism: The Appeal to Reason and the Radical Press in Turn-of-the-Century America," *Media, Culture & Society* 7 (April 1985): 161. See also Elliott Shore, *Talkin' Socialism* (Lawrence: University Press of Kansas, 1988); James Green, "The 'Salesmen-Soldiers' of the 'Appeal' Army: A Profile of Rank-and-File Socialist Agitators," in *Socialism and the Cities*, ed. Bruce Stave (Port Washington, N.Y.: Kennikat, 1975); James Green, *Grass-Roots Socialism* (Baton Rouge: Louisiana University Press, 1978); Howard Quint, "Julius A. Wayland, Pioneer Socialist Propagandist," *Mississippi Valley Historical Review* 34 (March 1949): 585–606; David Nord, "The Appeal to Reason and American Socialism, 1901–1920," *Kansas History* 1 (1978): 75–89; George Allan England, *The Story of the Appeal* (Girard, Kans.: Appeal to Reason, 1914); John Graham, ed., *"Yours for the Revolution": The Appeal to Reason, 1895–1922* (Lincoln: University of Nebraska Press, 1990).

29. Weinstein, *The Decline of Socialism*, 90–91. I discuss the impact of the wartime repression and other postal policies on working-class newspapers in " 'These Great and Dangerous Powers': Postal Censorship of the Press," *Journal of Communication Inquiry* 15 (Winter 1991): 55–71. See also Dorothy Fowler, *Unmailable: Congress and the Post Office* (Athens: University of Georgia Press, 1977).

30. "The Work of the Jackals," *La Parola Dei Socialisti*, August 22, 1914 (Chicago Foreign Language Press Survey, reel 30); Bruno Cartosio, "Italian Workers and Their Press in the United States," in *The Press of Labor Migrants in Europe and North America* ed. Christiane Harzig and Dirk Hoerder (Bremen, Germany: Labor Newspaper Preservation Project, 1985), 434–36.

31. Cook County Socialist Party Executive Committee Minutes, February 21, 1919 (Archives, University of Illinois at Chicago).

32. Hong, "They Hang Editors, Don't They?"

33. The editor was acquitted after Polish socialists spent nearly $600 in his defense. Theodore Schroeder, "Prosecuted for 'Obscenity,' " *Truth Seeker*, April 29, 1911, 266; *Dziennik Zwiazkowy*, December 5, 1910 (Chicago Foreign Language Press Survey, reel 50). Similar prosecutions were brought against the publishers of a Slovene socialist weekly and the *Appeal to Reason*.

34. CFL Minutes, February 16, 1919, 6, 12 (Chicago Historical Society); "Off Again-On Again!" *New Majority*, October 15, 1919, 15; "Union Newsboys Boost The New Majority," *New Majority*, January 24, 1920, 1.

35. *Who Is Back of the Gun-Men in the Chicago Trust Newspaper Lockout?* (copy in Fitzpatrick Papers). This violence was not so much an attack upon socialist politics as it was an effort to shut down one of the few newspapers not crippled by the publishers' lockout of union pressmen, which prompted a sympathy strike by union newsboys, drivers, and stereotypers. Philip Taft, "The Limits of Labor Unity: The Chicago Newspaper Strike of 1912," *Labor History* 19 (1978): 100–129.

36. See, for example, Daniel Fusfeld, *The Rise and Repression of Radical Labor* (Chicago: Charles H. Kerr, 1980); David Corbin, *The Socialist & Labor Star* (Huntington, W. Va.: Appalachian Movement Press, 1971); Roger Baldwin, "Wartime Restrictions on the Freedom of Speech, Press and Assemblage," in *American Labor Yearbook 1919–1920*, ed. A. Trachtenberg (New York: Rand School of Social Science, 1920); Gilbert Fite and Horace Peterson, *Opponents of War* (Madison: University of Wisconsin Press, 1957); Dorothy Gallagher, *All the Right Enemies* (Princeton, N.J.: Princeton University Press, 1988).

37. *Den Nye Tid*, quoted in Nelson, *Beyond the Martyrs*, 119–20.

38. CFL Minutes, *Union Labor Advocate*, February 1910, 8–10. The *Advocate* had been paid $300 in the previous year for publishing the minutes, but paid the Federation $30 a month for office rental. The CFL minutes ran seven pages that month, including a protest from publisher George Hodge that they took up too much space (p. 11). The Union Label League paid the *Advocate* $20 the previous month for its space, as well as $5.50 for editorial expenses (p. 34).

39. Nelson, *Beyond the Martyrs*, 123–25; Trade and Labor Assembly Minute Book, 1887–89 (Chicago Historical Society); Chicago Federation of Labor Minutes, April 3, 1909, *Union Labor Advocate*, May 1909, 5–9; Chicago Federation of Labor Minutes, November 6, 1910, 13–14; CFL Minutes, January 20, 1918, 12; CFL Minutes, June 16, 1918, 8; " 'Union Labor News' a Fake Publication," *Federation News*, September 13, 1924, 5; *Chicago Labor News*, October 7, 1921.

40. "The New Majority," *New Majority*, January 4, 1919, 1; John Keiser, "John Fitzpatrick and Progressive Unionism, 1915–1925," doctoral dissertation, Northwestern University, 1965.

41. Minutes of Special CFL Meeting, January 29, 1928 (John Fitzpatrick Papers, box 16, folder 116).

42. *Painters Bulletin* 6 (July 1920) (John Fitzpatrick Papers). Such local union organs have not generally been preserved, and this is the only copy of this title I have been able to locate.

43. *Ayer's Newspaper Annual* (Philadelphia: N. W. Ayer, 1921); Hoerder, *The Immigrant Labor Press*.

44. *Daily Labor Bulletin*, May 24–June 5, 1905 (Chicago Historical Society).

45. "Culinary Strikers Start Daily Paper," *New Majority*, May 15, 1920, 7.

46. Josef Barton, "Eastern and Southern Europeans," in *Ethnic Leadership in America*, ed. John Higham et al. (Baltimore: Johns Hopkins University Press, 1978); Karel Bicha, "Community or Cooperation? The Case of the Czech-Americans," in *Studies in Ethnicity*, ed. Charles Ward et al. (Boulder, Colo.: East European Monographs, 1980); Frank Renkiewicz, "An Economy of Self-Help: Fraternal Capitalism and the Evolution of Polish America," in *Studies in Ethnicity*, ed. Charles Ward et al. (Boulder, Colo.: East European Monographs, 1980); Myron Kuropas, "Ukrainian Chicago: The Making of a Nationality Group in America," in *Ethnic Chicago*, ed. Peter d'A. Jones and Melvin Holli (Grand Rapids, Mich.: William B. Eerdman, 1981).

47. Mary Cygan, "Political and Cultural Leadership in an Immigrant Community: Polish-American Socialism, 1880–1950," doctoral dissertation, Northwestern University, 1989; see especially pp. 48–82.

48. Editorial, *Dziennik Ludowy*, February 4, 1908 (Chicago Foreign Language Press Survey, reel 50). When the Chicago Federation of Labor launched its own Labor party, *Ludowy* backed the CFL ticket. When the paper began to run deficits in the 1920s, several Chicago unions—including the International Ladies Garment Workers Union, the Laborers, Meatcutters, Machinists, and Amalgamated Clothing Workers, all with substantial Polish memberships—donated funds and resolved to promote its circulation. "Unionists Consider Aid for Chicago Polish Labor Daily," *New Majority*, March 29, 1924, 2.

49. Record Books of the Society of Blessed Lithuania, January 12, 1919 (Chicago Foreign Language Press Survey, reel 43).

50. "*Naujienos* Observes Second Anniversary," *Naujienos*, March 20, 1916 (Chicago Foreign Language Press Survey, reel 42). The paper survives to this day.

51. These structures, and their connections to a broader oppositional German working-class culture, are discussed more fully in "The Socialistic Publishing Society," chapter V of my dissertation. For published accounts, see Renate Kiesewetter, "German-American Labor Press: The *Vorbote* and the *Chicagoer Arbeiter-Zeitung*," in *German Workers' Culture*, ed. Hartmut Keil (Washington, D.C.: Smithsonian Institution Press, 1988); Eric Hirsch, *Urban Revolt* (Berkeley: University of California Press, 1990); Nelson, *Beyond the Martyrs*.

52. Richard Schneirov and Thomas Suhrbur, *Union Brotherhood, Union Town* (Carbondale: Southern Illinois University Press, 1988); Clyde Barrow, "Counter-Movement within the Labor Movement: Workers' Education and the American Federation of Labor, 1900–1937," *Social Science Journal* 27 (1990): 399.

53. Cohen, *Making a New Deal*, 64–75, 218–38.

54. The following is based upon my " 'This Paper Is Owned by Many Thousands of Workingmen and Women': Contradictions of a Socialist Daily" (paper presented at the meeting of the Association for Education in Journalism and Mass Communication, Boston, August 1991).

55. Richard Schneirov, "Free Thought and Socialism in the Czech Community in Chicago, 1875–1887," in *"Struggle a Hard Battle,"* ed. Dirk Hoerder (De Kalb: Northern Illinois University Press, 1986); "A History of United Brotherhood of Carpenters Local 54," trans. H. Vydra (U.B.C. papers, box 9, folder 5, Chicago Historical Society); John Jelinek, ed., *Padesatilete Jubileum ceskeho narodniho hrbitova v Chicagu Illinois* (The Fifty-Year Jubilee of the Bohemian National Cemetery Association) (Chicago: Bohemian National Cemetery Association, 1927; English-language translation available at the Chicago Historical Society.

56. CFL Minutes, June 1, 1919, 17–18.

57. The working-class, nonprofessional character of early twentieth-century labor leaders is documented in my "A Collective Biography of Editors of U.S. Workers' Papers: 1913 & 1925" (paper presented at the meeting of the American Journalism Historians Association, Charleston, S.C., October 1988), and in chapter X of my dissertation.

58. Molek first edited a local weekly and then a succession of Chicago socialist organs—and was also active in Slovene cultural, political, and mutual-benefit institutions, living out his life largely within the Slovene community. But while his position as elected editor was influential, Molek was forced to step down when he persisted in criticizing Tito's government in *Prosveta*. Ivan Molek, *Slovene Immigrant History* (Dover, Del.: Mary Molek, 1979); Ivan Molek papers (Chicago Historical Society).

59. "A Call to the 30,000," *Chicago Daily Socialist*, January 21, 1908, 1; "Some Suggestions to the Staff," *Chicago Daily Socialist*, February 8, 1907, 4; H. G. Creel, "The Hustler's Column," *Chicago Daily Socialist*, August 25, 1909.

60. "To Our Workers' Correspondents: Instructions and Suggestions," *Radnik*, January 11, 1927 (Chicago Foreign Language Press Survey, reel 9). The article urged writers to avoid sloganeering and offered instructions on writing leads, structuring news reports, and keeping sentences short, and stressed that "the utmost accuracy is necessary." See also "To Our Correspondents," *Radnicka Straza*, October 14, 1914; "School for Workers' Correspondents in Chicago," *Radnik*, November 24, 1937 (Chicago Foreign Language Press Survey, reel 9).

61. *Union Labor Advocate*, April 8, 1911, 1, 14. This was the third issue that year

identified as Volume 12, Number 1—the others being January and March 1, 1911, the first issue of a quickly abandoned daily edition.

62. See, for example, Fred Glass, "A Locally Based Labor Media Strategy," *Labor Studies Journal* 14 (Winter 1989): 3–17; Fred Glass, "Labor and New Media Technology: A Union of Necessity," *Labor Studies Journal* 9 (Fall 1984): 131–50; Jon Bekken, "Labor and the Media: A Historical Perspective" (paper presented at the conference, Labor Technology: Communications Tools for the 1990s, Burlingame, Calif., 1990).

63. While workers might belong to an ethnic political party or union local, these were actively involved in broader class activities and struggles. Carpenters might meet in ethnic locals, but they worked together under the same conditions, struck together to improve those conditions, and went to jail together when their strikes were outlawed. Ethnic socialist locals frequently participated in transethnic cultural and political activities, ranging from picnics (at which workers' choirs and speakers typically performed in several languages) to demonstrations and electoral campaigns. See, for example, Schneirov and Suhrbur, *Union Brotherhood, Union Town*; Cohen, *Making a New Deal*.

64. C. Wright Mills, *The Power Elite* (New York: Oxford University Press, 1956), 298–302.

65. James Monaghan, "A New Source of Information for Historians," *Illinois State Historical Society Journal* 30 (July 1937): 163. Monaghan suggests that this support accounted for Roosevelt's overwhelming reelection.

Chapter 8

The Commercialization of the Black Press and the Rise of Race News in Chicago
Albert Kreiling

In the first half of this century, large numbers of blacks entered common orbits of racial experience as readers of local, regional, and national commercial weekly newspapers started around the turn of the century and later. The papers included four with huge nationwide followings by the 1920s — the *Baltimore Afro-American*, the *Chicago Defender*, the *Norfolk Journal and Guide*, and the *Pittsburgh Courier* — and many local and regional papers such as the *Cleveland Call and Post* and the *Philadelphia Tribune*.[1] The papers replicated the successes of white commercial papers starting with the penny press in the 1830s. Moreover, the triumph of commercial papers over earlier church, lodge, political, and opinion papers paralleled the stages in the history of the immigrant press charted by Robert Park.[2]

This chapter takes the *Chicago Defender* as a case study of several interrelated developments that contributed to the triumph of the commercial press, among them the following: (1) Numerous earlier journalists, usually amateurs who wrote or edited as a sideline, paved the way but soon were overshadowed by the professional press corps that developed later. (2) Numerous black entrepreneurs created large businesses, including publishing firms, that developed marketing strategies in the expanded urban black communities, as well as nationally. (3) Middle-class southern migrants arriving in Chicago since the close of Reconstruction, including businessmen and professional journalists, provided staffs, advertising support and readers. (4) Subject matter for a varied diet of "race news" came from the organized activities created by the expanding middle class, including professional sports, commercial entertainment, business and professional associations, social and civic organizations, and women's clubs. (5) The later Great Migration of the World War I years brought a huge lower class, which posed a threat to the dominance of middle-class styles of life in the community, but also provided a clientele for commercial papers and the products advertised in them. (6) Professional journalists created mass-appeal styles and techniques, or borrowed them from white papers, to attract lower-class readers. (7) After a wave of "modernization" or "secularization" of urban styles of life, middle-class hostility to new urban customs, products, and entertainment subsided, making readers receptive to consumer products.

The most legendary and successful of the national black papers, the *Chicago Defender*, was started by Robert Sengstacke Abbott in 1905. In the midst of industrial development and cultural change, the *Defender* became a stage to elevate the varied doings of blacks, as well as far-flung slights and injustices to them, into a unified and vivid drama that sustained a nationwide orbit of collective racial life. "The Defender was, in a cultural sense, the midwife of an important American revolution," Charles Johnson, sociologist and president of Fisk University, said on the paper's fiftieth birthday.[3] On the same occasion, poet Langston Hughes paid tribute to the role of the paper in awakening a common racial outlook:

> As a child in Kansas I grew up on "The Chicago Defender" and it awakened
> me in my youth to the problems which I and my race had to face in
> America. Its flaming headlines and indignant editorials did a great deal to
> make me the "race man" which I later became, as expressed in my own
> attitudes and in my writing.[4]

Abbott and the Start of the *Defender*

In *The Lonely Warrior*, Roi Ottley presented a factual account of the *Defender* under Abbott.[5] An overview, drawing upon Ottley's book and other sources as well as the paper itself, will be presented as a preface to the analysis that follows. Abbott was born in 1868 on St. Simon's Island, off the coast of Georgia, to former slaves. His father died shortly after his birth, and Robert grew up in Savannah and Woodville, Georgia, in the home of his mother's second husband, John H. H. Sengstacke, who had been reared in Germany. For a time, Sengstacke published a newspaper, on which Robert gained journalistic experience.

Abbott learned the printing trade at Hampton Institute, where Booker T. Washington. a Hampton graduate, occasionally visited. Abbott later advocated industrial training, and he idolized Washington. Yet the *Defender* steered clear of the strife between the rival black factions rallied behind Washington and W. E. B. Du Bois (often called the conservatives and the radicals). Moreover, like some other northern editors, although Abbott endorsed industrial training and other conservative enthusiasms, he also made the *Defender* an outspoken organ for the militant protests favored by the radicals. The paper thus illustrated the fusion of the styles of the rival factions in Chicago and elsewhere following Washington's death in 1915.

In his early years, the dark-skinned Abbott received his first taste of color discrimination among blacks. His first love, a light-skinned mulatto, spurned his marriage proposal at the insistence of her family. Later in Chicago, he experienced rude disdain from lighter-skinned residents, for skin color was an attribute in the social hierarchy ruled by the elite of earlier settlers. Moreover, as in Abbott's case, skin color often correlated with the time of migration from the South to northern cities. Abbott developed a deep-seated phobia about color and the *Defender* banned such words as *Negro, colored,* and *Afro-American,* instead using the term *Race.*

In 1893, as a member of the Hampton quartet, Abbott visited the Chicago World's Fair, where his racial sentiments were quickened by Frederick Douglass and Ida B. Wells, the militant journalist and anti-lynching crusader, who soon settled in the city. Abbott settled in Chicago late in the 1890s and tried to find work as a printer, but mostly met discrimination and discouragement. He attended weekly meetings to discuss race problems with community leaders, and he talked incessantly of the need for vigorous race papers.

A roomer who lived alone until he married in 1919, when he was nearly 50, Abbott led an ascetic life. He shunned bars and cabarets, but he talked to everyone on the street. His contact with the swelling ranks of black laborers and service workers gave him an edge in building a mass readership over other editors, who shunned people outside their own circles. He eventually became a leader in the business society, but he knew the sentiments of wider circles and spoke for them.

The *Defender* first appeared on May 5, 1905, as a six-column, four-page paper, sixteen by twenty inches. For five years, it was an unimpressive collection of local news and syndicated "plate matter," with the news gathered and the papers sold mainly by Abbott himself. The *Defender* began to assume its legendary character in 1910, with the aid of men more attuned to journalistic techniques than Abbott was. At first, most of them worked without pay. Soon the paper expanded to eight pages, then to twelve in 1915, to twenty in 1921, and on upward until the Great Depression. Meanwhile, according to the publisher's reports, circulation climbed from 1,000 in 1908 to 16,000 in 1915 and 130,000 in 1918. Ottley estimated the circulation at 230,000 in 1920.[6]

Abbott moved the paper's headquarters to his landlady's flat when he could not pay the rent on the first office. The *Defender* moved into a spacious and well-equipped printing plant in 1922, but in the early years, staff members gathered in Abbott's landlady's flat to put the paper together. Sketches of a few staff members will point to shifts between successive generations of black journalists and styles of journalism.

Representative of the earliest tradition of black journalism was W. Allison Sweeney, "dean" of the Chicago press corps. Sweeney was born to free blacks in the North in 1851, and had ties to Frederick Douglass and other black abolitionist editors and Republican politicians of the nineteenth-century convention movement. He worked on white dailies before he entered black journalism, but attained his greatest prominence as editor of the *Indianapolis Freeman*, where he generally was regarded as a spokesman for Douglass. The *Freeman* was the most widely read and influential black paper in the Midwest, with a large Chicago following, and Sweeney had considerable local standing when he moved to the city in the 1890s. Sweeney wrote editorials and columns for the *Defender* — lengthy essays full of impassioned pleas and profuse in flowery language. Also noted as an orator, he committed a nineteenth-century oratorical style to prose. Although idolized by younger journalists, he epitomized a departing style of black journalism that was giving way to modern techniques of reporting the rising commodity of race news.[7]

An early writer of society news was Julius Avendorph, assistant to the president of the Pullman Company, and a leader of the premigration elite. Avendorph became involved in the new activities spearheaded by later middle-class migrants. He was active in the rise of black professional baseball and wrote sports news for the *Defender*. Even so, he never approved of the shift from the social standards of the nineteenth-century elite to those of the later middle-class society.

In the *Defender*'s earliest years, radical leader Ida B. Wells-Barnett was writing anti-Washington polemics for the *Chicago Conservator*, the leading radical organ. After the radical-conservative controversy waned, she occasionally reported in the *Defender* on her investigations of lynchings and other injustices to blacks. She had been a columnist for black papers in the 1880s and editor of the Memphis *Free Speech* in the early 1890s, until she was driven from the city by whites incensed by a militant editorial. She settled in Chicago in the mid-1890s, married Ferdinand Barnett, principal founder of the *Conservator*, and edited the paper for a time. She and her husband exemplified the journalistic style of the first southern migrants — the "Afro-American Agitators," as Henry Grady dubbed them. They represented a transitional style of black journalism between that of northern free blacks such as Sweeney and that of the professional press corps of the twentieth century.[8]

Lucius C. Harper and Frank Young exemplified the younger men of the press corps. Both stayed with the *Defender* into the 1950s, and their columns drew large followings. Harper joined the staff in 1916 and became the longtime managing editor, as well as the author of a front-page column, "Dustin' Off the News." At first, railroad porter "Fay" Young helped Abbott in his off-hours. Like other cooperating porters, he brought back newspapers and periodicals left on his train, which the staff culled for news. Later he became a full-time employee and attained prominence as the longtime sports editor and "dean" of black sports writers.

Pullman porters, traveling entertainers, and 2,000 agents promoted the *Defender* throughout the South. The most effective promoter was Roscoe Conkling Simmons, Republican politician, orator, journalist, and nephew of Booker T. Washington's wife, who addressed large crowds throughout the South. Simmons appealed to a mass following and drew scorn from middle-class blacks. He started a column in the paper in 1921.

The contrast between some early writers and some later ones illustrates the greater acceptance of urban entertainment and customs under the impact of cultural modernization or secularization. For example, the first music critic, Nora Douglass Holt, and the first drama critic, Sylvester Russell, advocated the formal culture of "civilization" for blacks and despised much of the music and entertainment on the urban scene. Russell's successor, Tony Langston, used his position on the paper to establish close and reportedly lucrative ties with show-business people. Russell charged that Langston was interested only in money, not art. Of course, the charge reflected personal rivalry, but it also pointed to the commercialization of black publishing and entertainment.

The man most responsible for transforming the *Defender* into a fighting, sensation-seeking paper was J. Hockley Smiley, the first paid employee, who joined the staff in 1910 and remained until his death in 1915. The flamboyant, hard-drinking Smiley was the wayward son of successful caterer Charles Smiley, a leader of the small premigration elite. Smiley copied features and journalistic techniques from the *Chicago Tribune* and the Hearst papers. He introduced banner headlines, sometimes printed in red, invented southern atrocities when none had occurred, and carried out Abbott's plan to departmentalize the paper. Among the earliest departments were columns on churches, theater, and the YMCA, as well as features for women and children. Departmentalization proceeded to new heights for black journalism, and by the 1920s the paper carried lengthy sections on sports, society, and other subjects.

The development Smiley set in motion was the broadening of the *Defender*'s appeal to capture a mass following. Previously, black editors had produced papers strictly for middle-class readers — self-conscious in their respectability and in their disdain for the lower class. The *Defender* was not a working-class organ, for Abbott was rather conservative on matters other than race. Instead, the *Defender* became a mass medium *par excellence* — dependent upon a large and diverse following, but operated by and in the interest of the middle class. For the most part, the journalists of the press corps worked harmoniously with the owners of the largest businesses, including Abbott, who dominated the expanded black society. This resulted not only from mutual interest, but, more important, from shared outlooks stemming from their common middle-class backgrounds.

Growth and Group Conflict in Chicago's Black Community

Chicago's South Side black community grew enormously with the southern migrations, beginning with a trickle of the Talented Tenth in the 1880s and culminating with the flood of lower-class blacks in the World War I years. Changes in the community's social structure and middle-class styles of life, as well as sheer growth, were facilitating conditions for the success of the *Defender*.[9]

Free blacks, most of whose ancestors had never been slaves, lived in the North before the Civil War. From their ranks, in Chicago and elsewhere, came small community elites who identified with the abolitionist tradition and its heroes. Some members of the elite achieved success in service trades and other occupations catering to whites, but the distinguishing mark of elite status was a genteel, respectable way of life, not wealth or success.[10]

Following Reconstruction, with black political hopes dashed in the South, small numbers of blacks started to move to Chicago and other northern cities. Many were the most talented and educated of southern blacks, and many had learned Yankee frugality and Puritan piety in the schools set up by New England missionaries to aid the freedman after the Civil War. Some newcomers assimilated into the premigration elite in Chicago and elsewhere and assumed its outlook and customs.

But young Afro-American Agitators, including both newcomers and established residents, exhibited increased race consciousness and ambition for professional achievement. By the turn of the century, the young professionals dominated the elite. Thus, although young blacks in the 1880s and 1890s entered the elite and assumed its culture, they transformed the badge of elite membership from a way of life to achieved marks of status.[11]

In Chicago and elsewhere, Afro-American Agitators started newspapers that introduced some characteristics later taken up by the commercial press, including the constant flaying of southern lynchings and the habit of judging political parties and everything else from the standpoint of what they did for the race. Also apparent was the start of secularization, as the editors scorned other-worldliness as a distraction from the problems of this world. Starting the pattern of national circulation, the papers were distributed outside their home cities, and the editors often reprinted or commented on items from one anothers' papers. Thus the papers contributed to the rise of a nationwide orbit of racial experience, although it was limited to middle-class blacks. The later commercial papers drew far larger and more diverse followings.

The Afro-American Agitators' papers lacked some characteristics that enabled commercial papers to overshadow them quickly after the turn of the century. They usually depended upon partisan support and carried little advertising. They usually were just four pages, although parties and candidates might pay for longer issues near election time. With a few exceptions, the scope of their content was fairly narrow. Much of the content was opinion, with little reporting, and most of it was written by one or two staff members, submitted by free-lancers, supplied by syndicates, or reprinted from other publications. Moreover, most editors were amateur journalists and depended upon other lines of work for a living, such as Ferdinand Barnett, repeatedly in and out as editor of the *Conservator* according to the fluctuating demands of his law practice.[12]

A subtler shift typically separated the Afro-American Agitators from the journalists of the later professional press corps on the level of general mood, outlook, or sensibility. It was a characteristic difference between the early, backward-looking and the later, forward-looking activists of the Populist-Progressive years. On the surface, the only difference between the antilynching protests in Barnett's *Conservator* and Abbott's *Defender* was the *Defender's* more garish, flamboyant style. But, more important, the *Conservator* also reflected a generally fearful, pessimistic mood, while, in spite of constant protest, the *Defender* reflected an unshakable optimism concerning the future of the race and the United States.

The Afro-American Agitators' rhetoric linked their fears with the perceptions of many Americans who nervously watched changes in the industrializing society of the late nineteenth century. Central to their outlook was the perception that the rule of principles and morality had lost sway in the land, eclipsed by naked power struggles waged for self-interest by rising power blocs in business and politics.[13] To blacks, lynchings, the displacement of abolitionists by industrialists in the Republican party, and other events symbolized the demise of morality and the triumph of naked power in American life. The anxiety of the age was especially acute among groups such as blacks, who felt unattached to the dominant power blocs. Heightened identification with the racial group and constant goading of blacks to enter the power struggles were the Afro-American Agitators' characteristic responses. By contrast, the later professional journalists had found their niche in the new order in the exciting life of the expanded black South Side world.

By the turn of the century, the tide of southern migrants rose, and the old elite, now headed by the Afro-American Agitators, was challenged by striving businessmen and professionals building a segregated economy on the South Side. The newcomers, often called Bookerites, did not assimilate the culture and outlook of the old elite, but transformed it as they rose to become the dominant elite by the 1920s. In the radical-conservative skirmishes that started in the first decade of the century and subsided in the second, members of the old elite usually rallied behind W. E. B. Du Bois and, locally, such leaders as Ferdinand and Ida Barnett, while the newcomers usually supported Booker T. Washington and, on the local scene, such leaders as attorney S. Laing Williams, physician George Cleveland Hall, and businessmen Anthony Overton and Theodore W. Jones.

Members of the old elite found the behavior of the newcomers vulgar and offensive. They typically rejected and ridiculed Bookerites such as Robert Abbott, whom they called "that black man." Edward

Wilson, a member of the old elite, condemned the striving Bookerites in the *Voice*, a magazine in the radical camp:

> Their method of obtaining and holding leadership is largely one of aggression and vulgar display. . . . They push in everywhere. . . . In their process of rising—as they think—advertisement is as necessary as it is to the life of trade.[14]

The tension between the camps surfaced in the clash over alternative programs for advancing the race. Bookerites advocated a conservative policy of economic development rather than political action and protest, vocational training rather than liberal education, and the construction of black institutions rather than assimilation into white institutions. Radicals supported the NAACP in its early assimilationist phase when Bookerites shunned it, favored outspoken protest against injustices and discrimination, and called for liberal education for "manhood" instead of industrial training, which seemed to accept a servile role for blacks in America.[15]

A few observers at the time, and many later, wondered why some blacks were so vehemently committed to one side or the other on the issues the warring camps feuded about. For example, while Du Bois insistently called for higher education and Washington for industrial training, both occasionally admitted that some blacks needed each form of education. Briefly, I submit that commitment to positions on the issues symbolized identification with one side or the other in a status battle for leadership of the race.[16]

In the second decade of the century, the two factions were coming together in a reconstituted and expanded elite. Some themes from both sides were incorporated in a common middle-class outlook of "moderate racialism," as St. Clair Drake called it, that reflected the conservatives' pride in separate institutions but took up the radicals' militance.[17] This posture became dominant in commercial newspapers in the North, including the *Defender*.

However, in coupling the new shared outlook with sensationalism and other features appealing to the lower class, the *Defender* offended many middle-class blacks, including members of both sides in the former radical-conservative feud. Over the years, readership studies consistently found that many middle-class blacks had negative attitudes toward mass-appeal papers such as the *Defender*.[18] In Chicago, the attitudes were sometimes reflected in the preference of middle-class blacks for other publications, especially the *Chicago Bee*. Anthony Overton, a leading businessman who owned a cosmetics firm second only to Madame C. J. Walker's famous enterprise, branched out into banking, insurance, and publishing. He started the *Half-Century* magazine in 1916 and in 1925 converted it into the weekly *Bee*, which had a sizable readership for about two decades.[19]

Partly, the radicals and conservatives were drawn together by common foes. The wave of hostility toward blacks after World War I contributed to heightened race consciousness and unity. The middle-class factions also were drawn together as both felt threatened by the enormous lower-class population that arrived in the Great Migration of the war years. Nevertheless, the lower class provided a mass clientele for the businesses controlled by the middle class, including Overton's cosmetics firm and Abbott's *Defender*.

Moreover, the customs and outlooks of both factions were challenged by younger middle-class blacks reaching maturity on the urban scene, who by the 1920s were often called the New Negroes. The architects of wartime radicalism and artistic freedom in Harlem, the New Negroes brought an intensified racial consciousness and an increased acceptance of worldly pleasures into the ethos of urban middle-class life.[20] The New Negroes were highly visible in Chicago, although their interest in art and radicalism was slight compared with that of their Harlem counterparts. However, they constantly taunted their elders in a newspaper they started in 1919, the *Chicago Whip*.[21]

At first, older blacks were shocked by their children's behavior. As Edward Shils notes, in modernizing urban communities, middle-class youth and the lower class crossed the line between the "respectable" and "shady" worlds first by taking up worldly styles of life, with a carefree acceptance of pleasure, glamour, materialism, and hedonism. Older middle-class blacks made the leap later and more haltingly, but in the 1920s they too increasingly abandoned traditional attitudes and restraints to take up the carefree worldly *Zeitgeist* of the Jazz Age.[22] In the previous several years, however, newspapers and magazines on Chicago's South Side reflected considerable anxiety and debate about such new urban customs as cosmetics, fashion, and jazz music. The trend of modernization or secularization was evident in the churches, which tended to become clubs and social service agencies as they lifted old strictures against urban pleasures.[23] Thus the 1920s saw the culmination of the secularization started decades earlier by the Afro-American Agitators, although it had led in directions they never imagined or intended.

When the smoke cleared away after the radical-conservative skirmishes, the most significant development was the modernization of middle-class styles of life, with the development led by expanded urban populations. As both earlier observers and recent historians have noted, this was also true among Americans generally. After the Progressive hopes faded and postwar disenchantment set in, Americans beheld the modernized, secular, materialistic life-styles of the Jazz Age, which had supplanted the genteel life-styles of the nineteenth century.[24]

In the 1920s, the relatively prosperous middle class created an ostentatious, materialistic social world on Chicago's South Side — a prototype of others across the nation, and the cultural vortex in which were rising the habits and customs of modern consumerism. This development was crucial to the success of commercial papers such as the *Defender*, as readers became receptive to the consumer products advertised and to advice on their use from columnists. Moreover, in black publications as elsewhere, a major shift was the advance of "heroes of consumption" over "heroes of production."[25]

Themes and Imagery in the *Defender*

This section will present some major themes and imagery found in the *Defender* in the second and third decades of the century, although the volume and scope of the *Defender*'s coverage preclude a comprehensive analysis. In part, I will identify major recurring subjects and the treatment of them, as is commonly done in discussions of media content. I have long felt, however, that news media often engage their followings more by drawing them into ritualistic and dramatic action than by spreading information or "attitudes" (in the sense of opinions). Empirical social scientists have operationalized the term *attitude* as a verbalized opinion, and it has filtered into popular usage in that sense. In the earlier usage of the Chicago school of sociology, an attitude was a symbolic act, and communication was a process that engaged people in symbolic acts rather than one that spread facts or opinions.[26] Such later writers as Kenneth Burke and Orrin Klapp extended this approach.[27] In my view, it remains a powerful perspective for interpreting mass communication, and it underlies some of what follows.

The *Defender* reflected mass-appeal techniques, the middle-class outlook of the staff, and Abbott's ambivalent mix of sympathy and scorn for the masses of his race. In the second decade of the century, as the paper was refining the techniques of mass appeal, it simultaneously bore frequent signs of middle-class hostility to the lower class. The posture surfaced in attempts to inculcate middle-class deportment among the migrants. This material in the *Defender* was little different from the defense of middle-class customs in Bookerite publications such as the *Half-Century* and the *Bee*. Middle-class hostility to the migrants surfaced in front-page headlines such as "State Street a Breeding Spot for Evil" and "Influx of Southern Bullies Brings Disgrace to Chicago."

Signs of hostility to the lower class were less blatant in the 1920s. By this time, the *Defender* was brazenly appealing to lower-class readers with sordid front-page stories of crimes and love triangles. The shift was partly related to the greater acceptance of worldly pleasures and cultural diversity by middle-class blacks, but it also reflected the development of a stable alliance among the groups in the community. Secure in its dominance of community life, the middle class no longer felt threatened by other groups and a changing cultural milieu.

The *Defender* paid more attention than other papers to the activities of blacks outside middle-class circles. Abbott felt attached to the masses of his race, at least as an abstraction, although he despised lower-class customs. In news stories and in such columns as "Hotel News" and "In the Railroad Center," the *Defender* covered labor and service trades. It repeatedly supported the porters in their disputes with the Pullman Company.

The *Defender* also broadened the appeal of the previously staid middle-class press by adding its notorious sensational coverage of crimes and love triangles. Sensational coverage of local affairs began under Smiley, but reached new heights in the 1920s. The sensationalism, as well as advertisements for good-luck charms and patent medicines, aroused middle-class antipathy.

However distasteful to critics, sensationalism should not be dismissed as a perverse gimmick, motivated by crass commercial incentives and permitted by the low taste of a mass following. Such peremptory denunciations have forestalled interpretation of the ritualistic significance of the sensational material to readers. Crime, love triangles, conjugal instability, and other subjects of the *Defender*'s sensational stories were pervasive features of urban black life. The paper made dramatic rituals out of central events in personal and community experience and thereby contributed to a kind of "urban folklore." Representative titles of the love-scandal stories included " 'Greater Love' Leads Woman to Murder," "Kills Wife Because She Disobeyed," and "Beheads Wife in Love Quarrel."

The stories helped make lower-class urban life into a continuous and compelling drama, punctuated by excitement and tragedy. Music and jive talk contributed more than the press to a body of ritualistic expressions that sustained the dramatic representations, but the *Defender* played its part. The dramatic representations became symbolic of the feelings of persons caught up in lower-class urban rounds of life. The drama of love quarrels, marital breakups, and crime assumed the form of a pervasively felt presence, experienced by blacks as some personified force.

Another form of "modern folklore" that surfaced in the *Defender* was a realm of public figures — "symbolic leaders," as Orrin Klapp called them. They are the ephemeral contemporary equivalents of the more durable folk heroes of traditional societies. Among the symbolic leaders celebrated in the *Defender*, numerous types could be sorted out. They would include revered "race heroes," such as the famous surgeon Daniel Hale Williams. Somewhat less sanctified were the leaders of race businesses, such as Madame C. J. Walker. Distinguishable from "race heroes" were "race men," such as politician Oscar DePriest. Dauntless fighters for the race, they frequently gained stature through bold displays of defiance toward powerful whites. The worlds of sports and entertainment also supplied a growing covey of celebrities.

The most publicized celebrity in the early *Defender* was Jack Johnson, heavyweight boxing champion, who aroused fervid white animosity. The *Defender* made front-page stories out of Johnson's everyday activities, but publicized more heavily his fights, his persecution by whites, his trial for violation of the Mann Act, and his marital affairs. Cartoons depicted him as a symbol of the race, opposed by white prejudice.

Many middle-class blacks disliked Johnson, although perhaps ambivalently. As a symbol of race manhood, he probably kindled widespread sparks of at least grudging admiration. Upon the death of Adam Clayton Powell, *Ebony* said in an editorial that whites failed to understand his import as a symbol of race manhood to blacks, even to those who disapproved of his habits.[28] To some extent, probably, white contempt for such symbols of race manhood contributes to their appeal to blacks. Nevertheless, Johnson was preeminently the hero of the lower class.

Johnson represented a nascent urban lower-class type who flaunted fearlessness and a vicious style of masculinity. William Wiggins argues that Johnson personified the "bad nigger" — the stereotype in

southern folk tradition of the black man so enraged by white persecution that he lashes out brutally and hopelessly at whites. Johnson
and the "bad nigger" shared the traits of sexual virility, wanton ex-
travagance, hedonism, and a fearlessness of death and the white
man, Wiggins points out.[29] There are obvious similarities between the
"bad nigger" and not only Johnson, but numerous heroes raised in
the urban milieu. However, surrounded by such appurtenances as
fast women and fast cars, Johnson personified as well a distinctively
urban symbolic type.

In spite of critics' frequent attention to its sensationalism, the early
Defender was most remembered as the ardent champion of the race.
The paper kept the problem of interracial affairs alive in the minds of
blacks. This is not to say that the problem would not exist without
publicity, or that indignities and injustices would not be felt and resented. Rather, out of a welter of disconnected injustices, the *Defender*
created a unified, vivid, and continuous drama and kept it at the core
of the feelings of blacks.

The *Defender* bolstered a race-conscious outlook in many ways. The
front page frequently heralded black Achievements in government,
business, and elsewhere. The first black to attain any distinction
scored a victory for the race as well as himself. Regular front-page
cartoons pitted the suffering race against its white oppressor. In one
cartoon, Christ looked down on a lynching party under the caption
"Easter Morn in America." In "The New Year Dinner," Uncle Sam
carved a turkey and served helpings to other groups, but overlooked
blacks. The caption said, "Someone Overlooked — As Usual."

Sometimes the *Defender* made a *cause célèbre* for many weeks out of
a case regarded by blacks as unjust persecution of an individual because of his color. Such was the case of "Chicken Joe" Campbell, a
trusty at Joliet Prison, who was sentenced to death as a result of a fire
in which the warden's wife died. Saying that his guilt remained un-
proved, the *Defender* carried a cartoon in which a blindfolded detec-
tive selected the murderer from a row of men. The paper sometimes
made the persecution of an individual into a cause for itself and the
race, urging readers to write letters of protest or to send contributions
for legal or other assistance.

The *Defender* adopted the role of community watchdog and cru-
saded against the mistreatment of groups in the community. In 1912,
the paper investigated and denounced insurance collectors who were
insolent to black clients. In the same year, it took up the cause of

black hotel waiters, who were forced to eat in unclean basements. Occasionally, the *Defender* launched crusades against local white merchants.

The major recurrent drama in the life of the race was the continual appearance of Jim Crow. The *Defender*'s front page carried accounts of discrimination in restaurants, theaters, transportation, schools, employment, and even cemeteries. The paper counseled vocal protest and legal action under the state's equal-rights law, and it scorned the submissiveness of people who preferred to avoid the embarrassment of hostile encounters. Thus, it dramatized and encouraged a self-confident posture. It brought to far wider sectors of the black population the symbolism of assertive, forward-looking styles of life created by successive middle-class groups.

The racial perspective surfaced baldly in the selection of political news and editorials. Normally the paper reported only political developments that had a perceived impact on the race, and it judged politicians solely on the basis of their favorableness to the race. The paper promoted efforts to elect blacks as well as black representation on government bodies. Much attention went to Edward H. Wright's unsuccessful runs for alderman in 1910 and 1912 — early signs of mounting political ambitions. Considerable coverage also went to the performance as race watchdogs by candidates who were successful.

Abbott was impressed by Progressive Charles Deneen's stands for the race and, consequently, was hesitant to side with the opposing Republican "machine" candidate when "Big Bill" Thompson entered his first mayoral race in 1915. But the *Defender* enthusiastically joined the Thompson groundswell when "Big Bill" loudly opposed the showing of *The Birth of a Nation*. The film, which casts blacks in a derogatory light, sparked widespread hostility among blacks in northern cities, and the *Defender* publicized efforts to ban it across the country.

Thompson's gestures in defense of blacks, as well as appointments and assists to black politicians, made him an unparalleled hero to the *Defender*, as he was to most of the black community. In office, he developed durable symbolic appeals to blacks, which added to the obvious value of his frequent public praise of the race. In his later terms, whites often blamed blacks for putting him in office. These cries brought delight to the *Defender*, for they lent credence to the notion that blacks held the balance of political power. Thompson also acquired the aura of the little man who stood up to privileged interests.

The *Defender* applied the same racial perspective in its surveillance of the federal government. It presented a steady parade of official villains held responsible for slights to the race. The paper kept up a never-ending war on discrimination in employment and promotions in government departments and the armed services.

Central in the mythos of the race was the image of the South as a hell on earth. The *Defender* attacked southern politicians, peonage, and the Ku Klux Klan, but paid its greatest attention to lynchings. Dewey Jones, a former staff member, claimed the paper had a policy on the content of lynching stories regardless of the facts.[30] The southern atrocity stories carried such headlines as "Man Brutally Murdered: Georgia Man Lynched by Drunken Brutes" and "Family Driven from South by Mob: 'Armenia' Outdone by White Cannibals in Paris, Texas."

Showing an intense political consciousness, black papers tended to focus on events, such as lynchings, that could be construed as political issues for which political remedies could be sought. Pleas for remedies became "secular prayers," in Kenneth Burke's sense, in a political religion of the race. The *Defender* publicized and supported a federal antilynching bill throughout the 1920s.

The *Defender*'s most famous campaign was the effort to spur southern peasants northward in the wartime migration. To southern blacks brought up on Old Testament tales, the move assumed the mythic form of the flight from Egypt to the Promised Land. The *Defender* arranged group excursions to Chicago. For several years, it constantly tempted blacks to forsake the backwardness and injustice of the southern hellfire for the manhood and prosperity of the North. Scholars generally have regarded the primary cause of the migration as economic. However, standing behind the economic incentive was a far-reaching cultural transformation of the former slave population. The *Defender* did not cause this development, although the paper contributed to it. The *Defender* stepped into a cultural milieu receptive to new cultural orientations and to the drama of nationwide racial experience, with northern meccas such as Chicago the centers of race progress.

Southerners who turned to the *Defender*, those who stayed home as well as those who came North, gropingly entered a new orbit of collective life. They adopted the identity of membership in a self-conscious nationwide group as they embraced outlooks and sentiments rooted in the mythos of the race. This development paralleled the psychic transformation of immigrants who came to America.[31]

To Abbott and his staff, the migration symbolized the entry of the race into the world of modernity. The *Defender* reveled in such developments as the adoption by blacks of psychic mobility and an assertive, forward-looking personality, freed from the lethargy of passivity and the fetters of tradition. The paper declared that "the members of the Race have the manhood to make an effort to go north." A cartoon revealed that the paper saw in the migration not only a movement, but an "awakening."

The *Defender* did not originate these sentiments. They appeared often in the writings of the Afro-American Agitators in the 1880s and 1890s, but the *Defender* spread them far more widely and in a style that appealed to far larger numbers. The cultural movements of Afro-American Agitators, Bookerites, and other middle-class groups were collective enterprises in self-definition, accompanied by a vehement sloughing off of tradition. As the styles spread, increasing numbers of blacks haltingly tasted attitudes and outlooks of modernity. As early as the turn of the century, the new styles were sufficiently visible to bring occasional observations that a "New Negro" had appeared. By the postwar period, the visibility of the new styles and the number of people influenced by them had increased greatly. These developments were not peculiar to blacks, who merely exemplified the modernization of American life and culture in the Progressive era.

During the migration, the United States entered the war. By mid-1914 the *Defender* advocated U.S. entry, after opposing it briefly. The paper promoted patriotism in spite of racial grievances and supported bond drives. It constantly hammered at racial injustice during the war and demanded black rights in return for the race's show of patriotism.

Like other black journals, the *Defender* felt omens of government surveillance during the war, as black papers did again during World War II. The government watched more closely the handful of radical publications from Harlem's New Negroes. Recently, some journalists and journalism scholars have again taken these cases as examples of massive government efforts to suppress freedom of the press.[32] A more apt reaction probably is that the government's actions were merely ludicrous. The radical publications had tiny readerships and minuscule influence. Mainstream papers such as the *Defender* were staunch proponents of American ideals and called only for their realization for blacks.

The *Defender* devoted much attention to black participants in the war, especially the Eighth Regiment of the Illinois National Guard, the pride of Chicago's black community. The paper gave the unit a lavish ovation when it returned from the European campaign. The *Defender* carried many editorials on the war, discussing discrimination in the services, the patriotic duty of blacks to support the war, the insistence of blacks on justice at home after the conflict, and worldwide affairs brought to the attention of blacks by the conflict. Greatly increased attention to racial strife on the world scene developed during the war and continued after it. Long before, small coteries of blacks had glorified the potential impact of nonwhite nations on world affairs, but the posture spread to far larger numbers during the war.

Hostility between the races mounted in Chicago during the war. With the migration came a swift rise in the frequency and bitterness of interracial disputes over housing, labor, and other matters. The migration brought intense pressure to expand the "black belt" as blacks tried to move into white neighborhoods, and the *Defender* assailed white resistance. The influx of tens of thousands of blacks touched off scurrilous attacks from associations of white property owners and inflammatory accounts in daily newspapers. The *Defender* assailed whites on many fronts as racial friction mounted on streetcars, beaches, and elsewhere.

On July 27, 1919, the seething animosity exploded in a race riot, that lasted five days and left 38 people dead, 537 injured, and 1,000 homeless. The *Defender* denounced the rioters of both races and distributed an extra issue urging restraint by blacks. But the paper took some pride in attributing the riot partly to the manhood of blacks who irritated whites by refusing to submit to outrages and discrimination. The riot probably contributed to a trend already under way, as middle-class blacks placed greater emphasis on race manhood and self-reliance.

The prewar fabric of institutions and community life had expanded enormously by the 1920s. With this development, as well as the riot, middle-class blacks became more involved in community life. In 1920, blacks operated 1,500 business firms in Chicago, of which 651 were near the community center on State Street. Abbott was a director of Jesse Binga's bank, in which 1,100 people deposited $200,000 on opening day. These developments marked the triumph of Bookerite society, which now incorporated the previously antagonistic middle-class factions. The now-common middle-class spirit drew added strength from the black response to the riot and from economic prosperity and political gains in the twenties.

With its mass following, costly plant, and fat editions filled with advertising, the *Defender* stood at the forefront of the commercial black press. Its success signaled the triumph of commercial papers over those for which profit was a minor or nonexistent consideration. The paper carried news gathering to heights previously undreamed of, as it brought the new commodity of race news to large local and national followings.

The *Defender*'s success depended crucially upon the cultural reorientation of middle-class life in urban centers, while in turn the paper became a major stage for the celebration of the proud, optimistic social world that arose with the cultural shift. Front pages carried photographs of well-dressed, light-skinned young women. Such features signaled the triumph of a middle-class style of life that was forward-looking, materialistic, and race proud. Middle-class blacks increasingly found identities and outlooks not in the shattered moral absolutes and fixed character ideals of a bygone age, but in the parade of celebrities, dramatic events, and changing fashions of urban life.

Epilogue: Later Developments in the Black Press

The circulation of the *Defender* and the other national weeklies declined during the Great Depression, then surged upward again in the 1940s. As in the World War I years, black papers led a mounting spirit of racial consciousness and assertiveness, again calling for justice at home in return for black support of the war.[33] Yet severe and lasting drops in circulation were just over the horizon. What happened was not, as some observers predicted in the 1950s and 1960s, that the black press died as blacks assimilated into white society and abandoned race consciousness in the wake of the civil rights movement.

Instead, after conflicting signals in another period of cultural turmoil, a huge new middle class had become readers of an increasing array of black consumer magazines. The gradual displacement of national newspapers by commercial magazines began after World War II, but was clouded by the brief skyrocketing of such militant organs as *Muhammad Speaks* and the *Black Panther* in the tumultuous 1960s. The distraction of "radical chic" in the 1960s was as irrelevant to long-run trends as the radical-conservative feud was in the Progressive years.

Blacks frequently started commercial magazines from late in the nineteenth century through the 1930s, although the ventures usually were short-lived. At least thirty-five black magazines appeared in Chicago before the Depression. Robert Abbott contemplated starting a magazine in the mid-1920s and brought out *Abbott's Monthly* in 1929, but it died in the Depression. The magazines published by organizations such as fraternal orders may have gained large circulations and lasted for long periods, but none of the commercial magazines was notably successful. Before the triumph of commercial papers, the newspapers with the largest circulations were the organs of organizations such as churches and lodges. Similarly, the magazines with the largest national followings before World War II were the organs of organizations, the NAACP's *Crisis* and the Urban League's *Opportunity*.

Anthony Overton, who started the *Half-Century* in Chicago in 1916, was a staunch supporter of Booker T. Washington and traveled the country speaking in behalf of the Washington-controlled National Negro Business League. The *Half-Century* probably gained as large a readership as any commercial magazine in Chicago before *Ebony*. It is likely, however, that Overton subsidized it to promote the products and services of his other firms, especially High Brown cosmetics, which were featured in most of the ads. Over the decade in which the magazine appeared, the content reflected the shift from "heroes of production" to "heroes of consumption" documented in general magazines by Leo Lowenthal.[34] Overton personified the culture of production. Yet, his most successful enterprise manufactured cosmetics for the culture of consumption, and his magazine promulgated the styles of the new culture. The transition to the culture of consumption laid the foundation for the far greater success of black consumer magazines after the Great Depression and World War II.

Overton was mentor to John H. Johnson as Johnson planned and built the publishing empire that included *Ebony*, *Jet*, and other magazines. Overton's grandson, Anthony Overton III, has said that Johnson was "quite thick" with his grandfather.[35] Starting in the 1940s, Johnson led the triumph of the commercial magazine from Chicago, as Abbott had catapulted the commercial newspaper to success in the city four decades earlier.

There are obvious similarities in the success stories of Abbott and Johnson, but both similarities and differences in their publications. Both men came from the South, Johnson arriving with his mother for the Chicago World's Fair in 1933. Both started with little money,

Johnson mortgaging his mother's furniture for $500 to start *Negro Digest* in 1942. Both were better businessmen than journalists. Johnson's biggest money-maker, *Ebony*, started in 1945, reached a circulation unprecedented for black magazines only after Johnson hired journalists more skilled than he was at employing mass-appeal techniques. *Ebony*'s circulation passed a million in 1967, and advertising revenue was $7 million that year. Like the *Defender*'s J. Hockley Smiley, Johnson and his staff copied features of white publications. *Negro Digest* was patterned after *Reader's Digest*, *Ebony* after *Life*, and *Jet* after the white weekly news digests of the time.[36]

Like Abbott's *Defender*, Johnson's operation catered to both the lower class and the middle class, but with different publications. *Tan*, a confession magazine, cultivated lower-class readers, while middle-class blacks flocked to *Negro Digest*, *Ebony*, and *Jet*. The *Defender* stood astride an uneasy alliance in catering to both the lower class and the middle class, for content aimed at the lower class offended middle-class readers. Many middle-class blacks found publications more in step with their sensibilities when they shifted from national weeklies such as the *Defender* to consumer magazines such as *Ebony* after World War II, although some readers wrangled about such things as liquor and cigarette ads.

In addition, the liberals of the 1950s and the radicals of the 1960s complained about *Ebony*'s conservative or "bourgeois" slant. Middle-class blacks had long charged that the sensational content of the weeklies demeaned the public image of the race and called on the papers to accentuate the positive side of black life. Like Overton's publications, *Ebony* did just that, perhaps to an absurd degree, as the liberals and radicals charged, and as Paul Hirsch has shown in a content study.[37]

Sociology texts of a generation ago commonly proclaimed Chicago the most segregated city in the country, with blacks fenced into a compact black belt stretching from Eighteenth Street to Sixty-Third Street on the South Side. There, middle-class blacks lived in close proximity to the lower class. Since their start in the 1870s, the city's black papers often carried complaints from middle-class blacks about the difficulty of rearing children in such an environment. Frazier identified seven distinctive zones within the black belt that reflected progressively higher status as one moved southward.[38] Abbott's *Defender* enjoyed its heyday in that world, and the middle-class aversion to content aimed at the lower class reflected the same status battle as the middle-class moral wars to control public life in the spatial zones.

Equally evident in some readers' complaints about the paper were status struggles between and among middle-class factions, such as the antipathy of traditionalists to stories about new urban entertainment.

The well-known ecological studies of the Chicago school of sociology showed how the entire city was divided into zones reflecting tensions among status groups. Similarly, later sociologists and political scientists of the "status politics" school showed how battles over laws and government policies often expressed conflicts over the legitimacy of the habits and customs of the contending groups, as well as conflicts over their respective tangible interests.[39] As I have argued elsewhere, public debates about media content often reflect similar status conflicts over rival sensibilities about contested customs.[40]

After World War II, in Chicago and other cities, middle-class blacks increasingly fled from the compact inner-city ghettos, usually to new residential areas, also segregated but exclusively middle class, miles from the city center. They put enough distance between themselves and the lower class that class conflict over such things as entertainment places subsided. Reader surveys as well as casual observation suggest that as blacks left inner-city ghettos, they often abandoned the black weeklies, which they associated with the ghettos they had escaped, and turned to the growing consumer magazines.

Controversies over the Johnson magazines reflected animosities between and among middle-class factions. Most conspicuous from Johnson's start through the mid-1960s was antipathy from black liberals, whose sensibilities and concerns were similar to those of postwar white liberals. Probably the most popular manifesto of the black liberals was Frazier's *Black Bourgeoisie*, published in 1957. *Ebony* receives considerable unflattering mention in the book, which charges that the black press "promulgates the bourgeois values of the make-believe world of the black bourgeoisie."[41] The liberals' criticism of *Ebony* and similar publications was overshadowed by attacks from black militants. For a time, Johnson tried to add the militants as a market by transforming *Negro Digest* into *Black World*, with articles by and for the militants. This trend had parallels in white magazines, for example, in the brief taking up of "radical chic" in *Time*. Many former liberals became known as "neoconservatives" when they decided that the new critical groups on the scene were worse threats than the "bourgeoisie" and middle-class culture they had formerly opposed.

Some of the enthusiasms of what I have called the "New Class" in previous writings were those formerly held but since discarded by neoconservatives.[42] In what Orrin Klapp has called the "style rebellions" of the late 1960s, broad segments of the middle class took up poses and trends popular in elite circles, mainly in the Northeast and at liberal universities, decades earlier.[43] Some of the New Class poses reflected middle-class take-ups of the enthusiasms of the New York circles described by Russell Lynes in 1950.[44] In *The Tastemakers*, Lynes shows how artistic styles popular with highbrows in one period were discarded by them but picked up by middlebrows later, subsequently to be discarded by them but picked up by lowbrows.[45] Apparently, the same taking up and discarding of fashions occurs in politics, journalism, ideas, and other realms.

Various parallels exist between the 1960s and 1970s and the Populist-Progressive years. The *Defender* and other papers were both platforms and targets for rival sects of prophets and critics in the Progressive era, including the black radicals and conservatives, as Johnson's publications and other media were in the later period. In both periods, prophets assumed that the eclipse of previous settled social worlds had made any imaginable future possible, and much public rhetoric in the media, including that of the black radicals and conservatives, reflected the imagined futures espoused by rival visionaries. Chicago was a major center for the expression of the Progressives' imagined futures. (I have analyzed some of the rhetoric of white as well as black liberals in the city in previous writings.)[46]

In his studies of "styles of life," Max Weber regarded the spirit or ethos, not content, as the essence of the meaning of customs and cultural artifacts. Talcott Parsons and other Americans often translated Weber's focus upon style or spirit into the typical American obsession with content or messages, as in so much discussion of the media by communications scholars and others alike. Not surprisingly, in studies of black leaders, scholars have often classified them according to the content of their imagined futures — such as the classification of black Progressives as radicals, who wanted assimilation into white society, or conservatives, who favored the development of a separate black society. The more striking fact, it seems to me, is the shared spirit of the prophets on both sides, who believed they could build new worlds through rhetoric. Moreover, historically, many black leaders have favored assimilation at one time and separate development at another.

Throughout U.S. history, many prophets regarded mass media as the requisite agents to build the futures they envisioned, or feared the power of media promulgating futures they opposed. The debates

of the 1960s and 1970s about the assumed positive or negative consequences of content in "the media" were paralleled in the Progressives' debates about "the press." Historically, many journalists have
regarded black media as pivotal agents, for good or ill, to shape the
future of "the race." Abbott and Johnson considered their publications to be needed agents to lead black advances. In a speech in 1987,
Johnson portrayed America as in a crisis stemming from the erosion
of communities, and he pointed to the media as the proper agencies
to create new communities.[47] The faith in media as instruments of
"change" continues unabated today in the campaigns to promote
"awareness" or "consciousness" of one thing or another.

On the whole, the outcome of the Progressives' debates has been
replicated since the debates of the 1960s and 1970s. All of the
Progressive-era prophets were partly wrong, and all of their imagined futures proved to be off the mark. Similarly, in 1987 *Ebony* ran a
special issue on "The New Black Middle Class."[48] But it was nothing
like what Johnson had in mind when he started his magazines to
advance his race.

Notes

1. This chapter incorporates revised portions of my previously unpublished
paper, "The Rise of Black Consumer Magazines: The Case of the *Half-Century*," (presented to the History Division, Association for Education in Journalism, Boston,
August 1980), and my doctoral dissertation, "The Making of Racial Identities in the
Black Press: A Cultural Analysis of Race Journalism in Chicago, 1878–1929," University of Illinois, 1973.

2. Robert E. Park, *The Immigrant Press and Its Control* (New York: Harper &
Brothers, 1922), 328 et passim.

3. *Chicago Defender*, August 6, 1955, 2B.

4. Ibid., 4B.

5. Roi Ottley, *The Lonely Warrior: The Life and Times of Robert S. Abbott* (Chicago:
Henry Regnery, 1955). Other accounts include Dewey Jones, "The Effect of the
Negro Press on Race Relationships in the South," master's thesis, Columbia Uni-
versity, 1932; Ralph Nelson Davis, "The Negro Newspaper in Chicago," master's
thesis, University of Chicago, 1939, 46–122; Metz T. P. Lochard, "Phylon Profile XII:
Robert S. Abbott—'Race Leader,' " *Phylon* 8 (1947): 124–32; Armistead S. Pride,
"Robert Sengstacke Abbott," in *Dictionary of American Biography*, vol. 22, suppl. 2,
ed. Robert Livingstone Schuyler (New York: Charles Scribner's Sons, 1958), 2–4;
Chicago Defender, 1905–1955, mim. (Chicago: Robert S. Abbott, c. 1955); Fay Young,
"People Who Helped Make Defender Great," *Chicago Defender*, August 6, 1955, 3A,
15A, 20A; "The Realization of a Dream; An Epic of Negro Business: The Story of
Abbott and the Chicago Defender," *Messenger* 5 (November 1923): 871–74.

6. Ottley, *The Lonely Warrior*, 139.

7. On Sweeney, see *Chicago Defender*, October 29, 1921, 1, 3; *Chicago Whip*, October 29, 1921, 1; *Who's Who of the Colored Race: A General Biographical Dictionary of Men and Women of African Descent* (Chicago, 1915), 257; Alan H. Spear, *Black Chicago: The Making of a Negro Ghetto, 1890–1920* (Chicago: University of Chicago Press, 1967), 80–81.

8. Albert Kreiling, "The Rise of the Black Press in Chicago," *Journalism History* 4 (Winter 1977–78): 132–36, 156; Albert Kreiling, "Ida B. Wells as Columnist: Pioneer of Modern Black Journalism" (paper presented to the National Council for Black Studies, Charlotte, N.C., February 29–March 4, 1984); Albert Kreiling, "Ida B. Wells' Appeal to International Opinion to Stop Southern Lynching" (paper presented to the Minorities and Qualitative Studies Divisions, Association for Education in Journalism and Mass Communication, Gainesville, Fla., August 1984); Kreiling, "The Making of Racial Identities," 101–225; Ida B. Wells, *Crusade for Justice: The Autobiography of Ida B. Wells*, ed. Alfreda M. Duster (Chicago: University of Chicago Press, 1970).

9. In this chapter, I use the term *style of life* in the sense in which Max Weber introduced it in sociological and historical scholarship. In Weber's usage, the term refers to the taken-for-granted ethos or framework of sensibilities and customs built and sustained by a group. It roughly corresponds to Raymond Williams's "structure of feeling"; Raymond Williams, *The Long Revolution*, rev. ed. (New York: Harper & Row, 1966), 48–71 et passim. Obviously, the term has nothing to do with the popular middle-class cliché, *life-style*, which seems to refer to a set of practices consciously chosen by an individual. Max Weber, *From Max Weber: Essays in Sociology*, ed. and trans. H. H. Gerth and C. Wright Mills (New York: Oxford University Press, 1946), 186–94 et passim. The most discussed study in which Weber employed the "style of life" concept is Max Weber, *The Protestant Ethic and the Spirit of Capitalism*, trans. Talcott Parsons (New York: Charles Scribner's Sons, 1958). As Hugh Duncan has argued, Parsons's flawed translation probably contributed to the American misinterpretation of Weber's work. See Hugh Dalziel Duncan, *Symbols and Social Theory* (New York: Oxford University Press, 1969), 32, 88, et passim.

10. St. Clair Drake and Horace R. Cayton, *Black Metropolis: A Study of Negro Life in a Northern City* (New York: Harcourt, Brace, 1945), 543 et passim; E. Franklin Frazier, *The Negro Family in the United States* (Chicago: University of Chicago Press, 1966), 295–96 et passim.

11. Fenton Johnson, "Chicago Negro Aristocrats," ms. in Illinois Writers Project, Chicago Public Library; E. Franklin Frazier, *On Race Relations: Selected Writings*, ed. G. Franklin Edwards (Chicago: University of Chicago Press, 1968), 205 et passim; Frazier, *The Negro Family*, 295–96; Edward A. Shils, *The Bases of Social Stratification in Negro Society*, Carnegie-Myrdal Study, 1940, ms. in Schomburg Collection, New York Public Library, 61–65.

12. For a detailed discussion of Barnett, the *Conservator*, and other papers and journalists in Chicago in the nineteenth century, see Kreiling, "The Rise of the Black Press."

13. This analysis of the imagery and outlook of early protesters in the Populist-Progressive years draws insight from John M. Dobson, *Politics in the Gilded Age* (New York: Praeger, 1972); Eric F. Goldman, *Rendezvous with Destiny: A History of Modern American Reform*, rev. ed. (New York: Random House, 1955); Samuel P. Hays, *The Response to Industrialism, 1885–1914* (Chicago: University of Chicago Press, 1957);

Richard Hofstadter, *The Age of Reform: From Bryan to F.D.R.* (New York: Random House, 1955); Robert H. Wiebe, *The Search for Order, 1877–1920* (New York: Hill & Wang, 1967).

14. Edward E. Wilson, "Negro Society in Chicago," *Voice*, July 1907, 307.

15. The fullest analysis of the programs of the two camps is presented in August Meier, *Negro Thought in America, 1889–1915* (Ann Arbor: University of Michigan Press, 1963).

16. I have developed this argument in "The Making of Racial Identities," 226–333. To one who had studied the rhetoric of the Progressive period, the debates of the 1970s had a familiar ring, as people proclaimed their commitment to one side or the other on a series of issues: educational testing, school busing, abortion, and so forth.

17. St. Clair Drake, *Churches and Voluntary Associations in the Chicago Negro Community*, mim. (Chicago: Works Progress Administration, 1940).

18. For example, Consuelo C. Young, "A Study of Reader Attitudes toward the Negro Press," *Journalism Quarterly* 21 (June 1944): 148–52.

19. On the *Half-Century* and the *Bee*, see Kreiling, "The Rise of Black Consumer Magazines" and "The Making of Racial Identities," 257–80.

20. Studies of the political and literary journalism of the New Negroes include Theodore Kornweibel, Jr., *No Crystal Stair: Black Life and the Messenger, 1917–1928* (Westport, Conn.: Greenwood, 1975); Theodore G. Vincent, ed., *Voices of a Black Nation: Political Journalism in the Harlem Renaissance* (San Francisco: Ramparts, 1973); Abby Arthur Johnson and Ronald Maberry Johnson, *Propaganda and Aesthetics: The Literary Politics of Afro-American Magazines in the Twentieth Century* (Amherst: University of Massachusetts Press, 1979).

21. On the *Whip*, see Kreiling, "The Making of Racial Identities," 393–421.

22. Shils, *The Bases of Social Stratification*, 61–65.

23. On the secularization of the urban black church, see E. Franklin Frazier, *The Negro Church in America* (New York: Schocken, 1963).

24. Frederick Lewis Allen, *Only Yesterday* (New York: Harper & Brothers, 1931); William E. Leuchtenberg, *The Perils of Prosperity, 1914–32* (Chicago: University of Chicago Press, 1958); Samuel P. Hays, "The Social Analysis of American Political History, 1880–1920," *Political Science Quarterly* 80 (September 1965): 373–94; David M. Kennedy, "Overview: The Progressive Era," *Historian* 37 (May 1975): 453–68; William L. O'Neill, *The Progressive Years* (New York: Dodd, Mead, 1975); Robert H. Wiebe, "The Progressive Years, 1900–1917," in *The Reinterpretation of American History and Culture*, ed. William H. Cartwright and Richard L. Watson, Jr. (Washington, D.C.: National Council of Social Studies, 1973), 425–42.

25. Leo Lowenthal, "The Triumph of Mass Idols," in *Literature, Popular Culture, and Society* (Englewood Cliffs, N.J.: Prentice-Hall, 1961), 109–36.

26. Examples of the Chicago school perspective include George H. Mead, *Mind, Self, and Society: From the Standpoint of a Social Behaviorist*, ed. Charles W. Morris (Chicago: University of Chicago Press, 1934); W. I. Thomas, *On Social Organization and Social Personality: Selected Papers*, ed. Morris Janowitz (Chicago: University of Chicago Press, 1966); Robert Ezra Park, *Society: Collective Behavior, News and Opinion, Sociology and Modern Society*, ed. Everett Cherrington Hughes et al. (Glencoe, Ill.: Free Press, 1955); James F. Short, Jr., ed., *The Social Fabric of the Metropolis: Contributions of the Chicago School of Urban Sociology* (Chicago: University of Chicago

Press, 1971); Jerome G. Manis and Bernard N. Meltzer, eds., *Symbolic Interaction: A Reader in Social Psychology* (Boston: Allyn & Bacon, 1967); Herbert Blumer, *Symbolic Interactionism: Perspective and Method* (Englewood Cliffs, N.J.: Prentice-Hall, 1969); Anselm L. Strauss, *Mirrors and Masks: The Search for Identity* (Glencoe, Ill.: Free Press, 1959).

27. For example, Kenneth Burke, *Language as Symbolic Action: Essays on Life, Literature, and Method* (Berkeley: University of California Press, 1968); Orrin E. Klapp, *Symbolic Leaders: Public Dramas and Public Men* (Chicago: Aldine, 1964).

28. "Ebony Photo-Editorial: Adam Lives," *Ebony*, June 1972, 150.

29. William H. Wiggins, Jr., "Jack Johnson as Bad Nigger: The Folklore of His Life," *Black Scholar* 2 (January 1971): 35–46.

30. Jones, "The Effect of the Negro Press," 34.

31. As W. I. Thomas observed:

> Polish peasant communities, before 1860, lived as practically self-sufficient groups. They knew by report that there was a great world, and they had some relations with it. . . . But practically the extent of their world was the "okolica," "the neighborhood round about," and their definition of this was, "as far as a man is talked about." . . . The peasant did not know he was a Pole; he even denied it. The lord was a Pole; he was a peasant. We have records showing that members of other immigrant groups realize first in America that they are members of a nationality. (Robert E. Park and Herbert A. Miller, *Old World Traits Transplanted* (New York: Harper & Brothers, 1925), 145–46).

The above-cited book was published under the names of Park and Miller, but it was widely believed that the principal author was Thomas, who had difficulty securing a publisher after his forced departure from the University of Chicago in the wake of a scandal.

32. For example, see Kornweibel, *No Crystal Stair*, 77–80; Vincent, *Voices of a Black Nation*, 33–34.

33. Lee Finkle, *Forum for Protest: The Black Press During World War II* (Cranbury, N.J.: Associated University Presses, 1975).

34. Lowenthal, "The Triumph of Mass Idols."

35. Interview with Overton's grandson, Anthony Overton III.

36. On Johnson and his publications, see Walter Goodman, "Ebony: Biggest Negro Magazine," *Dissent* 15 (September–October 1968): 403–9; A. James Reichley, "How John Johnson Made It," *Fortune*, January 1968, 152–53, 178, 180; " 'Failure Is a Word I Don't Accept': An Interview with John H. Johnson," *Harvard Business Review* 54 (March–April 1976): 79–88; Walter Morrison, "Ebony: 30 Years of Heritage," *Chicago Daily News*, October 30, 1975, 5, 6; Roland E. Wolseley, *The Black Press, U.S.A.* (Ames: Iowa State University Press, 1971), 61–65 et passim.

37. Paul M. Hirsch, "An Analysis of Ebony: The Magazine and Its Readers," *Journalism Quarterly* 45 (Summer 1968): 261–92.

38. E. Franklin Frazier, *The Negro Family in Chicago* (Chicago: University of Chicago Press, 1932).

39. For example, Joseph Gusfield, *Symbolic Crusade: Status Politics and the American Temperance Movement* (Urbana: University of Illinois Press, 1963).

40. Albert Kreiling, "Toward a Sociological Approach for the Sociology of Pop-

ular Culture," *Communication Research* 5 (July 1978): 240–63; Albert Kreiling, "Television in American Ideological Hopes and Fears," in *Interpreting Television: Current Research Perspectives*, ed. Willard D. Rowland, Jr., and Bruce Watkins (Beverly Hills: Sage, 1984), 39–57.

41. E. Franklin Frazier, *Black Bourgeoisie* (New York: Free Press, 1957), 179.

42. Albert Kreiling, "Communication and the New Class" (paper presented to the Qualitative Studies Division, Association for Education in Journalism and Mass Communication, Memphis State University, August 1985); Albert Kreiling and James E. Swartz, "Ethics and Other New Class Fads in Historical Perspective" (paper presented to the Qualitative Studies Division, Association for Education in Journalism and Mass Communication, University of Oklahoma, Norman, August 1986).

43. Orrin E. Klapp, *Collective Search for Identity* (New York: Holt, Rinehart & Winston, 1969).

44. Russell Lynes, *Snobs* (New York: Harper, 1950).

45. Russell Lynes, *The Tastemakers* (New York: Harper & Brothers, 1949).

46. Albert Kreiling, "The Chicago School and Community," *Critical Studies in Mass Communication* 6 (September 1989): 317–21; Albert Kreiling and Norman Sims, "Symbolic Interactionism, Progressive Thought, and Chicago Journalism," in *Foundations for Communication Studies*, ed. John Soloski (Iowa City: Center for Communication Study, School of Journalism and Mass Communication, University of Iowa, 1981).

47. John H. Johnson, "The Crisis: Community and Communication," *University of Chicago Magazine*, Autumn 1974, 23–24.

48. *Ebony*, August 1987.

Chapter 9

Heads of Household and Ladies of the House: Gender, Genre, and Broadcast Ratings, 1929–1990

Eileen R. Meehan

In 1928, advertisers, national radio networks, program producers, and ratings firms divided the adult audience for broadcasting into two categories: heads of household and ladies of the house. The former category comprised male wage earners whose productive labor allowed the latter category to stay home as unpaid (hence, in capitalist terms, unproductive)[1] housekeepers, baby sitters, nannies, and domestic purchasing agents. Based on this division of labor, the broadcasting industry developed its own forms of industry wisdom and traditional practices.[2]

In this essay I will examine the political economy of ratings in order to add to our understanding of the business practice of categorizing people as ladies or heads or working women, as well as the programming practice of selecting genres for genders and discriminating by parts of the day. I will analyze how the audience figures in the trans-industrial market where ratings firms sell to advertisers, networks, and program producers the documents that define, describe, and measure the audience. At stake are the definitions of *audience, women's concerns, men's genres, children's television,* and similar terms that imply our personal and collective responsibility for the content of broadcasting.

The historical context and corporate struggles transformed wireless into radio and the listening audience into the commodity audience. In that context and those structures are rooted the modern structure of television, whether broadcast or cable. I begin by tracing the history of the ratings industry, with particular attention to the effects of demand on methodology and definitions of demographics. Next, I will contextualize the ratings industry within the larger trans-industrial structure of broadcasting, which is organized around two levels of activity. Finally, I will consider changes in the consumerist caste, the emergence of the "working woman" as a ratings category, and the relationship between industrial culture and popular culture.

From Audience to Commodity Audience

The modern structure of the broadcasting industry emerged in the period directly after World War I and was consolidated by 1928. National networks comprised local radio stations interconnected by AT&T and earned revenues through the sale of time slots to advertisers, which had designed programs in an attempt to influence the purchasing habits of the audience.[3] The business of broadcasting had apparently become the business of selling time to advertisers.

If advertisers were really buying time, however, one would expect that the cost of any particular time slot should be the same, regardless of daypart. That is, fifteen minutes on Sunday at 7:00 p.m. should cost the same as fifteen minutes on Monday at noon or Tuesday at midnight or Wednesday at 5:30 a.m. However, each of these time slots had a different price. Clearly, advertisers were not buying time, but rather access to an audience. And advertisers did not want to pay for just anybody who happened to tune in; they targeted the consumerist caste,[4] which was but one part of the vast listening public.[5] Thus, toll broadcasting earned its revenues from an invisible commodity, as the consumerist caste became the commodity audience.

Advertisers had to be convinced that the size and quality of broadcasting's product — the commodity audience — were sufficient to balance the costs of programming and the costs of access over the network. Both NBC and CBS produced materials designed to assure advertisers that the networks attracted huge audiences of dedicated consumers: Mrs. Consumer listened to the programs of soap manufacturers during the day, Mr. Consumer took control of the radio set at night, and the little Consumers sat glued to the set from after school to bedtime.[6] Advertisers distrusted these "studies" as self-serving, since NBC and CBS also based their prices on these reassuring measurements of consumerist audiences.[7] Yet advertisers needed information about demographics to select the proper times for their commercial-length programs and to evaluate the efficiency of those programs to reach the right audiences. Advertisers also needed information on the sizes of the targeted audiences, to evaluate the prices charged by networks.

In 1928, the Association of National Advertisers (ANA) hired Archibald Crossley to design a measurement technique that would provide advertisers with their own proprietorial information about audience quality and quantity.[8] A year later, Crossley unveiled his method: telephone interviews soliciting respondents' reports on what shows with which sponsors they listened to yesterday. The ANA embraced this approach, creating a subsidiary organization, the Cooperative Analysis of Broadcasting (CAB), to produce audience measurements for circulation only among advertisers. By 1930, CAB provided its ANA subscribers with ratings that showed radio programs drew a high-quality, low-quantity audience.

Crossley's method favored advertisers' interests. First, it relied on telephone interviews to inquire about radio use. By 1929, radio was well on its way to becoming a ubiquitous feature of American life: 13 million radio sets had been sold.[9] With penetration rates of more than 50 percent in households and radios situated in many public places (diners, soup kitchens, department stores, taverns, and so on), radio's status as a mass medium was undisputed. While anybody might have a radio or have consistent access to radio broadcasts, however, residential telephones remained rather a luxury. Although 41 percent of the private homes in the United States subscribed, being listed in the telephone book was still a mark of social status. During the Great Depression, households often cut back on luxuries; between 1929 and 1931, residential telephone subscriptions fell 10 percent. In contrast, radio presented no subscription costs; while radio homes might lack telephony, telephone homes were likely to have radios. In this way, Crossley sampled not radio homes, but telephone homes that had radios. To be included in the sampled radio audience, a household had to have sufficient income to afford monthly telephone charges, had to desire the social status signaled by a telephone listing, and had to live in an area deemed sufficiently profitable for AT&T to provide service. In short, Crossley's method ensured that he counted only the consumerist caste.

But if CAB was guaranteed high-quality audience by Crossley's telephone sample, it also was guaranteed low-quantity audience by Crossley's questions. In 1929, most radio programs ran fifteen minutes; asking someone to recall an entire day's listening was certainly an imposition. More important, the imposition was targeted at a social stratum that valued the symbols of middle-class status at a time when the middle-class code of conduct emphasized indirection and politeness as ways to avoid conflict and maintain face. Confronted by an unreasonable imposition, one might correctly extract oneself by deploying the social lie. Asked to remember twenty-four hours of programming for a perfect stranger on the telephone, one could easily escape the unpleasantness by suddenly "remembering" that one had not listened yesterday. Crossley could not separate true reports of no listening from white lies about not listening.

Unsurprisingly, Crossley and CAB "found" that radio audiences were indeed small. Further, households that either could afford luxuries such as the telephone or were unwilling to lose the social status associated with telephone subscription might also have been able to finance the middle-class ideal of the "unproductive" wife. Calls, then, could be timed to reach the particular gender targeted by the particular daypart. Measuring Mrs. Consumer would mean daytime calls; measuring Mr. Consumer would require evening calls and specific requests to speak with the head of the household.[10] In any case, Crossley's methodology produced ratings that defined the audience as the consumerist caste while delivering estimates of audience size that suited advertisers' vested interest in lowering networks' prices.

High Quality, High Quantity

As networks sought some way to counter the CAB ratings, the C. E. Hooper Company (CEH) was designing a methodology that would be attractive to *both* advertisers and networks. When Hooper began to consider challenging the CAB in 1930, that task must have seemed almost impossible. How could one resolve the contradictory demands of advertisers for low quantity and of networks for high quantity? How could one persuade advertisers to buy ratings from an independent firm when their own ANA ran a ratings operation? Yet, by 1932, CEH had developed a strategy based on measurement technique and on the syndication of ratings reports that would secure a monopoly over ratings production for CEH by 1936.

With telephone subscription dropping in the early 1930s, a sample based on telephone subscribers was an even better guarantee that radio listeners in such households would have sufficient disposable income and desire to qualify as bona fide consumers. Those in such a sample also were more likely to maintain the middle-class ideal of housebound wives and day-working husbands, thus satisfying advertisers' demand for women during the day and for men at night. CEH — like CAB — used telephone directories as the basis for its audience measurements. To CAB's design, however, CEH added the fillip of using urban directories, thus ensuring that the sample would have easy access to national brands through large retailers in cities and suburbs. During the Depression, middle-class folks in small-town and rural America simply were less desirable as members of the audience. They might maintain their telephones, consumerist ideology, and disposable income, but their access to national brands was through mom-and-pop retailers or mail-order catalogues. During the Depression, the constriction of national distribution to rural areas further decreased the attractiveness of these middle-class populations. This slight narrowing of the sample promised a higher-quality audience than that measured by CAB.

A more significant departure from CAB's approach was incorporated into CEH's telephone interview. Called the "telephone coincidental," this interview was a model of efficiency and ease. Respondents were asked if the radio was on when the telephone rang. A positive answer triggered a simple request for the name of the program and the sponsor. This was followed up by soliciting the demographics of the respondent and any other listeners. Finally, the respondent was queried about the fifteen minutes prior to the telephone call. This produced information about listening immediately before, and coincidental to, the telephone call. The task required little effort, but it yielded important results: suddenly, radio audiences were gigantic.[11] Thus, CEH could offer an increase in audience quantity to networks and significantly more accurate information about the listening habits and availabilies of the consumerist caste for advertisers. This improved information was but one element designed by CEH to offset the higher prices that networks would demand, given higher quantity of audience. The second element was CEH's decreasing costs of audience measures for advertisers. Because CAB's ratings were circulated only to subscribing advertisers, those sponsors paid all of CAB's operational costs through the price of their subscriptions. In contrast, CEH offered its reports to any firm that could pay the price. Termed "syndicated" ratings, these reports were sold to all comers, including advertisers, networks, program producers, and stations. This allowed CEH to spread its costs of operation over considerably more purchasers, hence lowering the cost per purchaser on any ratings report.

Consumerist Caste versus Listening Public

From 1936 to 1942, CEH's monopolization of ratings suggests that the company's strategy for measuring high-quality consumers, who replicated the idealized middle-class division of labor by gender, was successful. The C. E. Hooper Company monopolized the most profitable niche in the ratings industry — the production of ratings for national advertising over radio networks. This position also gave CEH an edge in the production of ratings for local markets.

During this period, radio's listening public clearly was larger and more diverse than the commodity audience reported in the ratings.[12] Then as now, the listening public included households where men were unemployed or absent, where the primary wage earners were women or children. Then as now, some people rejected consumerism in favor of self-sufficiency; others embraced the ideology of consumption but lacked either the money or the access to enact it. Then as now, U.S. culture comprised multiple heritages; society was divided along lines of gender, class, race, ethnicity, religion, and sexual orientation. This diversity, however, was not reflected in the ratings.

Rather, as commodities themselves, the ratings were constructed in response to market pressures, including competition and monopolization as well as continuities and discontinuities in demand. The ratings producer was no scientist motivated by curiosity, but rather a company seeking its self-interest through the profitable manipulation of demand. By targeting the consumerist caste, the new broadcasting industry adopted the ideals of that caste as an operational definition of internal divisions in the commodity audience: the employed male as head of household, the unpaid wife as lady of the house, and their requisite children. In this way, ideology and economics interpenetrated to "naturalize" both the consumerist ideal of domestic division of labor and the artificial market definition of the "real" audience for radio.

This raises questions about the appropriate use of language in discussions of industrialized popular culture. To whom does a genre belong? Scholars of popular culture generally have divided genres by gender, speaking of womens' genres, men's genres, even juvenile genres.[13] The use of the possessive suggested that the particular gender was intimately linked to the particular genre. From that perspective, one could interpret audience research or sales figures as feedback mechanisms for industrialized popular culture. If many women found pleasure in radio soap operas, then the soap operas earned high ratings; this encouraged soap manufacturers to produce soap operas that connected strongly to women's lives, so that women listened to radio soaps, and so on. From this perspective, the industrialization of culture did not interfere with relations between the populace and culture. Popular culture still belonged to the people, despite the presence of Procter & Gamble, Lever Brothers, RCA's NBC, CBS, and the C. E. Hooper Company. The companies remained in the cultural system, but their influence was limited by audience measures that accurately identified what people liked.

Such a position has long marked the public discourse of program producers, advertisers, networks, and ratings firms. However, the discourse is seriously undermined by the market structures that define the ratings commodity and the commodity audience. Women's genres are designed to target the women in the consumerist caste, and ratings are designed to measure only those ladies of the house. Similarly, men's genres target men within that consumerist caste; "kids' shows" target the offspring of the idealized middle-class household firmly rooted in a particular division of labor and a particular sexual orientation.

This is not to argue that women, men, and children outside the consumerist caste were unmoved by *Ma Perkins*, *Suspense*, or *The Shadow*. Rather, one must recognize that their listening and their pleasures were economically irrelevant. For industrial purposes, such folks were eavesdroppers who simply could be picked up as an incidental, secondary, and free audience. Because they lacked any value in the market, such listeners were literally priceless. Advertising vehicles (programs) were not designed for the public, but the technology of broadcasting and the costing of radio receivers did not bar the public from listening. People outside the consumerist caste might produce alternative or oppositional readings of the radio texts, but such increased cultural labor would not bar the listening public from escaping into the future via *Buck Rogers* or finding inspiration in *Mary Noble, Backstage Wife* or identifying with the suave Philo Vance.

Changing Players on a Constant Field

With CEH's success in 1936, the transindustrial market structure for broadcasting was fully articulated and firmly in place. That structure would persist until the introduction of peoplemeters in 1987, although surface changes did occur in the "players" and the "rules of the game." This section discusses such changes in terms of the continuing deep structure of broadcasting.[14] That structure was organized into two levels. The first determined how broadcasting functioned as a programming service; the second determined how audiences were defined, measured, and commoditified. The second level provided the rationale behind and empirical justification for programming policies guiding decisions in the first level.

On the first level, ownership of networks and broadcast technology changed. NBC was forced to divest its second radio network to ABC in 1943, which subsequently followed NBC and CBS into television. Radio was replaced by television as the technology of national network broadcasting. The new technologies of television emerged from government contracts for wartime research in radar granted to RCA and CBS, indicating the persistence of broadcasting's ties to the military.

Another organizational shift was triggered by combined economic and political pressures that emerged around the innovation of television. Television meant higher production costs for programs, with low rates of viewership until television sets were widely purchased for household use. The networks recruited some new sponsors, which typically used inexpensive genres such as game shows. Indeed, the desire to keep costs low while attracting increasingly larger audiences resulted in the systematic rigging of game shows. Revealed in a dramatic congressional hearing, the resulting "quiz show scandals" rocked network television.[15] Networks took over program selection and programming costs, gaining the ability to control their own schedules. Advertisers gave up sponsorship and programming costs, gaining access to the entire broadcast day by buying thirty-second or one-minute slots. This rearrangement of responsibilities persists to the present day. Thus, the period 1936 to 1987 saw shifts in responsibilities, technology, and firms on the first level, where programs were selected, advertisers and networks interacted, and national distribution was achieved via AT&T.[16]

The second level organized relations among advertisers, networks, and ratings producers. Continuities in demand for quality audience limited ratings methodologies to measurement of the consumerist caste. Discontinuities in demand over quantity of audience, rooted in the conflicting interests of advertisers and networks in price for the broadcast audience, opened up the possibility of some independence from demand for ratings producers. In the 1930s, this opening was used by CEH to rebalance relations between advertisers and networks, and to gain monopoly over national ratings production. That monopoly was protected by an ancillary need: advertisers and networks needed a "floor" upon which to stand when buying and selling broadcast slots. In terms of capitalist economics, it simply was irrational to start every deal for every broadcast slot by negotiating which ratings report from which ratings company would be used to set prices. Over time, companies challenged or replaced a ratings monopolist through the use of measurement methods that rebalanced discontinuities in demand. In 1942, CEH was seriously challenged by the A. C. Nielsen Company (ACN), which achieved monopoly over national ratings production by 1950. From 1959 to 1965, ACN faced challenges from two rivals (Sindlinger & Co. and ARB) and congressional hearings, which pressured ACN into changing its sample in 1970 and installing its Audimeters in a more urban and youthful sample.[17] These combined pressures and ACN's careful adaptations resulted in ACN's continued dominance over national ratings, ARB's emergence as "the" local rater, and creation of the Broadcast Ratings Council by the National Association of Broadcasters to protect ratings from government regulation.

During the post-World War II period, the consumerist caste expanded appreciably as the economy boomed. ACN's measurement methods suited the wider definition of the caste as well as the networks' new position as schedulers and programmers. For ACN's Audimeters, any television set that was turned on became a television set that was carefully watched. ACN gathered its demographics from diaries kept by viewers who were not in the Audimeter sample and then mapped the demographics from the diaries onto the Audimeters' reports of tuning. From 1965 to 1987, ACN weathered various challenges from ratings firms and from increasing penetration rates for cable television.

Starting in 1975, the U.S. economy underwent periodic recessions that triggered a slow decline in the consumerist caste.[18] This contraction in the consumerist caste set the stage for an expansion in the types of "players" measured by ACN. The rating firm had long resisted pressure from cable networks, which wanted inclusion in the national ratings. This policy changed as the Turner Broadcasting System subsidized ratings for its cable-distributed superstation. Rising interest from advertisers encouraged the full-blown measurement of cable, which by definition meant a decrease in network audiences as the same ACN sample was split across more television channels.[19] With the introduction of its peoplemeter in 1987–89, ACN achieved a rebalancing of advertisers and networks, plus the introduction of cable networks as a major source of demand for ratings. The expansion of ratings buyers and the replacement of CEH by ACN are surface changes on the second level of organization; they are not structural changes. Differences in pricing still trigger discontinuities in demand over audience quantity: advertisers seek lower quantity to lower network prices, and networks still seek to increase quantity.

In this regard, cable presents an interesting case of pressure and adaptation. New networks (satellite/cable channels) have used a new technology in attempting to increase their audience quantity at the expense of old networks using an old technology. At the same time, old networks have joined in ventures that have founded new networks and have purchased stock in the companies that own new networks. Despite this rivalry on the surface of the market, the deep structure of the market remains the same: the network oligopoly may have expanded, but it remains an oligopoly. The constraints at this level produce the immediate conditions in which audiences are measured and ratings are produced. The interaction of advertisers, networks (broadcast or cable/satellite), and the ratings monopolist generate the definition of the commodity audience, which is then operationalized through the ratings.[20]

The two levels intertwine to create the transindustrial market that constitutes broadcasting, a market in which manufacturers of nationally advertised brands interact with a network oligopoly, an interconnection monopolist,[21] and a ratings monopolist in order to deliver commercials to the consumerist caste via broadcast and telecommunications technologies.[22] While the first level manufactures, sells, and purchases the commodity audience, the second level proves that the commodity audience has been duly manufactured and sells that proof primarily to those companies that operate on the first level.

Yuppies versus Yuffies: Peoplemeters 1987–90

Broadcasting, then, revolves around the commodity audience. Absent from this ratings process is the actual audience — the audience that comprises actual listeners or actual viewers, regardless of their relationship to the consumerist caste. This realization is borne out by ACN's response to major social trends encouraged by the Reagan administration: increasing class stratification, downward social mobility, and increasing participation in the labor force by middle-class women.[23] The periodic recessions starting in the mid-1970s were exacerbated by the economic policies of the Reagan administration in the 1980s. As with Thatcherism, some corporations and segments of cities boomed under policies fostering speculation, deregulation, privatization, deindustrialization, and militarization. But the bulk of the population experienced significant loss of income in terms of real dollars. Some also lost employment as unionized manufacturing jobs were exported. Replacement jobs developed in an expanding service sector generally paid low wages with no medical benefits. Further, the service sector did not grow sufficiently to absorb all displaced workers, and the Reagan administration's anti-Keynesian policies severely limited the federal role in job creation. The result was significant transfer of wealth from the middle class and working class to the ruling class.

For the consumerist caste, this made the the concept of "the lady of the house" increasingly anachronistic. Most nuclear households simply could not afford a division of labor in which women worked without pay. This pushed increasing numbers of women into the labor force. Multiple low-paying jobs and teenage employment became facts of life. In the 1980s, the economic status of the consumerist caste was more akin to its status during the Great Depression than during the postwar boom when economic growth had been generalized across classes.

For the transindustrial market constituting broadcasting, these changes posed serious — but not radical — problems. Changes in methodology were necessary to ensure the quality of the commodity audience measured by ratings. Similarly, methodological changes were necessary to respond to pressures from cable networks for inclusion in the official ratings. When this connected with increasing interest among advertisers in cable audiences and the shrinkage of the consumerist caste, it culminated in a shift in demand: cable households began replacing television households as the population from which the peoplemeter sample was drawn. Like telephone subscription during the Great Depression, cable subscription during the current depression signaled a household's place in the consumerist caste. Despite cable's penetration rate of roughly 50 percent, cable subscription still effectively separates consumers from public, particularly as fees for basic service easily have doubled under deregulation. Further, working women were added to the ratings as economics dislodged the middle-class ideals regarding division of labor.

The resulting changes in the definition of the commodity audience, in the categories of women, and in the methods used to generate ratings were used by the ACN to fend off challenges from two rival firms that had proposed using peoplemeters. ACN's own version of the peoplemeter recorded television tuning and accepted input from viewers identifying themselves. Every fifteen minutes, a red light came on to remind viewers to touch the button that identified them to the machine. This simplified the construction of ratings by allowing demographics and tuning to be measured simultaneously.

It also depressed ratings by underreporting the quantity of viewers. For example, children often failed to respond, which resulted in wholesale drops in the quantity of the child audience for Saturday morning cartoons. Similarly, the engendering of household tasks affected peoplemetered ratings. Men responded to the technology; in diary studies, women had been the primary respondents. Further, broadcast networks questioned ACN's policy of installing a peoplemeter in a household for ten years. One would expect that a respondent's willingness to enter data every fifteen minutes would diminish as the decade wore on. For the interim, however, advertisers were well pleased with the new ratings, which ensured high-quality and low-quantity audience. Joining the advertisers were the cable networks, which found their positions considerably enhanced as network ratings diminished. Only the networks complained, using TBS's tactic of paying ACN for the maintenance of a diary-meter sample and other considerations while adjusting to the new facts of the marketplace.

Those adjustments have been difficult indeed. Not only have the ratings been reshaped against the broadcast networks' main interests, but the overwhelming adoption of videocassette recorders has further decreased dependence on locally broadcast signals for televised entertainment during prime time. For some households, video stores and public libraries have become important sources of prime-time television. In others, the lady of the house has became a working woman, time-shifting her viewing of soap operas via a VCR to the evening. Surveys suggest that working women maintain some control over their incomes but also remain the primary house worker.[24] Such women have become sufficiently attractive to advertisers that ABC/Hearst designed the cable network Lifetime as a women's channel. In network broadcasting, ABC joined CBS, NBC, and newcomer Fox in the creation of mixed-genre programs designed to appeal to the consumerist couple. The logic was simple: build programs that combined male and female genres in order to attract heads, ladies, and working women who have missed or time-shifted their soaps.

A brief glance back at network television of the 1980s indicates broadcast schedules that combined gender-specific genres with gender-mixed genres. Let us consider *Hill Street Blues* and *Alien Nation* in terms of gender stereotypes. While he watched shoot-outs and car chases on *Hill Street Blues*, she watched the continuing stories of

Renko and Bobby, Faye and Frank, Pizza Man and the Counselor. While he watched shoot-outs, car chases, and seminaked aliens simulating sex on *Alien Nation*, she watched the continuing stories of one man's family and its human friend as the Franciscos struggled to make a home and Matt struggled with his xenophobic upbringing, his partnership with George, his adoption by the family, and his increasing attraction to his alien neighbor.

Similarly, during daytime television, soap operas have been revamped in recognition of an audience beyond the housebound mother. Romantic melodrama has been extended to include relatively explicit depictions of sexual violence as well as consensual sexual liaisons. Among the standard population of soap opera doctors, nurses, lawyers, and extended families have been mixed urbane detectives, high-tech spies, international terrorists, European royalty, and industrial saboteurs. Higher production values, more on-location shooting, and a more expensive mise-en-scène have moved soap operas out of Ma Perkins's kitchen and into Scorpio's combination luxury home and high-tech control center.

As television's task became attracting the young urban professional and ignoring the young urban failure, the old genres became increasingly "upscale" and increasing intermixed. The economic downswing sharpened advertisers' demands for the consumerist caste and opened the way for an expansion in the network oligopoly to include cable networks. In the deep structure of the transindustrial market for broadcasting, the oligopoly in networking was expanded; the monopoly over ratings remained intact. As broadcast networks adjusted to the newly measured rivalry of cable channels and the new populations targeted by ratings, they built into their schedules new programs that combined old genres that had been reliable producers of either male or female audiences. This tactic sought to recapture the mass of the consumerist caste. However, in the 1990s, the very shape of the market for ratings has made it unlikely that network broadcasting will recapture its quantity audience.

Popular Culture, Industrial Culture, People's Culture

Neither commercial radio nor television, broadcast or cable, is a genuine mass medium. Nor are the cultural artifacts distributed via those media genuinely popular culture. Rather, the transindustrial structure that binds together these technologies and their artifacts is organized to tap and manipulate only one sector of the population —

the consumerist caste. The artifacts manufactured within that structure are designed to assemble the consumerist caste for measurement and sale. Further, the programs themselves exist only as vehicles for advertisements targeting that caste. The industrialization of such artifacts differentiates them from popular culture: broadcast/cable materials are neither of the people nor by the people, and they are not intended to be popular with the people.

Yet people do derive something from radio and television, both broadcast and cable.[25] Although intended only for the consumerist caste, access to radio and television is not restricted to that caste. Broadcast media are almost universal in the United States; cable subscribers are not automatically compulsive shoppers in this period of the "new frugality." Despite differences of ethnicity, gender, race, sexual orientation, religion, and class, most people assume that all of us are familiar with the cultural products distributed by these technologies. Industrialized culture has become part of our lives, as constant companion, news source, least objectionable entertainment, favorite show, background noise, or focus for fandom. We seem to work very hard at producing the alternative and oppositional readings that transform industrialized culture into shared visions and acceptable representations. From a political economic perspective, our labor is unsurprising: the cultural products are not designed for us and so must be reworked to be used. However, the fact that we actually exert our labor on such objects is quite surprising. To understand the need of human collectivities to construct people's cultures from the products of culture industries, we must turn to cultural studies and social history. By taking a political economic approach, we can see that the industrialized culture distributed via media, as well as the gender-specified genres constituting much of that product, is not popular culture, people's culture, or mass culture. Public taste has little to do with the manufacture of commodity audiences, ratings, and programming.

Notes

1. For an analysis of domestic labor and gender, see Christine Delphy, *Close to Home: A Materialist Analysis of Women's Oppression*, ed. and trans. Diana Leonard (Amherst: University of Massachusetts Press, 1984).

2. For descriptions and chronologies of industrial wisdom regarding gender differentiation of audiences, compare Erik Barnouw, *The Sponsor: Notes on a Modern Potentate* (Oxford: Oxford University Press, 1975), 9–74, especially 68–73 on

demographics; and Harry J. Skornia, *Television and Society: An Inquest and Agenda for Improvement* (New York: McGraw-Hill, 1965), 17–68, 88–142; with Hugh Malcolm Beville, Jr., *Audience Ratings: Radio, Television, Cable* (Hillsdale, N.J.: Lawrence Erlbaum, 1985) 1–82; and Karen S. Buzzard, *Chains of Gold: Marketing the Ratings and Rating the Markets* (Metuchen, N.J.: Scarecrow, 1990), 3–48, 86–96. The critical analyses presented by Barnouw and Skornia contrast sharply with the standard "industry insider" account given by Beville or the nonanalytic historical account constructed by Buzzard. Both Beville and Buzzard naturalize industrial wisdom and traditional practices; Barnouw and Skornia use an analytic approach to uncover how and why such wisdom and practices have been constructed by firms in particular ways. This essay takes a similarly critical and analytic approach to the economic history of ratings, genre, and gender commodities.

3. During the Patent Pool's internal troubles, William Paley first purchased and then reorganized a third national network, dubbed the Columbia Broadcasting System. For greater detail on networks and network programming, see Barnouw's three volumes as well as Laurence Bergreen, *Look Now, Pay Later: The Rise of Network Broadcasting* (Garden City, N.Y.: Doubleday, 1980); A. Frank Reel, *The Networks: How They Stole the Show* (New York: Charles Scribner's Sons, 1979); J. Fred MacDonald, *One Nation under Television: The Rise and Decline of Network TV* (New York: Pantheon, 1990); Todd Gitlin, *Inside Prime Time* (New York: Pantheon, 1983).

4. By "consumerist caste," I mean persons who met three criteria: first, they had sufficient disposable income to afford a life-style based on the consumption of manufactures that were nationally distributed and advertised; second, they had adopted the ideology of consumerism over the ideology of self-sufficiency; and third, they had easy access to the developing system of national distribution and national retailing.

5. Compare Beville, *Audience Ratings*; and Buzzard, *Chains of Gold*; with Eileen R. Meehan, "Why We Don't Count: The Commodity Audience," in *Logics of Television: Essays in Cultural Criticism*, ed. Patricia Mellencamp (Bloomington: Indiana University Press, 1990), 117–37.

6. Early internal studies that were reprinted for advertiser consumption include *Does Radio Sell Goods?* (CBS, 1931); *Has Radio Sold Goods in 1932?* (CBS, 1932); *Ears and Incomes* (CBS, 1934); *Little Books on Broadcasting*, series 1–12 and A–F (NBC, 1927–31); and from the same period, *A New Measurement of the Size, Locations, and Occupations of NBC Radio Audiences, Supplemented by Dealers Opinions of Radio Advertising* (NBC, n.d.). Networks have continued to issue such promotional materials disguised as objective, neutral studies. Erik Barnouw features an especially interesting CBS brochure, called *Where the Girls Are*, in *Tube of Plenty: The Evolution of American Television*, 2d rev. ed. (Oxford: Oxford University Press, 1990). The CBS brochure included a dial that advertisers could turn to determine what age group among females purchased a product type, hence what age group should be targeted by the manufacturer of that product type. While one may be tempted to dismiss the obvious sexism of the brochure's title as an artifact of the "bad old days," it is noteworthy that the brochure is presented as an illustration of how networks and advertisers used demographic ratings in the 1970s.

7. For "industry insider" discussions of ratings measurement techniques and advertiser interests, see Archibald Crossley, *Watch Your Selling Dollar* (New York: B. C. Forbes, 1930). An interesting comparison can be made with the apologia published by Crossley's successor, C. E. Hooper in Matthew N. Chapell and C. E.

Hooper, *Radio Audience Measurement* (New York: Steven Daye, 1944) and later self-justifications published by A. C. Nielsen, Sr., *Greater Prosperity through Market Research: The First Forty Years of the A. C. Nielsen Company* (Northbrook, Ill.: A. C. Nielsen Company, 1963) and A. C. Nielsen, Jr., *If Not the People. . . . Who?* (Northbrook, Ill.: A. C. Nielsen Company, 1966).

8. Compare Mark James Banks, "A History of Broadcast Audience Research in the United States, 1920–1980, with an Emphasis on the Ratings Services," doctoral dissertation, University of Tennessee, Knoxville, 1981; with Beville, *Audience Ratings*; and Buzzard, *Chains of Gold*. Where Banks takes an entirely descriptive, chronological approach to the topic, Donald Lee Hurwitz adopts an idealist culturalist position in analyzing the rhetoric of ratings firms in "Broadcast Ratings: The Rise and Development of Commercial Audience Research and Measurement in American Broadcasting," doctoral dissertation, University of Illinois, Urbana, 1983. For an approach utilizing rhetorical analysis and political economic analysis, see Eileen R. Meehan, "Neither Heroes nor Villains: Towards a Political Economy of the Ratings Industry," doctoral dissertation, University of Illinois, Urbana, 1983. For an institutional approach, see Eileen R. Meehan, "Ratings and the Institutional Approach: A Third Answer to the Commodity Question," *Critical Studies in Mass Communication* 1 (1984): 216–25.

9. For penetration rates, see U.S. Bureau of the Census, *Statistical History of the United States from Colonial Times to the Present* (New York: Basic Books, 1976), 783–84, 796. For a discussion of radio sales, see Barnouw, *Tube of Plenty*, 30–40; and Frederick Lewis Allen, *Only Yesterday: An Informal History of the 1920s* (New York: Harper, 1964 [1931]), 137–39.

10. In telephone surveys, men are generally more difficult to reach than women. Researchers have coped with differential rates of answering the telephone by asking for the "head of household," which has traditionally meant the senior male. The practice is less efficacious now as a means of snagging male respondents, because of both changing consciousness and the feminization of poverty.

11. See C. E. Hooper and Matthew Chapell, *Radio Audience Measurement* (New York: Stephen Daye, 1944); *Hooperatings Hi-lites*, 1932–40, various volumes; Banks, "A History of Broadcast Audience Research."

12. Much current historical research documents the multiplicity of the "American experience." For example, the American social history project directed by Herbert G. Gutman published the first volume of *Who Built America? Working People and the Nation's Economy, Politics, Culture, and Society* in 1989 (New York: Pantheon). The volume's attention to the differentiated experiences of working people whose lived experience connected them to distinct subcultures based on gender, race, ethnicity, religion, and politics provides a sharp contrast to Daniel J. Boorstin's three volumes of *The Americans* (New York: Vintage, Random House, 1974), which posits a homogeneous nation awakened to consumerism and the good life.

13. Compare Tania Modleski, *Loving with a Vengeance: Mass Produced Fantasies for Women* (New York: Methuen, 1982), 11–34 on feminine forms and 85–109, on soap operas; Janice A. Radway, *Reading the Romance: Women, Patriarchy, and Popular Literature* (Chapel Hill: University of North Carolina Press, 1984), 3–45; John Fiske, *Television Culture* (London: Methuen, 1987), 179–223 on feminine and masculine television; Jackie Byars, *All That Hollywood Allows: Re-reading Gender in 1950s Melodrama* (Chapel Hill: University of North Carolina Press, 1991), 1–24.

14. I rely on the traditional methods of political economy that address the

intertwining of macroscopic structures and systems, particularly institutional analysis and aggregate analysis. For exemplars, see Adam Smith, *The Wealth of Nations*, ed. Edward Cannan (London: Methuen, 1961 [1776]); Karl Marx, *A Contribution to the Critique of Political Economy*, ed. Maurice Dobb (New York: International Publishers, 1981 [1859]); Rudolf Hilferding, *Finance Capital*, ed. Tom Bottomore (London: Routledge & Kegan Paul, 1985 [1910]); Gunnar Myrdal, *The Political Element in the Development of Economic Theory* (New York: Simon & Schuster, 1969 [1954]); Howard J. Sherman, *Elementary Aggregate Economics* (New York: Appleton-Century-Crofts, 1966).

15. William Boddy, "The Seven Dwarfs and the Money Grubbers: The Public Relations Crisis of US Television in the Late 1950s," in *Logics of Television: Essays in Cultural Criticism*, ed. Patricia Mellencamp (Bloomington: Indiana University Press, 1990), 98–116.

16. PBS's experiments in the late 1970s with satellite distribution of broadcast signal eventually opened the door for companies—including RCA—to sell interconnection services via satellite. By the late 1980s, satellite capacity was very much in demand. However, recent decisions by the Federal Communications Commission will allow telephone companies to deliver video over fiber-optic cable. It remains to be seen whether AT&T or the "baby Bells" will attempt to monopolize interconnection through this newly sanctioned use of fiber optics, thereby respectively taking on satellite interconnection services and cable operating companies.

17. For a detailed account of these hearings and previous congressional inquiries into ratings, see Meehan, "Neither Heroes nor Villains."

18. For an authoritative account of this process, see Barry Bluestone and Bennett Harrison, *The Deindustrialization of America: Plant Closings, Community Abandonment, and the Dismantling of Basic Industry* (New York: Basic Books, 1982).

19. For an insider account, see Mark Christensen and Cameron Stauth, *The Sweeps* (Toronto: Bantam, 1985); see also Gitlin, *Inside Prime Time*, 325–35. Also, please note that the expansion of the ratings sample to include cable audiences automatically meant a decrease in network audience and corresponding increase in cable audience.

20. For advertisers, the ratings achieve three ends. First, ratings demonstrate the existence of the commodity audience. Next, ratings rationalize decisions about the purchase of advertising times and the placement of ads in particular genres targeted by demographics. Last, ratings justify network prices. For networks, ratings serve similar functions. Besides facilitating business relations with advertisers, ratings guide networks' scheduling decisions, identifying when the particular demographic group will be available for "its" genres and determining if a particular example of the genre is delivering enough audience to warrant renewal. In this way, surface changes in the second organizational level had a direct impact on the business practices of the first organizational level.

21. As noted previously, the interconnection monopoly has come under recent pressure by the oligopoly in satellite ownership. However, demand for satellite capacity has outstripped the availability of satellites, leaving satellite-distributed cable channels rather at the mercy of the satellite divisions of AT&T, Western Union, and GE (including GE's RCA). It may well be that the monopoly in interconnection will also expand to an oligopoly. However, AT&T's new technologies and its divestment of regional operating companies may reinstate its old oligopoly.

22. Masking the basic structure, however, is a plethora of surface detail: ratings rise and fall; shows are canceled; fans protest; network executives bet their careers on the upcoming fall's lineup; commercials interrupt shows; new measurement techniques are announced; once more, new technologies are touted as offering a whole new world of programming choice and efficient access to consumers. Beneath this avalanche of detail rests a bilevel market that has been constructed by multiple industries and in which these industries go about the business of broadcasting.

23. Bluestone and Harrison, *The Deindustrialization of America*, 25–48, 82–107.

24. For a full discussion of gender, class, consumerism, and deindustrialism, see Katherine S. Newman, *Falling from Grace: The Experience of Downward Mobility in the American Middle Class* (New York: Random House, 1988).

25. The concept of negotiated readings and a potentially obstreperous audience has attracted much attention from cultural theorists, textual analysts, and audience researchers. See Raymond Williams, *Marxism and Literature* (Oxford: Oxford University Press, 1977); Janet Woollacott, "Messages and Meanings," in *Culture, Society, and the Media*, ed. Michael Gurevitch, Tony Bennett, James Curran, and Janet Woollacott (London: Methuen, 1982), 91–111; Stuart Hall, "The Rediscovery of 'Ideology': The Return of the Repressed in Media Studies," in *Culture, Society, and the Media*, ed. Michael Gurevitch, Tony Bennett, James Curran, and Janet Woollacott (London: Methuen, 1982), 56–90; Charlotte Brunsdon and David Morley, *Everyday Television: 'Nationwide'* (London: British Film Institute, 1978); David Morley, *The 'Nationwide' Audience* (London: British Film Institute, 1980); Ien Ang, *Watching Dallas: Soap Opera and the Melodramatic Imagination* (New York: Methuen, 1985); Byars, *All That Hollywood Allows*, particularly 25–66.

Chapter 10

Conflict, Not Consensus: The Debate over Broadcast Communication Policy, 1930–1935
Robert W. McChesney

In the decades that followed the emergence of radio broadcasting in the United States in the 1920s and 1930s, much of the scholarship on the origins of the U.S. broadcasting setup was congratulatory. It assumed that the United States had adopted the best broadcast system imaginable and that the laws that had permitted and encouraged the development of a regulated commercial system had been the products of well-intentioned public servants. Sometimes the U.S. broadcasting system was characterized as being the result of a painstaking study and debate of a variety of alternatives; at other times, the notion that any debate or study had even been necessary was dismissed categorically, as the existing system was the sole conceivable system appropriate for U.S. democracy. In either case this perspective, which had been encouraged strongly by the commercial broadcasting industry, remained prominent in mass communication circles well into the 1970s.[1]

With the emergence of the work of Erik Barnouw, Philip Rosen, and others, this congratulatory perspective collapsed. When historians abandoned the presupposition that a network-dominated, advertising-supported broadcasting system was the only rational choice for a freedom-loving and democratic society, and then scrutinized radio's early years, a different picture emerged. Rather than being the result of public debate and conscientious public servants, the emerging system tended to be seen as the consequence of business, government, and military elites successfully installing a system to suit their self-interests, with minimal public participation.[2] Some, such as Mary Mander, replaced the consensus notion with a deterministic argument that it was "unavoidable" that broadcasting would become a commercial enterprise, given the domination of U.S. society by "the habits of industrial capitalism."[3] Others, such as Susan

222

Douglas, looked to broadcasting's "prehistory," the era preceding the emergence of broadcasting in 1919 and 1920, as the decisive era in which the radio corporations established their irrevocable hold on the medium. By 1922, she argues, the U.S. broadcasting system was in place "technically, economically, legislatively, and ideologically." There would be "no major break in this ideological frame," that private corporations should dominate broadcasting thereafter.[4]

Whereas the congratulatory school regarded the public as enthusiastic about the emergence of a commercial broadcasting setup, the more critical historians tend to see the public as ignorant if not apathetic in this regard. Insofar as both schools have concentrated on the period preceding 1927, these conclusions are understandable; this is precisely what most scholars do when assessing the origins and consolidation of the U.S. broadcasting system. However, if one extends one's gaze to the era from 1927 to the early 1930s, a very different picture emerges. For it was only in this period that network-dominated, advertising-supported broadcasting came to exist, let alone to dominate the ether. And it was during this key period that many Americans expressed extreme displeasure with the nature of commercial broadcasting fare and more than a few of them attempted to recast U.S. broadcasting radically to establish a viable nonprofit and noncommercial sector.

This chapter will review this overlooked episode in U.S. broadcasting history and suggest that a recognition of it requires that the existing critical school be reformulated accordingly. While the economic, cultural, and regulatory roots of commercial broadcasting may be traced to the early 1920s and points earlier, the economic, political, and ideological consolidation of the commercial broadcasting setup would not be completed until various points in the 1930s. Further, the path to consolidation for the commercial broadcasters was fraught with opposition, conflict, and, for a brief glimmer of historical time, the slight possibility of radically transcending the status quo.

Key Developments in U.S. Broadcasting, 1927–29[5]

U.S. broadcasting in the middle 1920s was far different from the system that would be entrenched only a few years later. Several hundred nonprofit broadcasters had commenced operations in the first half of the decade, the majority of which were affiliated with colleges and universities, and well over 200 of these, or approximately two-fifths of all stations, remained on the air in 1925.[6] Although still largely overlooked in the mass communications literature, these nonprofit broadcasters are now recognized as the "true pioneers" of U.S. broadcasting, who were, as one of the leading radio engineers of the period observed, "at the start of things distinctly on the ground floor."[7] The for-profit broadcasters were hardly professional broadcasters in the modern sense of the term. The majority were owned and operated by newspapers, department stores, electric power companies, and other private concerns, and their raison d'être was to generate favorable publicity for the owner's primary enterprise, not to generate profits in their own right.[8] As late as 1929 it was commonly posited by broadcasters, the Federal Radio Commission, and analysts that few if any private broadcasters were earning profits from the business of broadcasting, and there was little sense, in public discourse at least, that they ever would.[9]

Almost all of the scholarship on this subject has emphasized the establishment of the American Telephone & Telegraph Company's WEAF in 1922, with its formal commitment to time sales as the basis of support, as the first step in the inexorable march toward network-dominated, advertising-supported broadcasting. This was certainly not how the matter was perceived throughout the 1920s. Radio Corporation of America executive David Sarnoff made statements in 1922 and 1924 calling for the creation of a nonprofit and noncommercial broadcasting network to be subsidized by "those who derive profits" from the manufacture of radio receivers and related industries.[10] Commercial advertising, the other pillar of the emerging status quo, did not begin its stampede to the ether in earnest until 1928.[11] As late as 1927, the radio committee of the American Newspaper Publishers Association reassured its membership that "fortunately, direct advertising by radio is well-nigh an impossibility."[12] As has been amply documented in the major studies of the period, the very notion of commercial advertising was very controversial and more than a little unpopular throughout the 1920s. Even Secretary of Commerce Herbert Hoover, who was a pronounced advocate of advertising per se, was opposed to having it play more than a marginal role in radio broadcasting.[13]

Moreover, the two major networks, the National Broadcasting Company and the Columbia Broadcasting System, established in 1926 and 1927, respectively, did not have much impact until after the passage of the Radio Act of 1927. Throughout the late 1920s, NBC presented itself as a public service corporation rather than a traditional for-profit corporation, which would sell only the advertising that was necessary to subsidize high-quality noncommercial fare, "the finer things which are not sponsored commercially," as NBC President Merlin Aylesworth put it.[14] Few, if any, observers at the time projected the eventual role that NBC, CBS, and commercial advertising soon would assume within the U.S. broadcasting system. In all public discourse on the matter prior to 1927, there was general agreement that nonprofit broadcasting should play a significant role in the U.S. system, and that commercial advertising should be regarded with great skepticism as to its potential contributions to the field.[15]

Hence, there is little reason, on the surface, to regard the passage of the Radio Act of 1927 as some sort of mandate for network-dominated, advertising-supported broadcasting. That system barely existed at the time, and absolutely no one was discussing the issue in those terms. The Radio Act of 1927 was emergency legislation, hurriedly passed in February after a federal judge in 1926 had ruled the Department of Commerce's licensing of stations unconstitutional. Without regulation, the ether became chaotic; 200 new broadcasters immediately commenced operations, the total wattage increased by nearly 75 percent, and few stations respected the frequencies occupied by other broadcasters.[16] The committee deliberations and floor debate concerning the Radio Act of 1927 were what one might expect for emergency legislation; there was almost no discussion of the legislation's meaning for the type of broadcast system to be created.[17]

The Radio Act of 1927 established the FRC on a one-year basis, to allocate broadcast licenses and to bring order to the airwaves by reducing the total number of stations. The only directive that the law gave the FRC, in determining which applicants would get preference for the scarce channels, was that the FRC should favor those station applicants that best served the "public interest, convenience or necessity." The primary reason that even this many criteria were put into the statute was to ensure the bill's constitutionality; otherwise the bill's sponsors argued that it was essential to give the FRC complete latitude to operate as it saw fit.[18] The commercial broadcasters were vocal in their support of having the FRC, rather than Congress, determine licensing criteria.[19] During the FRC's first year, budgetary problems and the deaths of two members prevented it from taking any significant action to reduce the number of stations.[20] Congress renewed the FRC in 1928 for a year and then in 1929 indefinitely. There was no sense during this period that the Radio Act of 1927 and the FRC were anything more than temporary measures. The topic of broadcast regulation was before Congress at each and every session, right up until the passage of the Communications Act of 1934.

When Congress conducted committee hearings on whether to extend the FRC in early 1928 and again in early 1929, the FRC members were questioned about the unchecked and stunningly rapid emergence of network broadcasting over the previous two years, as well as the noticeable decrease in the number of nonprofit broadcasters. "The great feeling about radio in this country," commented Senator C. C. Dill, Democrat of Washington and one of the authors of the Radio Act of 1927, "is that it will be monopolized by the few wealthy interests."[21] FRC members were admonished repeatedly to protect the nonprofit broadcasters and to be certain to prevent all the choice frequencies from falling into the hands of NBC or CBS.[22] "It seems the chains are being the object of attack," a commercial broadcasting executive wrote an FRC member in 1928, "by all of Congress."[23] In this spirit, in 1928 Congress passed the Davis Amendment, which required the FRC to make a general reallocation of the entire spectrum, in order to provide more stations to the underrepresented southern and western regions of the nation.[24]

The resulting reallocation, mandated by the FRC in late 1928 in the form of General Order 40 and a number of follow-up directives, established the framework for modern U.S. broadcasting. Three of the five FRC members were appointed to an "allocating committee" that was responsible for determining the plan for the general reallocation. One member, Harold Lafount, had served as a director for several radio manufacturing firms in his native Utah and was a proponent of the capitalist development of the ether. "What has education contributed to radio?" Lafount asked in 1931. "Not one thing. What has commercialism contributed? Everything — the lifeblood of the industry." Commending the "wonderful programs" of the two chains, Lafount noted in 1931 that "experts everywhere now agree" that U.S. broadcasting "is as perfect as it could be made."[25] The other two members of the allocating committee included a McGraw-Hill utility trade publication editor who was on loan to the FRC for a year, and a broadcaster who would leave the FRC in 1929 to spearhead the expansion of the CBS network from forty-seven affiliated stations in 1929 to ninety-one affiliates four years later.[26]

The allocating committee held a number of meetings with radio engineers and representatives of the networks and the commercial broadcasters' trade association, the National Association of Broadcasters. These conferences and sessions were not publicized; nonprofit broadcasters and concerned nonbroadcasters did not have an opportunity to present their opinions. The resulting reallocation clearly had the look of one that would favor the fledgling commercial broadcasting industry: in short, the FRC would recognize and crystallize the dominant trends within broadcasting over the previous two years and make no effort to counteract these trends through public policy.[27]

In August 1928 the FRC announced its reallocation plan under General Order 40. Forty of the ninety available channels were set aside to be 50,000 watt clear channels that would have only one occupant nationally. The other fifty channels would house the remaining 600 or so broadcasters, who could operate simultaneously on the same channels at much lower power levels. Broadcasters in the same region would share the same frequency by using it at different times of day. To lower the number of stations, the FRC utilized a process whereby anybody could challenge an existing broadcaster for a frequency assignment at the end of a three-month term. In general, the FRC would have the various applicants for a particular frequency share its usage, allocating the majority of the hours to the station it deemed most worthy. In the long run, the station accorded the fewest hours on a shared channel often found it very difficult to stay on the air. This direct head-to-head competition for the scarce broadcast channels created great antipathy between the contending applicants, particularly, as was often the case, when commercial broadcasters successfully challenged nonprofit broadcasters.[28] Without the FRC having to turn down the license renewal applications of very many broadcasters, there were 100 fewer stations on the air by the autumn of 1929.[29]

With General Order 40 all stations, with the exception of a handful of network-affiliated clear-channel stations that had been established by the FRC the previous year, were assigned to new frequencies and new power levels.[30] The networks were the big winners. Whereas in 1927 NBC had twenty-eight affiliates and CBS had sixteen, for a combined 6.4 percent of the broadcast stations, within four years they combined to account for 30 percent of the stations. And this vastly understates their new role, as all but three of the forty clear-channel stations were owned by or affiliated with one of the two networks. Indeed, when the number of hours broadcast and the level of power are factored into the equation, NBC and CBS accounted for nearly 70 percent of U.S. broadcasting by 1931.[31] By 1935, only four of the sixty-two stations that broadcast at 5,000 watts power or greater did not have network affiliation.[32] Moreover, commercial advertising revenues, which barely existed on a national level prior to 1928, grew by leaps and bounds to an annual total of $72 million by 1934.[33] By 1931, surveys indicated that explicit sales talks occupied twelve to fifteen minutes of the broadcast hour, which alone understates the influence of advertisers, as they or their agencies usually also produced the programs that surrounded their advertisements. The growth of the networks and the emergence of commercial advertising, though distinct, were mutually reinforcing. One study has found that 80 percent of radio advertising revenues in 1929 went to 20 percent of the stations, all network owned or affiliated.[34] One commentator noted in 1930, "Nothing in American history has paralleled this mushroom growth." This point has become a staple insight among broadcast historians.[35]

The other side of the coin was reflected in the equally dramatic decline in nonprofit and noncommercial broadcasting. Nonprofit broadcasters found themselves in a vicious cycle: the FRC, noting their lack of financial and technological prowess, lowered their hours and power to the advantage of well-capitalized private broadcasters, and thus made it that much more difficult for the nonprofit broadcasters to generate the funds they needed to become successful. "Now the Federal Radio Commission has come along and taken away all of the hours that are worth anything and has left us with hours that are absolutely no good for commercial programs or for educational programs," wrote the despondent director of the soon to be extinct University of Arkansas station. "The Commission may boast that it has never cut an educational station off the air. It merely cuts off our head, our arms, and our legs, and then allows us to die a natural death."[36] The number of stations affiliated with colleges and universities declined from ninety-five in 1927 to less than half that figure by 1930, while the total number of nonprofit broadcasters declined from some 200 in 1927 to less than a third that total in 1934. Moreover, almost all of these stations operated with low power on shared frequencies. By 1934, nonprofit broadcasting accounted for only 2 percent of total U.S. broadcast time.[37] For most Americans, it effectively did not exist.

The FRC defended the reallocation in its *Third Annual Report*. It equated capitalist broadcasters with "general public service" broadcasters, since, in their quest for profit, they would be motivated to provide whatever programming the market desired. In contrast, those stations that did not operate for profit and that did not derive their revenues from the sale of advertising were termed "propaganda" stations, since, according to the FRC, these stations were more interested in spreading their particular viewpoints than in satisfying audience needs. Hence, the FRC argued that it had to favor the capitalist broadcasters because there were not enough stations to satisfy all the "propaganda" groups. These groups would have to learn to work through the auspices of the commercial broadcasters.[38]

The Emergence and Contours of the Broadcast Reform Movement

In the aftermath of General Order 40 there developed, for the first time, a coherent and unrepentant opposition to the emerging capitalist domination of the airwaves. "The battle was begun in earnest," noted one of the leading opposition groups, "in the summer of 1928 soon after the enactment of the Commission's General Order 40."[39] The primary elements of what could be characterized as an opposition movement or broadcast reform movement came from the ranks of the displaced and harassed nonprofit broadcasters, particularly those affiliated with colleges and universities. To many educators, their stations were being left "unprotected" by the FRC, as they were "attacked constantly by commercial broadcasters."[40]

In 1929 and 1930 educational broadcasters repeatedly protested to the U.S. Office of Education and the FRC that they were "being driven off the air at a rate that threatened their complete extinction."[41] Secretary of the Interior Ray Lyman Wilbur, at the urging of the National Education Association in 1929, authorized a group of educators and commercial broadcasters to study the issue of how to promote educational broadcasting. But the group split along institutional lines, with the network representatives claiming that independent educational stations were unnecessary, as the networks were more than willing to accommodate the educators. The final report of the Wilbur Committee, issued in early 1930, presented both sides on the matter but refused to recommend the reservation of a fixed number of channels for educational broadcasting. It recommended, instead, that the educators learn to cooperate with the commercial broadcasters.[42] The commercial broadcasters were delighted and thought the report settled the matter for all time; the educators, on the other hand, thought the report simply ignored the crisis of survival in which they were enmeshed.

Finally, in the summer of 1930, U.S. Commissioner of Education

William John Cooper, after repeated demands by educators, called a conference of educational and nonprofit broadcasters to organize a plan of attack before Congress for "new radio legislation" that would protect nonprofit broadcasters before the "commercial stations will have practically monopolized the channels open for radio broadcasting."[43] The October meeting in Chicago led to the creation of the National Committee on Education by Radio, which would be composed of representatives of nine leading national education organizations.[44] Although this would be a nongovernmental body, Cooper arranged for the NCER to receive a five-year $200,000 grant from the Payne Fund and appointed Joy Elmer Morgan, editor of the NEA *Journal*, to be the NCER's director. The Payne Fund was a small foundation drawing from the wealth of a Cleveland industrialist family; it had a strong interest in both education and mass communication, which led it to radio in the middle 1920s. After being rebuffed by the networks in its efforts to produce and broadcast educational programming, however, the Payne Fund resolved that the only way to assure the use of the ether for education and culture would be to establish independent nonprofit and noncommercial stations.[45] The NCER was established for the purpose of having Congress reserve 15 percent of the channels for educational use, assisting the educational stations in their seemingly endless hearings before the FRC, and conducting research to enhance education by radio.

For the next five years the NCER would lead a relentless fight to arrest the capitalist domination of the ether. The NCER had a full-time staff of at least three people, and it published a monthly newsletter, *Education by Radio*, with a controlled circulation that reached 11,000 by 1934. To the NCER, it was axiomatic that cooperation between educators and commercial broadcasters was "not possible." "That practice has been tried for nearly a decade and has proved unworkable," Morgan stated in 1931. "It is no longer open to discussion." Although the educational community was not unanimous or necessarily vociferous in its support of the NCER, the NCER legislative agenda received the formal support of the majority of educational organizations. And at times, some educational groups, such as the National Congress of Parents and Teachers, which resolved for the complete nationalization and decommercialization of broadcasting in 1932, called for much more radical reform of broadcasting than that proposed by the NCER.[46]

Yet the NCER was not some sort of trade organization that simply was trying to cut the best deal it could for itself. Morgan, in particular, was a Midwest populist who had cut his teeth on the public utilities movement of the Progressive Era. "Private monopoly in industry is bad enough; monopoly in the agencies which control the distribution of ideas and the dissemination of information is infinitely worse," Morgan wrote to Congress in January 1933. "It strikes at the very roots of free democratic government."[47] He brought to the broadcast struggle a missionary's zeal for reform. Morgan's was a very broad and deeply political definition of education and educational broadcasting. "As a result of radio broadcasting," he informed one audience in 1931,

> there will probably develop during the twentieth century either chaos or a world-order of civilization. Whether it shall be one or the other will depend largely upon whether broadcasting be used as a tool of education or as an instrument of selfish greed. So far, our American radio interests have thrown their major influence on the side of greed. . . . There has never been in the entire history of the United States an example of mismanagement and lack of vision so colossal and far-reaching in its consequences as our turning of the radio channels almost exclusively into commercial hands.[48]

"I believe we are dealing here," Morgan told the national convention of the National University Extension Association in 1932, "with one of the most crucial issues that was ever presented to civilization at any time in its entire history."[49]

The NCER was not alone in its campaign to recast U.S. broadcasting. Several other nonprofit broadcasters that found little support from the FRC became active in the fight for broadcast reform. The two most active of these were the Chicago Federation of Labor, which maintained the only labor station in the nation, WCFL of Chicago, and the Paulist Fathers religious order of New York, which operated WLWL, the only Catholic station in the northeastern United States. Both of these stations began in the mid-1920s with tremendous aspirations for public service; by the end of the decade both were struggling for survival, as the FRC assigned most of the hours they previously had been occupying to affiliates of NBC and CBS, respectively. In the early 1930s both WCFL and WLWL, after continued frustration with the FRC, would lead efforts to enact reform legislation.[50] The director of WCFL, Edward Nockels, would also represent the American Federation of Labor on broadcast legislation on Capitol Hill in the early 1930s. After General Order 40, Nockels stated that "all of the 90 channels for radio broadcasting" had been "given to capital and its friends and not even one channel to the millions that toil."[51] Nockels brought the same sense of mission to the battle for broadcast reform as the NCER's Morgan. "With the exception of the right to organize," Nockels enthused in 1930,

> there is no goal more important of attainment to the American labor movement than one radio wavelength with a nation-wide network over which it can broadcast Labor's message to all citizens of our country. This is the modern phase of the right of free speech. . . . whoever controls radio broadcasting in the future will eventually control the nation.[52]

In addition to displaced nonprofit broadcasters, some elements of the newspaper industry agitated for restrictions on the commercialization of the ether, particularly since this was regarded as a prime reason for the economic woes of the print media in the depths of the Great Depression. In both Britain and Canada, for example, the daily newspapers played major roles in encouraging the noncommercial development of their respective national broadcasting systems.[53] And in the United States in the early 1930s, major newspaper trade unions frequently resolved for the complete or near-complete nationalization and decommercialization of broadcasting on explicitly selfish grounds.[54] Among the newspaper publishers, there was considerable hostility to the increasing use of the ether as an advertising medium, especially in the late 1920s and at the beginning of the 1930s.[55] The most active daily newspaper publisher in the fight to reform broadcasting was H. O. Davis, owner of California's *Ventura Free Press*, who published two books critical of the status quo, promoted reform ideas before the ANPA, and even hired a full-time Washington, D.C., lobbyist to work on behalf of broadcast reform throughout the early 1930s.[56] Davis's broadcast reform activities, similar to those of the NCER, were subsidized by the Payne Fund, in this case surreptitiously, which provided him with more than $50,000 between 1931 and 1933 to generate support for reform. The *Ventura Free Press* radio campaign was explicitly radical. "We are going to the very root of the evil," Davis wrote in one open letter to newspaper publishers. "In order to reconstruct we must first destroy the present structure," he wrote in another open letter.[57]

An alarmed commercial broadcasting industry was able to defuse quickly any threat to their control of the ether that might be brought by the newspaper industry. By 1932 or 1933 Davis had been effectively marginalized, and the major newspapers had become allies of the commercial broadcasters in their efforts to thwart the opposition movement. The commercial broadcasters approached the newspaper industry on two levels. First, they emphasized that government restrictions on commercial broadcasting could easily be extended to newspapers. As an NBC vice president told the San Francisco Advertising Club in 1932, he and William Randolph Hearst had discussed the reform efforts and had agreed that "any threat to commercial advertising on the radio is a threat to all forms of advertising."[58]

Second, the commercial broadcasters strongly encouraged newspapers to either purchase their own stations or establish an affiliation with a local station in their community. By late 1931, 139 radio stations had newspaper owners or affiliations; another 100 stations would be added to this fold in the next twelve months.[59] The networks were especially aggressive in their efforts to establish newspaper affiliations, such that thirty-five of the ninety CBS network stations had newspaper owners or affiliations by 1932. "We only know here that newspaper-owned stations have increased their revenues through network broadcasting," CBS President William S. Paley commented, citing instances of newspapers tripling their broadcast advertising revenues in a single year. "Nor are these examples exceptions."[60] This strategy paid off quickly. In 1932 the chairman of the radio committee of the ANPA quit in disgust, noting that the newspapers that owned radio stations were stonewalling all of his efforts to develop a coherent broadcast anticommercialism platform for the organization.[61] "So long as a goodly array of journalists are close corporate allies of radio," the trade publication *Broadcasting* assured its readers, the broadcasting industry would be able to "pay no heed to the tempest in the teapot that certain press interests have been trying to create."[62]

The opposition to the status quo also was joined by many civic groups that had no particular material stake in the outcome of the fight. The most important of these was the American Civil Liberties Union. Prior to 1932, the ACLU had stayed out of legislative efforts to recast U.S. broadcasting, not regarding it as a free expression issue. However, by early 1933 the ACLU had become overwhelmed with criticism of U.S. broadcasting for its censorship of radical and nonmainstream opinions and for its unwillingness to air controversial public affairs broadcasting. "Censorship at the stations by the managers is constantly exercised in a most unenlightened fashion," ACLU director Roger Baldwin observed in a memo in 1933,

> all this with an eye to protecting the status quo. Only a comparatively few small stations voice critical or radical views, and these are in constant danger of either going out of business or being closed up. Protests by the Civil Liberties Union when the larger stations censor programs have resulted in no relief. The Federal Radio Commission pays no attention to such complaints.[63]

Shortly thereafter, the ACLU established its Radio Committee to deal with "the restrictions on broadcasting inherent in the American system."[64] The Committee was advised to study the "whole matter" of broadcasting, with the aim of developing a "practical plan" to reform the system and better meet the free expression requirements of a democratic society.[65] For the balance of the decade the ACLU would be active in the battle for broadcast reform.

The ACLU's response to the emergence of the status quo mirrored the broader response of the U.S. intelligentsia to network, commercial broadcasting: it was almost entirely negative. The NCER's Morgan was not far from the truth when he stated in 1933 that it was impossible to find *any* intellectual in favor of the status quo, unless that intellectual was receiving money or airtime from a commercial broadcaster.[66] This is not to suggest that the subject of broadcasting was foremost on the minds of U.S. intellectuals during this period; given the economic and political crisis embracing the world, the subject of radio was well down the list of concerns. Yet more than a few prominent intellectuals, including John Dewey, Walter Hale Hamilton, Alexander Meiklejohn, Charles A. Beard, Norman Thomas, Jane Addams, Upton Sinclair, Frederick Lewis Allen, E. P. Herring, Bruce Bliven, and H. L. Mencken, published articles and gave speeches damning the status quo and arguing on behalf of major reform.[67] Others, such as William Orton of Amherst College, Jerome Davis of the Yale Divinity School, social critic James Rorty, and pioneer radio inventor Lee DeForest, published and spoke actively on behalf of the opposition movement, often coordinating their activities with the NCER, the ACLU, and other opposition groups.[68]

Among the various elements of the broadcast reform movement there were three themes that underscored virtually all of their criticism of the status quo. First, the opposition movement argued that the airwaves should be regarded as a public resource and broadcasting as a public utility. By this reasoning, reformers argued that turning broadcasting over to a relative handful of private broadcasters so that they could satisfy selfish goals was a scandalous misuse of a public resource. Moreover, the policy by which the FRC had established the existing system had been entirely outside of public view; even Congress seemed largely oblivious to what had taken place. Hence the public had yet to exercise its right and duty to determine broadcast policy. Second, the broadcast reform movement argued that a network-dominated, for-profit, advertising-supported broadcast system would invariably shade its programming to defend the status quo and that it would never give fair play to unpopular or radical opinions. It would be difficult to overemphasize how much of the broadcast reform movement's critique revolved around this insight; the entire movement was propelled by a profound desire to create a broadcasting system that would better promote a democratic political culture, as the broadcast reformers defined it.

Third, the reformers criticized the nature of broadcast advertising and the limitations of advertising-subsidized programming, particularly in regard to the lack of cultural, educational, and public affairs programming that the system seemed capable of generating profitably. Some of this criticism had a distinctly elitist tone. *New Republic* editor Bruce Bliven, for example, wrote that "even the so-called entertainment aspects of programs are such that no civilized person can listen to them without nausea. This is often the result of a deliberate policy on the part of the advertiser, who finds people of low intelligence respond most readily to his commercial appeal, and therefore baits his trap with material intentionally designed to reach those who are not quite bright." Another writer stated that his "ideal broadcasting station" would make "no hypocritical pretense" of attempting "to present something for everyone." Rather, all the programming would "be aimed at and above a frankly upper-middle class" audience.[69] This bias reflected, to some extent, the class bias of the reform movement, but such sentiments were not held universally. The labor movement and some of the populists associated with the NCER were unwilling to concede that entertainment programming was incompatible with nonprofit and noncommercial broadcasting. They also disputed the notion that commercial broadcasts were "giving the people what they want," as the networks claimed and as the elitists were willing to concede. To the extent that such elitism permeated the reform movement, however, it rendered the generation of popular support that much more improbable. Much of this entire range of criticism, which largely has been overlooked by subsequent media critics, ages rather well and anticipates much of the best modern media criticism, from Herbert Gans, Gaye Tuchman, and Ben Bagdikian to Noam Chomsky and Edward S. Herman.[70]

The broadcast reform movement was insistent in its belief that increased regulation of the existing system could not produce the desired social results. At best, noted the NCER's Morgan, "this kind of arrangement would result in perpetual warfare."[71] In addition, it was a perpetual warfare that the broadcast reform movement invariably would lose. In the words of one naval captain who was critical of the corporate domination of broadcasting, the "large companies" would invariably triumph in any regulatory scheme that left the ownership and support mechanisms of the industry unaltered: "With clever executives and high-priced lawyers, the Government administrators have little chance in the long run to resist such pressure, due to the ever-changing personnel in the Government, regardless of the unquestioned faithfulness of the employees."[72] Few among the broadcast reform movement were willing to concede the "unquestioned faithfulness" of FRC members and employees, many of whom went on to lucrative careers with the networks or the NAB, or as commercial broadcasting attorneys. "Practically all the engineers and commissioners of this first radio commission," Morgan reflected, "were absorbed by the corporations to whom they had voted privileges worth millions of dollars."[73] One trade publication even commented in 1934 that Washington, D.C., had become a "happy hunting ground" for "former members of the FRC legal staff" as they parlayed their government experience into lucrative retainers from commercial broadcasting interests.[74]

The broadcast reform movement advocated any number of plans to re-create U.S. broadcasting, but three in particular received the most attention in the early 1930s. One plan was to have the government set aside a fixed percentage of the channels, generally either 15 percent or 25 percent, for the exclusive use of nonprofit broadcasters. The second plan was to have Congress authorize an extensive and independent study of broadcasting, with the aim of providing for an entirely new broadcast system. This plan was based on what had transpired in Britain and, particularly, Canada, which in 1932 announced that it was establishing a nonprofit and noncommercial broadcasting system, to no small extent due to distaste for what it saw taking place to the south.[75] To the reformers, it was axiomatic that any independent study of broadcasting would resolve to alter the status quo. The third plan was to have the government establish a series of nonprofit and noncommercial stations on a local, regional, and national basis that would be subsidized through taxes and operated by a congressionally approved board of directors of prominent citizens. This plan, too, was inspired by the experiences in Britain and Canada, and, indeed, in most of the world. The government stations would supplement, not replace, the existing commercial networks.

One basic and overriding problem plagued the broadcast reform movement throughout its existence: how to subsidize high-quality nonprofit broadcasting. Clearly, the existing system of nonprofit stations, with dilapidated facilities, restricted hours, and low power, attempting to rely upon donations from listeners, handouts from philanthropists, and grants from nonprofit groups had proven unsatisfactory, particularly in a grim economy. To many members of the movement the answer was obvious: have the government subsidize nonprofit broadcasting through the establishment of a series of government stations à la Britain, to be bankrolled by annual license fees. "A charge of $1.00 per set would provide America ten times the funds which we would need for a generous program of broadcasting," Morgan informed a convention of educators in 1932.[76] This was a touchy subject in U.S. politics, however: some elements of the broadcast reform movement, such as the ACLU, were more than a little skeptical about granting the government a larger role in communications. Even those elements of the reform movement, such as the NCER, that did not share the ACLU's innate skepticism toward the state began lobbying for a state-subsidized system only years after most of their leaders, including Morgan, had gone on record in favor of a government network as the only viable alternative to the status quo.[77] There was a general belief among the reformers in the early 1930s that the public would not accept government-controlled broadcasting. "A government-controlled radio system," two reformers noted in 1931, "whether or not hypothetically desirable, is highly impracticable, almost impossible."[78]

The only real alternative to having the government play a larger role was having advertising subsidize nonprofit broadcasting. This idea was anathema to the NCER, the ACLU, and much of the broadcast reform movement, which regarded advertising as every bit as bad as network domination. Indeed, it was its revulsion with advertising that led the NCER to disband its efforts to have a fixed percentage of the airwaves reserved for nonprofit broadcasters, since that measure would leave the issue of funding entirely unanswered. However, some elements of the reform movement, particularly nonprofit stations such as WCFL and WLWL, repeatedly defended their right to sell advertising to subsidize their operations.[79] This became the basis of the fundamental tactical split in the broadcast reform movement, as the various elements never worked in unison for the same proposal. "Every son-of-a-gun and his brother has a definite idea about the way it should be handled," bemoaned one reformer.[80] As an indication of the reformers' general confusion on this matter, as late as 1934, the NCER's research director, Tracy Tyler, "confessed" that he still had no notion regarding "what would be the best proposal for a general reorganization."[81]

In addition to the division over tactics and programs, at least three other major barriers stood between the broadcast reform movement and success. First, the radio lobby — NBC, CBS, and the NAB — had quickly emerged "as one of the most effective trade associations in the United States."[82] It was universally characterized as one of the very most powerful lobbies in Washington.[83] In addition to the usual political clout that accompanies wealth, the radio lobby had even greater leverage over publicity-conscious politicians because of its control of the airwaves. This point was not lost on either the commercial broadcasters or the opposition movement.[84] "I wanted to do something that would call attention to the inherent evils of our present commercialized form of broadcasting," wrote a freshman member of the House of Representatives in a "confidential" letter to the NCER in 1932. After explaining why he was abandoning the reform campaign after the radio broadcasters in his district had condemned him "in the most uncertain terms for my stand," he observed that the NCER "may not understand the complete control that the broadcasting stations have over the Members of Congress." He concluded that this was a problem the NCER must "overcome if you are to get anywhere with your program."[85]

The commercial broadcasters spared no expense in the early 1930s in a public relations campaign to establish the status quo as the only innately "American" and only truly "democratic" method for organizing broadcasting services.[86] With its abundant resources, the radio lobby was able to overwhelm the underfunded communications of the broadcast reform movement, which angered the reformers no end.[87] Also, the networks established "advisory councils" of prominent citizens to advise them on their public affairs programming and to reassure the public that the networks would be responsible and socially neutral in their broadcasting. Although even the most cursory examination of these "advisory groups" indicates that they had little effect on network operations, they were given heavy emphasis by the commercial broadcasters before Congress and the public.[88] As one NBC internal memo observed regarding that network's advisory council, "a great deal of weight will be put to it in the public mind."[89]

Second, given the clear contrast in the relative political strength and financial wherewithal of the radio lobby and the broadcast reform movement, the reformers had a great need for extensive and, they hoped, sympathetic coverage in the print news media. Unfortunately, the issue received very little coverage in the press, and what coverage it did receive was heavily oriented toward presenting the position of the commercial broadcasters. This point delighted the radio lobby, which placed great emphasis upon providing the press with a continual stream of press releases.[90] It angered and puzzled the reform movement, for the most part, which could not understand why their cause seemed to be getting short shrift.[91] As one reformer commented, "publicity . . . has been the weakest part of our whole setup."[92]

Third, the legal community, with few exceptions, rallied to the defense of the status quo. The American Bar Association established a Standing Committee on Communications in the late 1920s, with "the duty of studying and making recommendations on proposed radio legislation."[93] This committee was chaired by Louis G. Caldwell, who had been the FRC's first general counsel during the implementation of General Order 40 and had emerged as one of the leading commercial broadcasting attorneys in the nation.[94] Staffed almost entirely by commercial broadcasting attorneys, the ABA committee turned out annual reports ranging from forty to a hundred pages that argued in no uncertain terms that any reform of the status quo would be disastrous. Although these reports were never voted upon by the ABA, they were relied upon by Congress and presented to Congress and the public as the expert, neutral opinion of the U.S. legal community. The broadcast reform movement was appalled by this apparent conflict of interest, but it had little success in challenging the ABA committee's legitimacy.[95] Curiously, during the period from 1928 to 1933 the ABA committee, like the commercial broadcasting industry, was opposed to Congress's concerning itself with broadcast policy whatsoever. The committee favored granting the FRC unconditional power to act as it pleased. "The radio administration within a nation," Caldwell wrote in 1930, "must have a life-and-death power over the radio conduct of its subjects such as it neither has nor desires over their conduct in other matters." Caldwell argued that "such matters cannot safely be prescribed by statute" and are "unsuited for decision by a legislative body."[96] As for the seeming threat to free expression implicit in granting the FRC arbitrary power to license broadcasters, the legal community was not particularly concerned. "If all this be censorship," the ABA committee reported in 1929, "it seems unavoidable and in the best interests of the listening public."[97]

The Battle for the Airwaves, 1930–35

The campaign to restructure U.S. broadcasting had two distinct phases. The first, from 1930 until President Herbert Hoover left office in the spring of 1933, clearly was the high-water mark for popular discontent with U.S. broadcasting. One reformer confided to another that 95 percent of the people were dissatisfied with commercial broadcasting and that "more than one-half [of them] are ready to support any kind of a movement for a drastic change."[98] Even the proponents of the status quo were constantly mapping their strategy to reflect the public distaste for commercial broadcast fare. And this dissatisfaction was being communicated repeatedly to members of Congress. "Many members on both sides of the Capitol are aroused by local conditions," *Broadcasting* informed its readers on the status of broadcasting legislation, and they "have heard protests from constituents" regarding the nature of the U.S. system.[99] WCFL's Edward Nockels estimated that 70 percent of the Senate and 80 percent of the House supported legislation that would have set aside channels for nonprofit broadcasters, whereas the NAB warned its membership that the broadcast reformers had received pledges of support from fully 90 percent of the members of Congress.[100]

Nevertheless, reform legislation failed to get through Congress during this period, for two reasons. First, this was the trough of the Great Depression, and the preponderance of congressional activity was dedicated to legislation regarding economic recovery. "Were it not for the disturbing economic situation," *Broadcasting* observed in 1931, "Congress might blunder into the political radio morass camouflaged by these lobbying factions."[101] Second, while there was considerable support for reform among the rank-and-file members of Congress, this support tended to wane the less theoretical the issue became and the more the commercial broadcasters directed their fire against it, as the above-quoted letter to the NCER indicated. Moreover, the relevant committee leaders were nearly unanimous in their support for the status quo. "We have been lucky," observed NAB

President Harry Shaw, with perhaps too much modesty, in a speech to the NAB Board of Directors on the legislative situation in 1932. "We have been content to leave the protection of this industry to a few of our friends in certain places."[102] "If it were not for a little group of reactionary leaders in both branches of Congress," an incensed Nockels observed in 1931, reform "legislation would have been passed by this time."[103] And, indeed, when the Senate eventually passed a rider to a bill in 1931 that would have established a national, nonprofit labor network, the congressional leaders were able to have the bill tabled at the end of the session.[104]

The most important congressional leader in this regard was Senator C. C. Dill, who by the early 1930s had established himself as, in the words of *Broadcasting*, "unquestionably" having "the most influential voice in federal radio control of any figure in public life."[105] As ACLU counsel Morris Ernst stated emphatically in 1931, "There is no use in drafting material which will not be acceptable to him."[106] Behind a veneer of progressive rhetoric, Dill repeatedly stonewalled all efforts to get reform legislation through his Senate Committee on Interstate Commerce. An irate H. O. Davis noted in June 1932 that Dill constructed "a noisy radical front by going through the motions of attacking the broadcasting monopoly for home consumption, while behind the front he is working hand and glove with the broadcasters themselves."[107] In January 1932 Dill and another senator, responding to the public outcry for broadcast reform, had the Senate pass a measure authorizing the FRC to study the broadcast reform movement's criticisms of the status quo.[108] The FRC report, *Commercial Radio Advertising*, was based largely on the uncritical acceptance of commercial broadcasters' responses to a short questionnaire. The report, released that summer, praised the status quo and dismissed the broadcast reform movement's concerns as without merit.[109] The commercial broadcasters were elated, while the NCER dismissed the FRC report as "not a fact-finding document but a defense of the present radio system."[110] Davis termed the report "a joke."[111] Yet the report successfully defused the momentum for broadcast reform and left the movement in a sober state regarding its prospects. By 1933 the ACLU and the NCER came to accept Davis's stance regarding Dill, Dill's rhetoric notwithstanding. Senator Dill was a "weak sister" who would provide no assistance to the reform movement, the NCER's Tyler wrote the ACLU's Roger Baldwin.[112]

The second stage, from March 1933 until the Communications Act of 1934 was signed into law in June 1934, was the decisive period.

This was when Congress finally enacted permanent legislation on broadcasting. The reform movement initially was quite encouraged by the change in administrations and hoped that President Roosevelt would assist their cause. Indeed, there was considerable reason for optimism as many key proponents of the New Deal were outspoken critics of commercial broadcasting and advocates of sweeping reform of the status quo.[113] Moreover, one of Roosevelt's closest political and personal friends, Ambassador to Mexico Josephus Daniels, was an unabashed proponent of completely nationalized broadcasting. "There is no more reason why other communications industries should be privately owned than the mails," he wrote the president in one of many letters on the subject.[114] Nevertheless, Roosevelt elected not to take a public position on the broadcast debate, while his aides worked behind the scenes to assist the commercial broadcasters with their legislative agenda. Roosevelt was in no mood to take on an uphill fight against a powerful and entrenched communications industry, particularly when he enjoyed less-than-perfect relations with the nation's largely Republican newspaper industry. As even Daniels advised him, he had more important battles to fight.[115]

By 1933 the broadcasting industry largely had stabilized after the shake-up following General Order 40. The commercial broadcasters determined that the time was ripe for permanent legislation on broadcasting, which would eliminate the annual forum on Capitol Hill for "attacks by unfriendly groups" and "speed up the movement toward a more thoroughly stabilized broadcasting industry."[116] The commercial broadcasters' ideal situation would be to have the Radio Act of 1927 reenacted verbatim and to have a body similar to the FRC established on a permanent basis; indeed, the commercial broadcasters were the only group uniform in its praise of this otherwise most controversial body.[117] The fundamental problem was that the industry had no desire for Congress to debate or discuss how best to organize the U.S. broadcasting system, let alone have any public discussion of the issues involved. This would have been impossible in earlier sessions of Congress, but the commercial broadcasters were confident of their support among the key figures in Washington, most notably Senator Dill and the president.

In order to expedite the movement to pass permanent communications legislation, in the fall of 1933 President Roosevelt had Secretary of Commerce Daniel Roper appoint a committee of government department representatives to prepare recommendations for the "construction of needed legislation" in the area of communications.[118] This Roper Committee operated in secrecy, took no outside testimony, and recommended in January 1934 that the status quo be maintained but that all communications regulation be housed under one administrative agency. This was precisely what the commercial broadcasters had desired.[119] The committee did not even discuss broadcasting in its deliberations, yet included it in the report's final recommendations. This point was brought to the president's attention by a committee member who filed a "minority report" to indicate his displeasure with the lack of attention broadcasting had received.[120]

At the request of Secretary Roper, in January 1934 President Roosevelt authorized Roper to establish an independent Federal Committee to Study Radio Broadcasting under the Office of Education. This panel would take up the thorny issue of how best to structure and regulate U.S. broadcasting, which had been neglected by the Roper Committee.[121] The broadcast reformers were elated; for once they would have a forum. The commercial broadcasters and Senator Dill, on the other hand, were confounded. They informed the president in no uncertain terms that such a study was unnecessary, due to the aforementioned FRC study of 1932, and that it would not be used in the drafting of legislation, as was its ostensible purpose.[122] The president quietly canceled the FCSRB in late February. The NCER was informed that "this matter, for the time being, will be entirely handled by the Congress."[123]

The congressional strategy of Dill and his counterpart in the House, Representative Sam Rayburn, Democrat of Texas, was to rush the proposed legislation through committee hearings and have it brought to the floors of the House and Senate for a vote as quickly as possible.[124] Their bills essentially reenacted the Radio Act of 1927 and created a Federal Communications Commission to regulate all the communications industries. In short, with minor qualifications, these bills were precisely what the commercial broadcasters had desired. Dill hoped to stem any potential opposition to the proposed legislation by having his bill authorize the FCC to make a thorough study of communications and report back with any suggestions for reform legislation the following year. "If we leave out the controversial matters," Dill stated, "the bill can be passed at this session."[125] Indeed, Dill announced that he was not even intending to permit broadcasting to be discussed during the upcoming committee hearings on the legislation, since the unresolved broadcasting issues would now be taken up by the new FCC.[126] The commercial broadcasters announced their approval of this tactic; they had long felt more secure with their fate in the hands of regulators than in those of elected officials.[127]

While some elements of the reform movement had become demoralized and had given up any hope for immediate attention from Congress, the Paulist Fathers' John B. Harney submitted an amendment to the Dill communications bill during the committee hearings that would have required the FCC to set aside fully 25 percent of the channels for the use of nonprofit broadcasters. While the committee voted against the Harney proposal, Senators Robert Wagner, Democrat of New York, and Henry Hatfield, Republican of West Virginia, agreed to introduce the amendment on the floor of the Senate. Father Harney and the Paulists engaged in a whirlwind campaign to generate support for the measure, particularly from Catholic organizations and parishes around the nation. Within a few weeks the Paulists had more than 60,000 signatures on petitions supporting the measure, and had the active support of Edward Nockels and a portion of the labor movement.[128] In April the trade publication *Variety* reported that the now-termed Wagner-Hatfield amendment stood "better than a 50–50 chance of being adopted."[129]

The radio lobby attacked the Wagner-Hatfield amendment in late April and early May as if, as an NAB representative later explained, its passage "obviously would have destroyed the whole structure of broadcasting in America."[130] Both the White House and the FRC lobbied members of Congress against the legislation.[131] When the amendment was defeated on the Senate floor on May 15 by a vote of forty-two to twenty-three, one factor was instrumental in undercutting the sentiment for reform. After it became apparent that Father Harney would have his amendment introduced in the Senate, Senator Dill had installed a clause in his communications bill, section 307(c), that would require the FCC to hold hearings concerning the idea of reserving 25 percent of the channels for nonprofit broadcasters and then report back to Congress with recommendations the following year. This was enough to convince wayward senators that the Wagner-Hatfield amendment was not necessary.[132]

Immediately after voting down the Wagner-Hatfield amendment, the Senate approved Dill's communications bill with section 307(c) by a voice vote. In the House, Rayburn was able to keep the Harney amendment from getting to the floor for a vote or even being discussed in the floor debate. After the House passed the Rayburn communications bill in early June, the bills went to conference. After the revisions, Senator Dill telephoned Henry Bellows, the NAB's chief lobbyist, and informed him, "We have been very generous to you fellows." Bellows later commented, "When we read it, we found that every major point we had asked for was there."[133]

President Roosevelt signed the Communications Act of 1934 into law on June 18. The bill was lost in the media coverage of the stack of New Deal bills that had been passed at the end of the congressional session. When it was covered, it was characterized as a "New Deal in Radio Law" that was aimed at "curbing monopoly control in radio," and that boldly harnessed antagonistic private power and forced it to act in the public interest. Neither the Roosevelt administration nor Senator Dill did anything to discourage this interpretation, despite the patently bogus nature of the claim.[134] Indeed, some broadcasting historians assert this argument despite the fact that the Communications Act of 1934 restated the Radio Act of 1927 virtually verbatim and had been the conscious result of keeping the public and Congress itself as far removed as possible from any debate over broadcasting issues.[135]

With the passage of the Communications Act of 1934, Congress effectively removed itself from substantive broadcast policy issues for the balance of the century. The only "legitimate" opportunity remaining for the broadcast reform movement to present its case was in the FCC hearings in October 1934, mandated by section 307(c), which required the FCC to evaluate the Wagner-Hatfield fixed-percentage concept. The outcome of the hearings was never in doubt: most elements of the broadcast reform movement regarded them as a "setup for the broadcasters," and, indeed, two of the three FCC members who would be at the hearings announced to the NAB convention in September that there was no way they would alter the status quo, regardless of what transpired at the upcoming hearings.[136] In January 1935, the FCC formally issued its report to Congress: there was no need to alter the status quo, efforts should be made to assist disenfranchised nonprofit groups so that they could utilize the commercial broadcasters' facilities.[137]

Although this was no surprise, it was still a bitter blow for the reform movement; it constituted, in effect, the final nail in its coffin. The FCC made it clear that it would regard the status quo as the officially authorized broadcasting system henceforth, until notified otherwise by congressional statute. At the same time, however, Congress showed no interest in reopening the political can of worms represented by broadcast regulation after the passage of the Communications Act of 1934.

The immediate legacy of the reform movement was that it had forced the delay of the full stabilization of the airwaves from 1929 or 1930 to 1935. What the FCC had in fact successfully recommended was the cooperation thesis advanced by the Wilbur Committee in 1930 and rejected at that time. All those who wished to continue to participate in the legitimate debate over broadcast policy had to accept the status quo as unalterable. Ironically, precisely as the window for reform was being slammed shut, the NCER formally proposed the creation of a federal chain of noncommercial stations, in 1935.[138] The proposal fell on deaf ears; the broadcast reform movement quickly unraveled. The Paulist station WLWL simply sold its license to Arde Bulova in 1937 and went out of business. Labor station WCFL disbanded its efforts to be supported by membership contributions and became an advertising-supported NBC affiliate by the mid-1930s; despite its labor pedigree, it became largely indistinguishable from the capitalist broadcasters. After 1935 the NCER's funding became contingent upon its willingness to accept the status quo; after attempting to improve relations between educators and commercial broadcasters and the FCC, it closed down in 1941. The ACLU Radio Committee remained active with a somewhat radical broadcast legislative platform well into the second half of the decade, when it finally discontinued these efforts in view of their complete lack of success. By the end of the decade the ACLU had formally accepted the capitalist and commercial basis of the industry as legitimate, as much for pragmatic reasons as for any philosophical change of heart, and it began to resume its traditional concern with government, rather than capitalist or commercial, censorship. The broadcast system now was deemed fundamentally sound rather than fundamentally flawed.[139]

In the second half of the decade, the commercial broadcasters strove for ideological closure. They located commercial broadcasting next to the newspaper industry as an icon of American freedom and culture, and, with considerable historical revisionism if not outright fabrication, removed it from critical contemplation. The broadcast reform movement was written out of the dominant perspective on the development of U.S. broadcasting, and the conflict of the early 1930s was erased from historical memory. "Our American system of broadcasting," Radio Corporation of America President David Sarnoff told a nationwide audience over NBC in 1938,

> is what it is because it operates in the American democracy. It is a free system because this is a free country. It is privately owned because private ownership is one of our national doctrines. It is privately supported, through commercial sponsorship of a portion of its program hours, and at no cost to the listener, because ours is a free economic system. No special laws had to be passed to bring these things about. They were already implicit in the American system, ready and waiting for broadcasting when it came.[140]

The implications of this logic were not always left unspoken. "He who attacks the fundamentals of the American system" of broadcasting, CBS President Paley told an audience in 1937, "attacks democracy itself."[141]

Also quickly forgotten was the position of the legal community and the commercial broadcasting industry prior to 1934 in favor of arbitrary and unchecked commission regulation of broadcasting. Now that the industry was entrenched and beyond political challenge, any further regulation was determined to have more negative than positive possibilities. Louis Caldwell led the campaign, beginning in late 1934, to recognize existing property rights in the ether and eliminate all government licensing and regulation of broadcasting, all in the name of the First Amendment. Caldwell compared the Communications Act of 1934 to "the ordinances of the Star Chamber" and argued that with the legal recognition of the government's right to regulate broadcasting, "the clock of liberty has been set back three hundred years."[142] The campaign for deregulation was unsuccessful, but the resulting system by the late 1930s acknowledged the government's right to regulate broadcasting only after the marketplace and industry self-regulation had proven abject failures. In effect, there developed a de facto privatization of the airwaves and, with that, what broadcast historian Philip Rosen has termed the "myth of regulation."[143]

By the end of the decade, and thereafter, the notion that the citizenry had a right to determine whatever broadcast system they deemed superior for society was effectively dead; the issue had become off-limits as a legitimate political issue. By 1945 Paul Lazarsfeld would conclude his study of broadcasting by observing that the American people seemed to approve of the private and commercial basis of the industry. "People have little information on the subject," he noted. "They have obviously given it little thought."[144]

Conclusion

There was a debate over the private, for-profit, and commercial basis of the U.S. broadcasting system. This did not emerge as the result of a consensus, but as a result of conflict in which there were clear winners and losers. Because much of U.S. broadcasting history has underemphasized this opposition, it has had the earmarks of a "history written by its victors." Even the otherwise outstanding critical scholarship, with its emphasis on the period preceding 1927, seemingly has accepted the notion that the American people went along with the establishment of the status quo.

Yet the broadcast reform movement was unable to generate much popular momentum. Certainly, the might of the commercial broadcasters was such as to make any alternative system highly problematic. Nonetheless, it is an error to argue that the system was thoroughly consolidated by the middle 1920s or to assume that the American people were ignorant, apathetic, or even enthusiastic about commercial broadcasting. The commercial broadcasters and their allies did everything within their (substantial) powers to keep people and even Congress ignorant of their right and ability to determine broadcast policy throughout the period in question. And, in this sense, there has never really been a legitimate public debate over the issues the broadcast reform movement attempted to raise. Moreover, subsequent trends in the mass media industries suggest that some of the concerns of the broadcast reformers in the 1930s have not gone away; rather, they may indeed be more pressing today than at any other time in U.S. history. If this is the case, an understanding of this chapter in U.S. communication history may be all the more necessary.[145]

Notes

1. See, for example, Sydney Head, *Broadcasting in America* (Boston: Houghton Mifflin, 1956); Joseph P. McKerns, "Industry Skeptics and the Radio Act of 1927," *Journalism History* 3 (Winter 1976–77): 136; Frederick W. Ford, "The Meaning of the Public Interest, Convenience and Necessity," *Journal of Broadcasting* 8 (Winter 1964): 8.

2. The best treatment probably has been that by Philip T. Rosen, *The Modern Stentors: Radio Broadcasting and the Federal Government 1920–1934* (Westport, Conn.: Greenwood, 1980), 161–78. Because the Communications Act of 1934 largely restated the Radio Act of 1927 verbatim, the preponderance of the scholarship seem-

ingly concludes that the "real debate" over broadcasting must have taken place prior to 1927. If one concentrates upon that period, one would be perfectly justified in arguing that the status quo emerged without significant opposition. See also Erik Barnouw, *A Tower in Babel* (New York: Oxford University Press, 1966).

3. Mary S. Mander, "The Public Debate about Broadcasting in the Twenties: An Interpretive History," *Journal of Broadcasting* 25 (Spring 1984): 185.

4. Susan J. Douglas, *Inventing American Broadcasting 1899–1922* (Baltimore: Johns Hopkins University Press, 1987), 317.

5. A more substantial treatment of the themes in this chapter is found in Robert W. McChesney, *Telecommunications, Mass Media, and Democracy: The Battle for the Control of U.S. Broadcasting, 1928–1935* (New York: Oxford University Press, 1993).

6. S. E. Frost, *Education's Own Stations* (Chicago: University of Chicago Press, 1937), 4; Federal Communications Commission, *Digest of Hearings, Federal Communications Commission Broadcast Division, under Sec. 307(C) of "The Communications Act of 1934" October 1–20, November 7–12, 1934* (Washington, D.C.: Federal Communications Commission, 1935), 180–249 (hereafter cited as *FCC Digest*).

7. C. M. Jansky, Jr., "The Problem of the Institutionally Owned Station," in *Radio and Education: Proceedings of the Second Annual Assembly of the National Advisory Council on Radio in Education, Inc., 1932*, ed. Levering Tyson (Chicago: University of Chicago Press, 1932), 214 (hereafter cited as *Radio and Education 1932*); Werner J. Severin, "Commercial vs. Non-commercial Radio During Broadcasting's Early Years," *Journal of Broadcasting* 20 (Fall 1978): 491–504.

8. Jansky, "The Problem," 215; Henry A. Bellows, "The Right to Use Radio," *Public Utilities Fortnightly* 3 (June 27, 1929): 770–74.

9. "Federal Control of Radio Broadcasting," *Yale Law Journal* 32 (1929), 250; U.S. House of Representatives, 70th Cong., 1st Sess., *Hearings before the Committee on the Merchant Marine and Fisheries on H.R. 8825* (Washington, D.C.: U.S. Government Printing Office, 1928), January 31, 1928, 129 (hereafter cited as *House Hearings 1928*); Martin Codel, "Who Pays for Your Radio Program?" *Nation's Business* 17 (August 1929): 39ff.

10. See Wilbur Schramm, ed., *Mass Communications* (Urbana: University of Illinois Press, 1960), 43; David Sarnoff, "Address to Chicago Chamber of Commerce, April 1924," in Samuel L. Rothafel and Raymond Francis Yates, *Broadcasting: Its New Day* (New York: Arno, 1971), 171–84.

11. See John W. Spalding, "1928: Radio Becomes a Mass Advertising Medium," *Journal of Broadcasting* 8 (Winter 1963–64): 31–44.

12. "Report of the Committee on Radio," *American Newspaper Publishers Association Bulletin*, No. 5374, May 5, 1927, 285.

13. See Edward F. Sarno, "The National Radio Conferences," *Journal of Broadcasting* 13 (Spring 1969): 189–202; Carl J. Friedrich and Jeanette Sayre, *The Development of the Control of Advertising on the Air* (New York: Radiobroadcasting Research Project, 1940); "Opening Address by Herbert Hoover," in *Proceedings of the Fourth National Radio Conference and Recommendations for the Regulation of Radio* (Washington, D.C.: U.S. Government Printing Office, 1926), 5; Herbert Hoover to Harold G. Ingham, December 13, 1924, and Herbert Hoover to Col. Arthur Woods, December 10, 1924, Herbert Hoover Papers, Herbert Hoover Presidential Library, West Branch, Iowa, Commerce series, Box 490 (hereafter cited as Hoover Mss).

14. Merlin H. Aylesworth, "Radio's Accomplishment," *Century* 118 (June 1929): 214–21.

15. Jansky, "The Problem," 214–17; *Education by Radio*, February 12, 1931.

16. Stephen B. Davis, "The Law of the Air," in *The Radio Industry: The Story of Its Development*, ed. Anton de Haas (Chicago: A. W. Shaw, 1928), 169; Daniel E. Garvey, "Secretary Hoover and the Quest for Broadcast Regulation," *Journalism History* 3 (Autumn 1976): 66–70, 85; Marvin R. Bensman, "The Zenith-WJAZ Case and the Chaos of 1926–27," *Journal of Broadcasting* 14 (Fall 1970): 423–40; "Pending Litigation Marks Beginning of Radio Jurisprudence," *American Bar Association Journal* 15 (March 1929): 173–78.

17. "Report of the Committee on Radio Broadcasting," in *Proceedings of the Twelfth Annual Convention of the National University Extension Association 1927*, vol. 10 (Boston: Wright & Potter, 1927), 182; Donald G. Godfrey, "The 1927 Radio Act: People and Politics," *Journalism History* 4 (Autumn 1978): 78; Barnouw, *A Tower in Babel*, 281; Carl J. Friedrich and Evelyn Sternberg, "Congress and the Control of Radio-Broadcasting I," *American Political Science Review* 37 (October 1943): 799–800.

18. See Louis G. Caldwell, "The Standard of Public Interest, Convenience or Necessity as Used in the Radio Act of 1927," *Air Law Review* 1 (July 1930): 295–330; Clarence C. Dill, "Safe-Guarding the Ether—The American Way," *Congressional Digest*, August-September 1933, 196.

19. See James M. Herring, "Public Interest, Convenience or Necessity in Radio Broadcasting," *Harvard Business Review* 10 (April 1932): 280–91.

20. See "Report of the Standing Committee on Radio Law," in *Report of the Fifty-Second Annual Meeting of the American Bar Association, 1929* (Baltimore: Lord Baltimore, 1929), 404–506 (hereafter cited as *1929 ABA Report*); see also Laurence F. Schmeckebier, *The Federal Radio Commission* (Washington, D.C.: Brookings Institution, 1932), 22–23.

21. U.S. Senate, 70th Cong., 2nd Sess., *Hearings before the Committee on Interstate Commerce on S. 4937* (Washington, D.C.: U.S. Government Printing Office, 1929), February 4, 1929, 24 (hereafter cited as *Senate Hearings 1929*).

22. *House Hearings 1928*, January 27, 1928, January 31, 1928, 68, 74, 108–9; U.S. Senate, 70th Cong., 1st Sess., *Hearings before the Committee on Interstate Commerce on the Confirmation of Federal Radio Commissioners, Part Two* (Washington, D.C.: U.S. Government Printing Office, 1928), February 3, 1928, 192 (hereafter cited as *Senate Hearings 1928*).

23. President, National Association of Broadcasters, to Harold Lafount, January 23, 1928, Federal Communication Commission Papers, National Archives, Suitland, Md., Record Group 173, General Correspondence 1927–1946, Box 395.

24. See *1929 ABA Report*, 404–506; Murray Edelman, *The Licensing of Radio Services in the United States, 1927 to 1947* (Urbana: University of Illinois Press, Illinois Studies in the Social Sciences, 1950), 38–39.

25. Harold A. Lafount, "Educational Programs in Radio Broadcasting," *School and Society* 34 (December 5, 1931), 758–60; Statement by Radio Commissioner Harold A. Lafount, August 5, 1929, Harold Lafount to Paul Wooten, June 11, 1931, Hoover Mss, Box 148.

26. *Senate Hearings 1928*, Part One, 151, 191; *Senate Hearings 1929*, 142; "And All Because They're Smart," June 1935, 11, Columbia Broadcasting System Corporate Press Services, New York.

27. For an elaboration of this point, see Bethuel M. Webster, Jr., "Notes on the Policy of the Administration with Reference to the Control of Communications," *Air Law Review* 5 (April 1934): 107–31.

28. *1929 ABA Report*, 459.

29. Lucas A. Powe, Jr., *American Broadcasting and the First Amendment* (Berkeley: University of California Press, 1987), 65.

30. U.S. House of Representatives, 70th Cong., 2nd Sess., *Hearings before the Committee on the Merchant Marine and Fisheries on H.R. 15430*, Part One (Washington, D.C.: U.S. Government Printing Office, 1929), 75.

31. Christopher H. Sterling, *Electronic Media: A Guide to Trends in Broadcasting and Newer Technologies 1920–1983* (New York: Praeger, 1984), 12; Thomas Porter Robinson, *Radio Networks and the Federal Government* (New York: Columbia University Press, 1943), 26–27; "The Menace of Radio Monopoly," *Education by Radio*, March 26, 1931, 27; "The Power Trust and the Public Schools," *Education by Radio*, December 10, 1931, 150.

32. Cited in "Radio Censorship and the Federal Communications Commission," *Columbia Law Review* 39 (March 1939): 447.

33. Herman S. Hettinger, "Some Fundamental Aspects of Radio Broadcasting," *Harvard Business Review* 13 (1935): 14–28; "Chain Income from Time Sales," *Variety*, January 8, 1935, 40.

34. *Education by Radio*, January 5, 1932, 2; Rosen, *The Modern Stentors*, 158; J. Fred MacDonald, *Don't Touch That Dial: Radio Programming in American Life, 1920–1960* (Chicago: Nelson-Hall, 1979), 29–34; Michele Hilmes, *Hollywood and Broadcasting: From Radio to Cable* (Urbana: University of Illinois Press, 1990), 52.

35. Henry Volkening, "Abuses of Radio Broadcasting," *Current History* 33 (December 1930): 396–400; Rosen, *The Modern Stentors*, 12; Barnouw, *A Tower in Babel*, 270.

36. W. S. Gregson to B. B. Brackett, February 25, 1932, National Association of Educational Broadcasters Manuscripts, Wisconsin Historical Society, Madison, Wis., Box No. 1a, General Correspondence, 1932.

37. *FCC Digest*, 180–249; *Congressional Record* 78 (May 15, 1934): 8830–34; "Superpower," *Education by Radio*, May 7, 1931, 50.

38. Federal Radio Commission, *Third Annual Report of the Federal Radio Commission to the Congress of the United States* (Washington, D.C.: U.S. Government Printing Office, 1929), 31–36.

39. *Education by Radio*, May 7, 1931, 49.

40. Armstrong Perry, "The College Station and the Federal Radio Commission," in *Education on the Air: Second Yearbook of the Institute of Education by Radio*, ed. Josephine H. MacLatchy (Columbus: Ohio State University, 1931), 16–17.

41. Statement of Joy Elmer Morgan, "On Behalf of the National Committee on Education by Radio and the National Education Association," in *Official Report of Proceedings before the Federal Communications Commission . . . Hearing In Re before the Broadcast Division of the Federal Communications Commission on Section 307(c) of the Communications Act of 1934*, vol. 1 Smith & Hulse, official reporters (Washington, D.C.: Federal Communications Commission, 1935), 20.

42. See Advisory Committee on Education by Radio, *Report of the Advisory Committee on Education by Radio Appointed by the Secretary of the Interior* (Columbus, Ohio: F. J. Heer, 1930).

43. Letter of Transmittal of Commissioner Cooper, Office of Education Manuscripts, National Archives, Washington, D.C., RG 12, Box 31 (hereafter cited as Education Mss); Minutes of the Conference on Educational Radio Problems, Steven Hotel, Chicago, October 13, 1930, At the Invitation of the U.S. Commissioner of Education, Education Mss, RG 12, Box 31; Discussion of Future Possibilities of Radio in Educational Institutions, Led by Commissioner Lafount, October 13, 1930, Education Mss, RG 12, Box 32, General Correspondence.

44. The nine organizations included the NEA, the National University Extension Association, the American Council on Education, the National Council of State Superintendents, the Association of College and University Broadcasting Stations, the Jesuit Educational Association, the National Catholic Educational Association, the Association of Land Grant Colleges and Universities, and the National Association of State Universities.

45. For a longer treatment of the Payne Fund's radio activities, see McChesney, *Telecommunications*, ch. 3.

46. Joy Elmer Morgan, "Education's Rights on the Air," in *Radio and Education: Proceedings of the First Assembly of the National Advisory Council on Radio in Education, 1931*, ed. Levering Tyson (Chicago: University of Chicago Press, 1931), 128; "Education Demands Freedom of the Air," *Education by Radio*, April 28, 1932, 64.

47. See Joy Elmer Morgan and E. D. Bullock, *Selected Articles on Municipal Ownership* (Minneapolis: Wilson, 1911); Joy Elmer Morgan, "An Open Letter to Members of Congress," January 20, 1933, Payne Fund Inc. Manuscripts, Western Reserve Historical Society, Cleveland, Ohio, Container 39, Folder 750 (hereafter cited as Payne Fund Mss).

48. Morgan, "Education's Rights on the Air," 123, 128, 120–21.

49. Joy Elmer Morgan, "The Radio in Education," in *Proceedings of the 17th Annual Convention of the National University Extension Association 1932*, vol. 15 (Bloomington: Indiana University Press, 1932), 79.

50. For more detailed accounts of each of these stations, see Robert W. McChesney, "Crusade against Mammon: Father Harney, WLWL and the Debate over Radio in the 1930s," *Journalism History* 14 (Winter 1987): 118–30; Robert W. McChesney, "Labor and the Marketplace of Ideas: WCFL and the Battle for Labor Radio Broadcasting, 1928–1934," *Journalism Monographs* 134 (August 1992); Nathan Godfried, "The Origins of Labor Radio: WCFL, the 'Voice of Labor,' 1925–1928," *Historical Journal of Film, Radio and Television* 7 (1987): 143–59.

51. Edward N. Nockels, *Public Interest, Convenience, and Necessity, and the Last of the Public Domain* (pamphlet) (Washington, D.C., 1936), 13.

52. Edward N. Nockels, "The Voice of Labor," *American Federationist*, 37 (April 1930): 414.

53. William Leiss, Stephen Kline, and Sut Jhally, *Social Communication in Advertising* (New York: Metheun, 1986), 78; Frank W. Peers, *The Politics of Canadian Broadcasting 1920–1951* (Toronto: University of Toronto Press, 1969), 77. For a longer treatment of press-radio relations during this period, see Robert W. McChesney, "Press-Radio Relations and the Emergence of Network, Commercial Broadcasting in the United States, 1930–1935," *Historical Journal of Film, Radio and Television* 11 (1991): 41–57.

54. "Government Operation Proposed," *Education by Radio*, October 17, 1935, 51.

55. Robert S. Mann, "After All, Why Radio Advertising?" *Editor & Publisher*, June 6, 1931, 12; "A Mistake to Broadcast Advertising by Radio," *Printer's Ink*, February 22, 1923, 157; "Broadcasting Doesn't Belong in Advertising Account," *Printer's Ink*, August 6, 1925, 125–28; "A.N.P.A. Fails to Renew Radio Attack, California Body Urges European System," *Broadcasting*, December 1, 1931, 8.

56. See H. O. Davis, *Empire of the Air* (Ventura, CA: Ventura Free Press, 1932); *American Broadcasting: An Analytic Study of One Day's Output of 206 Commercial Radio Stations Including Program Contents and Advertising Interruptions* (Ventura, CA: Ventura Free Press, 1933).

57. H. O. Davis to S. H. Evans, November 10, 1931; H. O. Davis to O. J. Hardy, September 5, 1931, Payne Fund Mss, Container 59, Folder 1143.

58. "Radio Threat Concerns Press, Says Don Gilman," *Broadcasting*, February 15, 1932, 8.

59. "Radio and the Press," *Broadcasting*, November 15, 1931, 18.

60. Caleb Johnson, "Newspapers Share Radio's Revenue," *Broadcasting*, May 15, 1932, 17.

61. "Elzy Roberts Quits Press Radio Post," *Broadcasting*, May 15, 1932, 17.

62. "Radio and the Press," *Broadcasting*, November 15, 1931, 18.

63. Roger Baldwin, "Memorandum on Radio in Relation to Free Speech," May 19, 1933, American Civil Liberties Union Manuscripts, Princeton University, Princeton, N.J., 1933, vol. 599 (hereafter cited as ACLU Mss).

64. Harry F. Ward to Federal Communications Commission, August 24, 1934, ACLU Mss, 1934, vol. 694; Roger Baldwin to Harris K. Randall, April 4, 1933, ACLU Mss, 1931–33, vol. 513.

65. Roger Baldwin to Harris K. Randall, October 30, 1933, ACLU Mss, 1933, vol. 510.

66. Joy Elmer Morgan, "The New American Plan for Radio," in *A Debate Handbook on Radio Control and Operation*, ed. Bower Aly and Gerald T. Shively (Columbia, Mo.: Staples, 1933), 82 (hereafter cited as *Debate Handbook*).

67. For a longer treatment of the critique of commercial broadcasting generated by the reformers, see Robert W. McChesney, "An Almost Incredible Absurdity for a Democracy," *Journal of Communication Inquiry* 15 (Winter 1991): 89–114. For Hamilton's influence, see Richard Joyce Smith, "The Ultimate Control of Radio in the United States," in *Radio and Education 1932*, 181–94; E. Pendleton Herring, "Politics and Radio Regulation," *Harvard Business Review* 13 (1935): 167–78; E. Pendleton Herring, *Public Administration and the Public Interest* (New York: McGraw-Hill, 1936); Alexander Meiklejohn, *Political Freedom* (New York: Harper & Brothers, 1948), 86–87; John Dewey, "Radio—for Propaganda or Public Interest," *Education by Radio*, February 28, 1935, 11; John Dewey, "Our Un-Free Press," *Common Sense*, November 1935, 6–7. For Sinclair's position, see *Education by Radio*, December 24, 1931, 156; Fredrick Lewis Allen, "Radio City: Cultural Center?" *Education by Radio*, May 12, 1932, 65–68, "H. L. Mencken," *Education by Radio*, August 27, 1931, 101–2; Bruce Bliven, "Shall the Government Own, Operate, and Control Radio Broadcasting in the United States?" in *Radio and Education: Proceedings of the Fourth Annual Assembly of the National Advisory Council on Radio in Education, Inc., 1934*, ed. Levering Tyson (Chicago: University of Chicago Press, 1934), 76–83, 106–15.

68. William Aylott Orton, *America in Search of Culture* (Boston: Little, Brown, 1933); Jerome Davis, *Capitalism and Its Culture* (New York: Farrar & Rinehart, 1935);

James Rorty, *Order on the Air!* (New York: John Day, 1934); James Rorty, *Our Master's Voice: Advertising* (New York: John Day, 1934).

69. Bruce Bliven, "For Better Broadcasting," *New Republic*, October 3, 1934, 201; Anonymous, "I'm Signing Off," *Forum*, February 1932, 114; see also "The Dominant Moron," *Catholic World*, May 1934, 135–37.

70. Ben H. Bagdikian, *The Media Monopoly*, 3d ed. (Boston: Beacon, 1990); Herbert J. Gans, *Deciding What's News* (New York: Pantheon, 1979); Edward S. Herman and Noam Chomsky, *Manufacturing Consent: The Political Economy of the Mass Media* (New York: Pantheon, 1988); Gaye Tuchman, *Making News* (New York: Basic Books, 1978).

71. Morgan, "Education's Rights on the Air," 122.

72. Comments on Report of Majority Members of Committee and Discussion of Position of Minority Member, Franklin Delano Roosevelt Manuscripts, Franklin Delano Roosevelt Presidential Library, Hyde Park, New York, OF 859a, 1933–45 (hereafter cited as FDR Mss).

73. "The Ideals of a Great Citizen," *Education by Radio*, April 7, 1932, 56; Joy Elmer Morgan, Unpublished Memoirs, 19–20, Joy Elmer Morgan Papers, National Education Association, Washington, D.C., FCB 1, Drawer 1.

74. Cited in "Radio's Legal Racket," *Education by Radio*, May 10, 1934, 19.

75. "Nationally-Owned Radio System for Canada," *Education by Radio*, July 7, 1932, 81–82; Martin Codel, "Canadian Broadcasting to Be Nationalized," *Broadcasting*, May 15, 1932, 7–8; "Canadian Radio Proposal Is Challenge to U.S. Broadcasters, Dill Tells Senate," *Broadcasting*, May 15, 1932, 8.

76. Morgan, "The Radio in Education," 83.

77. Morgan, "Education's Rights on the Air," 124; Joy Elmer Morgan, "Should the U.S. Adopt the British System of Radio Control?" *Congressional Digest*, August-September 1933, 206; Joy Elmer Morgan, "Radio and Education," in *Radio and Its Future*, ed. Martin Codel (New York: Harper & Brothers, 1930), 76–77.

78. Vita Lauter and Joseph H. Friend, "Radio and the Censors," *Forum*, December 1931, 364.

79. U.S. Senate, 73rd Cong., 2nd Sess., *Hearings before the Committee on Interstate Commerce on S. 2910, 1934* (Washington, D.C.: U.S. Government Printing Office, 1934), 186 (hereafter cited as *Senate Hearings 1934*); "Advertising Is Basis of Radio Existence," *Federation News*, August 5, 1933, 6.

80. S. H. Evans to W. V. Woehlke, February 15, 1932, Payne Fund Mss, Container 60, Folder 1165.

81. T. F. Tyler to J. O. Keller, November 10, 1934, Payne Fund Mss, Container 41, Folder 798.

82. David R. Mackey, "The National Association of Broadcasters: Its First Twenty Years," doctoral dissertation, Northwestern University, 1956, 1.

83. Tracy Tyler to Roger Baldwin, October 26, 1933, ACLU Mss, 1933, vol. 599; personal interview with Bethuel M. Webster, Jr., February 18, 1987; Eddie Dowling, "Radio Needs a Revolution," *Forum* February 1934, 69.

84. Morgan, "Should the U.S. Adopt," 204; Sol Taishoff, "Session of Radio-Minded Congress Nears," *Broadcasting*, December 1, 1931, 5.

85. T. R. Amlie to T. F. Tyler, May 24, 1932, Payne Fund Mss, Container 43, Folder 825.

86. For two classic statements, see National Association of Broadcasters,

Broadcasting in the United States (Washington, D.C.: National Association of Broadcasters, 1933); National Broadcasting Company, *Broadcasting. vols. 1–4* (New York: National Broadcasting Company, 1935).

87. Morgan, "The New American Plan," 82.

88. See Francis D. Farrell, *Brief History of the Advisory Council of the National Broadcasting Company* (New York: National Broadcasting Company, 1939), 2; Barnouw, *A Tower in Babel*, 204–6; Confidential Memorandum from Levering Tyson to Dr. Robert Hutchins, January 14, 1933, R. M. Hutchins Papers Addenda, University of Chicago, Chicago, Ill., vol. 99 (hereafter cited as Hutchins Add Mss); Orrin E. Dunlap, Jr., "Council Reviews Effect of Radio on American Life," *New York Times*, April 29, 1934, sec. IX, p. 9. See also Louise M. Benjamin, "Birth of a Network's 'Conscience': The NBC Advisory Council, 1927," *Journalism Quarterly* 66 (Autumn 1989): 587–90.

89. Suggested Memorandum to Mr. Aylesworth from Mr. Patterson, 1933, Hutchins Add Mss, vol. 99.

90. See James E. Pollard, "Newspaper Publicity for Radio Programs," in *Education on the Air: Fifth Yearbook of the Institute for Education by Radio*, ed. Josephine H. MacLatchy (Columbus: Ohio State University, 1934), 222–23.

91. See, for example, "Can America Get the Truth about Radio?" *Education by Radio*, March 15, 1934, 9. For a detailed analysis of the role of the ABA and the legal community, see Robert W. McChesney, "Free Speech and Democracy: Louis G. Caldwell, the American Bar Association and the Debate over the Free Speech Implications of Broadcast Regulation, 1928–1938," *American Journal of Legal History* 35 (October 1991): 351–92.

92. J. F. Wright to T. F. Tyler, March 30, 1934, Payne Fund Mss, Container 42, Folder 820.

93. "Discussion following Friday Morning Session, May 21, 1931," in *Radio and Education 1931*, 144.

94. "Four Stations Appeal Radio Orders," *New York Times*, November 12, 1929, 42; "Assails Chicago Station," *New York Times*, April 19, 1932, 34; "Caldwell Off to Madrid," *Broadcasters' News Bulletin*, July 30, 1932.

95. "Legal Racketeering?" *Education by Radio*, August 27, 1931, 101; "Radio from the Citizen's Point of View," *Education by Radio*, October 8, 1931, 112.

96. Louis G. Caldwell, "Radio and the Law," in *Radio and Its Future*, ed. Martin Codel (New York: Harper & Brothers, 1930), 226–31.

97. *1929 ABA Report*, 459.

98. W. H. Woehlke to S. H. Evans, December 12, 1932, Payne Fund Mss, Container 60, Folder 1167.

99. Taishoff, "Session of Radio-Minded Congress," 6.

100. Edward N. Nockels, "Labor's Rights on the Air," *Federation News*, February 7, 1931, 2; "Labor Resolution Presented," *Broadcasters' News Bulletin*, January 12, 1931; "Labor Bill Headed for Congress," *Broadcasters' News Bulletin*, February 21, 1931.

101. Taishoff, "Session of Radio-Minded Congress," 6.

102. "President Shaw Warns," *Broadcasters' News Bulletin*, January 11, 1932.

103. Nockels, "Labor's Rights on the Air," 2.

104. "Labor's Big Fight for Freedom of the Air," *Federation News*, March 21, 1931, 9; "Labor Bill Headed for Congress."

105. Martin Codel, "Dill and Davis Seen Powers in Radio Rule under Roosevelt," *Broadcasting*, November 15, 1932, 8.

106. Morris Ernst to Gordon W. Moss, November 19, 1931, ACLU Mss, 1931–33, vol. 513.

107. H. O. Davis to W. H. Cowles, June 24, 1932, Payne Fund Mss, Container 59, Folder 1145.

108. *Congressional Record* 75 (January 4, 1932): 1194–95; *Congressional Record* 75 (January 7, 1932): 1412–13; Sol Taishoff, "Commission Opens Sweeping Radio Inquiry," *Broadcasting*, February 1, 1932, 5, 28.

109. Federal Radio Commission, *Commercial Radio Advertising* (Washington, D.C.: U.S. Government Printing Office, 1932).

110. "A Congressional Investigation of Radio," *Education by Radio*, December 8, 1932, 105. For the industry position see, for example, "Indisputable Facts," *Broadcasting*, June 15, 1932, 20.

111. H. O. Davis to W. H. Brooks, October 5, 1932, Payne Fund Mss, Container 59, Folder 1145.

112. Tracy Tyler to Roger Baldwin, October 26, 1933, ACLU Mss, 1933, vol. 599.

113. Most prominent were Eddie Dowling; Dr. Arthur Morgan, chairman of the Tennessee Valley Authority; Ambassador to Mexico Josephus Daniels; and economist Adolph A. Berle. See, for example, Dowling, "Radio Needs a Revolution"; Arthur E. Morgan, "Radio as a Cultural Agency in Sparsely Settled Regions and Remote Areas," in *Radio as a Cultural Agency: Proceedings of a National Conference on the Use of Radio as a Cultural Agency in a Democracy*, ed. Tracy F. Tyler (Washington, D.C.: National Committee on Education by Radio, 1934), 81.

114. Josephus Daniels to Franklin D. Roosevelt, January 15, 1935, FDR Mss, PPF 86, 1935.

115. Ibid.; for additional analysis of the Roosevelt administration and broadcast policy, see Rosen, *The Modern Stentors*, 170–80; Robert W. McChesney, "Franklin Roosevelt, His Administration, and the Communications Act of 1934," *American Journalism* 5 (1988): 204–30.

116. Sol Taishoff, " 'War Plans' Laid to Protect Broadcasting," *Broadcasting*, March 1, 1933, 5; see also "Report of the Standing Committee on Communications," in *Report of the Fifty-Fifth Annual Meeting of the American Bar Association, 1932* (Baltimore: Lord Baltimore, 1932), 452.

117. See, for example, *Senate Hearings 1934*, March 10, 1934, 53–55; also, Bellows to Early, February 28, 1934, FDR Mss, OF 859a, 1933–45.

118. *Study of Communications by an Interdepartmental Committee, Letter from the President of the United States to the Chairman of the Committee on Interstate Commerce Transmitting a Memorandum from the Secretary of Commerce Relative to a Study of Communications by an Interdepartmental Committee* (Washington, D.C.: U.S. Government Printing Office, 1934).

119. Ibid.; "Control Board Planned for All Communications; with Mergers Permitted," *New York Times*, December 14, 1933, 2; James Couzens, "The Channels of Information," *Public Utilities Fortnightly* 4 (August 22, 1929): 216–20; Rosen, *The Modern Stentors*, 178.

120. Comments on Report of Majority Members of Committee and Discussion of Position of Minority Member, FDR Mss, OF 859a, 1933–45.

121. Sol Taishoff, "Roosevelt Demands Communications Bill," *Broadcasting*,

February 15, 1934, 6; "President Orders Broadcast Survey," *NAB Reports*, February 3, 1934, 287.

122. "Dill Will Push Communications Bill," *NAB Reports*, February 10, 1934, 299; "Broadcasting Survey Postponed," *NAB Reports*, February 24, 1934, 309; "Broadcast 'Study' Shelved as Futile; Roper-Proposed Investigation Discouraged by Congress," *Broadcasting*, March 1, 1934, 15.

123. Daniel C. Roper to Hohenstein, March 6, 1934, Department of Commerce Manuscripts, National Archives, Washington, D.C., NARG 40, General Correspondence, File 80553/13-G.

124. "Communications Bill Speeded," *NAB Reports*, March 10, 1934, 323.

125. "Roosevelt Approves Communications Board to Rule Radio Telephone, Telegraph, Cable," *New York Times*, February 10, 1934, 12.

126. Taishoff, "Roosevelt Demands," 5.

127. *New York Times*, February 10, 1934, 12; *Senate Hearings 1934*, March 13, 1934, 106.

128. U.S. Senate Interstate Commerce Committee Manuscripts, National Archives, Washington, D.C., Sen 73A-J28, tray 155; James McVann, *The Paulists, 1858–1970* (New York: Society of St. Paul the Apostle, 1983), 896; "Labor Aids Bill for Free Radio," *Federation News*, April 7, 1934, 6; "Labor Toils for Radio Freedom," *Federation News*, May 26, 1934, 1, 3.

129. "Air Enemies Unite Forces," *Variety*, May 8, 1934, 37, 45.

130. Henry A. Bellows, "Report of the Legislative Committee," *NAB Reports*, November 15, 1934, 618.

131. Francis T. Maloney to Eugene Sykes, April 25, 1934; Eugene Sykes to Francis T. Maloney, April 28, 1934, FCC Mss, FCC General Correspondence, Box 38; Rosen, *The Modern Stentors*, 179; Sol Taishoff, "Powerful Lobby Threatens Radio Structure," *Broadcasting*, May 15, 1934, 6.

132. Rosen, *The Modern Stentors*, 179.

133. Bellows, "Report of the Legislative Committee," 618.

134. "New Communications Bill Is Aimed at Curbing Monopoly in Radio," *New York Times*, May 20, 1934, sec. IX, p. 9; Orrin E. Dunlap, Jr., "New Deal in Radio Law to Regulate All Broadcasting," *New York Times*, June 24, 1934, sec. XIII, p. 19. For an immediate response by a liberal FCC member to the asininity of this interpretation of the Communications Act of 1934, see George Henry Payne, *The Fourth Estate and Other Addresses* (Boston: Microphone, 1936), 42.

135. Walter B. Emery, "Broadcasting Rights and Responsibilities in Democratic Society," *Centennial Review* 8 (1964): 306–22.

136. Clifton Read to Hadley Cantril, October 25, 1934, ACLU Mss, 1934, vol. 699; "Government Interference Fear Groundless, Say Commissioners," *Broadcasting*, October 1, 1934, 18.

137. "Federal Communications Commission Reports to Congress," *Education by Radio*, January 31, 1935, 5.

138. Arthur G. Crane, "Safeguarding Educational Radio," in *Education on the Air . . . and Radio and Education, 1935*, ed. Levering Tyson and Josephine MacLatchy (Chicago: University of Chicago Press, 1935).

139. For a longer treatment of the ACLU Radio Committee, see Robert W. McChesney, "Constant Retreat: The American Civil Liberties Union and the Debate over the Meaning of Free Speech for Radio Broadcasting in the 1930s," in *Free Speech*

Yearbook, 1987, vol. 26, ed. Stephen A. Smith (Carbondale: Southern Illinois University Press, 1988).

140. Cited in "In Their Own Behalf," *Education by Radio*, June–July 1938, 21.

141. William S. Paley, "The Viewpoint of the Radio Industry," in *Educational Broadcasting 1937*, ed. C. S. Marsh (Chicago: University of Chicago Press, 1937), 6.

142. Louis G. Caldwell, "Comment on the Current Problems of the Law of Communications," *American Bar Association Journal* 22 (December 1936): 848–52; Louis G. Caldwell, "Freedom of Speech and Radio Broadcasting," in *Radio: The Fifth Estate*, ed. Herman S. Hettinger, *Annals of the American Academy of Political and Social Science* 117 (January 1935), 179–81.

143. Rosen, *The Modern Stentors*, 180.

144. Paul F. Lazarsfeld, *The People Look at Radio* (Chapel Hill: University of North Carolina Press, 1946), 89.

145. For a more theoretical discussion of why fundamental media issues have remained "off-limits" in U.S. political culture, see Robert W. McChesney, "Off-Limits: An Inquiry into the Lack of Debate Concerning the Ownership, Structure and Control of the Mass Media in American Political Life," *Communication*, 13 (1992): 1–19.

Chapter 11

Seducing the Innocent: Childhood and Television in Postwar America
Lynn Spigel

In August 1991, Pee-wee Herman moved out of his kidvid playhouse into the pornhouse of the nightly news when a mug shot of the children's idol revealed him to be a fully grown man, a man arrested for exposing himself in an adult movie theater. In true Pee-wee style, the arrest sparked a series of nervous reactions. Psychologists appeared on local newscasts, advising parents on ways to tell children about their TV play-pal, offering tips on how to make youngsters understand the scandal of Pee-wee's adult desires. All grown up and seemingly all washed up, Pee-wee was axed from the CBS lineup, and Pee-wee dolls and paraphernalia were removed from the shelves of the local Toys 'Я' Us.

Pee-wee is a perfect example of what Jacqueline Rose has called the "impossibility" of childhood. As Rose argues in her work on *Peter Pan*, the child is a cultural construct, a pleasing image that adults need in order to sustain their own identities. Childhood is the difference against which adults define themselves. It is a time of innocence, a time that refers back to a fantasy world where the painful realities and social constraints of adult culture no longer exist. Childhood has less to do with what children experience (since they too are subject to the evils of our social world) than with what adults want to believe.[1] In this regard, the problem with Pee-wee is not so much his indecent exposure, but the fact that he exposes the fantasy of childhood itself. Pee-wee, as a liminal figure somewhere between boy and man, is always on the verge of revealing the fact that children are not the pleasing projection of an adult imagination. He is always threatening to disrupt adult identities by deconstructing the myth of childhood innocence.

The Pee-wee panic is the most recent skirmish in an older battle to define and preserve childhood on television. Since the medium's rise

in the late 1940s, educators, citizen groups, the clergy, and other social organizations have attacked television for its unwholesome effects on children. Graphic violence, suggestive sexuality, and bad
behavior of the Bart Simpson kind are continually seen as threats to
youngsters, threats that need to be researched and controlled. But,
rather than examine television's effects on children per se, I want to
look at the *image* of the child that television, and the debates around
it, have constructed. In order to do so, I will return to the years following World War II, when television was first defined as a "family"
medium. In particular, I want to explore the efforts in that period to
make distinctions between adult and children's entertainment, and
the need, among the adult population, to keep those distinctions intact. Critics in the popular press established a set of taste standards
and reception practices for children's programs that were predicated
on middle-class ideals for child rearing, ideals that stressed the need
to maintain power hierarchies between generations and to keep children innocent of adult secrets. But even if the advice literature suggested such controls and regulations, the actual children's television
programs that emerged in this period played with the culturally prescribed distinctions between adults and children. Drawing upon the
fantasy figures of children's literature, puppet shows, the circus,
movies, and radio programs, these television shows engaged the
hearts of children (and often adults as well) by presenting a topsy-
turvy world where the lines between young and old were blurred and
literally re-presented by clowns, fairies, and cowboys who functioned
as modern-day Peter Pans. Indeed, as we shall see, the narrative
pleasure these programs offered was based in large part on the
transgression of generational roles that were idealized in the child-
rearing advice literature of the period.

Presumed Innocent: Childhood and Cultural Power

After World War II, the American public was deluged with images of
nuclear family bliss. The ravages of war, it was suggested, could in
part be assuaged through the protection of a stable home, a home far
removed from the horrors experienced in previous decades. Films
such as *It's a Wonderful Life* (Frank Capra, 1947) showed how family
values could insulate individuals from economic hardships and compensate for wartime sacrifices, encouraging Americans to return to
the "basics" — Mom, Dad, and the kids.[2] Advertisements for luxury
goods told women to leave their wartime jobs and return home,

where they could rekindle romance and purchase their share of washing machines and electric blenders. Meanwhile, in social reality, people were marrying at record rates, and the baby boom, which began during the war and lasted through 1964, created a nation of children who became a new symbol of hope.[3] Children, after all, were innocent; they did not know what their parents knew; they hadn't lived through the hardships of the Great Depression and the war, nor did they bear the blame.

The concept of childhood innocence — and the investment in youth as a symbolic future — was, of course, not a new invention. Since the early centuries of industrialization, children have been conceptualized as blank slates upon whom parents "write" their culture.[4] In the American context, this tabula rasa conception of the child gained new force and meanings with the transition from an agrarian to an industrialized society that took place over the course of the nineteenth century. While the agrarian child had been a worker in the farm economy, in the industrial society children were no longer crucial to the family income. This was particularly true for white middle-class households, where the family income was high enough to sustain a comfortable life without the contribution of a child's wages. Stripped of immediate ties to the family economy, the white middle-class child emerged as a new sociological category in whom the middle-class adult culture invested new hopes and dreams. By the turn of the century, with falling birthrates and advances in medical science that decreased infant mortality, parents placed increased focus on individual children, regarding them as distinct personalities who needed guidance and moral support. At the same time, the exploitation of child laborers (who came largely from black, immigrant, and working-class families) created a common cause for "child-saving" movements that attempted to combat child abuse by proposing wide-reaching reforms for children of all classes and races.

While this focus on children had humanitarian goals, the particular battles fought over childhood were linked to power struggles in the adult culture. At the core of this concentration on children was a battle between women and men for cultural, social, and political authority. Especially in middle-class households, the focus on children was linked to women's role in the new economy. Like the child's, the woman's place in patriarchal industrial culture was in the home, and her confinement to the domestic sphere was legitimated by the idea that women were morally obliged to be the caretakers and nurturers for their children. The sentimentalization of the mother-child bond worked to secure the middle-class woman's exclusion from the public sphere. Importantly, however, many women at the time perceived the mother role as an empowering one, and for this reason numerous women turned to mothering as an avenue for increased dominion and prestige.

The "mothers' movement," which took institutional form as the National Congress of Mothers in 1897, gave a public voice to women's issues. Although for some this movement was a complicit embrace of women's domestic confinement, for others it served as a venue for expressing what we might now call "feminist" values. At a time when "genteel" women were expected to leave matters of civic governance to men, women activists justified their interests in the suffrage struggle and other social reforms by invoking the more acceptable female concerns of motherhood and child welfare. "The Age of Feminism," one spokeswoman claimed, "is also the age of the child."[5] As this woman must have understood, the child had become a key to power in the public world. The child, after all, was a link to the future. In a world where Darwin's theories of evolution were taking hold, the child became a vehicle for changing the course of history, for bettering the world through imparting one's goals upon a new generation.

Just as women saw the child as a means to their own social power, men began to turn to children as a way to reinvent their authority in the alienating conditions of the industrial world. According to Margaret Marsh, a sentimental vision of childhood was at the core of the "male domesticity" that gained force at the turn of the century. Faced with white-collar desk jobs and increasing feelings of anonymity in the urban world, men were advised to turn toward their homes — and particularly their children — to regain a sense of authority and prestige. Camping trips, family games, and other child-rearing activities promised to refortify men's diminishing power in public life.[6] Again, at the heart of this endeavor was the notion that children were innocent creatures who needed guidance into a world that they would help transform.

This image of children — as both innocents and arbiters of progress — was not only at the center of power struggles at home; it also served to legitimate the institutional power of scientists, policymakers, and media experts who turned their attention to chidren's welfare. Policy reform movements of the Progressive Era fashioned an image of the child as the means to modernization: as a new generation, children linked the past with the future, tradition with progress. As such, the child was no longer simply the responsibility of the private family, but also a prime concern of public agencies. In 1912, the federal government gave official credence to this logic by establishing the Children's Bureau as an official administration for overseeing the care of the young. The twentieth century thus emerged as the "century of the child," an era in which children became discrete individuals who, with the proper socialization, would carry the nation into the future.[7]

While social reforms and public institutions were based on humanitarian efforts, they often worked to diminish the regional, class, ethnic, and racial diversity of family life by disseminating an American "norm" based largely on white, middle-class values and life experiences. By 1915, the emphasis on creating standards for child rearing changed from reform per se to scientific investigation of what constituted the "normal" child, and such investigations became the basis for further social policy.[8] In both its reform and investigatory modes, the child-saving movement was a bedrock for a new organization of childhood experiences: the rise of public schools and decline of child labor ensured that the "normal" child would be an individual educated according to the standards of the dominant class, race, and sex (that is, according to white, patriarchal, middle-class curricula). In addition, the child-saving movement set out to regulate children's play: the rise of municipal playgrounds and national organizations such as the Boy Scouts (1910) and Girl Scouts (1912) helped institutionalize ideas about what constituted children's appropriate use of leisure time.

This normalization of childhood experience and formation of standards for child development were promoted by a stream of media experts who disseminated professional advice. In their book on the history of expert advice to women, Barbara Ehrenreich and Deirdre English have shown how the original goals of the mothers' movement were co-opted by a stream of professional scientists who spoke through the venues of women's media to teach women how to raise their young.[9] Rather than finding increased authority through child rearing, women were repositioned as consumers of information that only scientists and institutions of higher education could produce.

By the 1920s, then, child rearing was no longer seen as a natural instinct of the mother; rather, it was a professional skill that women had to learn by heeding the wisdom of (mostly male) professionals. Women were confronted with a host of scientific advice from "experts" who spoke to them through such popular venues as women's magazines and radio shows. At the heart of this advice was the idea that children were pliable, innocent creatures who needed to be guided by adults. It was the adult's responsibility to generate moral values in the young by guarding the gates to knowledge. By doling out adult secrets only at the proper stages in child development, parents could ensure that children would carry the torch of progress for future generations. A mistake in this regard, the experts warned, could prove fatal — not only for the individual child, but for the moral character of the entire nation. And it is in the context of this moral discourse on knowledge and cultural power that the debates on television should be viewed.

Television and the Gates to Knowledge

As the above brief sketch suggests, childhood is something that adults attempt to maintain through various systems of governance, surveillance, and prescriptive science. And while the protection of children appears to be a consequence of "natural" instinct, the way in which our social system goes about this task is also a function of particular material conditions, ideological concerns, and struggles over social and political power. Childhood, then, historically has been an unstable category, one that must be regulated and controlled constantly. Childhood — or at least the image of the innocent youth to which this category refers — can exist only through a certain disciplinary power that, as Michel Foucault has shown, operates to regulate knowledge.[10] Adulthood brings with it authority, and even more a civic duty, to control the dissemination of information about the world. And childhood — as a moment of purity and innocence — exists only so long as the young are protected from certain types of knowledge.

Given this, it is not surprising that mass media typically have been viewed with trepidation by the adult culture. Be it the 1920s movie matinee or the contemporary video game, mass media have been seen as a threatening force that circulates forbidden secrets to children, and that does so in ways that parents and even the state cannot fully control. Worse still, parents may not even know how and where their children have acquired this information. With the mass, commercial dissemination of ideas, the parent is, so to speak, left out of the mediation loop, and the child becomes the direct addressee of the message. Perhaps for this reason, the history of children's involvement with mass media has been marked by a deep concern on the part of adult groups to monitor their entertainment and survey their pleasure. From Anthony Comstock's crusade against dime novels to the more liberal approach of matinee mothers who chaperoned children at the movies, the adult culture has continually tried to filter the knowledge that mass media transmit to the young.[11]

After World War II, this legacy of child saving, and the skepticism about mass media that it presupposed, was taken to its logical extreme when local, state, and federal governments focused with unparalleled concern on the figure of the "juvenile delinquent." Although it is by no means certain that actual incidents of juvenile crimes multiplied after the war, it is clear that law enforcement agencies began to police criminal youth in more rigorous ways.[12] In the late 1940s, the federal government established the Continuing Committee on the Prevention and Control of Delinquency, and law enforcers began to count instances of youth crimes more thoroughly than ever before. It was also at this time that the Senate took a profound interest in juvenile delinquency, and in 1952, under the auspices of Senator Estes Kefauver, began a series of investigations that continued into the 1960s. Meanwhile, women's magazines and child psychologists such as Dr. Benjamin Spock (whose *Common Sense Book of Baby and Childcare* was first published in 1946) advised mothers how to prevent their children from becoming antisocial and emotionally impaired. Although it is hard to determine how many parents actually followed the experts' advice, the popularity of this literature (for example, by 1952 Spock's book had sold more than four million copies), attests to the fact that people were eager to hear what the experts had to say.[13]

Juvenile delinquency was blamed primarily on two separate but related causes — a bad family life and mass media.[14] According to the popular wisdom, the splintering of families during the war left children vulnerable to outside forces that encouraged the development of immoral habits and criminal behavior. Experts argued that the rise in juvenile crimes during the war was largely caused by working mothers who did not properly devote their energies to their young. Thus, as in the past, the mother-child bond served to justify the idea that women's place was in the home. Indeed, at a time when the female labor force was being told to relinquish their jobs to returning GIs, the mass media (and the scientific experts who spoke through these venues) promoted a romantic ideal of motherhood that must have helped to encourage middle-class women to spend the lion's share of their energies on domestic concerns. Then, too, men were told to invest more concern in family life. Like the male domesticity at the turn of the century, this postwar version of the child-centered family provided men with a conduit to power that promised to compensate for their increasing loss of authority in the bureaucratic corporate world. Magazines such as *Esquire* and *Popular Science* told men to take renewed interest in all facets of family life, particularly those that involved family fun and leisure (as opposed to the actual work women performed as housekeepers and mothers). Whether the advice was aimed at men or women, the child emerged as a terrain on which to assert adult power, and the parent in turn relied on the experts' wisdom. Failure to follow this advice could result in "problem" children or, worse still, criminals.

In the advice literature of the period, mass media became a central focus of concern as the experts told parents how to control and regulate media in ways that promoted family values. As a domestic medium that brought the outside world directly into the home, television was at once ally and enemy. Television was often considered to have beneficial effects because it would bring the family together for recreation. In 1952, when the House of Representatives held hearings on the content of radio and television programs, government officials speculated that television was a necessity for family bliss. Representative Joseph Byrson from South Carolina admitted:

> My two younger children spent much of their time watching the neighbor's television. In a year or two, when my youngest son had graduated from a local junior high school, he wanted to go away to school. I believe, if I had purchased a television set at that time, he would have finished high school here in Washington.[15]

Similar sentiments were expressed in audience research of the day. In *The Age of Television* (1956), Leo Bogart summarized a wide range of audience studies that showed many Americans believed television would revive domestic life. Drawing upon these findings, Bogart concluded that social scientific surveys "agree completely that television has had the effect of keeping the family at home more than formerly."[16] The respondents in studies around the country testified to the particular ways that television enhanced their family life. In a 1950 study of families from Evanston, Illinois, one parent claimed that television "has given the children a happier home where they can laugh," while another admitted, "My two 16-year-olds like to stay home now. I'm so glad, as I would not know where they were otherwise."[17]

Popular magazines publicized, and perhaps encouraged, such sentiments by advising parents on ways to use television as a tool for family cohesion. In 1948, *Parents Magazine* (which generally took a favorable attitude toward television) published the advice of April Ella Codel, who claimed that television repaired the damage radio had done in her home:

> Our family is rather closely knit, anyhow, yet with practically every room having a radio, it was not uncommon for all to scatter to enjoy particular programs. With the one television set, our family is brought together as a unit for a while after dinner.

The following year, another author for *Parents Magazine* claimed, "All the mothers I have talked to are enthusiastic about television for their children. Certainly it has brought back the family circle in the living room." And in 1955 *Better Homes and Gardens* published a readership survey in which parents praised television's ability to unify the family.[18]

Even while critics praised television as a source of domestic unity and benevolent socialization, they also worried about its harmful effects, particularly its dissemination of debased knowledge and its related encouragement of passive minds and bodies. In 1951, *Better Homes and Gardens* complained that the medium's "synthetic entertainment" produced a child who was "glued to television."[19] Worse still, this new addiction would reverse good habits of hygiene, nutrition, and decorum, causing physical, mental, and social disorders. A cartoon in a 1950 issue of *Ladies' Home Journal* suggests a typical scenario. The magazine showed a little girl slumped on an ottoman and suffering from a new disease called "telebugeye." According to the caption, the child was a "pale, weak, stupid looking creature" who grew "bugeyed" from sitting and watching television for too long.[20] Perhaps responding to these concerns, advertisements for television sets depicted children spectators in scenes that associated television with the "higher arts," and some even implied that children would cultivate artistic talents by watching television. In 1951, General Electric showed a little girl, dressed in a tutu, imitating an on-screen ballerina, while Truetone showed a little boy learning to play the saxophone by watching a professional horn player on television.[21]

As the popular wisdom often suggested, the child's passive addiction to television might itself lead to the opposite effect of increased aggression. According to this logic, television decreased children's intellectual abilities, leaving them vulnerable to its unsavory content. The discussions followed in the wake of critical and social scientific theories of the 1930s and 1940s that suggested mass media inject ideas and behavior into passive individuals. The popular press circulated stories about a six-year-old who asked his father for real bullets because his sister didn't die when he shot her with his toy gun, a seven-year-old who put ground glass in the family's lamb stew, a nine-year-old who proposed killing his teacher with a box of poison chocolates, an eleven-year-old who shot his television set with his B.B. gun, a thirteen-year-old who stabbed her mother with a kitchen knife, and a sixteen-year-old babysitter who strangled a sleeping child to death — all, of course, after witnessing similar murders on television.[22] In reaction to the popular furor, as early as 1950, the Television Broadcasters' Association hired a public relations firm to write protelevision press releases that emphasized the more positive types of programming television had to offer.[23] But, as I have shown elsewhere, the controversies grew more heated as grass-roots groups and government officials battled to censor the airwaves.[24] Even after the National Association of Broadcasters adopted its code in 1952 (a code that included a whole section on children), the debates continued.[25] In that same year, Representative Ezekiel Gathings of Arkansas spearheaded a House investigation of radio and television programs that presented studies demonstrating television's negative influence on youth.[26] By 1954, Estes Kefauver's Senate subcommittee hearings on juvenile delinquency were investigating television's relationship to the perceived increase in youth crimes, focusing particularly on the "ideas that spring into the living room for the entertainment of the youth of America, which have to do with crime and with horror, sadism, and sex."[27] In the face of such criticism, parental control over children's use of this new medium and the knowledge it disseminated emerged as a number-one concern.

Mastering the Child

The anxieties about television's effects on youth were connected to more general fears about its disruption of generational roles, particularly with regard to power struggles over what constituted proper children's entertainment. At the 1952 House hearings, for example, government officials expressed their discomfort with programming that they found offensive, but that delighted the hearts of children.

When describing *You Asked for It* (a half-hour variety format premised on viewers' requests to see various acts), Ezekiel Gathings claimed that while most of the program was "wholesome . . . something like a vaudeville show," he could not abide one act that featured "a grass-skirted young lady and a thinly clad gentleman dancing the hoochie-coochie. They danced to a very lively tune and shook the shimmy. . . . My children saw that, and I could not get it turned off to save my life."[28] This problem of controlling children's program choices was voiced more generally by popular critics, who warned that television might disrupt family unity by inverting the power dynamics between children and adults. According to this logic, the television image had usurped the authority previously held by parents. As television critic John Crosby claimed, "You tell little Oscar to trot off to bed, and you will probably find yourself embroiled in argument. But if Milton Berle tells him to go to bed, off he goes."[29]

Women's magazines published articles and cartoons showing how parents might lose dominion over TV-addicted children who refused to eat dinner, go to bed, contribute to family conversations, finish their chores, or do their homework.[30] In 1950, *New York Times* critic Jack Gould wrote, "Mealtime is an event out of the ordinary for the television parent; for the child it may just be out." In that same year, a cartoon in *Better Homes and Gardens* showed parents seated at the dining room table while their children sat in the living room, glued to the television set. Speaking from the point of view of the exasperated mother, the caption read, "All right, that does it! Harry, call up the television store and tell them to send a truck right over!"[31]

Television's potential inversion of power relationships between child and adult gave way to humorous speculations about the ways in which adults themselves were becoming more like children. In numerous popular comedies of the period, parents — epecially fathers — were shown to regress to a childlike state after watching too much television. In a 1955 episode of *The Adventures of Ozzie and Harriet* titled "The Pajama Game," Ozzie Nelson and his sons, Ricky and David, are shown seated before the TV set. The boys are able to do complicated algebra formulas while watching television, and they maintain their general capabilities for industrious behavior. Ozzie, on the other hand, becomes mesmerized by television, and after his wife Harriet has already gone to bed, he decides to read a novelization of the movie he had been watching on television most of the night. The next morning, Ozzie is in a stupor, unable to wake up on schedule. The episode thus humorously inverts the popular fear that television would interfere with children's activities. Now it is the father who is unable to use the new medium in a responsible, adult way.

In 1954, *Fireside Theatre*, a filmed anthology drama series, evoked a similar theme in an episode titled "The Grass Is Greener." Based on the simple life of a farm family, the program begins with the purchase of a television set, a purchase that the father, Bruce, adamantly opposes. Going against Bruce's wishes, his wife, Irene, makes use of the local retailer's credit plan and has a television set installed in her home. When Bruce returns home for the evening, he finds himself oddly displaced by the new center of interest as his family sits enthralled by a TV western. When he attempts to get their attention, his son hushes him with a dismissive "Shh," after which the family resumes its fascination with the television program. Not only does Bruce lose control over his youngsters, but in the next scene, he actually regresses to the behavior of his children when he too finds himself enthralled by a TV western, slumped in an easy chair, passively addicted to the new medium.

The most explicit and humorous case of infantilization took place in the first episode of *The Honeymooners*, "TV or Not TV" (1955), when Alice and Ralph Kramden chip in with neighbor Ed Norton to buy a television set. Ralph and Norton become classic couch potatoes, sprawled before the set and enthralled by mindless entertainment. Midway into the teleplay, Ralph sits before the TV set with a smorgasbord of snacks, ready to tune in to a movie. But Norton has other ideas; he wants to watch the children's serial *Captain Video*. Norton takes out his Captain Video helmet and begins reciting the club member pledge, promising Captain Video to obey his mommy and daddy and drink milk after every meal. In case the sense of male regression is not yet clear enough, at the end of the episode Alice scolds the men, saying, "Stop acting like babies and try to grow up a little." Finally, Ralph and Norton fall asleep before the set and Alice tucks them in for the night, covering them with a blanket and shaking her head with motherly condescension.

While the infantilized fathers that such television programs portrayed might have been hyperbolic, they spoke to a more general set of anxieties about television's inversion of the power dynamics between adults and children. Summarizing parents' attitudes toward television, Leo Bogart claimed, "There is a feeling, never stated in so many words, that the set has a power of its own to control the destinies and viewing habits of the audience, and that what it 'does' to parents and children alike is somehow beyond the bounds of any individual set-owner's power of control."[32] In this context, popular media offered solace by showing parents how they could reclaim power in their own homes — if not over the medium, then at least over their children. Television opened up a whole array of disciplinary measures that parents might exert over their youngsters.[33]

Indeed, the bulk of discussions about children and television were offered in the context of mastery. If the machine could control the child, then so could the parent. Here, the language of common sense provided some reassurance by reminding parents that it was they, after all, who were in command. As Jack Gould wrote in 1949, "It takes a human hand to turn on a television set."[34] But for parents who needed a bit more than just the soothing words of a popular sage, the media ushered in specialists from a wide range of fields; child psychologists, educators, psychiatrists, and broadcasters recommended ways to stave off the evils of the new medium.

At the heart of the advice on children and television was a marked desire to keep childhood as a period distinct from adulthood. Critics of the medium feared that television might abolish such distinctions by making children privy to adult secrets. In 1951, television critic Robert Lewis Shayon claimed, "Television is the shortest cut yet devised, the most accessible backdoor to the grownup world."[35] More generally, the issue of accessibility became the primary cause for alarm. Television's immediate availability in the home threatened to abolish childhood by giving children equal access to the ideas and values circulated in the adult culture. In 1950, Phyllis Cerf, the wife of the publisher of *Parents Magazine*, claimed that "television, like candy, is wonderful, provided you don't have too much of it. You can run out of candy, or carefully place it out of your children's reach, but television, once it has come into your home, can go on and on."[36] If Cerf addressed the problem of accessibility mostly through fears about the quantity of television that children consumed, others also worried about the quality of messages that it distributed to old and young alike. Television, it was often suggested, failed to discriminate among its audiences; it addressed all family members with the same message. As *Parents Magazine* claimed in 1952:

> A large part of what children see and hear is intended mainly for adult eyes and ears. Of the things that are intended for children, many are unsuitable or questionable. Some people see no problems or dangers in this. "TV keeps the children from underfoot," they say. Or "TV keeps Billy off the streets. It's a built-in baby sitter." But other adults are concerned. "It's not

healthy. All day long it's machine guns, murder and gangs. You can't tell me children don't get dangerous ideas from TV."[37]

As such statements imply, television increased parental dilemmas because it undermined their dominion over the kinds of knowledge that their children might acquire.

In the wake of such criticism, popular media advised parents how to protect their young by filtering out television's undesirable elements. One method of purification came in the form of disciplining the child's use of televison by establishing a schedule. Drawing on cognitive and behavioralist theories of childhood that had been popular since the 1920s, and mixing these with the liberal approach of Dr. Spock, the experts recommended ways for parents to instill healthy viewing habits in their children, advising methods of punishment and reward that would reinforce particular viewing routines that adults deemed appropriate for youngsters.

But even if children adopted "healthy" viewing habits and routines, they still might see programs unsuited for innocent eyes, particularly in the early 1950s, when crime, mystery, and sexually suggestive programs often appeared during early prime-time hours. Thus, experts advised parents on how to establish a canon of wholesome programs. A readership survey in *Better Homes and Gardens* indicated that some parents had, in fact, set standards for appropriate and inappropriate entertainment:

> Forty percent of all the parents answering do not approve of some of the programs their children would like to see—chiefly crime, violent mystery or horror, western, and "emotional" programs. . . .
>
> About one-fourth of the parents insist on their children viewing special events on TV. In this category they mention parades, children shows, educational programs, great artists, and theater productions.[38]

In many ways this canon of good and bad TV recalled Victorian notions of ideal family recreation. Overly exciting stimuli threatened to corrupt the child, while educational and morally uplifting programs were socially sanctioned. In the years to come, magazines such as *Reader's Digest* and *Saturday Review* internalized this canon of wholesome and culturally enriching programs, particularly giving their seal of approval to educational fare such as *Ding Dong School* and *Captain Kangaroo*. In all cases, critical judgments were based on adult standards. Indeed, this hierarchy of television programs is symptomatic of the more general efforts to establish an economy of pleasure for children spectators that suited adult concepts of appropriate children's entertainment.

The idea that fun should promote industrious behavior rather than passive reflection was paramount in critical discussions. According to a 1954 article in *Parents Magazine*, the best shows are " 'programs designed for children with understanding of their growth and development, and which give, if possible, some opportunity for participation.' "[39] With this assumption in mind, *Parents Magazine* commended programs with drawing and essay contests, claiming that they promoted active forms of play:

> The idea of the drawing program—what used to be called "Chalk Talks" in the old Chatauqua days—promises to become very popular on television. WJZ-TV and its affiliates show *Cartoon Teletales*, with one artist drawing illustrations for stories told by his companion. On WABD New York's *Small Fry Club*, and WTMJ Milwaukee's *Children's Corner*, drawings sent in by children are shown on the screen. And on WCBS-TV there is a program which shows real television originality and inspires creative activity by the young audience: *Scrapbook, Jr. Edition*; among its features is a cartoon strip beginning a new adventure story, and the children are asked to write in their ideas for an ending; then the winning conclusion is drawn by the artist in another cartoon strip shown the following week.[40]

Such programs acted as a Band-Aid cure for the deeper political and economic demands of commercial broadcasting's one-way communication structure. But, while television critics frequently argued that children's shows should encourage participatory forms of play, they never demanded that adult programming should elicit these active forms of reception. Perhaps in this sense, adults wished to protect their young from the undemocratic aspects of their one-way commercial broadcast system, even while they accepted that system as the dominant forum for communication.

The critical expectations for children's television voiced in magazines like *Parents* tell us more about adult taste standards than they do about what children actually found pleasurable. Indeed, adults seem to have watched the shows supposedly aimed at children. Since children's shows were often scheduled during late afternoon and early evening hours, adults would have ample occasion to view these programs. *Kukla, Fran and Ollie*, for example, had a strong appeal for grownups, so much so that when NBC attempted to split it into two fifteen-minute shows in 1951, the network was, in the words of one executive, "swamped" with audience mail from angry adults. Robert

G. Pilkington, an insurance underwriter, wrote to the network, complaining:

> I have read with interest your general letter sent to me among others in answer to the protests regarding Kukla, Fran and Ollie [*sic*]. . . .
>
> The biggest reason for the change is obviously the greater revenue that can be derived from two 15-minute shows, combined with the lack of sponsorship on many stations. Which leads me to inquire, what is the matter with your Sales Department? Regardless of the popular conception that radio and television is directed to the 12-year-old mentality, there is a large enough segment of your viewing audience appreciative of the KFO type show and buying its sponsors' products to warrant a sales effort in its direction. After one program, I went out, simply in appreciation, and immediately bought some of the goods advertised.
>
> Who ever got the idea that Kukla, Fran, and Ollie is a juvenile show? It's an adult program, pure and simple, and contains too many subtleties to be successful completely except with that mind. Maybe your salesmen and sponsors overlooked that little detail.[41]

Mr. Pilkington's acknowledgment of his enjoyment of a children's show is vivid testimony to the paradox at the heart of television's attempts to make distinctions between adults' and children's narrative pleasures. While cultural ideals may have dictated that those pleasures be kept apart, in practice the situation was never so clear-cut. Adults seemed to enjoy what children should have liked, and children seemed to like the very things that adults deemed inappropriate juvenile entertainment.

Perhaps for this reason, the impartation of adult tastes onto children became the number-one goal in the popular media of the time. As Serafina Bathrick has argued, *Parents Magazine* showed mothers how to be "TV guides" who helped their children develop the right sensibilities.[42] In 1954, for example, the magazine claimed:

> We can only hope to cultivate good taste in our children by developing good taste in ourselves and helping our children to be sure to see the programs that are good programs. . . . Parents can accomplish a lot by pointing out sequences of bad taste, by reacting themselves to elements of bad taste, by appreciating aloud or indirectly programs which are in good taste. . . . as one expert put it, "Children cannot be protected, in life, from exposure to unwholesome influences, but they can be taught how to recognize and deal with them when they are exposed."[43]

Thus, according to the popular wisdom, by elevating children's taste standards, parents could better regulate the undesirable elements of mass culture. Even if they could not control entirely their children's access to the kinds of messages circulated by television, they could, at least, ensure that children internalized their parents' sensibilities toward program content. Revealingly in this regard, an audience study conducted in Columbus, Ohio, reported that parents found it particularly important to regulate the program choices of pre- and grade-schoolers, but high school students received less parental supervision because "their program tastes apparently are considerably closer to those of their parents."[44]

This preoccupation with the establishment of taste standards reflected a class bias. Summarizing numerous social scientific studies, Leo Bogart claimed that it was mainly the middle class who feared television's influence on children and that while "people of higher social position, income and education are more critical of existing fare in radio, television and the movies . . . those at the lower end of the social scale are more ready to accept what is available." But even if he believed that discriminating taste was a function of class difference, Bogart internalized the elitist preoccupation with canon formation, lending professional credence to the idea that adults should restrict their children's viewing to what they deemed "respectable" culture. As he suggested:

> If television cannot really be blamed for turning children into criminals or
> neurotics, this does not imply that it is a wholly healthful influence on the
> growing child. A much more serious charge is that television, in the worst
> aspects of its content, helps to perpetuate moral, cultural and social values
> which are not in accord with the highest ideals of an enlightened
> democracy. The cowboy film, the detective thriller and the soap opera, so
> often identified by critics as the epitome of American mass culture,
> probably do not represent the heritage which Americans at large want to
> transmit to posterity.[45]

Thus, while Bogart noted that working-class parents did not find a need to discriminate among programs, and that the formation of critical standards was mainly a middle-class pursuit, he nevertheless decided that television programs would not please the value systems of "Americans at large." Here, as elsewhere, the notion of an enlightened democracy served to justify the hegemony of bourgeois tastes and the imparting of those tastes onto children of all classes.

For their part, children often seemed to have different ideas. Like Senator Gathing's youngsters who wanted to watch dancers do the "hootchie coochie," children respondents in audience studies often claimed to prefer programs their parents found unwholesome, especially science fiction serials and westerns. Surveys also indicated that children often liked to watch programs aimed at adults and that "parents were often reluctant to admit that their children watched adult shows regularly."[46] Milton Berle's *Texaco Star Theater* (which was famous for its inclusion of "off-color" cabaret humor) became so popular with children that Berle adopted the persona of Uncle Miltie, pandering to parents by telling his juvenile audience to obey their elders and go straight to bed when the program ended.[47] But other programs were unable to bridge the generation gap. When, for example, CBS aired the mystery anthology *Suspense*, affiliates across the country received letters from concerned parents who wanted the program taken off the air. Attempting to please its adult constituency, one Oklahoma station was caught in the cross fire between parents and children. When the station announced it would not air "horror story" programs before the bedtime hour of 9:00 p.m., it received a letter with the words "We protest!" signed by twenty-two children.[48]

The Children's Hour

If the adult culture attempted to distinguish children's entertainment from adult shows, the actual children's programming that emerged in this period was based largely on the dissolution of age categories. Children's programs were filled with liminal characters, characters that existed somewhere in between child and adult, as the shows played with the cultural concepts of childhood that circulated at the time. Indeed, the pleasure encouraged by these programs was rooted in the transgression of taboos and regulations found in the advice literature aimed at adults.

In the TV playhouse, adults functioned for the sole purpose of fulfilling the child's wish. If in everyday life adults represented rules, knowledge, and the threat of punishment, on television they represented mayhem, entertainment, and prizes. On *Howdy Doody* (1947–60, NBC), host Buffalo Bob was ambiguously a grownup and a *cowboy*, who, like Peter Pan, had not abandoned the land of make-believe. Indeed, children's programs had their own never-never lands — impossible places like "Doodyville," places that mocked the confines of real domestic space.[49] Then, too, children's shows set aside the mundane nature of real time by presenting children with the marvelous antics of "Howdy Doody time," a time in which youngsters need not do their homework, go to bed, or wash behind their ears. In fact, *Howdy Doody* began with a cartoon depiction of a cuckoo clock — literally going cuckoo — as the hands span feverishly around the dial, signaling the temporary abandonment of the normal schedule for the next thirty minutes of fantastic clowns and puppets.

Johnny Jupiter (1953–54, DuMont and NBC) similarly transported children from the confines of their living room into a magical world. Johnny was a puppet who lived on Jupiter with his pals Reject the Robot and Major Domo. At their outer-space television station, Johnny, Reject, and Major Domo were contacted by earthling Ernest Duckweather, a teenage techno-nerd who invented a magic television set on which he spoke with his Jupiterian pals. Ernest was a 1950s Pee-wee, a liminal figure who straddled the categories of child and adult. And like Pee-wee (although without the campy wink), Ernest suffered from a case of arrested sexual development, underscored in numerous episodes by his disinterest in the advances of his boss's daughter. Johnny, like other children's hosts, played with the fantasy of childhood itself, presenting himself as a half boy/half man who defended himself against the constraints and cares of the grownup world.

By blurring the boundaries between adult and child identities, such programs presented a ripe environment through which to address children as consumers. As both authority figures and wish fulfillments, the casts of clowns and cowboys promised children a peek at toys and sweets behind their mothers' backs. The children's show was a candy store populated by dream parents who pandered forbidden products. Even more important, these programs taught children the art of persuasion, advising them how to tell their parents about the wondrous items advertised on the show. In a 1958 episode of *Howdy Doody*, for example, Buffalo Bob chats about Hostess Cupcakes with Howdy, who marvels at the delicious creamy centers. Bob then directly addresses the children at home, telling them to "make sure to tell your mom to put a package of Hostess Cupcakes in your lunch box when you go to school, or ask her to buy some as a special reward sometime during the week." In this imaginary transaction between Buffalo Bob and the child audience, the parent becomes a functionary through which the child accomplishes consumer goals. Children are taught how to influence their parents' product choices, and in the process the child's narrative pleasure is inextricably intertwined with the pleasure of consumption.

Winky Dink and You, (1953–57, CBS), a cult classic of 1950s TV, took this consumer logic to its extreme by making the program completely dependent upon the product it advertised. Winky was a flatly drawn Tinkerbell-like cartoon character who cohosted the show with the real-life Jack Barry. Although by current standards extremely low-tech in nature, the program was premised on an interactive use of television technology. *Winky Dink* offered children the possibility of drawing on the television set through the purchase of a special Winky Dink kit, complete with rub-off crayons, an erasing cloth, and the all-important "magic window," a piece of tinted plastic that, when sufficiently rubbed by the child's hands, stuck to the television screen. With this apparatus in place, the child could draw along to the animation on the screen, perhaps filling in features on cartoon characters' faces or completing story narratives by drawing in the necessary scenery and props. In a 1953 episode, Jack Barry showed children how the whole thing worked by picking up a remote feed from the home of Helen, a little girl in Pittsburgh, Pennsylvania. Helen demonstrated how the kit worked, and Barry reminded children (and no doubt their parents as well) of the prosocial skills that would be learned on the show. After Helen erected her plastic screen, Barry told the children at home to "share your Winky Dink kits" by evenly dividing the crayons. And, at a time when television was considered a major cause of eyestrain, Barry told the audience to "notice how that plastic is lightly tinted. That makes it much easier to watch our television show, even for your parents." The consumer message of the show was thus tempered with the rhetoric of public service. In the middle commercial, this mixture of commercialism and goodwill was drawn out in a long speech delivered by Barry, who looked directly into the camera to address the children at home:

> I tell you what, if you had your Winky Dink kits and played along with us, well, there's no reason for any of us to miss all the fun. It's so easy to get your Winky Dink kits. And, you know something, the fun starts as soon as you get your kit. Of course, you can watch the program without a kit, but you can't really be a part of the program without 'em. And you can't have the fun that the other boys and girls who have their Winky Dink kits do have. Now, I know you're just used to watching television shows and you just sit back and watch all the other shows, but not this show. This show you really get a chance to be a part of 'cause it's different. You get a chance at home to play right along with us, and what you at home draw actually becomes part of the program. But to be a part of the show, you must have

one of our Winky Dink kits [Barry holds up the kit and describes its contents].

Thus, the product pitch worked by drawing on the popular fears that television made children passive. Like the "chalk talks" applauded by *Parents Magazine*, *Winky Dink* encouraged participation from children, but participation came at a price. Buying the Winky Dink kit, the ad suggested, would ensure that children took an active part in the communication process, and with this prosocial message intact, Barry went on to pander to the child audience in the most crass and unabashed way. Still holding up the kit, he exclaimed:

> Now boys and girls you *must* have this kit, and here's how you get it. Mark down the address, will you? To get this Winky Dink kit for yourself or for your friends, you send fifty cents [Barry holds up a sign with fifty cents boldy printed on it]. Boys and girls, send fifty cents, got that? Fifty cents, with your name and address [Barry holds up a sign that says to print your name and address] and send it to Winky Dink, Box 5, New York 19, New York [Barry holds up a sign with the address]. Now, I do hope you'll all get your Winky Dink kit right away because you really can't have as much fun as if you have a kit.

Programs such as *Howdy Doody* and *Winky Dink* were products of a world in which the age limits of consumption were shifting, a world in which parents had less and less control over the kinds of objects children would desire and potentially own. Just as Jack Barry saw little need to worry where children would possibly get the fifty cents needed to purchase his kit, other industrialists were increasingly appealing directly to children, assuming that they would either buy products on their own or use their powers of persuasion to coax parents into purchasing them. In the postwar years, teenagers, who often held after school jobs, became a viable market for low-ticket consumer items such as clothing, makeup, and records.[50] And even in the case of high-ticket items — especially household commodities — advertisers discovered that tapping into the new consumer power of children and teens was also a way to urge adults to buy more. An editor of *Home Furnishings* (the furniture retailers' trade journal) claimed, "The younger generation from one to twenty influences the entire home furnishings industry."[51]

Children especially were considered to have "nagging" power in family purchases of television sets. Surveys indicated that families with children tended to buy televisions more than childless couples did. Television manufacturers quickly assimilated the new findings into their sales techniques. As early as 1948, the industry trade journal *Advertising and Selling* reported that the manager of public relations and advertising at the manufacturing company, Stromberg-Carlson, "quoted a survey . . . indicating that children not only exert a tremendous amount of influence in the selection and purchase of television receivers but that they are, in fact, television's most enthusiastic audience."[52] Basing their advertisements on such surveys, manufacturers and retailers formulated strategies by which to convince parents to buy products for the sake of their children. In 1950, the American Television Dealers and Manufacturers ran nationwide newspaper advertisements that played on parental guilt. The first ad in the series had a headline that read, "Your daughter won't ever tell you the humiliation she's felt in begging those precious hours of television from a neighbor." Forlorn children were pictured on top of the layout, and parents were shown how television could raise their youngsters' spirits. This particular case is especially interesting because it shows that there are indeed limits to which advertisers can go before a certain degree of sales resistance takes place. Outraged by the advertisement, parents, educators, and clergymen complained to their newspapers about its manipulative tone. In addition, the Family Service Association of America called it a "cruel pressure to apply against millions of parents" who could not afford television sets.[53]

Not surprisingly, the area of consumerism remains one of the most heatedly debated in the discourse on television and youth. Commercials induct the child into the market, and market values appear to be in direct opposition to conceptions of childhood innocence.[54] Yet, once again, while adults historically have argued against the commercialization of children's television, they too have been seduced by its consumer fantasies. Indeed, since the 1950s, children's programs have found ways to draw adults into the joys of spending money by offering them a ticket for a nostalgic return to a childhood dreamland of make-believe.

The appearance of *The Mickey Mouse Club* in the 1955 fall season is an emblematic example. This show and its 1954 predecessor, *Disneyland*, were created as one big advertisement for Walt Disney's theme park in Anaheim, California. Despite the blatant commercialism of *Disneyland*, it won a Peabody Award for its educational value and an Emmy for best adventure series, and was among the top ten programs in the ratings. Not surprisingly, the program's success paved the way for a new surge of sponsor interest in other children's fare. In its first season, *The Mickey Mouse Club* was similarly successful, although some television critics were initially wary of its Disney product endorsements and its overabundance of commercials (critic Jack Gould was outraged that the premier episode had about twenty ads, one of which cut off a Pluto cartoon).[55] Still, its syrupy dose of pro-social themes — respect for elders, family values, courage — must have tempered adult fears about the commercial aspects of the show.[56]

Like other children's programs, *The Mickey Mouse Club* contained a set of liminal characters that played with culturally prescribed generational roles. The opening credits began with Mickey Mouse himself, who then introduced the Mouseketeers, an odd blend of children — from toddlers to teens — and grown-ups Roy and Jimmy, who dressed just like the children in mouse ears and T-shirts. And like *Howdy Doody*, *The Mickey Mouse Club* existed in a kind of never-never land. But it took the concept one step further by promising children that its never-never land could in fact become a virtual reality, a real place where children might venture — that is, if they could persuade their parents to take them to Southern California. Of course, as with other Disney products, the theme park was predicated on the pleasure of playing with the culturally prescribed distinctions between child and adult. Disneyland was a place where adults could rediscover the joys of youth in fantasy replicas of narrative spaces (like Frontierland, Fantasyland, and Tomorrowland), which they once traversed in storybooks and movies. The roller coasters and teacup rides offered adults the chance to shake up their conceptions of normal time and space, to look at the world from the perspective of childhood exhilaration and curiosity. Indeed, the fact that Disneyland was promoted as a place of family amusement reminds us that the liminality of children's entertainment is often just as appealing to adults as it is to children. Moreover, as the biggest tourist attraction of the 1950s, Disneyland was dramatic proof that despite the arguments against it, children's commercial entertainment could be marketed as wholesome fun for the entire family.[57]

The End of the Innocence?

The controversy that surrounded children's television in the 1950s, and the assumption that children's viewing pleasures should be monitored by adults, continued into the next decades with increased force. In 1961, one of the first and most influential book-length studies of the subject, *Television in the Lives of Our Children*, reported that by the sixth grade children spent almost as much time watching television as they did in school. Moreover, authors Wilbur Schramm, Jack Lyle, and Edwin B. Parker speculated that television might contribute to "premature aging" by encouraging American youth to grow up too fast. The boundaries between children and adults might blur, particularly because, as the authors noted, children often watched programs that were made for an adult audience.[58]

As the 1960s came to a close, critics who grew up in the turmoil of the new youth movement began to blame television for the perceived generation gap between themselves and their parents. In his 1973 book *No Peace, No Place: Excavations along the Generational Fault*, Jeff Greenfield claimed that television threatened to abolish childhood innocence because it allowed youngsters to "eavesdrop" on adult secrets. Similarly, in *Looking Back: A Chronicle of Growing Up Old in the Sixties*, Joyce Maynard said that television played a major role in her premature sophistication.[59] And more recently, in *No Sense of Place*, Joshua Meyrowitz has claimed that television contributes to a "blurring of childhood and adulthood." According to Meyrowitz, television not only exposes "many adult secrets to children," it also "reveals the 'secret of secrecy.' " For example, Meyrowitz argues that by broadcasting warnings about programs that children are not supposed to see, television lets young viewers know exactly what is being forbidden. Television, in other words, makes children privy to the fact that adults are hiding knowledge from them.[60]

While debates about children and television continue to base themselves around the ideal of childhood innocence, the industrial producers of children's culture have learned more sophisticated ways to tap into children's enjoyment of entertainment that adults deem inappropriate. The 1950s debates over comics and television did not destroy the popularity of magazines such as *Mad*, nor did they diminish the next generation's penchant for the perverse pleasures of Ugly Stickers and Wacky Packs. The recent merchandising of "Toxic High" stickers, a set of Topps trading cards based on the perverse, violent, and authority-bucking antics at a typical high school, is a case in point. Cartoonist Mark Newgarden (also the brains behind the popular Garbage Pail Kids) admits gleefully, "We did a focus test where we showed it to kids behind one of those two-way mirrors, and the kids went wild for it. And then we showed it to their mothers, and their mothers were aghast."[61] As this "tasteless test" suggests, the strength of a child's toy is now predictable in part by the degree to which the parent disapproves.

Broadcast television has emerged, perhaps, as a more "protected" arena. At the time of this writing, the reform group Action for Children's Television (ACT) has discontinued its two-decade attempt to raise children's program standards. According to the organization's founder, Peggy Charin, ACT's work has been accomplished with the recent passing of the Children's Television Act, which mandates broadcasters' responsibility to young viewers. Ironically, however, these gains come at a time when more and more children are finding their entertainment outside the auspices of broadcast television. Now, cable television, VCRs, and Nintendo games offer youngsters alternative venues for pleasure, venues about which critics are more and more anxious.[62] And, as in the 1950s, such anxieties revolve around the central problem of keeping childhood separate from adulthood. In an episode of *The Simpsons*, for example, precocious son Bart is shown charging his school pals twenty-five cents to watch the Playboy channel on cable TV, while in another episode he beats his father Homer at a video game, to the degree that Homer is reduced to a child, yelling and screaming because he can't score points.

Like the child-saving movement in the early part of this century, the anxieties about children as victims of television and the urge to reform the commercial nature and degrading content of electronic media often have humanitarian goals. But, as in the past, this humanitarian urge is no more than a Band-Aid cure for the public's larger disempowerment and alienation from the channels of expression in our country. In fact, since the inception of television as a privately controlled commercial medium, the American public has rarely argued against its basic corporate structure. Little was said about the fact that television technology (with its inherent capability for two-way communication) was being developed as a one-way medium used mostly for the financial gain of major corporations.[63] Instead, the only widespread challenge to commercialization of the airwaves has taken place in the name of the child. The child in this configuration becomes an alibi and a conduit for larger issues regarding the commercialization of communication and the price tags attached to free speech on our country's mass media. The discourse of victimization that surrounds the child viewer might, in this sense, usefully be renamed and reinvestigated as a discourse of power through which adults express their own disenfrachisement from our nation's dominant mode of communication.

Notes

1. Jacqueline Rose, *The Case of Peter Pan: The Impossibility of Children's Fiction* (London: Macmillan, 1984).

2. It should be noted that many films of this period—particularly film noir and family melodrama—depicted dysfunctional families, showing, for instance, how infidelity, missing parents, overprotective mothers, or henpecked fathers could cause destruction for child and parent alike. See, for example, *Rebel without a Cause* (Nicholas Raye, 1955) or *Mildred Pierce* (Michael Curtiz, 1945).

3. In the early 1950s, the median marriage age ranged between twenty and twenty-one; the average family started having children in the beginning of the second year of marriage and had three to four children. For birthrates, see Rochelle Gatlin, *American Women since 1945* (Jackson: University Press of Mississippi, 1987), 51, 55, 61; Susan M. Hartmann, *American Women in the 1940s: The Home Front and Beyond* (Boston: Twayne, 1982), 25, 91, 170, 213; Glenna Matthews, *"Just a Housewife": The Rise and Fall of Domesticity in America* (New York: Oxford University Press, 1987), 265; Elaine Tyler May, *Homeward Bound: American Families in the Cold War Era* (New York: Basic Books, 1988), 7, 136–37. On marriage and divorce rates, see Hartmann, *American Women in the 1940s*, 163–65; Gatlin, *American Women since 1945*, 51; and Tyler May, *Homeward Bound*, 6–8, 21, 59, 117, 185.

4. For a detailed study of the social construction of childhood, see Philippe Aries, *Centuries of Childhood: A Social History of Family Life*, trans. Robert Baldick (New York: Vintage, 1962).

5. Beatrice Hale, cited in Barbara Ehrenreich and Deirdre English, *For Her Own Good: 150 Years of the Experts' Advice to Women* (Garden City, NY: Anchor, 1978), 194. Also see Ehrenreich and English's description of the mothers' movement, 192–96.

6. See Margaret Marsh, *Suburban Lives* (New Brunswick, N.J.: Rutgers University Press, 1990) and her article "Suburban Men and Masculine Domesticity, 1870–1915," *American Quarterly* 40 (June 1988): 70–83.

7. The phrase "century of the child" was used to describe the twentieth century's child-centeredness in Arthur W. Calhoun, *Social History of the American Family*, vol. 3, *Since the Civil War* (Cleveland: Arthur H. Clark, 1919), 131.

8. For a good overview of child saving in the early decades of the twentieth century, see Hamilton Cravens, "Child-Saving in the Age of Professionalism, 1915–1930," in *American Childhood: A Research Guide and Historical Handbook*, ed. Joseph M. Hawes and N. Ray Hiner (Westport, Conn.: Greenwood, 1985), 415–88.

9. Ehrenreich and English, *For Her Own Good*, 183–211.

10. The links between power and the regularization of knowledge through discourse runs throughout Foucault's body of research and methodological works. For a series of interviews with Foucault about these broad interests, see Michel Foucault, *Power/Knowledge: Selected Interviews and Other Writings 1972–1977*, ed. Colin Gordon, trans. Colin Gordon et al. (New York: Pantheon, 1977).

11. For more on this, see Mark West, *Children, Culture and Controversy* (Hamden, Conn.: Archon, 1988); Richard deCordova, "Ethnography and Exhibition: The Child Audience, the Hays Office and Saturday Matinees," *Camera Obscura* 23 (May 1990): 91–107.

12. For more on this and other aspects of the public concern over juvenile

delinquents, see James Gilbert, *A Cycle of Outrage: America's Reaction to the Juvenile Delinquent in the 1950s* (New York: Oxford University Press, 1986). Gilbert shows that while public officials, educators, psychologists, and other "experts" increasingly focused on criminal youth, "the incidence of juvenile crime does not appear to have increased enormously during this period." Gilbert goes on to show that crime statistics were imprecise and, since the definition of juvenile crime and the policing of it had changed over the course of the century, it is difficult to prove that the postwar period actually witnessed a substantial rise in teenage crimes. Given this, Gilbert argues that the perception of juvenile delinquency in the 1950s was based less on reality than on the way crime was labeled and reported, as well as the general worries about the future direction of American society (pp. 66–71).

13. For more on Spock's popularity and influence, see Charles E. Strickland and Andrew M. Ambrose, "The Changing Worlds of Children, 1945–1963," in *American Childhood: A Research Guide and Historical Handbook*, ed. Joseph M. Hawes and N. Ray Hiner (Westport, Conn.: Greenwood, 1985), 538–44. Strickland and Ambrose also point out that while it is impossible to say exactly how many parents actually practiced Spock's teachings, anthropological and psychological studies conducted during the period suggest that many parents, particularly of the middle class, did opt for the more permissive methods of child rearing that Spock advised.

14. For more on how juvenile delinquency was blamed on mass media (especially music and film), see Gilbert, *A Cycle of Outrage*, 143–95.

15. House Interstate and Foreign Commerce Committee, *Hearings before a Subcommittee of the Committee on Interstate and Foreign Commerce: Investigation of Radio and Television Programs*, 82nd Cong., 2d Sess., H. Res. 278 (Washington, D.C.: U.S. Government Printing Office, June 3, 1952), 23. The hearings reconvened on June 4, 5, and 26, 1952; September 16, 17, 23, 24, 25, and 26, 1952; and December 3, 4, and 5, 1952.

16. Leo Bogart, *The Age of Television: A Study of Viewing Habits and the Impact of Television on American Life* (New York: Frederick Ungar, 1958[1956]), 101. As a cautionary note, I would suggest that in his attempt to present a global, synthetic picture of the television audience, Bogart often smooths over the contradictions in the studies he presents. This attempt at global synthesis goes hand in hand with Bogart's view that the television audience is a homogeneous mass and that television programming further erases distinctions. He writes, "The levelling of social differences is part of the standardization of tastes and interests to which the mass media give expression, and to which they also contribute. The ubiquitous TV antenna is a symbol of people seeking—and getting—the identical message" (p. 5). Through this logic of mass mentalities, Bogart often comes to conclusions that oversimplify the heterogeneity of audience responses in the studies he presents.

17. Paul Witty, "Children's, Parents' and Teachers' Reactions to Television," *Elementary English* 27 (October 1950): 8, cited in Bogart, *The Age of Television*, 264.

18. Ella April Codel, "Television Has Changed Our Lives," *Parents Magazine*, December 1948, 64; Henrietta Battle, "Television and Your Child," *Parents Magazine*, November 1949, 58; *Better Homes and Gardens*, October 1955, 209.

19. William Porter, "Is Your Child *Glued* to TV, Radio, Movies, or Comics?" *Better Homes and Gardens*, October 1951, 125.

20. *Ladies' Home Journal*, April 1950, 237. For a similar cartoon, see *Ladies' Home Journal*, December 1955, 164.

21. *House Beautiful*, June 1951, 8; *Life*, November 26, 1951, 11.

22. For these examples, see "Bang! You're Dead," *Newsweek*, March 21, 1955, 35; Norman Cousins,"The Time Trap," *Saturday Review of Literature*, December 24, 1949, 20; Don Wharton, "Let's Get Rid of Tele-Violence," *Parents Magazine*, April 1956, 93.

23. Edward M. Brecher, "TV, Your Children, and Your Grandchildren," *Consumer Reports*, May 1950, 231.

24. For more on early censorship campaigns, see Lynn Spigel, *Make Room for TV: Television and the Family Ideal in Postwar America* (Chicago: University of Chicago Press, 1992).

25. The networks also tried to police themselves. As early as 1948, NBC executives considered problems of standards and practices in television. *NBC Standards and Practices Bulletin—No. 7: A Report on Television Program Editing and Policy Control*, November 1948, NBC Records, Box 157, Folder 7, Wisconsin Center Historical Archives, State Historical Society, Madison. In 1951, NBC became the first network to establish standards for children's shows, crime shows, mention of sex on programs, proper costuming, and so on. See *NBC Code*, 1951, NBC Records, Box 163, Folder 1, Wisconsin Center Historical Archives, State Historical Society, Madison. For a general explanation of the code, see "Catholic Council Plans TV Legion," 63.

26. House Interstate and Foreign Commerce Committee, *Hearings*.

27. Chairman Senator Robert C. Hendrickson, cited in Committee on the Judiciary United States Senate, *Hearings before the Subcommittee to Investigate Juvenile Delinquency : Juvenile Delinquency (Television Programs)*, 83rd Cong., 2d Sess., S. Res. 89 (Washington, D.C.: U.S. Government Printing Office, June 5, 1954), 1. The committee reconvened on October 19 and 20, 1954, and also met on April 6 and 7, 1955, to continue the debates.

28. House Interstate and Foreign Commerce Committee, *Hearings*, 10–11.

29. John Crosby, "Parents Arise! You Have Nothing to Lose but Your Sanity," in *Out of the Blue! A Book about Radio and Television* (New York: Simon & Schuster, 1952), 115. For more on television's threat to parental power, and particularly its threat to patriarchal dominion, see my book, *Make Room for TV*, and my chapter, "TV In the Family Circle: The Popular Reception of a New Medium," in *Logics of Television: Essays in Cultural Criticism*, ed. Patricia Mellencamp (Bloomington: University of Indiana Press, 1990), 73–97.

30. As Ellen Wartella and Sharon Mazzarella have observed, early social scientific studies suggested that children were not simply using television in place of other media; instead, television was colonizing children's leisure time more than any other mass cultural form ever had. Social scientists found this "reorganization hypothesis" to be particularly important because it meant that television was changing the nature of children's lives, taking them away from schoolwork, household duties, family conversations, and creative play. Ellen Wartella and Sharon Mazzarella, "A Historical Comparison of Children's Use of Leisure Time," in *For Fun and Profit: The Transformation of Leisure into Consumption*, ed. Richard Butsch (Philadelphia: Temple University Press, 1990), 183–85. This reorganization hypothesis was also at the core of early studies conducted by school boards around the country, which showed that television was reducing the amount of time children spent on homework. For early school board activities, see, for example, "TV Also Alarms Cleve. Educators," *Variety*, March 22, 1950, 29; "Students Read, Sleep Less," *Variety*, April 5, 1950, 38.

31. Jack Gould, "TV Daddy and Video Mama: A Dirge," *New York Times Magazine*, May 14, 1950; 56; *Better Homes and Gardens*, September 1950, 56. Audience research showed that people claimed television was disrupting mealtimes and other traditional occasions for family interaction. See Eleanor E. MacCoby , "Television: Its Impact on School Children," *Public Opinion Quarterly* 15 (Fall 1951), 428–30, 438; Bogart, *The Age of Television*, 261.

32. Bogart, *The Age of Television*, 268.

33. In the context of Dr. Spock's popularity, discipline was often a tricky matter. One of the central theses in that book was that parents should avoid conflict to ensure that their home created a democratic environment where children felt they too had a say in family matters. In this regard, much of the disciplinary advice centered on finding ways for different family members to coexist harmoniously with television—even in the face of family squabbles over program choices and viewing duration. As I detail elsewhere, much of the expert advice on television focused on ways to avoid conflict. For example, home magazines showed women how to divide domestic space so that family members of all sexes and generations could watch television separately, without interfering with the activities of others. See chapter 2 in my book, *Make Room for TV*, and my article, "Television in the Family Circle."

34. Jack Gould, "What Is Television Doing to Us?" *New York Times Magazine*, June 12, 1949, 7. *Popular Science*, March 1955, took the logic of human agency to its literal extreme, presenting a "lock-and-key" TV that "won't work until Mama sees fit and turns it on with her key" (p. 110).

35. Robert Lewis Shayon, *Television and Our Children* (New York: Longmans Green, 1951), 37.

36. Cited in "What Shall We Do About Television? A Symposium," *Parents Magazine*, December 1950, 37.

37. Paul Witty and Harry Bricket, "Your Child and TV," *Parents Magazine*, December 1952, 37.

38. *Better Homes and Gardens*, October 1955, 202.

39. Robert M. Goldenson, "Television and Our Children—The Experts Speak Up," *Parents Magazine*, December 1954, 76.

40. Dorothy L. McFadden, "Television Comes to Our Children," *Parents Magazine*, January 1949, 74.

41. Robert G. Pilkington, letter to Sylvester L. Weaver, December 17, 1951, NBC Records, Wisconsin Center Historical Archives, State Historical Society, Madison.

42. Serafina K. Bathrick, "Mother as TV Guide," in *From Receiver to Remote Control*, ed. Matthew Geller (New York: New Museum of Contemporary Art: 1990), 23–30.

43. Goldenson, "Television and Our Children," 78.

44. Freda Postle Koch, *Children's Television Habits in the Columbus, Ohio, Area*, Television Committee, Franklin County, Ohio Section, White House Conference on Children and Youth, 1952, cited and summarized in Bogart, *The Age of Television*, 262. Specifically, the study reported that 42 percent of kindergarteners to second graders, 47 percent of fourth through eighth graders, and 26 percent of high school students said that they disagreed with parents on program choices. According to Bogart, however, the bulk of children in this study said that parents primarily established schedules for children, rather than restricting content per se (p. 263).

45. Bogart, *The Age of Television*, 289. In the 1954 Kefauver hearings, similar findings about the relationship between social class and parents' attitudes toward television were made part of the official record. See Committee on the Judiciary United States Senate, *Hearings*, 21–23.

46. The Reverend Everett C. Parker, summarizing findings from the Information Service, Central Department of Research and Survey, National Council of the Churches of Christ in the United States of America, *Parents, Children, and Television: The First Television Generation* (New York: n.p., 1954); reprinted and summarized in Committee on the Judiciary United States Senate, *Hearings*, 28. The surveys included in Bogart's account include a 1955 study from the *New York Herald Tribune* that studied 1,200 schoolchildren; a 1952 and 1955 study by the American Research Bureau of children ages six to sixteen; H. H. Remmars, R. E. Horton and R. E. Mainer, *Attitudes of High School Students toward Certain Aspects of Television* (Indiana: Purdue University, 1953). These are all summarized in Bogart, *The Age of Television*, 252–56. Also see the *Better Homes and Gardens* survey cited above and also summarized in Bogart.

47. For example, in 1952, the American Research Bureau observed that by the age of seven, one child in four had stayed up to watch Berle. Bogart, *The Age of Television*, 254.

48. "Kids Not Kidding," *Variety*, March 29, 1950, 33.

49. In his ethnographic study of children who watch *Pee-wee's Playhouse*, Henry Jenkins shows how similar aspects of contemporary programming might appeal to child viewers. He claims that the ambiguity about Pee-wee's status as boy and man as well as the program's disruption of rule-governed behavior allow young viewers to work through anxieties about the day-to-day power hierarchies between children and adults as well as their own anxieties about becoming adults. See Henry Jenkins, " 'Going Bonkers!': Children, Play, and Pee-wee," *Camera Obscura* 17 (May 1988): 169–93.

50. For an overview of the rise of teenage consumer culture in the postwar period, see Thomas Doherty, *Teenagers and Teenpics: The Juvenilization of American Movies in the 1950s* (Boston: Unwin Hyman, 1988), 42–61.

51. Sylvia O'Neill, "Are You Guilty of Juvenile Delinquency?" *Home Furnishings* August 1954, 14.

52. "Video's Juvenile Audience," *Advertising and Selling*, August 1948, 99.

53. "Television Tempest," *Newsweek*, November 27, 1950, 62.

54. For two scholarly articles on the commercialization of contemporary children's culture, see Stephen Kline, "Limits to the Imagination: Marketing and Children's Culture," in *Cultural Politics in Contemporary America*, ed. Ian Angus and Sut Jhally (New York: Routledge, 1989), 299–316; Tom Englehart, "The Strawberry Shortcake Strategy," in *Watching Television*, ed. Todd Gitlin (New York: Pantheon, 1987), 74–108.

55. For a discussion of the success of *Disneyland*, see William Melody, *Children's Television: The Economics of Exploitation* (New Haven, Conn.: Yale University Press, 1973), 41; for a discussion critical responses to the premier episode, (including Gould's), see Jerry Bowles, *Forever Hold Your Banner High! The Story of the Mickey Mouse Club and What Happened to the Mouseketeers* (Garden City, NY: Doubleday, 1973), 16–17. *The Mickey Mouse Club* went off the air in 1957 and returned in syndication in 1962. Although its ratings did fall in 1956, its cancellation probably had more to do with disputes between Disney and ABC. See Bowles, 23–24.

56. In *Forever Hold Your Banner High!*, Jerry Bowles claims that "part of the show's impact had to do with its really not being a children's show at all but, rather, a show that featured children playing roles of little adults. All the values the show taught—reliability, reverence, bravery, loyalty, good behavior, the ickky-sticky grown-up stuff of romantic love—are things adults think kids like to be taught" (p. 21).

57. Disney's success with targeting a dual audience of children and adults was to become major marketing strategy by the next decade. Prime-time programs such as *The Flintstones* and *Batman* self-consciously aimed to attract different age levels by building in a range of interpretive possibilities. *Batman*, for example, was targeted to appeal as "camp" for adults and as action-adventure fantasy for children. For more on this, see Lynn Spigel and Henry Jenkins, "Same Bat Channel/Different Bat Times: Mass Culture and Popular Memory," in *The Many Lives of the Batman: Critical Approaches to a Superhero and His Media*, ed. William Uricchio and Roberta Pearson (New York: Routledge, 1991), 117–48.

58. Wilbur Schramm, Jack Lyle, and Edwin B. Parker, *Television in the Lives of Our Children* (Stanford, Calif.: Stanford University Press, 1961), 156. The authors based this speculation on numerous social scientific studies that also suggested television was making children grow up too fast.

59. Jeff Greenfield, *No Peace, No Place: Excavations along the Generational Fault* (Garden City, NY: Doubleday, 1973), 114–16; Joyce Maynard, *Looking Back: A Chronicle of Growing Up Old in the Sixties* (Garden City, NY: Doubleday, 1973), 51–52. Both of these books are cited in Strickland and Ambrose, "The Changing Worlds of Children," 560.

60. Joshua Meyrowitz, *No Sense of Place: The Impact of Electronic Media on Social Behavior* (New York: Oxford University Press, 1985), 247.

61. Mark Newgarden, cited in Bill Forman, "Sticker Shock," *Creem*, May 1992, 28.

62. A 1988 Nickelodian press release, "Kids Spend $15.8 Billion Annually," underscores the popularity of new technologies such as cable, VCRs, and personal computers with the younger generation. Some 72 percent of American children say they will subscribe to cable TV as adults, and among those already receiving cable in their homes, 85 percent say they will subscribe as adults. Among the 73 percent of American children in households that own VCRs, almost half (43 percent) report watching videotapes "every day or almost every day." And the press release reported that 24 percent of the nation's children own personal computers. These data were compiled by the Nickelodian/Yankelovich Youth Monitor. See the Children's Television clipping file, Doheny Cinema-Television Library, University of Southern California. In his recent book on video games, Eugene F. Provenzo, Jr., reports that video games took off in the late 1980s. For example, two years after its introduction in 1986, Nintendo had sold about 11 million units, and in 1990 alone it sold 7.2 million units. More generally, by February 1989, "16 of the 20 top selling toys in the country were video games or video-game related." See Eugene F. Provenzo, Jr., *Video Kids: Making Sense of Nintendo* (Cambridge: Harvard University Press, 1991), 8, 12. For more recent analysis of video games and children, see Marsha Kinder, *Playing with Power: In Movies, Television and Video Games* (Berkeley: University of California Press, 1991). For a general discussion of the children's marketplace in contemporary culture, see Kline, "Limits to the Imagination."

63. Although television's corporate structure was not heavily contested, there were heated debates about the commercial uses of radio broadcasting in the 1920s, and there were also alternative visions. See the chapter in this volume by Robert W. McChesney.

Chapter 12

Ready, Willing, Able: Network Television News and the Federal Government, 1948–1953
Nancy E. Bernhard

"Television? Oh, come on, that's a fad. It'll never last."[1] So spoke an ACME News Pictures editor in 1948, to Don Hewitt, who went on to create *60 Minutes* and earn almost $1 billion for CBS by 1991.[2] When Reuven Frank, later NBC News president, was first hired by that network in 1950, his boss told him, "Nobody in radio who is worth anything thinks [television's] gonna last."[3] The ABC, CBS, NBC, and Dumont television networks together lost $25 million in 1949.[4]

The individuals who by foresight, or luck, or lack of other prospects, came to create network television news worked in a medium dogged by financial instability, technical disaster, and political mine fields. But between 1948 and 1953, the network organizations invented television news before an audience that leapt from 5 percent to 45 percent of U.S. households during those five years.[5]

News programs brought little sponsor revenue to the national networks, but stations were required to provide public service programming for license to use the airwaves. However incidental to the networks' business purposes, television news, gradually through the 1950s, became a pervasive force in national political life, with power to set agendas and legitimate worldviews.

In delivering news, television combined the prerogatives of capitalism with the process of democracy. This essay explores the main institutional parameters of network television news production during its first five years: how the news divisions' relationships with advertisers and government agencies shaped news form and content. By exploring the institutional context in which network television news was produced — Who got access to the air? What constraints did journalists face? — we can see how such news defined political authority and conferred political legitimacy.

Scholars writing principally from the American studies discipline have explored the triumph of corporate order, the disintegration of a cultural critique of capitalism, and the Second Red Scare as the most significant transformations of American culture in the postwar era.[6] They agree that television played a key role in these changes by inscribing consumption as the principal mode of public life. George Lipsitz provides keen readings of how evolving situation comedies legitimated the triumph of consumer values in the postwar years.[7] I would add that audiences watched news as well as entertainment programs, and grappled directly with the issues at the heart of the transformation of their society. News programs claimed to present unbiased truths. Broadcast journalists' claims about their own independence and objectivity colored how many Americans conceived political reality and experienced public life.

Yet the audience plays no part in the institutional matrix I will describe here, except as a vast pool of potential consumers that broadcasters hoped to entertain or inform sufficiently with programs to keep them watching commercials. While television journalists, network managers, government public affairs officers, and advertising representatives struggled among themselves over access to the air and program content, they shared one need if the enterprise were to continue: to secure sponsors by attracting viewers. Although responsible broadcasters tried to expose injustices in U.S. society,[8] television contributed greatly to what C. Wright Mills described as the transformation of the U.S. public into a media market.[9]

Corporate ownership and sponsorship, the need for continuing access to government sources of film and information, and the blacklists constrained journalists and their programs. Not surprisingly, television presented only views that supported corporate capitalism.[10] Yet the notion persists that the commercial system of broadcasting is actually free and democratic. As television marginalized other forms of discourse, the narrow range of political contention it portrayed became the entire range most viewers encountered,[11] and the availability of alternative worldviews diminished.

Blacklisting and Business

Television came of age with the Cold War: as the networks first pursued and won wide audiences, well-placed extremists were able to exclude everyone but avowed anti-Communists from the broadcasting industry. Among the first major stories the network news divisions reported as they created new programs in 1948 were the

Communist coup in Czechoslovakia, the Soviet blockade of West Berlin, Whittaker Chambers's accusations against Alger Hiss, and the capture of Manchuria by Chinese Communists. Official and self-appointed loyalty investigators carefully watched those who controlled access to the air, and to whom access was accorded. They warned that in the hands of devious individuals, television technology had an unprecedented capacity to deceive. The *American Mercury* cautioned against leftists seeking to invade television, saying that "video is the answer to the thought-controller's dream."[12]

The entertainment industry was a particular target of anti-Communist activity because of this alleged danger of thought manipulation by leftists. In 1947, Alfred Kohlberg, an importer of Chinese textiles and ardent anti-Communist, gave money to three ex-FBI investigators to found American Business Consultants. They published *Counterattack: The Newsletter of Facts on Communism*. Subscribers to *Counterattack* were offered special reports, including the well-known *Red Channels: The Report of Communist Influence in Radio and Television*, issued in June 1950. Soon nicknamed "the Bible of Madison Avenue" for its ubiquity with networks, sponsors, and advertising agencies, *Red Channels* listed 151 people in the radio and television industries who were allegedly linked to "Communist causes."[13] Among network news personnel, *Red Channels* listed only William Shirer, Alexander Kendrick, and Howard K. Smith, all of CBS, but blacklisting created a pervasive climate that set unspoken codes for hiring and for news content.

American Business Consultants represented an extremist group of corporate and ex-government personnel. These right wingers, not Communists, managed to exercise inordinate control over the broadcasting industry, by their control over its advertisers.[14] Laurence Johnson, a zealous anti-Communist who owned a chain of supermarkets in Upstate New York, provided the mechanisms for control. He wrote to manufacturers, threatening boycotts, or to display their products with signs indicating that the manufacturer supported communism, if they did not withdraw sponsorship from programs he deemed un-American. The direct liaison between the sponsors and American Business Consultants was Jack Wren, a former Naval Intelligence officer, who oversaw "security" at the advertising agency of Batten, Barton, Durstine and Osborn.[15]

CBS and NBC responded to these accusations by instituting their own internal security systems. NBC had required new employees to sign loyalty oaths since the mid-1940s,[16] delegating the investigation of alleged risks to its legal department. CBS created a new vice presidency for this purpose. In December 1950, CBS also began to require loyalty oaths of its employees, on the model of the federal program instituted by President Harry Truman.[17] CBS Chairman William S. Paley required the oaths after he heard that FBI Director J. Edgar Hoover referred to the network as the "Communist Broadcasting System."[18]

But the danger to the networks from political controversy is often misconstrued. The executives who administered the loyalty oaths understood their cooperation in the blacklists to be a business decision rather than a political concession. An NBC spokesman characterized blacklisting as "a business safeguard."[19] Privately, many broadcasters abhorred the practice. Daniel T. O'Shea, who oversaw the oaths and investigated controversial personnel for CBS, also saw the network's motives as economic rather than political:

> They didn't do the blacklisting because of what people had done; they did it because of business. Shows were beginning to cost more. A client would say, "Listen, we can't have this. We're spending forty or fifty thousand dollars for good will. We don't want to be identified with this . . ." I kept some people off the air. Never deliberately unjustly. It wasn't that I felt myself in the middle of ridding the world of Communists—rather of some group or another who were affecting CBS's business.[20]

Thus, the accuracy of each accusation was unimportant to the network because the negative impressions created by false accusations still alienated the source of network revenue, the sponsors. The networks avoided political controversy as a matter of business policy. Profit motives, not political complicity, inspired the networks to cave in to the blacklisters.

Television Responds to the Korean Crisis

The networks practiced voluntarism and self-censorship in the government's first hot war against communism. The Korean War, which began in late June 1950, occasioned an unparalleled variety of collaborations between broadcasters and federal officials. At the outset, the television industry faced several scenarios that threatened both its survival and corporate control over broadcasting. By working closely with federal agencies for the duration, the networks preserved their ultimate control and made themselves indispensable to many federal officials.

Broadcasters feared that advertisers would flee the new medium for radio because of the days-long delay in getting film on the air. Viewership declined during the first days of the war because, according to *Variety*, "Americans had established the habit of turning to their radios for late developments during World War II."[21] Broadcasters also feared that television set manufacturing would stall due to the need for parts and factory retooling for war materiel, which could freeze both audience size and sponsor revenue.[22] The FCC had frozen the number of television stations since September 1948, while problems with frequency interference were solved.[23] Additionally, as operators of sensitive electronic equipment during wartime, broadcasters were required by law to cooperate with defense officials, who threatened them with federal takeover.[24] And as purveyors of wartime information, broadcasters had to grapple with censorship. These combined threats to the industry's viability and independence precipitated a unified, industrywide response.

When the war began, the National Association of Broadcasters[25] (NAB) pronounced itself "instantly available to the government."[26] The NAB Board of Directors met in Washington, D.C., on August 7 and 8, 1950, and presented a resolution to Dr. John Steelman, assistant to President Truman (a position equivalent to the contemporary chief of staff) declaring the broadcasting industry's eagerness to support the government's national security aims. They resolved: "The broadcasting industry is now in every respect ready, able and willing to take its full part in effectuating all measures necessary to insure the national security and to achieve those objectives to which our country is committed."[27]

The NAB thus grouped the entire broadcasting industry under the auspices of the new Broadcasters' Advisory Council (BAC). In the first year of its existence, the BAC returned to Washington several times to meet with Federal Communications Commissioner Wayne McCoy, Secretary of State Dean Acheson, Secretary of Defense George Marshall, and President Truman.

The threats to the industry from electronic shortages and sponsor flight never materialized. More than five million televisions were sold each year of the war.[28] But the danger to corporate control over broadcasting facilities remained acute. In January 1951, one month after the People's Republic of China entered the war, Assistant Secretary of Defense Marx Leva asked for legislation giving the president broad powers to control radio and television during emergencies, or "periods of critical international relationships,"[29] mainly to prevent the use of signals as navigation aids by enemy planes.

A cooperative effort by BAC executives, industry-employed engineers, the FCC, the Air Defense Command, and the Office of Civil Defense produced the voluntary CONELRAD (Control of Electromagnetic Radiation) Plan to prevent enemy use of broadcast signals.[30] Asked by station operators whether participation was fully voluntary, FCC officials admitted that "stations have a choice of going along with the plan or shutting down should an air raid occur."[31] In October 1951, after the BAC was consulted, legislation passed that gave the president power to control stations "upon proclamation of war, disaster, etc. and if he deems it to be in the public interest."[32] By working with the officials who threatened takeover of their facilities, the BAC preserved its corporate control and set precedents for close, voluntary collaborations in the years to come.

The wartime threat of military censorship proved qualitatively different from the other potential infringements on network independence, because it posed no financial threat to the networks. Acceding to censorship protected corporate interests, so the network managements welcomed it, working collaboratively with officials to set the procedures.

At the start of the war, General Douglas MacArthur gave to journalists in the field the responsibility for determining whether or not military information was classified. No consistent guidelines existed, so correspondents daily faced the choice of getting scooped or getting thrown out of Korea. The Army Public Information Office complained that "the press wasn't getting on the team, asked too many questions, interviewed the shell-shocked, followed reports of firing on human decoys."[33] Divulging military secrets was not the only grounds for getting thrown out. The High Command also proscribed "criticism of command decisions or of the conduct of Allied soldiers on the battlefield,"[34] but exercised no prior restraint.

During the first months of the war, CBS enforced its own strict self-censorship on dispatches from Korea. Three of the reports it refused to air, filed by Bill Downs and Bill Costello, concerned the conflict between correspondents and army information officers over censorship. The fourth, filed by veteran World War II correspondent Edward R. Murrow, described an unsuccessful United Nations offensive that senior U.S. officers had criticized. CBS executives feared the domestic consequences of appearing to give aid and comfort to the enemy.

The frustration of having no consistent guidelines thus triggered one of the oddest actions in the history of war journalism. To protect its members, one month into the war the Overseas Press Club and many senior correspondents actually requested the imposition of formal censorship.[35] Members of the BAC, along with representatives of the print media, met with Secretary of Defense George Marshall, the director of the Office of Public Information in the Defense Department, and the Army's chief of information to work out the procedures for implementation. By the end of December 1950, full censorship was in effect for stories originating at Eighth Army headquarters.[36] The censors deleted not only military information that might compromise the war effort, but also "comments indicating a low morale or poor efficiency on the part of United Nations troops,"[37] the word *retreat*, and any information that would "injure the morale of our forces" or "embarrass the United States, its allies or neutral countries."[38] Censorship and self-censorship prevented criticism of the war far more often than did the disclosure of military secrets. By way of comparison, although the U.S. Army did not censor reports from Vietnam, Secretary of State Dean Rusk could "recall no information by a reporter that led to serious harm to the nation."[39]

Network management preferred prior censorship to risking the displeasure of sponsors or officials. Television presented a far narrower range of opinion about the war than existed even in the military establishment that fought it. In Korea, broadcasters used the freedom of the press to volunteer as propagandists.

"This Program Is an Official Production of the U.S. Government"

On the domestic front, the BAC distributed a *Defense Bulletin* to all NAB member stations, providing texts for public service campaigns to aid various aspects of the war effort. The NAB public affairs staff worked closely with the Advertising Council to develop broadcast scripts to publicize campaigns such as armed services recruiting and savings bonds.[40] Each *Defense Bulletin* bore the NAB seal with a ribbon running through it, inscribed, "America's Broadcasters, Ready, Willing, Able."[41]

The BAC also had a hand in several television programs produced collaboratively by network and White House personnel. John Steelman, the assistant to President Truman who supervised the BAC, supervised and hosted a weekly television program on the NBC network for almost two years. He remembers that he or someone on his staff originally conceived the program, titled *Battle Report — Washington*. "We thought the people ought to understand, and so forth," he says of the conception. "So I took it up with someone at NBC. They liked the idea. They knew I was in a position to get the speakers."[42] NBC provided the studio and the technical support; Steelman provided guests, films, and other visual illustrations. NBC thus presented official government information, with no independent verification, as news.

More than twenty-five news and public affairs series made up of government films aired on network television between 1948 and 1953. In those years, simply filling the broadcast day with inexpensive programming posed enormous challenges. The great majority of news and public affairs programming aired without sponsors, or on a "sustaining" basis. The networks looked for cheap sources of news film, and they turned to the federal government, which provided hundreds of films for free. The Army Signal Corps produced a great deal of film footage each week. The networks also aired films produced by the Civil Defense Administration, the Economic Cooperation Administration, the Mutual Security Agency, the Federal Aeronautics Administration, and the U.S. Navy, Air Force, and Marine Corps, among other official bodies.

Bureaucracies formed within the federal government to administer the various exchanges. Many of the individuals who staffed these offices came from industry backgrounds, and many of the network personnel had military or other government experience. Conflicts erupted over the quality and scheduling of programs, but a mutual desire to please predominated. We can trace the dynamics of this relationship in the work of one federal bureau, the Radio-TV Branch of the Office of Public Information (OPI) of the Department of Defense (DOD).

"Consolidation Memorandum Number Three" for the creation of the DOD in 1947–48 states, "The mission of the Radio-Television Branch is to assist radio and television networks and independent stations in keeping the public informed of the activities of the National Military Establishment."[43] The Radio-TV Branch measured its success by estimating the value of the free airtime the networks donated to DOD programming. In 1950, for television alone, branch chief Charles Dillon estimated that figure to be more than $1.7 million (a high estimate because in 1950 many programs aired without sponsors). On the memo he prepared for his superiors reporting these figures, Dillon included the following explanation of his branch's work:

> The Radio-TV Branch, through its multitude of contacts in the Radio-TV industry, and through its own official Department of Defense programs . . . "makes friends and influences people" among the groups controlling what goes on the air. There is no way of putting an accurate dollar sign on the value of this service, because the figures shown on the attached page represent only the commercial time value. The general impact on the public is immeasurable.[44]

In return for the substantial value in airtime donated by the networks early in the decade, Dillon's staff provided free programming produced by the Army Signal Corps, public affairs announcements, personnel to appear on discussion programs, and archival footage. They even arranged for naval manuevers to be performed for network cameras. In a typical month, OPI might release six films for network use, provide thirty or forty newsreel-type clips, and send a speaker to a broadcasters' convention.[45] Dillon also briefed Pentagon officials who were scheduled to appear on network programs. When air surgeon Brigadier General Hall was invited to discuss brainwashing on Kate Smith's radio program, Dillon told him to "stay away from controversial issues."[46]

The variety of services the public affairs staff provided caused confusion as to its primary purpose, both within the huge Pentagon bureaucracy and at the networks. The Radio-TV Branch continuously received directives concerning the order of its priorities from DOD's Public Relations Advisory Council, chaired by Assistant Secretary of Defense for Administrative and Public Affairs Andrew Berding. In October 1952 Berding instructed Dillon to "concentrate on getting defense material on existing programs"[47] rather than to focus on the DOD-produced programs, which never attracted large audiences.

The networks preferred it that way. Ted Koop, Washington, D.C., bureau chief for CBS News, complained to Dillon that while he imagined that the DOD's own shows had to be the Radio-TV Branch's "principal duty and interest," CBS perceived a lack of cooperation on other projects. Dillon wished "emphatically to deny" that their own shows came first: "It is our mission, by directive, to provide the best possible service we can to the network industry, within the limits of our staff and resources." To placate Koop, Dillon prepared a list of all the instances of service the branch had provided to CBS A.M. radio and television in the first six months of 1951. The list numbered more than a hundred. He added, "The cooperation and good-will of CBS, and of you personally, are vital to the success of our mission. One of the real pleasures has been the association with you and the other members of the CBS organization. You can count on our doing our best to give you what you want."[48] While DOD still exerted control over the programs that used its film or personnel, Dillon made explicit efforts to keep his network collaborators happy.

Conflicts over the scheduling of government-produced programs intensified as the 1950s progressed and prime time became more valuable. The balance of power shifted in the mid-1950s from the federal agencies, who provided the news operations with film and services, to the networks, who provided government officials with valuable airtime. As advertising revenue doubled, tripled, and quadrupled later in the decade, the networks worked hard to satisfy their sponsors. Government sanction kept advertisers happily free from trouble with the blacklisters, but government-produced films generally had terrible production values, and audiences had learned to expect snappier programs.

Dillon's counterparts at the State Department administered a program that ran on the ABC network from June 1950 through January 1953. Initially titled *The Marshall Plan in Action*, after January 1951 the program was called *Strength for a Free World*. Produced by the Economic Cooperation Administration (ECA), the State Department bureau that administered Marshall Plan aid, the program aired on thirteen ABC stations. Until early 1952, ABC reedited old Mutual Security Agency films to fit the thirty-minute format. One of the first documentary series produced primarily for television use, *Strength for a Free World* aired more than 200 episodes.[49]

As it consisted of baldly propagandistic films, the program pleased no one at the State Department or ABC, and few in the television audience. In 1952 it earned a rating of 2.7. ECA Director of Information Robert Mullen wrote, "I feel compelled to state once again my strong belief that the program should be taken off the air. In my opinion it is actually doing more harm than good."[50] The State Department began to recognize that the increasing sophistication of television and its audiences shifted control over its coverage to the network.

For most of its run, *Strength for a Free World* aired in the 9:30–10:00 p.m. Sunday slot. In April 1952, ABC moved it to Tuesday night at 8:00 p.m., opposite the most popular program on television, Milton

Berle's *Texaco Star Theater*. Bishop Fulton J. Sheen, new to television but rapidly gaining an audience, and Frank Sinatra also broadcast programs in that time slot. The switch angered ECA officials, one of whom wrote: "I am frankly of the opinion that we are being used by ABC to fill a half-hour of their time when it would be impossible for them to put anything else on the air that could stand up to the competition at that time. Since they are getting our show free of charge, it is rather obvious what they are doing."[51] Unless ABC agreed to change the time, the ECA planned to scout options with other networks or independent stations. Used to control over their airtime, department officials chafed at the network's exertion of its scheduling prerogative. Two months later, *Strength for a Free World* moved again to Thursday at 9:00 p.m. for the summer of 1952, and then ran through most of the 1952–53 season on Sunday from 6:00 to 6:30 p.m. The program never earned a major audience.

Despite the off-air wrangling, little conflict surfaced between the journalists and government officials appearing together on cooperatively produced programs. During the summer of 1950, as a replacement series for *Overseas Press Club*, the State Department presented a discussion program titled *World Briefing* and then *Diplomatic Pouch*. The program consisted of State Department officials acquainting viewers with the background to policy, illustrating their remarks with maps and charts, and answering cordial questions from a panel of CBS correspondents.[52]

In preparation for his appearance on the program, the director of the Bureau of German Affairs, Henry Byroade, directed his staff to write questions for the CBS correspondents to ask him. He did not want questions pertaining to the rearmament of Germany or the proposed European army, but he wanted one question to be, "In view of Soviet regimentation of German youth, what are we doing with German youth?"[53] This memo, and one film of *Diplomatic Pouch* of Secretary of State Dean Acheson's appearance on the final program in the series, survive in the National Archives. They indicate that the CBS correspondents appeared only to provide the guise of free inquiry. The State Department determined the questions and answers that would best suit its policy needs.

The September 10, 1950, program opened with a voice-over, "What happens abroad, happens to you. The war in Asia is a war on the whole free world of which we are a part, and so foreign affairs are American affairs." The questions from CBS reporters Charles Collingwood, Edward R. Murrow, and Griffin Bancroft set up the secretary

to deliver apparently rehearsed speeches. The correct maps "spon-
taneously" materialized when his speeches turned to those areas of
the world. Collingwood lobbed this question: "You've often talked
about situations of strength. Is that a part of our foreign policy?"
Murrow broached a difficult subject, press criticism, "even from
radio," of the conduct of the Korean War. Just four weeks earlier, CBS
had suppressed one of Murrow's own broadcasts for being too critical
of U.S. policy. Rather than asking Acheson to respond to the criticisms, however, Murrow grinned broadly at the secretary and asked,
"What do you do for relaxation and relief from this constant tension?"

Both State Department and network personnel made a clear distinction between programs that treated officials in a friendly manner
and those that subjected them to serious questioning, but both types
of programs routinely were scripted in advance. When the summer
series *Diplomatic Pouch* ended, *Capitol Cloakroom* filled its time slot.
The previous spring, Charles Dillon tried to persuade the new secretary of the Army to appear on *Capitol Cloakroom*. Dillon described it
as "a friendly type of program in which a trio of CBS newsmen ask
questions and chat with the guest to enlighten the public. It is not the
type of program that puts guests 'on the spot.' The general format of
the program is always discussed beforehand and agreed to by all
concerned."[54]

Officials and journalists prepared their exchanges, even when they
claimed to be spontaneous. CBS produced a program similar in its
inception to NBC's *Battle Report*, titled *The Facts We Face*. Originally
designed to inform the public about the progress of the Korean War,
The Facts We Face rapidly broadened to feature guests from the State
Department with expertise on Europe,[55] and other agencies such as
the Atomic Energy Commission, whose representatives explained
"atomic warfare and ways to survive it."[56] Four State Department
officials appeared on the February 26, 1951, episode to discuss the
merits of the North Atlantic Community. An elaborate rundown of
the sequence and duration of topics to be discussed circulated among
the four officials and the program's host, Walter Cronkite.[57]

For the appearance of J. Thomas Schneider, chairman of the Personnel Policy Board, Schneider's staff prepared a statement followed
by "ad-lib" questions and answers to be performed by Schneider and
CBS correspondent Bill Shadel. No wonder the acting director of
the Defense Department's Office of Public Information wrote of the
program, "CBS television presentations of this kind are usually extremely well done."[58] Schneider wanted Undersecretary of Defense

Stephen Early to approve the format of his participation on the program, and sent him the prepared script of questions and answers. He wanted to be well prepared, but also to appear spontaneous. One memo read, "Mr. Schneider will not discuss any items not included in the attached statement but in view of the informal nature of the program will not read them word for word but will discuss their general sense with Mr. Shadel."[59]

Scripting discussions in advance helped the networks to secure prominent guests and produce smooth programs. It undermined the spontaneity and freedom fundamental to democratic debate, but many officials would not appear without guarantees that they would not be made to look foolish or calculating. Journalists provided important support for the officials who appeared on their programs: Why else would the officials appear? Sponsors relished programs that generated lively exchanges in patriotic settings, but shrank from those asking conceivably "dangerous" questions. These programs served government, sponsor, and network interests well.

CBS and the Central Intelligence Agency

At least one network, CBS, also provided support to one government agency for no immediate corporate benefit. Evidence of large-scale, long-term collaborations between CBS and the Central Intelligence Agency has accumulated since the congressional investigations of the intelligence services in 1976–77. I will survey this evidence in this section, and discuss how these collaborations differ from the others I have described.

To the CIA, journalists and news executives constitute "an intelligence asset of the first magnitude."[60] At a 1977 congressional hearing to investigate the relationship between the CIA and the news media, former Director of Central Intelligence Stansfield Turner observed that the CIA and journalists "are in the same business. Both the Agency and the journalists are out looking for information and both of them have something that the other one wants."[61] By 1977, according to both CIA and media sources, the heyday in the 1950s and 1960s of cooperation with large, prestigious media organizations was long over. In an exposé published in *Rolling Stone*, Carl Bernstein estimated at 400 the number of journalists "tasked," or given instructions, by the CIA in the preceding thirty years. But he added that "those officials most knowledgeable about the subject say that a figure of 400 American journalists is on the low side of the actual number who maintained covert relationships and undertook clandestine tasks."[62] According to CIA officials, the most active and rewarding relationships with media outlets were with the *New York Times*, *Time*, and CBS. (Almost all the evidence disclosed to date about television journalists concerns CBS, except the suggestion that ABC Moscow correspondent Sam Jaffe, formerly of CBS, had CIA ties.[63] I would guess that ABC and NBC participated, but less extensively than did CBS.)

Information gathering constituted the bulk of these activities, because it is so vital to the goals of both agents and journalists. They exchanged and confirmed information; agents prebriefed journalists traveling abroad and "tasked" them to look for certain information; agents debriefed journalists after they returned from abroad; and journalists provided agents with access to their notes, files, and film. Most journalists found nothing objectionable about such "reporting"; many described it as desirable or routine. CBS News President Sig Mickelson said "anyone newsgathering abroad who *didn't* check in with a station chief as part of his rounds would have been remiss in the performance of his duty."[64] Others noted that debriefing "got to be so routine you felt a little miffed if you weren't asked."[65] Sharing information benefited both agents and journalists. Ties of friendship and patriotism, as well as professional expediency, made informational contacts largely voluntary.

The explanation offered by the few executives who have admitted their participation is that at the height of the Cold War, collaboration with the CIA seemed a natural and necessary thing to do. Richard Wald, president of NBC News in the 1970s, expressed the unquestioned nature of the service: "It was a thing people did then."[66] The relationship was so friendly that Allen Dulles, CIA director from 1953 to 1961, held annual New Year's parties for CBS News staff at his home or at his private club, the Alibi, in Washington, D.C. They were, as Mickelson told Murrow biographer Ann Sperber:

> part of the long history of good relations between the CIA and the news media in those years, particularly with CBS, marked by annual briefing sessions. These were freewheeling discussions with the correspondents, delightful evenings—the Director set a good table—top newsmen, top agency men, good talk and cigars, each side out for what it could get but then, said one who was there, they were all adults; you took the point of view into consideration as you would anybody else's. And the fact was, some of these guys had the best information going and you were free to check it out.[67]

William Bundy, Dulles's chief aide, similarly described the exchange of information at these dinners as mutually beneficial and enjoyable:

> It was a terribly nice party. There would be about twenty-five of us all told, about fifteen of them from CBS. We had a CIA man next to each CBS, and there was general table conversation, very useful in giving the feeling of Allen's thinking without giving them secret material, and at the same time extracting their views and thoughts—he was particularly good at this. Later critics like David Schoenbrun and Eric Sevareid would be there, and it was a very warm and relaxed occasion.[68]

Clearly, at the time, no one who participated felt that these gatherings violated professional ethics: to be invited to share such prominent company indicated that one had reached the pinnacle of professional esteem. These men moved in the same social circles, shared a faith in U.S. institutions, and respected one another's work. The gatherings cultivated correspondents' friendly contacts in the corridors of power.

But journalists participated in more than dining with CIA personnel. They undertook roles in covert operations. They hosted parties, provided safehouses, and acted as couriers for agents abroad. They spotted, assessed, and recruited potential agents, and "handled" them once recruited. Participation in covert operations often entailed payments of money or gifts. Few journalists would contend that these actions did not compromise their reporting.

The associations most compromising to the media's independence did not involve professional journalists, but professional agents who used media credentials as "covers" for their operations. The ability to investigate and ask questions without appearing suspicious was indispensable to covert agents. Top-level media executives often arranged for their credentials. During the 1950s, the CIA even ran a formal school to train agents to act like journalists. But these cases seem to have been fairly rare. The majority of CIA-media personnel began as professional journalists and then voluntarily performed intelligence tasks.[69]

The systematic arrangement between CBS and the CIA in the 1950s operated through the network's Washington, D.C., bureau. CBS News President Sig Mickelson and Washington Bureau Chief Ted Koop administered regular exchanges of news film that lasted at least until 1971. Mickelson tired of using a pay telephone to call the CIA and finally installed a private phone line that bypassed the CBS switchboard.[70]

Intelligence operations involving the CBS news staff ranged from the nearly comical, as when Chairman Paley arranged for CIA agents to use the CBS broadcast booth at the United Nations to lip-read the whispered conversations of the Soviet delegation during Premier Nikita Khrushchev's visit in 1959[71] to far more systematic arrangements involving CBS News correspondents. Since both corporate and national security secrecy cloak these operations, we may presume the public record represents only a portion of the collaborations that occurred.

A case disclosed in 1976 by Mickelson and corroborated by John Day, a former manager of CBS News, concerned correspondent Frank Kearns, who began at the network as a stringer in Cairo in the mid-1950s. Mickelson and Day told John Crewdson of the *New York Times* that they heard a "rumor" in 1957 or 1958 that Kearns worked for the CIA.[72] The network liked Kearns's work and wanted to hire him as a full-time correspondent, but "was concerned about his CIA affiliation." Mickelson and Day then told CIA Director Allen Dulles at a Washington, D.C., dinner party, "in effect, that CBS wished to employ the man, but would not if he remained with the agency." Mickelson then "put it up to Frank" to choose between the two organizations, and sometime later a CIA agent showed Mickelson Kearns's letter of resignation from the agency. CBS then hired Kearns in September 1958.[73]

Former CBS correspondent Daniel Schorr footnotes this story with the epilogue that "Kearns subsequently resigned from the CIA and was appointed a CBS News staff correspondent, risking his life many times in the Middle East and Cyprus battles."[74] Whether Kearns actually resigned or not, CBS rewarded his dual allegiance with a staff position. The executives were not concerned with Kearns's willingness to serve CBS and the CIA at once, only with the formality of the arrangement. John Crewdson of the *Times* also named CBS writer Austin Goodrich and CBS correspondent Sam Jaffe, who later went to Moscow with ABC, as agents.[75]

When Richard Salant became CBS News president for the first time in 1961, a CIA agent telephoned to say he wanted to continue the "long-standing relationship" known to Paley and CBS Inc. President Frank Stanton. Stanton told Salant that he knew of no such relationship, so Salant refused persistent requests for outtakes from Eastern Europe. When CBS correspondent William Cole was thrown out of Moscow after interviewing dissidents, Salant refused to set up an interview with Cole for CIA officials.[76] Salant told Carl Bernstein that he also refused CIA officials access to all correspondents, and would let them see broadcast reports but not outtakes. This arrangement lasted until the early 1970s.[77] Salant's refusal to comply fully indicates growing conflict within the network after 1961 over the appropriate role for the network to take in intelligence gathering.

A partial exposure of network collaboration with the CIA came with the House and Senate Select Committees on Intelligence investigations of the mid-1970s. When the new CIA director, George Bush, took over in early 1976, CBS and *New York Times* journalists demanded full disclosure of the reporters who had worked with the agency.[78] Bush refused, but declared that the agency would no longer recruit accredited correspondents.[79] This gesture meant little, however, because by the 1970s most journalists serving the CIA worked as stringers, not as accredited correspondents, and were not agency recruits but provided information voluntarily.

Perhaps continuing declassification will fill in the sketchy record of CIA-media collaboration at the height of the Cold War. Unlike the comparably public collaborations involving programs, the intelligence operations involving news staff served network corporate interests in only the most general way, as support for the national security state. The networks' growing status as multinational corporations, and the personal allegiances of the correspondents who succeeded in those organizations, guaranteed both their cooperation and their long-term silence.

Conclusion: Commercial Television News and Political Authority

The networks thus supported government aims both as an expedient means to secure and keep sponsors in the era of the blacklist and out of an overarching commitment to the national security state. After all, as a generation of revisionist historians labored to say, the interests of the national security state were largely aligned with those of U.S. corporations.[80] Its rhetoric inscribes corporate capitalism as a set of institutions as crucial to U.S. defenses against encroaching communism as democratic government. The networks certainly acted as full-fledged participants in the domestic information campaigns of the Cold War.

In the late 1940s and early 1950s, the seeming danger of secret Communists overpowered the notion that the American blend of democracy and capitalism would ultimately triumph in a free marketplace of ideas. Network leaders asserted that democracy was a fragile luxury, and gave the public only information that supported the national security state. Yet they employed this same belief in the free marketplace of ideas, abandoned so routinely in their various official collaborations, as a rationale to program television for maximum profit. Defenders of the commercial system of broadcasting argued that the audience could choose the system of government it wanted, just as it could choose its brand of soap powder and automobile. But the government competed on television not against a political opposition, for no such voices found regular access to the frequencies, but against *I Love Lucy*, and Uncle Miltie, and *The $64,000 Question*.

Commercial television fostered a conception of the medium itself as a set of democratic institutions. Broadcasters and advertisers claim that the networks serve popular democracy by providing the people with what they want, as read by the numbers of people who watch their programs. But this assumes that audience size is the only requirement for sponsorship. During the Persian Gulf war, CBS reported that although their special reports drew higher ratings than competing entertainment programs, they sold only 20 percent of the commercial time on the programs because sponsors feared association with images of war dead, or because their upbeat messages seemed inappropriate during war programming.[81] A program must not only reach tens of millions of people, but must reinforce the ultimate beneficence of U.S. government and corporations.

During the early Cold War, the networks excluded from their employ anyone who would not embrace anticommunism. They supported the war in Korea more consistently than did U.S. generals. They aired propaganda in the guise of independently produced news programs. Network correspondents played roles scripted for them by federal officials. Television acknowledged less dissent than could be found in newspapers, within the government itself, or, indeed, in the households to whom the sponsors wished to sell their products. This marginalization of dissent eclipsed the more contentious aspects of liberal democracy, and reinforced the consensus view of U.S. history and politics vital to Cold War liberalism. By 1963, as the famous Roper poll announced, a majority of people cited television as their chief source of news.

Television has achieved a remarkable conflation of our notion of the public interest, which stations are required by law to serve, with the networks' corporate interests. Network television news did not introduce corporate capitalism to the public processes of U.S. government, but it surely cemented corporate control of mainstream political discourse.

Notes

1. Quoted in Gary Paul Gates, *Air Time: The Inside Story of CBS News* (New York: Harper & Row, 1978), 60.

2. Hewitt's figure is cited in Richard Campbell, *60 Minutes and the News: A Mythology for Middle America* (Urbana: University of Illinois Press, 1991), 2.

3. Desmond Smith, "TV News Did Not Just Happen—It Had to Invent Itself," *Smithsonian*, June 1989, 76.

4. Cobbett Steinberg, *TV Facts* (New York: Facts on File, 1985), 126.

5. Ibid., 85–86.

6. Lary May, "Introduction" in *Recasting America: Culture and Politics in the Age of Cold War*, ed. Lary May (Chicago: University of Chicago Press, 1989), 10–11.

7. See George Lipsitz, "The Meaning of Memory: Family, Class, and Ethnicity in Early Network Television," in *Time Passages: Collective Memory and American Popular Culture* (Minneapolis: University of Minnesota Press, 1990), 39–75.

8. At the network level, the most aggressive investigative reporting was done by documentary teams through the 1950s and 1960s: *See It Now* and *CBS Reports* at CBS, *Project XX* and *White Paper* at NBC, and *Close-Up!* at ABC.

9. C. Wright Mills, *The Power Elite* (New York: Oxford University Press, 1956), 298–324.

10. Herman and Chomsky have provided a useful model for the way monopolistic control of the media works systematically for the ends of a corporate elite. See their chapter "A Propaganda Model," in Edward S. Herman and Noam Chomsky, *Manufacturing Consent: The Political Economy of the Mass Media* (New York: Pantheon, 1988), 1–36.

11. I am indebted to Daniel Hallin for his useful model of the "spheres" of journalistic activity. Different procedures apply for stories in the shifting spheres of consensus, legitimate controversy, and deviance. Hallin used the model to explain the perception of oppositional reporting from Vietnam. See Daniel C. Hallin, "The Media, the War in Vietnam and Political Support: A Critique of the Thesis of an Oppositional Media," *Journal of Politics* 46 (1984): 2–24; and *The "Uncensored War": The Media and Vietnam* (New York: Oxford University Press, 1986), 116–18 et passim.

12. Harold Lord Varney, "How TV Molds Your Mind," *American Mercury*, April 1954, 51.

13. John Cogley, *Report on Blacklisting II: Radio and Television* (New York: Fund for the Republic, 1956), 1–2.

14. Other blacklisters targeted the entertainment industry union, AFTRA. Aware, Inc., Vincent Hartnett, and the Joint Committee Against Communism concentrated on the entertainment side of television. Foley argues that information about news personnel is harder to find, and that news departments were usually more insulated from sponsor pressures than their entertainment counterparts. See

Karen Sue Foley, *The Political Blacklist in the Broadcast Industry: The Decade of the 1950s* (New York: Arno, 1979), 13.

15. David Caute, *The Great Fear: The Anti-Communist Purge under Truman and Eisenhower* (New York: Simon & Schuster, 1978), 521–22.

16. Stephen J. Whitfield, *The Culture of the Cold War* (Baltimore: Johns Hopkins University Press, 1991), 166.

17. Cogley, *Report on Blacklisting*, 23, 68.

18. Robert Metz, *CBS: Reflections in a Bloodshot Eye* (Chicago: Playboy Press, 1975), 282.

19. Quoted in Caute, *The Great Fear*, 528.

20. Quoted in A. M. Sperber, *Murrow: His Life and Times* (New York: Freundlich, 1986), 365.

21. "Video Hypos War News Coverage to Keep Pace with Radio Rapidity," *Variety*, August 16, 1950, 33. See also Herb Golden, "Show Biz Eyes War Changes," *Variety*, July 19, 1950, 1.

22. *Broadcasting, Variety*, and *Television Digest* all carried many stories about potential rationing and shortages from July 1950 through mid-1951. See, for instance, "Truman Speech May Hold Key to Korean War's Effect on TV Industry," *Variety*, July 19, 1950, 25; "Civilian Radio-TV Cutbacks Mulled," *Broadcasting*, July 31, 1950, 23.

23. On the freeze, see J. Fred MacDonald, *One Nation under Television: The Rise and Decline of Network TV* (New York: Pantheon, 1990), 59–61.

24. President Truman's "Model State Civil Defense Act" of September 1950 included a plan for state seizure of communications in an emergency. See Dave Berlyn, "America's Sentinels: Radio, TV," *Broadcasting*, September 25, 1950, 19. The Defense Department proposed a plan in early 1951; see below.

25. The NAB was founded in 1923 to protect the rights and interests of the broadcasting industry. It consistently offered industry self-regulation as an alternative to government regulation, and in the 1950s was considered "one of the most effective trade associations in the United States." David R. Mackey, "The Development of the National Association of Broadcasters," *Journal of Broadcasting* 1 (Fall 1957): 303.

26. "News from NAB," press release, July 21, 1950.

27. Ibid.

28. Steinberg, *TV Facts*, 85.

29. "Radio Bill Hearing Set," *New York Times*, February 11, 1951, 40:1. See also "Emergency Role," *Broadcasting*, January 1, 1951, 20; "News from NAB," press release, February 21, 1951.

30. "Broadcasters to Huddle with FCC on Emergency Operation Setup," *Variety*, March 21, 1951, 24:1.

31. "Govt. Gives Plans of B'caster Role in Civil Defense," *Variety*, April 18, 1951, 28:4.

32. *Digest of General Bills with Index*, 82nd Cong., 1st Sess. (Washington, D.C.: Library of Congress Legislative Reference Section, 1951), xii.

33. Sperber, *Murrow: His Life and Times*, 345.

34. "Army Eases New Rules," *New York Times*, July 28, 1950, 5:2.

35. "Situation Not Normal," *Newsweek*, September 25, 1950, 61; "M'Arthur Sets Up New Security Code," *New York Times*, December 13, 1950, 8:1.

36. "Censorship Is Tightened," *New York Times*, December 27, 1950, 4:7.

37. "Korea Censorship Tightened Again," *New York Times*, January 7, 1951, 14:1.

38. "U.S. 8th Army Bars Word 'Retreat' as It Rivets Censorship onto Korea," *New York Times*, January 10, 1951, 1:6.

39. Loch K. Johnson, *America's Secret Power: The CIA in a Democratic Society* (New York: Oxford University Press, 1989), 202.

40. "News from NAB," press release, September 19, 1950.

41. The intent of those present at the August board meetings was to publish the *Bulletin* at least three times monthly. The first was published on September 25, 1950, and the last one I found was dated December 19, 1950. I was unable to find corroboration for the publishing frequency or duration.

42. John Steelman, personal telephone interview, March 14, 1989.

43. Frye to Pritchard et al., Consolidation Memorandum No. 3, April 22, 1949, Public Affairs Records 1949–1953, Office of the Secretary of Defense Historical Office, Department of Defense, the Pentagon, Arlington, Va. (hereafter cited as OSD Records).

44. "TOTAL Radio and TV," memo, April 10, 1950, Dillon Folder, OSD Records.

45. See monthly activity reports, Public Affairs Records 1949–53, OSD Records. The naval manuevers were reported on May 31, 1955.

46. "Meeting with Radio-TV Liaison Officers," May 11, 1953, Public Affairs Records 1949–53, OSD Records.

47. Minutes of the Public Relations Advisory Council meeting, October 30, 1952, OSD Records.

48. Dillon to Koop, July 9, 1951, Public Affairs Records 1949–53, OSD Records.

49. Alex McNeil, *Total Television: A Comprehensive Guide to Programming from 1948 to the Present*, 2d ed. (New York: Penguin, 1984), 406.

50. "Mutual Security Agency Program," unsigned memo (in all probability, Mullen) to J. V. Roscoe, April 15, 1952, Moving Pictures-Television-ABC File, Records of the Assistant Secretary of State for Public Affairs 1945–50, Record Group 59, General Records of the Department of State, Washington National Records Center, Suitland, Md. (hereafter cited as ASSPA-S Records).

51. Hutchison to Berding, April 28, 1952, ASSPA-S Records.

52. "State Department Officials to Outline U.S. Foreign Policy in CBS Video," *New York Times*, June 21, 1950.

53. Byroade to Hay et al., August 14, 1950, Files of the Assistant Secretary of State for Public Affairs, Decimal 911.44, Records of the Department of State, National Archives, Washington, D.C. (hereafter cited as ASSPA-NA Records).

54. Dillon to King, April 17, 1950, Files of the Office of Public Information, Department of Defense, 1950, Record Group 330, Entry 133, Decimal 311.25, National Archives, Washington, D.C. (hereafter cited as OPI Records).

55. "Connally, Russell Move to Bar Curb on Sending Troops," *New York Times*, February 26, 1951, 10:5.

56. J. Fred MacDonald, *Television and the Red Menace: The Video Road to Vietnam* (New York: Praeger, 1985), 41.

57. "Memo: Suggested Sequence and Topics for 'Facts We Face' Half Hour Television Show on Europe," ASSPA-NA Records.

58. Roberts to Schneider, August 22, 1950, OPI Records.

59. Marvin to Roberts, August 30, 1950, OPI Records.

60. Carl Bernstein, "The CIA and the Media," *Rolling Stone*, October 20, 1977, 66.

61. House Permanent Select Committee on Intelligence, Subcommittee on Oversight, *The CIA and the Media* (Washington, D.C.: U.S. Government Printing Office, 1979), 315.

62. Bernstein, "The CIA and the Media," 66.

63. John M. Crewdson, "TV Newsman Spied on Russians in U.N." *New York Times*, January 22, 1976, 36:7–8.

64. Sperber, *Murrow: His Life and Times*, 635.

65. Hugh Morrow, former *Saturday Evening Post* correspondent, quoted in Bernstein, "The CIA and the Media," 58.

66. Quoted in Ibid., 64.

67. Sperber, *Murrow: His Life and Times*, 635.

68. Quoted in Leonard Mosley, *Dulles: A Biography of Eleanor, Allen and John Foster Dulles and Their Family Network* (New York: Dial, 1978), 457.

69. Bernstein, "The CIA and the Media," 59.

70. Ibid., 62.

71. Lewis W. Paper, *Empire: William S. Paley and the Making of CBS* (New York: St. Martin's, 1987), 304; Daniel Schorr, *Clearing the Air* (New York: Berkley, 1978), 278–79.

72. A second story also came via Mickelson in 1976. Barry Lando, a CBS *60 Minutes* Washington reporter, alerted Daniel Schorr just before Crewdson's article about Kearns came out. Schorr immediately telephoned Mickelson, who told Schorr that he learned from Allen Dulles, not from a "rumor," in 1956, a year or two earlier than in the other version, that Kearns worked for the CIA. Schorr, *Clearing the Air*, 204

73. John M. Crewdson, "An Ex-CBS Writer Is Linked to C.I.A.," *New York Times*, February 11, 1976, 24:1.

74. Schorr, *Clearing the Air*, 204.

75. See Crewdson, "An Ex-CBS Writer," 24:1; "Pose as Journalists Laid to 11 in C.I.A.," *New York Times*, January 23, 1976, 1:3–8:3; "TV Newsman Spied on Russians at U.N.," *New York Times*, January 22, 1976, 1:3–36:3. Varying accounts of Goodrich's affiliation with the agency have been published. See also Paper, *Empire*, 304; and Schorr, *Clearing the Air*, 204, 277–79.

76. Schorr, *Clearing the Air*, 278.

77. Bernstein, "The CIA and the Media," 62.

78. "CIA Data Asked by Times and CBS," *New York Times*, February 10, 1976.

79. "C.I.A. Statement," *New York Times*, February 12, 1976, 13:8.

80. Among the most influential revisionist historians are William Appleman Williams, Gabriel Kolko, Walter LaFeber, Barton J. Bernstein, Athan Theoharis, Gar Alperovitz, and Lloyd C. Gardner.

81. Bill Carter, "Few Sponsors for TV War News," *New York Times*, February 7, 1991, sec. D, 1:3.

Chapter 13

U.S. Mass Communication Research, Counterinsurgency, and Scientific "Reality"

Christopher Simpson

Many people remember the CIA's Phoenix program in Vietnam as an assassination and political murder operation. Phoenix operatives killed about 20,000 Vietnamese rebels, according to CIA Director William Colby—about twice that many according to Vietnamese estimates.[1] Figure 13.1 shows a Phoenix "wanted" poster; most of the men illustrated in it were murdered. Colby says that an "imaginative U.S. Information Agency officer" came up with the poster design.

But reducing Phoenix to simply assassinations underestimates the program's sophistication and the CIA's ambitions for it. Colby insists that Phoenix would be better understood as a means of "establishing democratic legitimacy in the villages," and that it was primarily an intelligence project to "provide a non-communist structure to counter the claims of the [Vietnamese] Liberation Committees."[2] The posters were an "anti-terrorist" device, he says in his memoirs.

Colby's explanation is in part simply euphemism, but its importance goes beyond that. For the CIA, Phoenix was really an experiment in the state of the art of the social psychology of controlling unrest in U.S. client states—an experiment that Colby considers to have been a "great success."[3] Most simply, the CIA's idea was to encourage the cooperation of the Vietnamese population through a combination of terror, careful redefinition of Viet Cong rebels as the "real" terrorists, and orchestrated offers of purported democracy and progress to encourage compliance with the U.S.-sponsored regime.

Phoenix became a key aspect of the CIA's overall vision for "developing" Vietnamese society. It sought to coordinate the regime's police and military efforts to uproot the Viet Cong and replace it with a U.S.-sponsored alternative. Colby viewed the 20,000 killings carried out during the first phases of Phoenix as a scientific, rational, and even "humane"—his word—means of executing the war, at least

Phung - Hoàng

ĐÂY, NHỮNG CÁN BỘ CỘNG SẢN MÀ
CHIẾN DỊCH PHỤNG HOÀNG ĐANG TRUY NÃ

PHAN VĂN MẪM tự	TRẦN VĂN DŨNG tự	NGUYỄN VĂN MINH tự	MAI VĂN TỐC
MƯỜI THÀNH	HÙNG	BẢY MINH	sanh năm 1931
sanh năm 1908	sanh năm 1930	sanh năm 1937	Cán sự Nông Hội
Phó Ban Binh Vận	Trưởng Ban Nông Hội	Trưởng Ban Quân Sự	Ấp An Nhơn
Xã An Thái Trung	Xã An Thái Trung	Xã An Thái Trung	Xã An Hữu
Quận Giáo Đức	Quận Giáo Đức	Quận Giáo Đức	Quận Giáo Đức

Đồng bào thân mến,

Nếu đồng bào biết nơi ẩn trốn của các cán bộ Cộng Sản trên đây, yêu cầu thông báo cho nhân viên Cảnh Sát Quốc Gia hoặc Chánh quyền và Quân đội VNCH gần nhất. Đồng bào sẽ được tưởng thưởng và tên tuổi đồng bào sẽ được giữ kín.

Cùng các bạn cán bộ Cộng-Sản

Các bạn không thể lẩn trốn mãi được vì mọi người đã nhận diện các bạn.

Các bạn hãy ra hồi chánh để hưởng sự khoan hồng của Chánh Phủ. Các bạn sẽ được tiếp đón niềm nở và đối xử tử tế.

ỦY BAN PHỤNG HOÀNG
TỈNH ĐỊNH TƯỜNG

CC-703-70

Figure 13.1   A Phoenix "wanted" poster identifying suspected Vietcong

compared with conventional military action. This did not work in Vietnam, and perhaps it cannot work in any fundamental sense. Nonetheless, these tactics did prolong the agony of colonized peoples and they continue to be used for that purpose today.

The CIA's strategy was based in large part on sociological methods and theories on communication and society popularized by Daniel Lerner, Ithiel de Sola Pool, and other specialists at the Massachusetts Institute of Technology's Center for International Studies (CENIS), which during the 1950s and 1960s was one of the most important centers of communication research in the United States. It applied the most advanced sociological techniques to the challenge of controlling human attitudes and behavior on a mass scale. Various professors at the center had their own interests, but taken as a whole the CENIS project began with consideration of the impact of mass media on social development in the Third World, extended into research for Phoenix-type programs that combined media with various forms of coercion, then continued into devising strategy and tactics for nuclear war as a means of literally "sending messages" to the USSR during some final crisis for humanity.[4]

This essay deals with the evolution of the preconceptions and prejudices in one of the fields in which CENIS specialized, mass communication research. This is a small field in the social sciences, but an intriguing one. Communication research today provides the framework for the college- and graduate-level training of journalists, public relations and advertising personnel, and the related craftspeople who might be called the "ideological workers" of contemporary U.S. society. A relatively new specialty, it crystallized into a distinct discipline with colleges, curricula, the authority to grant doctorates, and so on, between about 1950 and 1955.[5] These characteristics permit researchers to make a clear study of the field's history and — more to the point here — to document the role of U.S. government psychological warfare and counterinsurgency programs in the creation of what are known as the dominant paradigms of U.S. mass communication research.

During the decades since World War II, the U.S. government's national security interests usually overlapped with the commercial ambitions of major advertisers and media companies, and with the aspirations of a particularly enterprising stratum of U.S. university administrators and professors. U.S. military, intelligence, and propaganda agencies helped bankroll substantially all of a generation's research into techniques of persuasion, advertising, interrogation, public opinion polling, political and military mobilization, propagation of ideology, and related questions. The persuasion studies, in particular, provided much of the scientific underpinning for modern advertising and motivational techniques. The government conducted security-related communication research on a scale that went well beyond what would have been possible with private sector money alone, often exploiting its unique access to pools of military recruits useful as test subjects.[6]

At least six of the most important U.S. centers of postwar communication research grew up as de facto adjuncts of government psychological warfare programs. For years, government money — although it was not always publicly acknowledged as such — made up more than 75 percent of the annual budgets of institutions such as Paul Lazarsfeld's Bureau of Applied Social Research at Columbia University, Hadley Cantril's Institute for International Social Research at Princeton, Ithiel de Sola Pool's CENIS Program at MIT, and others.[7] In one case, the U.S. State Department secretly (and illegally) financed the National Opinion Research Center's studies of U.S. popular opinion as part of the department's Cold War lobbying campaigns on Capitol Hill — thus making NORC's ostensibly private, independent surveys financially viable for the first time.[8] In another case, the CIA clandestinely underwrote American University's Bureau of Social Science Research studies of torture — there is no other word for it — of prisoners of war.[9] In sum, it is unlikely that mass communication research could have emerged in anything like its present form without constant transfusions of money for the leading lights in the field from U.S. military, intelligence, and propaganda agencies.

Government psychological warfare programs helped form mass communications research into a distinct scholarly field. The state usually did not directly determine what scientists could or could not say, but it did strongly influence the selection of who would do the "authoritative" talking in the field, who would be recognized as leaders, and which one of several competing scientific paradigms concerning communication would be funded, elaborated, and encouraged to prosper.

This essay is organized in two basic parts. First, I will look at how the concept "communication" came to be defined in U.S. social science circles. Next, I will examine psychological warfare and counterinsurgency programs sponsored by U.S. military, propaganda, and intelligence agencies since 1945, focusing on how these agencies applied social science research and analysis techniques to tasks of social control, covert operations, and intelligence missions. In both sections I will deal with how paradigms in the social sciences are constructed.

Before World War II

Two seminal works in modern U.S. communication research that remain in wide use in graduate programs today are Walter Lippmann's *Public Opinion* (1922) and Harold Lasswell's *Propaganda Technique in the World War* (1926).[10] Both were the product of the prototypical psychological warfare operations of World War I. Both investigated the impact of the then-new phenomenon of genuinely mass communication on Western, industrial society, and both were distinctly hostile to the professed values of democracy. They argued that new technologies for communication and transportation had awakened millions of disenfranchised people to a world outside their factories and villages, but that the traditional economic and political structures that had shaped Europe during the nineteenth century remained in place. This would lead to explosive situations, as Lippmann and Lasswell saw things, including the Bolshevik revolution of 1917 and the wave of labor rebellions that swept through Europe and the United States in the wake of World War I.

Lippmann concluded that "representative government . . . cannot be worked successfully, no matter what the basis of election, unless there is an independent, expert organization for making the unseen facts [of the new world] intelligible to those who have to make the decisions."[11] Lasswell developed a similar idea, emphasizing selective use of assassinations, violence, and other coercion, as well as propaganda, as a means of "communicating" with and managing people.[12]

Lippmann and Lasswell articulated a narrow paradigm that substituted, for communication as such, one particular manifestation of communication that is pronounced in hierarchical industrial states. They contended, in short, that communication's essence is its use as an instrument for imposing one's will on others, and often on masses of others. Their articulation of communication-as-domination permitted a rapid application of a positivist scientific method to the study of communication for the first time.

For Lasswell, the study of all communication could be reduced to "/who/ says /what/ to /whom/ with /what effect/" — a motto that is practically inscribed in stone over the portals of today's colleges of communication. It is a seemingly simple, logical approach, but it carries with it sweeping implications. With the Lasswellian method, it became possible to isolate and measure systematically those aspects of communications that were of greatest relevance to powerful groups in U.S. society. In the United States, consumer capitalism is based to an important degree on privately owned media's sales of the attention of mass audiences to advertisers. To market this commodity, media companies must have some means for measuring it. Thus, the field of mass communication research — its techniques, body of knowledge, institutional structure, and so on — evolved symbiotically with the evolution of the modern capitalist state generally, and particularly with the media industry and those segments of the economy most dependent on mass markets.[13]

World War and Early-Modern Communication Research

Through the end of the 1930s, the work of Lasswell, Lippmann, and other mass communication theorists and researchers remained mainly scholastic or commercial. There were a variety of intellectual currents in the field, ranging from Lasswell's self-consciously Machiavellian analysis to the radical reformism of Robert Lynd, Harry Field, and others. The sociologists and social psychologists of the day (from which the nascent field of communication research was gradually being born) seemed to many outside observers to call for progressive, even fundamental, changes in society.

World War II changed all that: the construction of a paradigm of communication-as-domination and the institutionalization of communication research took decisive steps forward during the conflict. Nazi intellectuals pioneered many of the strictly political uses of modern communication analysis and technologies. Josef Goebbels's work in social manipulation and in some forms of public communication is well known. On a more academic plane, a bright young Nazi security service agent, Otto Ohlendorf, established a German research center known as the Deutsche Lebensgebiete in 1939 to apply new tools such as opinion surveys to the problem of determining /who/ said /what/ to /whom/ with /what effect/ inside Germany. He was successful, on the whole, and his performance at the Deutsche Lebensgebiete laid the foundation for his later career as commandant of SS Einsatzgruppe D in the Caucasus, and as the senior manager of postwar economic planning for the SS. He had truly a remarkable career, in some ways, until he was convicted and hanged for organizing the murder of 90,000 people, most of them women and children.[14] Ohlendorf's principal sponsor and mentor was a leading SS intellectual, Dr. Reinhard Hoehn of the Institute for State Research at the University of Berlin. Hoehn managed to escape his pupil's fate and emerged after the war as one of Germany's most prominent experts on questions of public opinion and the state.[15] Several other leading German mass communication and public opinion specialists contributed their skills to Nazi publicity and opinion-monitoring projects. Notable among them was Elisabeth Noelle-Neumann, who began her career at the Goebbels intellectual journal *Das Reich* and eventually emerged as one of Europe's most celebrated communication theorists.[16]

The war spurred the emergence of psychological warfare as a particularly promising new form of applied communication research. The phrase *psychological warfare* first entered English in 1941 as a translated mutation of the Nazi concept *Weltanschauungkreig* (literally, "worldview warfare"), meaning the purportedly scientific application of propaganda, terror, and state pressure as a means of securing an ideological victory over one's enemies.[17] William "Wild Bill" Donovan, the director of the recently established U.S. intelligence agency OSS, viewed an understanding of Nazi psychological tactics as a vital source of ideas for "Americanized" versions of many of the same stratagems. Use of the new term quickly became widespread throughout the U.S. intelligence community. For Donovan, psychological warfare was a full fourth arm of the U.S. military, equal in status to the army, navy, and air force.[18]

The personal, social, and scientific networks established in U.S. social sciences during World War II, particularly among communication researchers, later played a central role in the evolution (or "social construction") of U.S. sociology after the war.[19] There were six main U.S. centers of psychological warfare research during the conflict. Several of them went through name changes and reorganizations in the course of the war, but they can be summarized as follows: (1) Samuel Stouffer's Research Branch of the U.S. Army's Division of Morale; (2) the Office of War Information (OWI), led by Elmer Davis; (3) the Psychological Warfare Division of the U.S. Army, led by Brigadier General Robert McClure; (4) the Office of Strategic Services, led by William Donovan; (5) Rensis Likert's Division of Program

Surveys at the Department of Agriculture, which provided field research personnel inside the United States for the Army, OWI, and other government agencies; and (6) Harold Lasswell's War Communications Division at the Library of Congress.

Dozens of prominent social scientists participated in the war through these organizations. The Office of War Information included Elmo Roper (of the Roper survey organization), Elmo Wilson (also of Roper), Leonard Doob (Yale), Wilbur Schramm (University of Illinois and later Stanford), Alexander Leighton (Cornell), Leo Lowenthal (Institut für Sozialforschung, USIA, and University of California), Hans Speier (RAND Corporation), Nathan Leites (RAND), Edward Barrett (Columbia journalism school dean and *Columbia Journalism Review* founder), and Clyde Kluckhohn (Harvard), among others. (The institutions in parentheses simply indicate the affiliations for which these scholars may be best known.) OWI simultaneously extended contracts for communication research and consulting to Paul Lazarsfeld, Hadley Cantril, Frank Stanton, and George Gallup, and to Rensis Likert's team at the Agriculture Department.[20]

In addition to his OWI work, Nathan Lietes served as Lasswell's senior research assistant at the Library of Congress project, as did Heinz Eulau (Stanford). Other prominent contributors to the Lasswell project included Irving Janis (Yale) and the young Itheil de Sola Pool (MIT), who, with Lietes, already had begun systematic content analysis of communist publications long before the war was over. Lasswell's Library of Congress project is remembered today as the foundation of content analysis in the United States.[21] The list presented in Table 13.1 summarizes some basic data about the work of prominent U.S. social scientists in World War II psychological warfare programs. The names here are simply a selection of those who have since played important roles in mass communication research; the list is not intended to be complete.

The day-to-day significance of these networks has been explored by social psychologist John Clausen, a veteran of Samuel Stouffer's Research Branch. Clausen made a systematic study during the early 1980s of the postwar careers of his former colleagues who had gone into mass communication research, sociology, or psychology. Twenty-five of twenty-seven veterans who could be located responded to his questionnaire; of these, twenty-four reported that their wartime work had had "lasting implications" and had been "a major influence on [their] subsequent career." Clausen quotes the reply of psychologist

Office of War Information

Staff

Elmo Roper (Roper Surveys)
Elmo Wilson (Roper Surveys)
Leonard Doob (Yale)
Wilbur Schramm (U. Illinois, Stanford)
Alexander Leighton (Cornell)
Leo Lowenthal (Frankfurt School, USIA, U. California)

Hans Speier (RAND Corporation)
Nathan Leites (RAND Corporation)
Edward Barrett (State Department, Columbia)
Clyde Kluckhohn (Harvard)

Consulting Contracts

Paul Lazarsfeld (Bureau of Applied Social Research)
Hadley Cantril (Princeton)
Frank Stanton (CBS)

George Gallup (Gallup Polls)
Rensis Likert (Institute for Social Research)
National Opinion Research Center

War Communications Division (Library of Congress)

Staff

Harold Lasswell (Yale)
Nathan Leites (RAND Corporation)
Heinz Eulau (Stanford)

Irving Janis (Yale)
Ithiel de Sola Pool (MIT)

Psychological Warfare Division (U.S. Army)

Staff

William Paley (CBS)
C. D. Jackson (Time/Life, Fortune)
W. Phillips Davison (Columbia, RAND Corporation)
Saul Padover (New School for Social Research)

Morris Janowitz (Frankfurt School, U. Michigan)
John W. Riley (Rutgers)
Daniel Lerner (MIT, Stanford)
Edward Shils (U. Chicago)

Office of Strategic Services

Staff

W. Phillips Davison (Columbia, RAND Corporation)
Saul Padover (New School for Social Research)
Morris Janowitz (Frankfurt School, U. Michigan)
Howard Becker (U. Wisconsin)

DeWitt Poole (State Department, Public Opinion Quarterly)
Alex Inkeles (Harvard)
Walter Langer (U. Wisconsin)
Douglas Cater (Aspen Institute)
Herbert Marcuse (Frankfurt School, U. California)

Consulting contracts

Stanford University
University of California (Berkeley)
Columbia University

Princeton University
Institute of Human Relations (Yale)
National Opinion Research Center

Table 13.1   Communication research scholars in World War II U.S. psychological warfare programs

Nathan Maccoby (Stanford): "The Research Branch not only established one of the best old-boy (or old-girl) networks ever, but an alumnus of the Branch had an open door to most relevant jobs and career lines. We were a lucky bunch." Nearly three-fifths of the respondents indicated that the Research Branch experience "had a major influence on the direction or character of their work in the decade after the war," Clausen continues, "and all but three of the remainder indicated a substantial influence. . . . fully three fourths reported the Branch experience to have been a very important influence on their careers as a whole."[22] To jump ahead for just a moment, Figure 13.2 shows a 1952 document from the U.S. Psychological Strategy Board, which was an interagency coordinating committee for U.S. psychological warfare efforts during the Korean War. It also clearly illustrates the durability of the social networks among these academics.[23]

Thus, the World War II experience of psychological warfare operations and research contributed substantially to the construction of a remarkably tight circle of men and women who shared important conceptions about mass communication research. They regarded mass communication as a tool for social management and as a weapon in social conflict. They expressed common assumptions concerning the usefulness of quantitative research — particularly experimental and quasi-experimental effects research, opinion surveys, and quantitative content analysis — as a means of illuminating what communication "is" and improving its application to social management. They also demonstrated common attitudes toward at least some of the ethical questions intrinsic to performing applied social research on behalf of a government.

These men and women were not obscure college professors. They were much of the central command of mainstream U.S. sociology, and the names discussed here were particularly prominent in various stages of communication studies. To a very large degree, it was they who wrote the textbooks, enjoyed the heavy government contracts that often are necessary for professional prominence in the United States, served on the editorial boards of the key journals, and became the deans and emeritus professors of the most influential schools of communication and journalism in this country. What can be seen here, in sum, is the construction of social networks whose specialty was claimed to be "knowledge" about a particular topic — in this case, communication.

PROPOSED CONSULTANT PANELS

1. Panel of top evaluation officers actually engaged in evaluating Government operations, particularly the activities of the departments represented on PSB. This would include such persons as

   Ben Gedalecia, State Department (PRS)
   and   Dr. Leo Lowenthal, Evaluation Chief,(State Dept.) OIB.

2. Policy Panel, consisting of individuals in Government who are working on plans and policy at a fairly high level. This would include such persons as

   Paul H. Nitze, Director, Policy Planning Staff (S/P), State Department,
   Howland H. Sargeant, Assistant Secretary for Public Affairs (State Dept.), or
   Joseph B. Phillips, Deputy Asst. Secy. for P (State), and others.

3. An Operational Panel - a group of individuals actually responsible for the operation of the various aspects of our psychological strategy, including, for example,

   Dr. Wilson S. Compton, Chief, International Information Administration, State Department,
   Frank Wisner, of CIA,
   George W. Perkins, Assistant Secretary for European Affairs, State Department, or
   (the head of whatever geographical area seems most appropriate).

In certain cases, it might be desirable for all three of these panels to meet together; in other circumstances it might be preferable to meet with each of them separately.

4. Panel of Social Science research experts outside Government. This should include such persons as

   Dr. Hadley Cantril of Princeton,
   Dr. Daniel Lerner of Stanford,
   Victor Hunt (or Dr. Hans Speier) of Rand Corporation,
   Dr. Harold Lasswell of Yale,
   and others.

5. A Panel

Figure 13.2   Psychological Strategy Board memo illustrates the durability of networks of state sponsors and communication scholars.

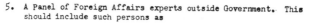

5. A Panel of Foreign Affairs experts outside Government. This should include such persons as

James Burnham
Erwin O. Canham
Hadley Cantril
J. Wallace Carroll
John Sherman Cooper
Gardner Cowles
Mark Foster Ethridge
George H. Gallup
Ben Hibbs
John D. Rockefeller, III
Nelson A. Rockefeller
Bertram D. Wolfe
and others.

James Perkins
George Franklin
Paul Hoffman
John Foster Dulles

6. A Panel of names of <u>individuals</u> to whom PSB could turn for advice and assistance on <u>appropriate occasion</u>. This list should cover a broad field, and might include such persons as

Dr. Hans Speier and
Philip Davidson - of Rand Corporation
Dr. Daniel Lerner of Stanford
Kingsley Davis of Columbia
Jerome Brunner of Harvard
Maurice Janowitz of the University of Michigan
Rensis Likert, University of Michigan
Wilbur Schramm, University of Illinois
John Riley, Rutgers
Gabriel Almond, Princeton
Elmo C. Wilson, President, International Public Opinion
    Research (IPR), New York
Clyde Kluckohn, Harvard
Willmoore Kendall, Operations Research Office, Johns Hopkins
Philip Selznick, UCLA
Alexander Leighton, Cornell

and Area Specialists, such as

David Rowe, Yale (China)
David Mandelbaum, UCLA (India)
Philip Moseley, Cornell (Soviet Union)
George Homans, Harvard

These persons (5. and 6.) are in addition to those already included in the <u>panels</u> above - and who might be consulted <u>individually</u>.

Figure 13.2   (contd.)

The Search for "Magic Keys"

In the first decade after the war, many social scientists and some government agencies believed that sociology, social psychology, and related fields were on the brink of decisive breakthroughs in engineering human affairs. The so-called hard sciences had employed the positivist scientific method to bring society radar, penicillin, and atomic energy. Now the social sciences would use the same methods to usher in a new era of reason, security, and social peace under the umbrella of the United States.

The rising U.S. intelligence community — the OSS at first, and later the CIA and the various military intelligence groups — placed itself at the forefront of this effort. Here is how Brigadier General John Magruder of the OSS put it in testimony at a U.S. Senate hearing in late 1945:

> In all of the intelligence that enters into waging war soundly and waging peace soundly, it is the social scientists who make a huge contribution. The government of the United States would be well advised to do all in its power to promote the development of knowledge in the field of the social sciences. . . . Were we to develop a dearth of social scientists, all national intelligence agencies servicing policy makers in peace or war would be directly handicapped. . . . research of social scientists [is] indispensable to the sound development of national intelligence in peace and war.[24]

Magruder introduced a chart into the Senate record to illustrate the OSS's perspective (see Figure 13.3). It is revealing on two counts.[25] First, in the OSS view, there was a seamless continuum between wartime and peacetime operations. While different tactics could be employed as situations changed, the intelligence community's fundamental perspective remained that U.S. interests would best be achieved by dominating rival powers, regardless of whether the United States was technically at peace or at war at any given time. Magruder saw relatively peaceful engineering of consent for U.S. aims as desirable, but the option of using violence remained essential. Second, as the chart illustrates, the OSS believed that virtually every aspect of postwar intelligence operations should make use of sociology or social psychology, or both.

This opened the era of what has been called the "search for magic keys" to communication.[26] Leo Lowenthal, who was formerly of the Frankfurt School and who during the Korean War became chief of research for the Voice of America, said in 1951 — only half jokingly — that the Voice was seeking "the ultimate miracle . . . the push button

USE OF SOCIAL SCIENCES IN OSS INTELLIGENCE

DESCRIPTIVE INTELLIGENCE : Detailed and Inclusive background information

BASIC SOCIAL SCIENCES

POLITICAL SCIENCE ◆

ECONOMICS ■

STATISTICS ◀

HISTORY ○

SOCIAL PSYCHOLOGY ◆

SOCIOLOGY ■

ANTHROPOLOGY ◀

GEOGRAPHY ●

STRATEGIC SURVEY

Governmental structure and authority
Political institutions
International relations

Social structure
Social institutions
Social ethics and customs
Biographical data
Population statistics
Health and sanitation

Nature of economy
Natural resources
Manufacturing and industry
Trade and commerce
Finance
Agriculture
National aspirations
Public morale

Terrain and climate
Utilities
Transportation

INTELLIGENCE FOR POLICY & OPERATIONS

e.g.

WAR

Character of invasion beaches
Strategic dependants of imports
Morale stamina of public

PEACE

Pressure groups
Trade and currency controls
Potential government leadership

Figure 13.3 Intelligence application of the social sciences, as viewed by the OSS, 1945

millennium in the use of opinion research in psychological warfare. On that distant day," he said, "the warrior would tell the research technician the elements of content, audience, medium and effect desired. The researcher would simply work out the mathematics and solve the algebraic formula," and the war would be won.[27]

Germany became a major testing ground for studies in social engineering, as the United States took as its mission the reeducation of Germans in the wake of the Nazi years. This helped open the door for reformist, liberal social scientists to undertake purportedly objective research studies that they might earlier have rejected as immoral or politically suspect.[28]

Figure 13.4 presents survey results from a widely disseminated U.S. textbook on communication of the period. It describes the impact of mass bombing on German civilian populations, with the bombs literally taken as a form of "communication" with their targets.[29] Note that the medium-strength bombing proved to be marginally more cost-effective, in many cases, in inducing the desire to surrender. That insight permitted more efficient targeting of U.S. atomic weapons, which at the time seemed to be in short supply, at least as the Air Force saw things.

How is it that liberal, social-democratic, and reform-minded social scientists become enmeshed in psychological warfare, counterinsurgency, and even preparations for nuclear war? One part of the answer lies in many scientists' ability to create self-contradictory conceptual structures that permit them to isolate themselves from the consequences of their acts. Here is one example. In late 1947, the U.S. National Security Council took two actions to provide the first bureaucratic-administrative structure for U.S. clandestine warfare during peacetime. These decisions illustrate the extent to which U.S. psychological warfare has had from its inception multiple, overlapping layers of cover stories, deceits, and euphemistic explanations. In this case, the NSC created two such layers simultaneously, each contradictory to the other.

First, the NSC approved a relatively innocuous policy document known as "NSC 4: Coordination of Foreign Information Measures."[30] It assigned the assistant secretary of state for public affairs responsibility to lead "the immediate strengthening and coordination of all foreign information measures of the U.S. government . . . to counteract effects of anti-U.S. propaganda." Importantly, NSC 4 was classified as "confidential," the lowest category of government secret. As a practical matter, this meant that word of this confidential action

TABLE 2

Percent Willing to Surrender

	Heavy bombing	Medium bombing	Light bombing	Un-bombed
Nazi party members	43	49	38	37
Nonmembers	60	57	50	53
Difference	17	8	12	16
Ideological Nazis	20	30	12	14
Non-Nazis	65	53	57	65
Difference	45	33	45	51

In the tables of this chapter the base of the percentages is the number of people falling in each cell. For example, in table 2, 43 percent of *Nazi Party members who were heavily bombed* said they were willing to surrender. Sixty percent of *nonmembers heavily bombed* were willing to surrender, etc.

TABLE 3

Percent Reporting War Weariness

	Heavy bombing	Medium bombing	Light bombing
Nazi party members	73	76	53
Nonmembers	73	73	63
Difference *	0	(3)-	10
Ideological Nazis	42	42	37
Non-Nazis	76	79	65
Difference	34	37	28

* Difference in parentheses is in direction opposite from expectation.

TABLE 13

Percent Willing to Surrender

	Heavy bombing	Medium bombing	Light bombing	Un-bombed
High status	55	59	38	33
Middle status	58	53	51	48
Low status	63	62	61	61

TABLE 14

Percent Willing to Surrender

	Heavy bombing	Medium bombing	Light bombing	Un-bombed
Catholic	66	63	73	57
Protestant	54	51	48	52

Figure 13.4 Bombing of civilians depicted as a form of communication, in Cold War era communication textbook

would likely be publicized in the news media as an NSC "secret decision" within days, perhaps within hours.

That is precisely what took place. In time, a series of public decisions grew up around NSC 4 involving policy directives and funding for the U.S. Information Agency, scholarly exchange programs, operation of America House cultural centers abroad, and similar overt information programs. Officially, the position of the U.S. government on such matters was that "truth is our weapon," as Edward Barrett — who was soon to be put in charge of the program — put it. This widely announced policy held that the U.S. openly presented its views on international controversies, and frankly discussed the flaws and advantages of U.S. society in a bid to win credibility for its point of view. This was not "propaganda" (in the negative sense of that word), Barrett insisted, it was "truth."[31]

In reality, only minutes after completing action on NSC 4, the NSC took up a second measure: NSC 4-A. This was classified "top secret," a considerably stricter security rating. This status bars the disclosure of even the existence of the decision to any person outside an authorized circle. In NSC 4-A, the NSC directed that "the foreign information activities of the U.S. Government," now supposedly led by the assistant secretary of state, "must be supplemented by covert psychological operations." The CIA was to organize and administer these officially nonexistent programs, in part under cover provided by the "confidential" program — that is, the public program — authorized under NSC 4.[32]

The NSC's action removed the U.S. Congress and public from any meaningful debate over whether or not to undertake clandestine psychological warfare abroad. More than that, the "deniability" of the psychological operations themselves ensured that the public would remain effectively excluded from decision making on this form of war for decades — a legacy that remains to this day.[33]

The scientists, operatives, and government administrators active in these programs created a euphemistic sublanguage of terms that permitted those who had been initiated into the arcana of national security to discuss psychological warfare and clandestine operations in varying degrees of specificity (depending upon the audience) while simultaneously denying the very existence of such programs when it was politically convenient to do so. In an added confusing twist, NSC 4 had established an officially confidential (but in reality public) program of bland "Foreign Information Measures" that sometimes also were referred to as "psychological measures" or "psychological warfare" in public discussions. Although officially confidential, these highly public activities became decoys to divert public and congressional attention away from more deadly affairs. These seemingly contradictory conceptual structures helped preserve the myth that the United States was dealing with the world in a straightforward manner consistent with its professed ideals, while the Soviets were waging a different sort of Cold War, one that relied upon deceit, "propaganda," and clandestine violence.

Building an Institutional Identity for Communication Research

For the first decade after 1945 — which is to say, the decade in which communication research crystallized into a distinct scholarly field, complete with colleges, graduate degrees, and so on — U.S. military, propaganda, and intelligence agencies provided the overwhelming majority of all project funding for the field. The earliest cumulative data concerning government funding of social science is provided by the National Science Foundation in 1952: it shows that more than 96 percent of all reported federal funding for social science at that time was drawn from the U.S. military. The remaining 4 percent of government funding was divided about equally between conventional civilian agencies (Department of Labor, Department of the Interior) and civilian agencies with clear national security missions (such as the Federal Civil Defense Administration). Social science funding rooted in national security missions totaled $12.27 million that year, the NSF reported, while comparable civilian funding totaled only $0.28 million.[34]

This extreme skew in favor of research to support military, intelligence, and propaganda missions was particularly pronounced in mass communication studies. A close review of *Public Opinion Quarterly* and other scholarly mass communication literature during the decade after 1945, for example, reveals several dozen medium- to large-scale communication research projects funded by the Office of Naval Research, the U.S. Air Force, CIA, and U.S. Information Agency. The only comparable "civilian" study appears to have been a 1950 Department of Agriculture survey of the effects of television on dressmakers — one of the earliest such studies of television effects — that apparently was never written up for scholarly mass communication journals.[35]

At least a half dozen of the most important centers of U.S. communication research were dependent for their survival on funding from a handful of national security agencies, although the limits of space here permit discussion of only three. Their reliance on psychological warfare money was so exclusive as to suggest clearly that the crystallization of mass communication research into a distinct scholarly field would not have come about during the 1950s without substantial military, CIA, and USIA intervention.

The Survey Research Center (SRC) at the University of Michigan (today known as the Institute for Social Research, or ISR), for example, was established by Rensis Likert in the summer of 1946 using a number of the personnel who had served under Likert during the war. The "SRC functioned during its first year as something of an outpost of the federal government," writes Jean Converse in *Survey Research in the United States*.[36] Major early contracts included a ten-year grant from the Office of Naval Research for studies of the psychological aspects of morale, leadership, and control of large organizations, and a series of contracts for surveys of Americans' attitudes on economics for the Federal Reserve Board, which in those years was deeply concerned about the potential for a renewed 1930s-style depression and social upheaval as veterans returned to the civilian work force. Early SRC/ISR research with strategic intelligence applications included U.S. Air Force-funded interview studies of Soviet defectors and refugees. The point of that enterprise was twofold: first, to identify social psychological attributes of the Soviet population that could be exploited in U.S. propaganda, and second, collection of intelligence on military and economic centers inside the USSR that would be targeted for atomic or conventional attacks in the event of war.[37]

SRC/ISR archival records show that federal contracts contributed fully 99 percent of the institution's revenues during its first full year in 1947, and well over 50 Percent of SRC/ISR revenues during its first five years of operation.[38]

At the National Opinion Research Center (NORC), perhaps the most liberal and reform-minded of the early centers of communication research, about 90 percent of the organization's work during the war years was made up of contracts from the Office of War Information, the U.S. government's principal monitor of civilian morale. This backing was "probably critical in making [NORC's] national capacity [for conducting surveys] viable," Converse writes. In 1944, Congress canceled the OWI project, but the NORC field studies of U.S. civilian morale and attitudes continued under secret "emergency" contracts with the Department of State. This arrangement became institutionalized and provided a survey vehicle onto which NORC later could market "piggyback" survey questions for commercial customers.[39]

A second noteworthy NORC contract during the center's first decade was a series of inquiries, for the U.S. Army Chemical Corps, into individual and group responses to community disasters. NORC used natural disasters such as earthquakes and tornados as analogues to model responses to an attack with chemical weapons. In time, NORC undertook a related series of disaster studies that became the U.S. government's main data base for evaluating the psychological effects of nuclear war.[40]

Funding for the Bureau of Applied Social Research (BASR) at Columbia University appears to have been more diversified. BASR records prior to 1950 are sketchy, but Converse concludes that approximately 50 percent of BASR's budget from 1941 through 1946 stemmed from commercial work such as readership studies for *Time* and *Life* magazines. But by 1949, the BASR was deeply in debt to Columbia University and lacked a cushion of operating funds with which to cover project expenses while waiting for clients to make payments. The cash-flow problem was so severe that Paul Lazarsfeld speculated in fund-raising appeals that BASR would be forced to close if help were not forthcoming.

By the end of that year, however, BASR's Kingley Davis won new military and intelligence contracts that substantially improved BASR's financial situation. By fiscal year 1950–51, BASR's annual budget had reached a new high, 75 percent of which consisted of contracts with U.S. military and propaganda agencies.[41] Major federally funded BASR projects of the period included two Air Force studies for intelligence gathering on urban social dynamics abroad, a large project for the Office of Naval Research, and a multiyear contract for the Voice of America for public opinion surveys in the Middle East.[42]

The Voice of America project began in September 1950. Extensive, methodologically ambitious surveys were conducted in Iran, Turkey, Egypt, and four other countries, each of which was a major target of U.S. psychological warfare efforts of the period. (Two of the countries, Iran and Egypt, underwent CIA-supported coups d'état while the study was under way.) Lazarsfeld helped compose the survey questions, which eventually were asked by native-language researchers in the field.[43] BASR designed the survey to elicit specific guidance for U.S. propaganda and intelligence operations in the region.

Still another important BASR contract focused on engineering public opinion in the Philippines, and particularly on measuring the effectiveness of psychological warfare and counterinsurgency operations against the Huk guerrillas. These programs helped generate several basic building blocks of today's communiction theory, including understanding of the key role of opinion leaders in shaping mass public sentiment and the well-known "personal influence" and "two-step" models of communications behavior.[44] The Philippines project simultaneously became the proving ground for techniques designed to monitor the impact on Filipino public opinion of U.S.-backed search-and-destroy counterinsurgency squads, counterguerrilla "hunter-killer teams," the "pacification" of peasant villages, and other tactics that later became well known in Vietnam, El Salvador, and similar conflicts.[45]

The public opinion studies and the hunter-killer teams developed as interlocking characteristics of a single theory for managing insurgencies in U.S. client states such as the Philippines. MIT's Center for International Studies played a particularly important role in the elaboration of these tactics during the second half of the 1950s. CENIS was funded largely by the CIA and the Air Force, often using the Ford Foundation as a cover.

CENIS might be called the second generation of postwar U.S. communications research. By the mid-1950s, both academics and policymakers gradually realized that the earlier search for "magic keys" and the "push-button millennium" in social engineering had largely failed. Audiences proved to be far more resilient and resistant than theorists first had thought.

CENIS articulated a new group of tactics for managing international conflicts, and these became quite popular with government funders. CENIS scholars such as Ithiel de Sola Pool, Daniel Lerner, and Max Millikan (who had been the CIA's assistant director for intelligence prior to becoming CENIS director) argued that propaganda could be more effectively blended with controlled economic development, arms transfers, police and military training, and counterinsurgency support for U.S.-backed regimes. These multifaceted tactics had developed more or less informally during U.S. interventions in Greece and the Philippines. Part of CENIS's job for the government was to articulate fully and systematize those insights into packages that included background data on various contested countries, plus tactics and systems for counterinsurgency that supposedly could be applied virtually anywhere in the world.[46] Among sociologists, these tactics took the name "development theory"; among military planners the same approach came to be called "limited

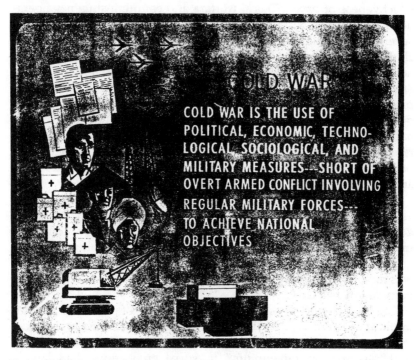

Figure 13.5 Sociology integrated into counterinsurgency: illustration from a 1962 U.S. Army symposium on "limited war"

warfare."[47] Figure 13.5 is a reproduction of a slide from a social science seminar organized for the U.S. Army in the spring of 1962, as counterinsurgency warfare in Asia was beginning to reach full velocity. Note the integrated tactics — and the B-52s.[48]

The CIA spent tens of millions of dollars on communication research projects throughout the 1950s. It typically passed money through a front organization such as the Human Ecology Fund, the RAND Corporation, or one of several foundations.[49] This sponsorship, and the ostensibly civilian cover it enjoyed, encouraged what many people would consider to be criminal enterprises to enter the intellectual mainstream in the United States. At the Bureau of Social Science Research (BSSR) at American University in Washington, D.C., for example, researchers under contract to the CIA systematically documented the use of drugs, electroshock, and other forms of torture in interrogation of prisoners. A related project traced the steps leading to the psychological collapse of prisoners of war. In time,

BSSR social scientists wrote up such projects for mainstream journals such as *Sociometry*, where they were received with some critical acclaim.[50] Another major CIA-funded communication research project provided a $1 million research grant to Hadley Cantril, a major figure in U.S. public opinion studies and a founder of the transactional analysis school of psychology.[51]

U.S. military projects also became central to the evolution of the discipline of communication research, including its *Zeitgeist* or overall perspective on communication itself. One example of U.S. Air Force programs will illustrate this. During the 1950s, the Air Force paid about a third of a million dollars to Stuart Dodd of the University of Washington to study the effects of propaganda leaflets dropped from airplanes. This became known as Project Revere, and it was one of the largest series of communication studies of its day. It since has been recognized as the foundation of what is known as diffusion research, the study of how messages move through a population.[52]

The project was both a study of propaganda and a propaganda project in its own right. Dodd's experiment consisted of dropping millions of leaflets (such as that shown in Figure 13.6) on rural communities and small towns in Washington State, Alabama, and the far West. Using survey research, his team then tracked the dispersal of this message — *Communist bombers might attack your neighborhood* — through the population.[53] In fact, many of the communities targeted by Dodd's study were inaccessible to American commercial airliners, much less Soviet bombers. Among the more interesting results: children, in particular, were inclined to pick up pretty, fluttery papers dropped from airplanes. One may wonder how much Dodd or the Air Force remembered of these results when the Air Force went about designing the pretty, fluttery, air-dropped antipersonnel mines that took such a devastating toll on Vietnamese children a few years later.

The Dodd project simultaneously became a major source of overt and tacit promotion for psychological warfare within the academic community. Figure 13.7 presents Dodd's own list of what he termed "Revere-connected papers" published in the scholarly literature as of 1958.[54] The list includes substantial representation of Revere papers in virtually every major U.S. sociological publication of the day.

Note particularly the titles. There is something interesting happening in the rhetoric of the field of communication research. The presentation of this work has taken on a strong aroma of "science," "objectivity," and "professionalism." The values and many of the political preconceptions of the psychological warfare projects are

Figure 13.6 U.S. Air Force-sponsored communication research as propaganda.
University of Washington scientists dropped millions of leaflets like this
one on towns in the northwestern United States at the height of the
"bomber gap" crisis.

THIS COULD HAVE BEEN A BOMB!
INVASION BY AIR IS POSSIBLE!

▼ EARLY DETECTION OF APPROACHING AIRCRAFT IS OUR ONLY DEFENSE.

▼ NOT ALL APPROACHES TO OUR COUNTRY ARE GUARDED BY RADAR.

▼ THESE GAPS CAN BE COVERED ONLY BY YOU AS A MEMBER OF THE AIRCRAFT WARNING SERVICE.

▼ THE A.W.S. FILTER CENTERS NEED PLOTTERS, TELLERS, AND RECORDERS.

Contact your filter center Today and learn how you can help in this program....learn how you can win your wings with the Aircraft Warning Service.

BOISE FILTER CENTER
6ᵗʰ Avenue & Main St.
PHONE 1116

Figure 13.7 Stuart Dodd's list of "Revere-connected" papers (1958)

1. Bowerman, Charles, with Stuart C. Dodd and Otto N. Larsen, "Testing Message Diffusion—Verbal vs. Graphic Symbols," *International Social Science Bulletin,* UNESCO, Vol. 5, September 1953.
2. Catton, William R., Jr., "Exploring Techniques for Measuring Human Values," *American Sociological Review,* Vol. 19, 1954, pp. 49-55.
3. ———, and Melvin L. DeFleur, "The Limits of Determinacy in Attitude Measurement," *Social Forces,* Vol. 35, 1957, pp. 295-300.
4. ———, and Stuart C. Dodd, "Symbolizing the Values of Others," in *Symbols and Values: An Initial Study,* Thirteenth Symposium of the Conference on Science, Philosophy, and Religion, New York, Harper, 1954, Chap. 34, pp. 485-496.
5. ———, and Richard J. Hill, "Predicting the Relative Effectiveness of Leaflets: A Study in Selective Perception with Some Implications for Sampling," *Research Studies of the State College of Washington,* Proceedings of the Pacific Coast Sociological Society, 1953, Vol. 21, pp. 247-251.
6. DeFleur, Melvin L., and Ørjar Øyen, "The Spatial Diffusion of an Airborne Leaflet Message," *American Journal of Sociology,* Vol. 59, 1953, pp. 144-149.
7. Dodd, Stuart C., "The Interactance Hypothesis—A Gravity Model Fitting Physical Masses and Human Groups," *American Sociological Review,* Vol. 15, 1950, pp. 245-256.
8. ———, "Sociomatrices and Levels of Interaction—for Dealing with Plurels, Groups, and Organizations," *Sociometry,* Vol. 14, 1951, pp. 237-248.
9. ———, "On Classifying Human Values—a Step in the Prediction of Human Valuing," *American Sociological Review,* Vol. 16, 1951, pp. 645-653.
10. ———, "On All-or-None Elements and Mathematical Models for Sociologists," *American Sociological Review,* Vol. 17, 1952, pp. 167-177.
11. ——— and staff, "Testing Message Diffusing in C-Ville," *Research Studies of the State College of Washington,* Proceedings of the Pacific Coast Sociological Society, 1952, Vol. 20, 1952, pp. 83-91.
12. ———, "Testing Message Diffusion from Person to Person," *Public Opinion Quarterly,* Vol. 16, 1952, pp. 247-262.
13. ———, "Controlled Experiments on Interacting—Testing the Interactance Hypothesis Factor by Factor," read at the Sociological Research Association Conference, Atlantic City, N. J., September 1952.
14. ———, "Human Dimensions—a Re-search for Concepts to Integrate Thinking," *Main Currents in Modern Thought,* Vol. 9, 1953, pp. 106-113.
15. ———, "Testing Message Diffusion in Controlled Experiments: Charting the Distance and Time Factors in the Interactance Hypothesis," *American Sociological Review,* Vol. 18, 1953, pp. 410-416.
16. ———, "Can the Social Scientist Serve Two Masters—An Answer through Experimental Sociology," *Research Studies of the State College of Washington,* Proceedings of the Pacific Sociological Society, Vol. 21, 1953, pp. 195-213.
17. ———, "Formulas for Spreading Opinion—a Report of Controlled Experiments on Leaflet Messages in Project Revere," read at A.A.P.O.R. meetings, Madison, Wis., Apr. 14, 1955.
18. ———, "Diffusion Is Predictable: Testing Probability Models for Laws of Interaction," *American Sociological Review,* Vol. 20, 1955, pp. 392-401.

Figure 13.7   (Contd.)

19. ——, "Testing Message Diffusion by Chain Tags," *American Journal of Sociology,* Vol. 61, 1956, pp. 425-432.
20. ——, "Testing Message Diffusion in Harmonic Logistic Curves," *Psychometrika,* Vol. 21, 1956, pp. 192-205.
21. ——, "A Predictive Theory of Public Opinion—Using Nine 'Mode' and 'Tense' Factors," *Public Opinion Quarterly,* Vol. 20, 1956, pp. 571-585.
22. ——, "Conditions for Motivating Men—the Valuance Theory for Motivating Behaviors in Any Culture," *Journal of Personality,* Vol. 25, 1957, pp. 489-504.
23. ——, "The Counteractance Model," *American Journal of Sociology,* Vol. 63, 1957, pp. 273-284.
24. ——, "A Power of Town Size Predicts Its Internal Interacting—a Controlled Experiment Relating the Amount of an Interaction to the Number of Potential Interactors," *Social Forces,* Vol. 36, 1957, pp. 132-137.
25. ——, with Edith D. Rainboth and Jiri Nehnevajsa, "Revere Studies on Interaction" (Volume ready for press).
26. Hill, Richard J., "A Note on Inconsistency in Paired Comparison Judgments," *American Sociological Review,* Vol. 18, 1953, pp. 564-566.
27. ——, "An Experimental Investigation of the Logistic Model of Message Diffusion," read at AAAS meeting, San Francisco, Calif., Dec. 27, 1954.
28. ——, with Stuart C. Dodd and Susan Huffaker, "Testing Message Diffusion—the Logistic Growth Curve in a School Population," read at the Biometrics Conference, Eugene, Ore., June 1952.
29. Larsen, Otto N., "The Comparative Validity of Telephone and Face-to-Face Interviews in the Measurement of Message Diffusion from Leaflets," *American Sociological Review,* Vol. 17, 1952, pp. 471-476.
30. ——, "Rumors in a Disaster," accepted for publication in *Journal of Communication.*
31. ——, and Melvin L. DeFleur, "The Comparative Role of Children and Adults in Propaganda Diffusion," *American Sociological Review,* Vol. 19, 1954, pp. 593-602.
32. ——, and Richard J. Hill, "Mass Media and Interpersonal Communication," *American Sociological Review,* Vol. 19, 1954, pp. 426-434.
33. Nehnevajsa, Jiri, and Stuart C. Dodd, "Physical Dimensions of Social Distance," *Sociology and Social Research,* Vol. 38, 1954, pp. 287-292.
34. Pence, Orville, and Dominic LaRusso, "A Study of Testimony: Content Distortion in Oral Person-to-Person Communication," submitted for publication.
35. Rainboth, Edith Dyer, and Melvin L. DeFleur, "Testing Message Diffusion in Four Communities: Some Factors in the Use of Airborne Leaflets as a Communication Medium," *American Sociological Review,* Vol. 17, 1952, pp. 734-737.
36. Rapoport, Anatol, "Nets with Distance Bias," *Bulletin of Mathematical Biophysics,* Vol. 13, 1951, pp. 85-91.
37. ——, "Connectivity of Random Nets," *Bulletin of Mathematical Biophysics,* Vol. 13, 1951, pp. 107-117.
38. ——, "The Probability Distribution of Distinct Hits on Closely Packed Targets," *Bulletin of Mathematical Biophysics,* Vol. 13, 1951, pp. 133-138.
39. ——, "'Ignition' Phenomena in Random Nets," *Bulletin of Mathematical Biophysics,* Vol. 14, 1952, pp. 35-44.

Figure 13.7 (Contd.)

40. ———, "Contribution to the Mathematical Theory of Mass Behavior: I. The Propagation of Single Acts," *Bulletin of Mathematical Biophysics,* Vol. 14, 1952, pp. 159-169.

41. ———, "Response Time and Threshold of a Random Net," *Bulletin of Mathematical Biophysics,* Vol. 14, 1952, pp. 351-363.

42. ———, and Lionel I. Rebhun, "On the Mathematical Theory of Rumor Spread," *Bulletin of Mathematical Biophysics,* Vol. 14, 1952, pp. 375-383.

43. ———, "Contribution to the Mathematical Theory of Contagion and Spread of Information: I. Spread through a Thoroughly Mixed Population," *Bulletin of Mathematical Biophysics,* Vol. 15, 1953, pp. 173-183.

44. ———, "Spread of Information through a Population with Socio-structural Bias: I. Assumption of Transitivity," *Bulletin of Mathematical Biophysics,* Vol. 15, 1953, pp. 523-533.

45. ———, "Spread of Information through a Population with Socio-structural Bias: II. Various Models with Partial Transitivity," *Bulletin of Mathematical Biophysics,* Vol. 15, 1953, pp. 535-546.

46. ———, "Spread of Information through a Population with Socio-structural Bias: III. Suggested Experimental Procedures," *Bulletin of Mathematical Biophysics,* Vol. 16, 1954, pp. 75-81.

47. Shaw, John G., "Testing Message Diffusion in Relation to Demographic Variables: an Analysis of Respondents to an Airborne Leaflet Message," submitted for publication.

48. Turabian, Chahin, and Stuart C. Dodd, "A Dimensional System of Human Values," *Transactions Second World Congress of Sociology,* International Sociology Association, 1954, pp. 100-105.

49. Winthrop, Henry, and Stuart C. Dodd, "A Dimensional Theory of Social Diffusion —an Analysis, Modeling and Partial Testing of One-way Interacting," *Sociometry,* Vol. 16, 1953, pp. 180-202.

Theses

50. M.A. Catton, William R., Jr., "The Sociological Study of Human Values," 1952.

51. M.A. Øyen, Ørjar, "The Relationship between Distances and Social Interaction— the Case of Message Diffusion," 1953.

52. Ph.D. Catton, William R., Jr., "Propaganda Effectiveness as a Function of Human Values," 1954.

53. Ph.D. DeFleur, Melvin Lawrence, "Experimental Studies of Stimulus Response Relationships in Leaflet Communication," 1954.

54. Ph.D. Hill, Richard J., "Temporal Aspects of Message Diffusion," 1955.

55. Ph.D. Larsen, Otto N., "Interpersonal Relations in the Social Diffusion of Messages," 1955.

56. Ph.D. Shaw, John G., Jr., "The Relationship of Selected Ecological Variables to Leaflet Message Response," 1954.

57. M.A. West, S. S., "Variation of Compliance to Airborne Leaflet Messages with Age and with Terminal Level of Education," 1956.

Monographs Published

58. DeFleur, Melvin L., and Otto N. Larsen, *The Flow of Information,* New York, Harper, 1958.

being absorbed into new, "scientificized" presentations of communication theory that tended to conceal the prejudices of the early 1950s programs under a new coat of "objective" rhetoric. Basic terms in the field began to change. Terms such as *propaganda* and *psychological warfare* fell out of favor; they became instead *international communications*, *development*, and *public diplomacy*. This was a refinement of the contradictory conceptual structures concerning communication discussed earlier.

This professionalization of the discipline brought with it a new rhetoric that downplayed the relatively blatant role of psychological warfare in mainstream mass communication research that had characterized the first decade after 1945. Scientists increasingly adopted a vocabulary that was self-consciously neutral, but that maintained (and in fact developed) the core conceptions of what communication "is" and what to do with it. This process of changing the labels while preserving the core paradigm can clearly be seen in the projects that were unfortunate enough to be caught on the cusp of the change.

At the Bureau of Social Science Research, for example, Chitra M. Smith prepared an extensive annotated bibliography in late 1952 titled *International Propaganda and Psychological Warfare*.[55] This was clearly an old-style presentation. It is useful from a historical point of view, because as an annotated bibliography, Smith's work provides a good indication of the scope of the concept of psychological warfare in 1952.

By 1956, however, the rhetorical tide had begun to turn. That year, the RAND Corporation published virtually the same bibliography with only two substantive changes: the title became *International Communication and Political Opinion* and two authors were credited — Bruce Lannes Smith and Chitra M. Smith.[56] The earlier acknowledgment of psychological warfare as the unifying theme of the collection — in fact, as its raison d'être — completely disappeared, *without* any change to the actual content of the work. This is one example of a broader process by which the "psychological warfare" of one generation became the "international communication" of the next.

A similar incident took place at Harvard's Russian Research Center. In 1954, Clyde Kluckhohn, Alex Inkeles, and Raymond Bauer prepared a psychological warfare study for the U.S. Air Force titled *Strategic Psychological and Sociological Strengths and Vulnerabilities of the Soviet Social System*.[57] Much of this work concerned the USSR's national communication system, which was Inkeles's specialty. In 1956, the authors deleted about a dozen pages of recommendations concerning psychological operations during nuclear war and published the remaining 400-page text under the title *How the Soviet System Works*. That book, in turn, became a standard graduate reader in U.S. studies of the USSR throughout the 1960s. The Kluckhohn, Inkeles, and Bauer text thus moved from its original incarnation as a relatively naive how-to manual for the exploitation of a rival system to make a much more sweeping — yet paradoxically more seemingly objective and scientific — claim concerning how Soviet reality "works."[58]

Conclusion

In conclusion, then, the following pattern becomes apparent. First, a prototypical paradigm of communication-as-domination and the research techniques for applying it emerged from the war, class conflict, and the early organization of mass markets via newspapers and radio during the first decades of this century. Lasswell's and Lazarsfeld's insights and methodologies, for example, permitted forms of audience measurement without which the structure of modern radio and television probably could not exist. In this way, early communication research often became one instrument in a broader campaign of suppression of discourse other than the messages and values promulgated by monopoly enterprises and central governments.

Second, World War II encouraged the construction of a network of scientists and state sponsors for psychological warfare. That is what the Clausen study showed.

Third, this network played a pivotal role in creating a new branch of social science, euphemistically termed "communication research," which in turn further developed and institutionalized a highly influential framework for how "communication" itself was to be regarded. That work helped enforce the preconceptions and worldview of mainstream U.S. social science and, in an indirect and more complex manner, of U.S. society as a whole. As James Carey has put it, "We first produce the world by symbolic work, and then take up residence in the world we have produced. Alas," he continues, "there is magic in our self deceptions."[59] By the 1970s, the institutions created during the evolution of communication research — graduate schools, social science think tanks, professional societies, and the like — had won considerable public and commercial sector funding and emerged as the main centers for advanced training in the United States of men and women who might well be called professional ideological workers.

Finally, this essay has discussed briefly the conceptual structures used for thinking about communication and social order, and
euphemism's important role in providing cover for scientific enterprises that many people might otherwise regard as criminal. Such
euphemisms seem to be essential in maintaining the otherwise obvious split between society's professed values — the reasons it claims
for doing things — and its actual behavior.

Notes

1. William Colby, with James McCargar, *Lost Victory* (Chicago: Contemporary
Books, 1989), 281, 331–33. Colby's figures, it should be noted, cover the period 1968–
71 only, although the program continued in various forms until at least 1975. Colby's
version seeks to distance the CIA from responsibility for murders, and stresses the
political and sociological aspects of Phoenix. For a detailed discussion from a more
critical point of view of the evolution and tactics of Phoenix, see Douglas Valentine,
The Phoenix Program (New York: William Morrow, 1990).

2. Colby, *Lost Victory*, 253.

3. Ibid., 259.

4. Massachusetts Institute of Technology, Center for International Studies,
"The Center for International Studies: A Description," MIT, Cambridge, July 1955.
See also U.S. Department of State, Foreign Service Institute, "Problems of Devel-
opment and Internal Defense," Country Team Seminar, June 11, 1962.

5. In order to maintain a tight focus, this essay exclusively tracks the role of
U.S. government psychological warfare, propaganda, and intelligence programs in
U.S. mass communication research. It is not intended to be a complete history of
the field or of the forces that shaped it. Commercial research and strictly academic
developments have also been important, of course. The latter is a comfortable topic
that continues to be discussed exhaustively in mainstream mass communication historiography, often without serious consideration of the social and economic context
in which the academic work was performed. The former often has been ignored
(with a few noteworthy exceptions), as has the government's psychological warfare
effort.

Some of the best overviews of the professionalization of communication research during the first half of the 1950s, the emergence of doctorate-granting institutions, and so on include Jean M. Converse, *Survey Research in the United States*
(Berkeley: University of California Press, 1987); Daniel Czitrom, *Media and the American Mind* (Chapel Hill: University of North Carolina Press, 1982); Jesse Delia, "Communication Research: A History," in *Handbook of Communication Science*, ed. Charles
Berger and Steven Chaffee (Newbury Park, Calif.: Sage, 1987), 20–98.

On ideological workers: today a substantial majority of employers of entry-
level television and radio reporters, newspaper and magazine editors and writers,
many types of advertising specialists, and public relations personnel (or, to use the
currently preferred term, "public communication" experts) require new hires to
arrive with advanced degrees in one of several varieties of mass communication

study. See W. W. Schwed, "Hiring, Promotion, Salary, Longevity Trends Charted at Dailies," *Newspaper Research Journal* (October 1981); Lee Becker, J. W. Fruit, and S. L. Caudill, *The Training and Hiring of Journalists* (Norwood, N.J.: Ablex, 1987); Lee Becker and Thomas Engleman, "Class of '87 Describes Salaries, Satisfaction Found in Jobs," *Journalism Educator*, Spring 1989.

6. Albert Biderman and Elizabeth Crawford, *The Political Economy of Social Research: The Case of Sociology* (Springfield, Va.: Clearinghouse for Federal Scientific and Technological Information, 1968).

7. On BASR, see Converse, *Survey Research*, 269, 275–76, 506–7, fn. 37, fn. 42. On Cantril's IISR, see John Crewdson and Joseph Treaster, "The CIA's 3-Decade Effort to Mold the World's Views," *New York Times*, December 25, 26, 27, 1977, with discussion of Cantril and the IISR on December 26. For Cantril's version, which conceals the true source of his funds, see Hadley Cantril, *The Human Dimension: Experiences in Policy Research* (New Brunswick, N.J.: Rutgers University Press, 1967). On CENIS, see Christopher Simpson, *Psychological Warfare and Communication Research: Science, Power, and Sociology in the Cold War* (New York: Oxford University Press, forthcoming); Ithiel de Sola Pool, "The Necessity for Social Scientists Doing Research for Governments," *Background*, August 1966. Other major communication research projects that depended heavily on funding from U.S. government psychological warfare agencies included the National Opinion Research Center, the Survey Research Center (now the Institute for Social Research), and the Bureau of Social Science Research, among others. The text that follows discusses these in more detail.

8. For details on the Department of State contracts, which produced a scandal when they were uncovered in 1957, see U.S. Congress, House, Committee on Government Operations, *State Department Opinion Polls*, 85th Cong., 1st Sess., June–July 1957 (Washington, D.C.: U.S. Government Printing Office, 1957).

9. Albert Biderman, "Social-Psychological Needs and 'Involuntary' Behavior as Illustrated by Compliance in Interrogation," *Sociometry* (June 1960); Louis Gottschalk, *The Use of Drugs in Information-Seeking Interviews*, Bureau of Social Science Research Report No. 322 (December 1958), BSSR Archives, series II, box 11, University of Maryland Libraries Special Collections, College Park, Md.; Albert Biderman, Barbara Heller, and Paula Epstein, *A Selected Bibliography on Captivity Behavior*, Bureau of Social Science Research Report No. 339-1 (February 1961), BSSR Archives, Series II, box 14, University of Maryland Libraries Special Collection, College Park, Md. Biderman acknowledges the Human Ecology Fund—a well-known CIA conduit—and U.S. Air Force Contract No. AF 49 (638)727 as the source of his funding for this work. For more on the CIA's use of the Human Ecology Fund and the related Society for the Investigation of Human Ecology, see John Marks, *The Search for the Manchurian Candidate* (New York: Times Books, 1979), 147–63.

10. Walter Lippmann, *Public Opinion* (New York: Harcourt Brace, 1922); Harold Lasswell, *Propaganda Technique in the World War* (Cambridge: MIT Press, 1971 [1926]).

11. Lippmann, *Public Opinion*, 31, 32. John Dewey wrote that Lippmann's writing style was so accomplished that "one finishes the book almost without realizing that it is perhaps the most effective indictment of democracy as currently conceived ever penned"; *New Republic*, May 3, 1922. W. S. Myers commented that Lippmann "is essentially a propagandist, and his work is influenced by this characteristic attitude of approach toward any subject"; *Bookmark*, June 1922. Lippmann was a

publicist for U.S. expeditionary forces during World War I, and later executive secretary of the Inquiry, an early U.S. intelligence agency set up to support U.S. negotiators at the Versailles peace talks.

12. Lasswell advocated what he viewed as a scientific application of persuasion and precise violence, in contrast to bludgeon tactics, to achieve more effective social control. "Successful social and political management often depends on proper coordination of propaganda with coercion, violent or non-violent; economic inducement (including bribery); diplomatic negotiation; and other techniques," he wrote. Harold Lasswell, Ralph Casey, and Bruce Lannes Smith, *Propaganda and Promotional Activities: An Annotated Bibliography*, (Chicago: University of Chicago Press, 1969 [1935]), 43. See also Harold Lasswell, "Propaganda," in *Encyclopedia of the Social Sciences*, vol. 11 (New York: Macmillan, 1937), 524–25. Although Lasswell's importance as a theoretician of social control has long been recognized, it has been brought to renewed public attention in the United States in recent years largely through Noam Chomsky's media studies. See Noam Chomsky, *Intellectuals and the State* (Netherlands: Johan Huizinga-lezing, 1977), 9ff.; Noam Chomsky, "Democracy and the Media," in *Necessary Illusions: Thought Control in Democratic Societies* (Boston: South End, 1989).

13. To carry this point further, the elaboration of the Lippmann-Lasswell model of what communication "is" permitted communication research to become in part a method for the *suppression* of indigenous, rival approaches to communication.

As noted in the text, the evolution of pervasive consumer capitalism is interlocked with development of techniques to measure the extent and responses of mass audiences to various forms of communication. The sales of products and services in a mass society, in turn, depend to an important degree on the advertiser's success in substituting its values and preconceptions for those previously held by its audience. Automobile marketers, for example, do not tout their products simply for their usefulness as transportation; they seek to define their customers' self-esteem in terms of owning or using the product to the greatest degree possible. Thus, people do not simply purchase commodities, they become them—both literally and figuratively—and that transformation can take place only at the expense of rival systems of human society and consciousness.

My thinking on this point was spurred by Oskar Negt's discussion of Horkheimer and Adorno in "Mass Media: Tools of Domination or Instruments of Liberation? Aspects of the Frankfurt School's Communications Analysis," *New German Critique* (Spring 1978): 61ff.

14. Arthur Smith, Jr., "Life in Wartime Germany: Colonel Ohlendorf's Opinion Service," *Public Opinion Quarterly* (Spring 1972): 72; Lawrence Stokes, "The Sicherheitsdienst (SD) of the Reichsfuhrer SS and German Public Opinion," doctoral dissertation, Johns Hopkins University, 1972.

15. Ibid.; Carsten Klingemann, "Angewandte Soziologie im Nationalsozialismus," *1999, Zeitschrift für Sozialgeschichte des 20 und 21 Jahrhunderts* (January 1989), 25; Christoph Cobet (Hrsg.) *Einfuhrung in Fragen an die Soziologie in Deutschland nach Hitler 1945–1950* (Frankfurt am Main: Verlag Christoph Cobet, 1988). For an examination of interlocking problems concerning German geographical studies of the same period, which overlapped in certain respects with communication studies, see Mechtild Roessler, *Wissenschaft und Lebensraum: Geographische Ostforschung im Nationalsozialismus* (Berlin: Dietrich Reimer Verlag, 1990).

16. Chris Raymond, "Professor Is Accused of Promulgating Anti-Semitic Views

as Journalist in Germany and U.S. in World War II," *Chronicle of Higher Education*, December 11, 1991.

17. Ladislas Farago, *German Psychological Warfare* (New York: Putnam, 1941). For history of the origin of the term, see William Daugherty, "Changing Concepts," in *Psychological Warfare Casebook*, ed. William Daugherty and Morris Janowitz (Baltimore: Operations Research Office, Johns Hopkins University Press, 1958), 12.

18. Alfred Paddock, *US Army Special Warfare: Its Origins* (Washington, D.C.: National Defense University Press, 1982), 5–8, 23–37.

19. John Clausen, "Research on the American Soldier as a Career Contingency," *Social Psychology Quarterly* 47 (1987), 207ff.; Simpson, *Psychological Warfare and Communication Research*.

20. On Roper and Wilson, see Converse, *Survey Research*, 171–72. On Doob and Lietes, see Daniel Lerner, *Propaganda in War and Crisis* (New York: George Stewart, 1951), vii–viii. On Kluckhohn, Leighton, Lowenthal, and Schramm, see William Daugherty and Morris Janowitz, eds., *Psychological Warfare Casebook* (Baltimore: Operations Research Office, Johns Hopkins University Press, 1958), xiii–xiv. On Speier, see Christine Nasso, ed., *Contemporary Authors* (1st rev.), vol. 21–24 (Detroit: Gale Research, 1969), 829. On Barrett, see Edward Barrett, *Truth Is Our Weapon* (New York: Funk & Wagnalls, 1953), 31–32. After Barrett's death, the Associated Press identified him as a former member of the OSS; see "Edward Barrett Dies; Started Columbia Journalism Review," *Washington Post*, October 26, 1989. On contracts with Lazarsfeld, Stanton, et al., see Converse, *Survey Research*, 163, 172, 309.

21. On Leites and Eulau, see Wilbur Schramm, "Beginnings of Communications Study," in *The Media Revolution in America and Western Europe*, ed. Everett Rogers and Francis Balle (Norwood, N.J.: Ablex, 1985), 205; Harold Lasswell and Nathan Lietes, *The Language of Politics* (New York: George Stewart, 1949), 298. On Ithiel de Sola Pool, see Lasswell and Lietes also, pp. 153, 334ff.

22. Clausen, "Research on the American Soldier."

23. Mallory Brown, "Evaluation of the National Psychological Effort of [the] U.S." with attachment "Proposed Consultant Panels," April 8, 1952, in records of the Psychological Strategy Board, File PSB 091.412, No. 2, Harry S Truman Presidential Library, Independence, Mo.

24. U.S. Congress, Senate, Committee on Military Affairs, *Hearings on Science Legislation (5.1297)*, 79th Cong., 1st Sess., October–November 1945, part 4, 899–902.

25. Ibid., chart follows 900.

26. Shearon Lowery and Melvin De Fleur, *Milestones in Mass Communication Research* (New York: Longman, 1983).

27. American Association for Public Opinion Research Conference Proceedings, "Contributions of Opinion Research to Psychological Warfare," *Public Opinion Quarterly* (Winter 1951–52): 802.

28. Biderman and Crawford, *The Political Economy of Social Research*, 40–44.

29. Lerner, *Propaganda in War*, 355–66. The data in Lerner are drawn from U.S. Strategic Bombing Survey, Morale Division, *The Effects of Strategic Bombing on German Morale*, vol. 1, 33–37.

30. U.S. National Security Council, *NSC 4: Coordination of Foreign Information Measures*, December 9, 1947, RG 273, U.S. National Archives, Washington, D.C.

31. Barrett, *Truth Is Our Weapon*.

32. U.S. National Security Council, *NSC 4-A: Psychological Operations*, December 9, 1947, RG 273, U.S. National Archives, Washington, D.C.

33. U.S. National Security Council, *NSC 10/2: Office of Special Projects*, June 15, 1948, RG 273, U.S. National Archives, Washington, D.C. For a good overview of modern U.S. clandestine warfare, see John Prados, *The Presidents' Secret Wars* (New York: Morrow, 1986).

34. National Science Foundation, *Federal Funds for Science* (Washington, D.C.: U.S. Government Printing Office, 1953), 39–40. The major private foundations cooperated closely with federal psychological warfare programs and became closely intertwined with them, despite frequent claims to the contrary. "Perhaps most intriguing" in this regard, Clausen writes in the same study cited earlier, "was the number of our members who became foundation executives. Charles Dollard became president of Carnegie. Donald Young shifted from the Presidency of SSRC [Social Science Research Council] to that of Russell Sage [a major funder and publisher of U.S. sociological studies], where he ultimately recruited Leonard Cottrell. Leland DeVinney went from Harvard to the Rockefeller Foundation. William McPeak . . . helped set up the Ford Foundation and became its vice president." Clausen also offers a list of further examples.

Some foundations provided cover for intelligence agency funds passed to scholars, and often provided seed money for psychological warfare and mass persuasion research projects considered too hot to handle by public propaganda agencies such as the Voice of America. Carl Hovland's now-classic studies at Yale, for example, tested the effects of various types of propaganda appeals on audiences, including use of threats, fear, atrocity stories, and neutral education. Hovland's work technically was funded by Carnegie, but remained closely coordinated with, and dependent upon, Department of Defense projects throughout its existence. Hovland's work remains widely recognized as the scientific foundation of much of modern advertising. See Carl Hovland, Arthur Lumsdaine, and Fred Sheffield, *Experiments on Mass Communication*, vol. 3 of the *American Soldier* series (Princeton, N.J.: Princeton University Press, 1949); Carl Hovland, Irving Janis, and H. H. Kelley, *Communication and Persuasion* (New Haven, Conn.: Yale University Press, 1953). For an overview of the Hovland work and its impact, see Werner Severin and James Tankard, *Communication Theories*, 2d ed. (New York: Longman, 1988), 159–77; for Hovland's role in psychological warfare research and operations, see Simpson, *Psychological Warfare and Communication Research*.

35. Harry Alpert, "Opinion and Attitude Surveys in the US Government," *Public Opinion Quarterly* (Spring 1952). Alpert states in the introduction of this article that virtually all military-, intelligence-, and foreign propaganda-related studies have been excluded from the scope of his article.

36. Converse, *Survey Research*, 340–41, 353, 357.

37. Clyde Kluckhohn, Alex Inkeles, and Raymond Bauer, *Strategic Psychological and Sociological Strengths and Vulnerabilities of the Soviet Social System* (USAF Contract No. 33[038]-12909) (Cambridge: Russian Research Center, Harvard University, 1954), 20–22 and Annex 1 (on ISR role) and 360–68 (on use in strategic air offensive against the USSR).

38. Converse, *Survey Research*, 353, 531, fn. 17.

39. Converse, *Survey Research*, 309, 321–22, 327. See also House Committee on Government Operations, *State Department Opinion Polls*.

40. Charles Fritz and Eli Marks, "The NORC Studies of Human Behavior in Disasters," *Journal of Social Issues* 10, no. 3 (1954): 26–41.

41. Converse, *Survey Research*, 269, 275–76, 506–7, fn. 37, fn. 42.

42. On Air Force and Office of Naval Research studies, see ibid., 290, 506, fn. 37. On the Voice of America study, see Daniel Lerner, with Lucille Pevsner, *Passing of Traditional Society: Modernizing the Middle East* (Glencoe, Ill.: Free Press, 1958), 79–80. The Lerner study, which was conducted by CENIS using BASR data, is widely regarded as the foundation of the U.S. school of "development theory," which specializes in U.S. tactics in developing countries. For more detailed work on the origins of development theory, see Rohan Samarajiva and Peter Shields, "Integration, Telecommunication, and Development: Power in the Paradigms," *Journal of Communication* (Summer 1990), 84ff.; Rohan Samarajiva, "The Murky Beginnings of the Communication and Development Field," in *Rethinking Development Communication*, ed. N. Jayaweera and S. Amunugama (Singapore, Asian Mass Communication and Development Centre, 1987).

43. Lerner, *Passing of Traditional Society*, 79–80.

44. Simpson, *Psychological Warfare and Communication Research*. See also Bruce Lannes Smith, "Trends in Research in International Communication and Opinion, 1945–1955," *Public Opinion Quarterly* (Spring 1956).

45. For the role of Philippines counterinsurgency in the evolution of U.S. limited war strategy, see D. Michael Shafer, *Deadly Paradigms: The Failure of U.S. Counterinsurgency Policy* (Princeton, N.J.: Princeton University Press, 1988), 205–39.

46. MIT, CIS, "The Center for International Studies"; U.S. Department of State, FSI, "Problems of Development and Internal Defense."

47. William Lybrand, ed., *The US Army's Limited-War Mission and Social Science Research*, symposium proceedings. (Washington, D.C.: Special Operations Research Office, 1962).

48. Ibid., chart follows 28.

49. For *New York Times* and Lloyd Free's acknowledgment of the CIA's $1 million grant to Cantril, see note 7. On the CIA's use of the Human Ecology Fund and the related Society for the Investigation of Human Ecology as a conduit for clandestine funding of social science research, see Marks, *The Search for the Manchurian Candidate*, 147–63. On CIA contracting with the RAND Corporation, see Bruce L.R. Smith, *The RAND Corporation* (Cambridge: Harvard University Press, 1966); RAND Corporation, *RAND 25th Anniversary Volume* (Santa Monica, Calif.: RAND Corporation, c. 1974).

50. For examples of CIA-funded studies of torture of prisoners, see note 9. For secret U.S. government research into use of LSD, electroshock, insulin shock, and related "interrogation" techniques, see Marks, *The Search for the Manchurian Candidate*; Martin Lee and Bruce Shlain, *Acid Dreams* (New York: Grove, 1985).

51. On funding for Cantril, see note 7. Cantril's first target became a study of protest voters in France, whom the CIA regarded as hostile to U.S. foreign policy. Cantril followed the French study with a tour of the USSR under private scholarly cover and public opinion and mass media analyses of a series of countries that might serve as a checklist for CIA interventions of the period: Cuba, Brazil, the Dominican Republic, Egypt, India, Nigeria, the Philippines, Poland, and so on. On Cantril's studies in France, see Hadley Cantril, *The Politics of Despair* (New York: Basic Books, 1958). On Cantril's studies in the USSR and the Third World, see Cantril, *The Human Dimension*, 1–5, 131–44.

U.S. public opinion about foreign affairs, particularly about the Vietnam War and other controversial issues, became a major preoccupation of the research institute that Cantril founded with CIA funds. In those surveys, Cantril introduced an important methodological innovation by breaking out Americans' political opinions by their demographic characteristics and their place on an ideological spectrum he had devised—a forerunner of the political opinion analysis techniques that have revolutionized U.S. election campaigns during the past decade. See Lloyd Free and Hadley Cantril, *The Political Beliefs of Americans* (New Brunswick, N.J.: Rutgers University Press, 1967). For an example of modern usage of a similar technique, see "Redefining the American Electorate," *Washington Post*, October 1, 1987, A-12, with data provided by the Times Mirror-Gallup organization.

52. Lowery and De Fleur, *Milestones*, 205–31. See also Stuart Dodd, "Testing Message Diffusion from Person to Person," *Public Opinion Quarterly* (Summer 1952), 247ff. Air Force contract No. AF 13(038)-27522 underwrote much of the Project Revere enterprise.

53. Copies of some Revere leaflets are available via the University Archives at the University of Washington Libraries and in the papers of the Marks *Manchurian Candidate* study, which are now held by the National Security Archive, Washington, D.C. On the key role of children in diffusing air-dropped messages, see Otto Larsen and Melvin De Fleur, "The Comparative Role of Children and Adults in Propaganda Diffusion," *American Sociological Review* 19 (1954): 593–602.

54. Stuart Dodd, "Formulas for Spreading Opinions," *Public Opinion Quarterly* (Winter 1958): 537.

55. Chitra M. Smith, *International Propaganda and Psychological Warfare: An Annoted Bibliography*, BSSR Archives, Series II, Box 7, Project 819, University of Maryland Libraries Special Collections, College Park, Md.

56. Bruce Lannes Smith and Chitra M. Smith, *International Communication and Public Opinion* (Princeton, N.J.: RAND Corporation and Princeton University Press, 1956).

57. Kluckhohn, Inkeles, and Bauer, *Strategic Psychological and Sociological Strengths*.

58. Raymond Bauer, Alex Inkeles, and Clyde Kluckhohn, *How the Soviet System Works: Cultural, Psychological and Social Themes* (New York: Vintage, 1961 [1956]).

59. James Carey, *Communication as Culture* (Boston: Unwin Hyman, 1989), 30.

Chapter 14

Will You Love Me Tomorrow? Changing Discourses about Female Sexuality in the Mass Media, 1960–1968
Susan J. Douglas

In December 1960, something new happened in American popular music. A girl group, composed of four black teenagers, had the number-one hit in the country. The song featured an adolescent female voice deliberating plaintively about whether or not she should succumb to the seductive promises of love from her boyfriend. Should she give in and have sex with him, or heed the advice she had heard all her life, that if she did so, he would lose all respect for her and jilt her once he had gotten what he wanted? The lyrics of the song, written by Carole King and Gerry Goffin, poignantly evoked the girl's struggle. In "Will You Love Me Tomorrow," Shirley Owens, lead singer for the Shirelles, wondered whether the tender looks, longing sighs, and declarations of love, so seemingly genuine that night, were actually to be trusted.

The song represented a pivotal cultural moment. It inaugurated that era in popular music when girl groups, as well as individual girl singers, became a regular feature of, and often topped, the top-forty charts. In the mid-1950s, when Elvis Presley dominated the charts — in 1956, five of the nine top singles of the year were by Elvis — there would be weeks, and sometimes months, when no women or female groups had hits among the top fifteen records. By the early 1960s, it was not unusual for five of the top fifteen hits to be by female artists.[1] Although songs and movies by Elvis continued to be released while he was in the army, his forced removal from the rock scene signaled a sea change in the music industry and, in fact, in the culture industry at large. By the early 1960s, Elvis's brand of raw, sexually aggressive masculinity, which resonated with other male rockers such as Chuck Berry, Jerry Lee Lewis, and Little Richard, had to compete with a new sound and a new "female-centered pop sensibility."[2] Usually these singers were still girls, often they were African American, and many sang in groups. And they were not singing about doggies in windows or old Cape Cod.

In 1960, the year of the Shirelles' first number-one hit, there were approximately 11.7 million girls between the ages of twelve and eighteen in the United States, and they were exerting increasing economic clout. The average of four dollars a week a girl received as an allowance was spent on cosmetics, magazines, movies, records, and clothes.[3] In an effort to tap into this flow of discretionary income, executives in the culture industry, from film producers to admen, sought to produce music, films, TV shows, ads, and magazines that these girls would buy, both literally and figuratively. The goal, of course, was to cash in on this newly identified market of female "baby boomers."

One unintended and ironic result was that all of this marketing attention helped cultivate a highly self-conscious sense of importance and difference among these girls. The rise of so much popular culture addressed to teenage girls was key to an emerging, prefeminist sense of their own power and autonomy. All these media products conveyed the message, despite the retrograde images of beach bunnies, pliant girlfriends, and aspiring brides, that as a generation these girls really mattered, economically and culturally. This new, female-centered pop sensiblity gave this huge cohort of girls and young women a sense, however inchoate and apolitical, of historical destiny. They sensed they were freer of constraints than their mothers had been, that they were modern, "with it," riding a wave of progress, less old-fashioned; they sensed that anything was possible. Such a message, reworked over and over in books, films, TV shows, and popular music, helped set the stage for the feminist revolution of the early 1970s.

What gave rise to this sensibility? Most obvious, and probably most important, was the coming of age of that huge demographic bulge in the population subsequently labeled the baby boom, those children born between 1942 and 1964.[4] While the segregation of adolescents into a distinctive "youth culture" had begun to emerge gradually in the United States since the turn of the century,[5] it was in the 1950s and 1960s that this culture became huge, formidable, and distinctive. In the late 1950s and early 1960s, the growth rate of the teenage population took off at four times the average of all other age groups.[6] Above all, and forged especially by the rise of rock and roll, was this cohort's sense of itself as a group to be reckoned with. This was true for girls as well as for boys.

This chapter examines the proliferation of pop culture texts geared to young women in the 1960s, focusing on magazine representations of the "sexual revolution," the pregnancy melodramas *A Summer Place* and *Susan Slade* as well as *Splendor in the Grass*, girl-group music, and the TV shows *Bewitched* and *I Dream of Jeannie*. These now are regarded either with amusement, as the ultimate in high kitsch, or with contempt for promoting trivializing, objectifying, sexist images of women. I intend to reclaim these texts, and to argue that they had important historical consequences. At first blush it might seem that a movie such as *A Summer Place* or a song such as "He's So Fine" has absolutely nothing to do with feminism, except that it contributed to an ideology many young women would ultimately react against. I would like to suggest that such texts played a different and much more complicated role in women's history, and that by rereading them we can come to a richer understanding of feminism's immediate prehistory. Embedded in much of the popular culture of the time were changing discourses about what constituted female sexuality, which included critiques of the double standard, an acceptance that girls' sexual desires were normal and healthy, and images of girls acting on those desires without suffering dire consequences.[7] We need to consider these media texts as profoundly serious cultural documents that addressed the percolating aspirations, frustrations, and conflicts within young women that ultimately would lead them to reject the gender ideology of the 1950s and to seek out something new.

This popular culture hardly was progressive in any feminist sense of the word, yet neither was it as monolithic and oppressive as we might think. Rather, much of this popular culture was marked by major rifts, major fault lines within its ideological terrain. One of the principal rifts is a representation of patriarchy in crisis. Because these texts contained major contradictions about the proper balance between female passivity and agency, they problematized the young girl's stance toward her place within American patriarchy and within a culture obsessed by consumerism. These simmering criticisms, embodied in new images of young girls with some agency in the world, marked the beginning of a prefeminist sensibility that eventually led to the rise of the women's liberation movement in the United States.

My project, then, is to extend the existing historiography of the women's movement, and to argue that this prehistory of the second wave of feminism, with its beach movies, girl groups, and flying nuns, is a cultural history too long dismissed and overlooked, both by male cultural critics and by feminists. The standard accounts of the women's movement look to the experiences of young women in the civil rights movement and the New Left in the 1960s, document what they learned and how they were patronized, and then recount how these disaffected, usually radical women began organizing the foundational groups of the women's liberation movement.[8] These same histories also track the organizational history of liberal feminism, beginning with the Kennedy Commission's 1963 *Report on the Status of Women* and then reviewing the establishment of NOW and WEAL and the push for congressional passage of the ERA.[9]

While these are, of course, essential and important histories, they also are the histories of a relatively small group of women and are, therefore, incomplete. As primarily political histories, they do not examine in depth the convergence of a range of cultural and social factors that made a huge cohort of mostly anonymous and apolitical young women move from prefeminism to some version of feminism over a ten- to fifteen-year period. By reviewing the evolution of this upheaval from a cultural perspective and analyzing how it played out in the mass media, I hope to add to our understanding of the myriad factors that affected — and were affected by — the changing identities of teenage girls in the 1960s. Without those millions of anonymous young women, the women's liberation movement would not have had the enormous impact it did. The mass media played a central, if often inadvertent, role in this shift from prefeminism to feminism.

By the early 1960s, there was no longer simply a teen culture, defined as it was in the 1950s primarily by male voices and male performers. Now there was a distinctive teen girl culture, with teenage girl performers directly addressing teenage girl listeners. These voices sang about the pull between the need to conform and the often overwhelming desire to rebel, about the tension between restraint and freedom, and about the rewards — and the costs — of prevailing gender roles. They foregrounded, in other words, teen female ambivalence in the face of the major cultural contradictions surrounding gender roles in the early 1960s. In between songs about going to the chapel or wanting to be Bobby's girl were other tunes, songs about rebel boyfriends, defiant daughters, and new, sexually aggressive young women.

At the core of most of this female pop culture, then, was a discourse of ambivalence and contradiction. Visual representations of freedom, power, and sexual liberation were counterbalanced by admonitions about the dangers of assertiveness, license, and letting go. More than ever, girls were presented with "on the one hand, on the other hand" positions, since there were so many appealing points of identification to inhabit simultaneously. They could identify with Sandra Dee, the girl who gave in in *A Summer Place*, and with Natalie Wood, who didn't, in *Splendor in the Grass*. They could sing "Goin' to the Chapel" and Leslie Gore's "You Don't Own Me" and fervently embrace both sentiments. In the process of trying to produce texts that girls would find most authentic, texts that would successfully hail the teenage girl, the culture industry produced odd deformities in which the spirit and incipient rebellion of teenage girl culture was overlaid with images of witches, identical twins, and go-go girls in cages. However symbolized and expressed, the common theme was girls breaking out of both the visible and invisible constraints of bourgeois society, with varying degrees of success and punishment.

Like other feminist scholars, I will argue that examining the centrality of contradiction and ambivalence in feminine pop culture texts is key to our understanding of how the mass media, in certain cases, exacerbate such contradictions in women's lives and in their personal politics. My major assumption about these female audiences draws heavily from the recent work on female readership and spectatorship advanced by Janice Radway, Linda Williams, and Judith Mayne.[10] Whether studying women's responses to romance novels, film, or music, these scholars have argued forcefully that women have been socialized to become proficient at multiple, sometimes conflicting, readings of media texts in which they empathize and identify simultaneously with several characters. As Williams notes succinctly, because the female spectator is in a "constant state of juggling all positions at once . . . she tends to identify with contradiction itself."[11] These scholars have dismissed any notion of the unified subject or self: women are theorized to be filled with contradictory, often conflicting, positions vis-à-vis the dominant culture and are capable of assuming, are even urged to assume, a range of different subject positions depending on the situation, media form, and method of signification. As a result of this kind of viewing process, and the range of options provided to women in media texts, women become even more ambivalent and fragmented as subjects, even more riven with contradictory positions toward establishment norms.

I want to extend this kind of analysis to what I regard as other key popular culture texts of the early and mid-1960s and to argue that the contradictions embedded and, at times, foregrounded in these texts actually helped change history. I do not mean to suggest that the popular culture of this period rejected the highly circumscribed images and roles for women that reinforced heterosexual love and marriage as the ultimate goal for young women. Finding and landing the right man was still paramount in all these different narratives. But these texts contained ample criticism of 1950s bourgeois moral codes — what Laura Mulvey and others have called "fissures" and what John Fiske has cast as the "polysemic" text filled with "semiotic excess."[12] They encouraged and invited oppositional reactions to the status quo of American sexual and gender norms and ultimately helped pave the way for a larger critique of American patriarchy.[13]

By 1964, with the widespread proliferation of *Sex and the Single Girl*, *The Feminine Mystique*, and *Sex and the College Girl*, it was clear that the gender ideology of the 1950s, especially the "double standard" prohibition against girls indulging in premarital sex, was collapsing. This gradual overthrowing of the double standard — what came to be called the sexual revolution — constituted an essential prerequisite of the rise of the women's liberation movement. Feminists at the time, and some feminist scholars since, have regarded the sexual revolution with contempt because of the way it pressured women into being constantly available, compliant sex objects for men.[14] While fully acknowledging the criticisms of the sexual revolution, I argue that changing discourses about female sexuality in the early 1960s constituted the first important step in raising the consciousness of young women around the country. In sexual relations, with the double standard significantly eroded, young women by the late 1960s could behave as men had: they weren't supposed to remain virgins until marriage, and they didn't even have to restrict their premarital sex to a potential husband. When women could start behaving like men sexually, but were told they could not behave like men in any other sphere, a sense of inequity began festering in many women that eventually would change history. So the sexual revolution, with its undisputed oppressions and deeply disturbing consequences, was, simultaneously, empowering to many women. Tracking the way the media portrayed and promoted the sexual revolution from the early

1960s onward, especially when addressing women, is key to this history.

Media Coverage of the Sexual Revolution

By 1964, ascertaining the breadth and impact of the sexual revolution had become an obsession in national magazines. Although scholars have argued that the term is an exaggeration, and that the real revolution in sexual mores in the United States began in the 1920s, what mattered in the early 1960s was the widespread perception that such a revolution was occurring.[15] According to the magazines, the country was experiencing the collapse of the official morality of the 1950s, what the magazines labeled American puritanism. This perception was reinforced by two key factors. First was the FDA's 1960 approval of the birth control pill, and the subsequent assumption that this medication, by itself, had the power to transform sexual behavior, especially that of unmarried women. Second was the incessant media attention lavished on the sexual revolution, in the form of news stories and articles, and in the increasing use of sex to sell products. Underlying much of this commentary is a keen if unspoken sense that the sexual revolution posed a real threat, unless managed properly, to male privilege and power.

From the more personalized "My Daughter Is in Trouble" and "If Only They Had Waited" to the simple "The Sexual Revolution," news and general-readership magazines, women's magazines, and men's magazines all covered the sexual revolution extensively, beginning with the release of the pill in 1960, and on through the free sex movements later in the decade. The classic pattern in these articles was to overstate the rapidity and amplitude of the change, and to suggest that the new sexual permissiveness already was widely accepted by and acted upon by young people. In 1961, *Esquire* noted that "attitudes toward sex among those who grew up after World war II—those under thirty, in other words—are strikingly different from those of earlier generations. It can be summed up this way: sex is one of life's principal goods. And . . . there is far less reluctance about premarital sex."[16] *Newsweek* commented on the "increasing gap between official academic morality and actual sexual practices among high-school and college students."[17] Margaret Mead complained succinctly, "We have jumped from puritanism to lust," while Pearl Buck observed, "The change is so abrupt, so far-reaching, that we are all

356 Susan J. Douglas

dazed by it."[18] "America," proclaimed *Reader's Digest*, "seems to be engaged in one vast, all-pervading, all-permissive sexological spree."[19] The *Saturday Review* listed the three immediate causes for the spree:

Loss of the three deterrants to free sex practice—morality (undermined by the Kinsey report); venereal disease (attacked by penicillin); and fear of pregnancy (avoided by contraceptives, including the pills that one college boy gave to his girl as a Valentine present)—have resulted in a breakdown of the former bastions of chastity.[20]

What was especially fascinating — and worrying — to many writers was the demise of the double standard; in other words, the increased sexual activity of young women. It was women, wrote Pearl Buck, who were really adopting new sexual standards, and doing so without "any feelings of guilt or loss of self-respect."[21] While Ann Landers and other writers in magazines and newspapers exhorted girls to remain virgins until marriage, three widely read and discussed texts, all by women, linked female sexual activity to sophistication, modernity, and enlightenment. Gloria Steinem's "The Moral Disarmament of Betty Coed," Helen Gurley Brown's *Sex and the Single Girl*, and Gael Greene's *Sex and the College Girl* all suggested that the old puritanism, the old repression, the old denials, were just that: old-fashioned, anachronistic, and, above all, self-limiting.

Why did the old threats — conception, infection, detection — begin to lose their power over teenage girls in the 1960s? Repeatedly, contemporary observers linked the sexual revolution to the rise of relativism, to the highly self-conscious sense of modernity in the 1960s, to existentialism and the post-atomic dread of the abyss, to psychoanalysis, and to the increased commercialization of American life. Also cited was the increased social authority of science, particularly medical science. And no upheaval in prevailing moral codes would be complete without blaming parents, especially mothers. These explanations were particularly prominent when the focus was a favorite topic, sex and the college girl. Consonant with the upper-middle-class white bias of mainstream magazines, the sexual mores of black and working-class teens received little attention; it was, as one writer put it, "not girls from lower income levels [but] girls from our so-called 'best' families" who were surprising adults with their sexual behavior.[22]

According to these articles, educated young people refused to perpetuate the moral authoritarianism of their parents; they refused to impose their judgments on others, especially when it came to sex. As one girl reportedly told *Esquire*, "I used to think it was terrible if people had intercourse before marriage. Now I think each person should find his own values."[23] Another boy simply asked, "Who's to judge what is right and wrong?"[24] Condemning the "insidious influence of relativism — nothing is or is not true; nothing is or is not wrong; no one is responsible for anyone else in this existential era," Donald Eldridge, president of Bennett College, observed that the new sins were "hypocrisy, dogma, absolutes, provincialism."[25]

Relativism supposedly reigned because puritanism had become discredited as a pernicious, destructive, and unhealthy moral code, especially so because of its rigid, unforgiving, yet arbitrary absolutism. The popularization of psychoanalysis in the hands of writers such as Norman Brown in *Life Against Death* cast repression as a hateful straitjacket promoting death-in-life. "There is a tendency to see in sex" maintained *Time*, "not only personal but social salvation — the last area of freedom in an industrialized society." *Time* then pronounced, "The Puritan ethic, so long the dominant moral force in the United States, is widely considered to be dying, if not dead, and there are few mourners."[26]

Also cited as fueling the sexual revolution was the threat of Armageddon: "Two world wars led people to believe that tomorrow may never come, and that it is more important to live fully in the moment," wrote a *Reader's Digest* contributor, the mother of a son who had to get married. She also cited the fear that "there may be no tomorrow — only today."[27] Such resignation led to a connection between existential dread and sexual sophistication. As one boy told *Newsweek* about the rise in cohabitation among college students, "Living together makes me feel like an intelligent person — like Sartre and his mistress.[!]"[28]

The commercialization of virtually every aspect of modern life, and particularly sex, was also foregrounded by magazines that were, after all, promoting the very media trend they derided. In a cover story titled "The Second Sexual Revolution," clearly designed to sell magazines, *Time* cited the "innumerable screens and stages, posters and pages" that flashed "larger-than-life-sized images of sex." The message of all these media was that "sex will save you and libido make you free."[29] But the media could not effect such change on their own and were not really culpable: it was the parents, and especially the mothers, who were responsible for the erosion of sexual standards.

Donald Eldridge, in The *Saturday Review*, chastised parents who "long ago abdicated their responsibility in the area of sex education," but had special contempt for "the mother who fosters sexual precocity in her daughters and who herself has a very shaky concept of values, responsibility, and true affection." He was especially outraged by "the girls who, sometimes with the connivance of their ambitious mothers, deliberately trap desirable young men by getting pregnant."[30] It was mothers, in other words, who reduced sexual liaisons to commodity relations, because of the unbridled social climbing and grasping, unprincipled materialism of middle-class, older women. In these and other popular culture texts (especially films), mothers represented, simultaneously, unhealthy sexual repression and untoward sexual license, but both were used in the service of status-seeking opportunism for their often less worldly, "unspoiled" daughters.

Although the hegemony of 1950s morality was beginning to crumble, and many young people were rebelling against American puritanism, the magazines overstated the scope and impact, not to mention the repercussions, of the sexual revolution, and even contradicted themselves throughout this period.[31] At war with this picture of sex-crazed young women tossing the double standard out the window, sleeping with whomever they fancied, and demanding sexual satisfaction was the persistence of the old morality and its normative codes defining male and female sexual behavior. Pushed especially fervently by Ann Landers and other writers, and still given widespread representation in films and TV shows, was the dogma that boys were more easily aroused than girls, that they enjoyed sex for its own sake more than girls, that they had an unconquerable physical need for sex that girls did not, and that they did not respect girls they could go all the way with. Yet in a host of new movies, girls could see important and deeply appealing exceptions to such rigid and dire warnings.

Pregnancy Melodramas

In the early 1960s, many films geared to a young audience confronted this clash between the old and new morality head on. There was the emergence of a new kind of film, a cross between the woman's film and the youth film: the pregnancy melodrama. *A Summer Place* (1959), *Splendor in the Grass* (1961), *Susan Slade* (1961), *Parrish* (1961), *Love with the Proper Stranger* (1963), and *Where the Boys Are* (1960) are just a few examples of films from this period that place the issue of premarital sex between young people at the center of the narrative.[32] At the heart of all these films is the battle between American puritanism, with its unnatural repression and stifling hypocrisy, and the new morality, which truly allowed for a more healthy marriage between love and sex. Eager to cultivate the youth market, and relying more regularly on sexual themes to lure viewers, the Hollywood studios confronted sexual taboos that television shows, for example, distinctly avoided.

A Summer Place is an especially rich exemplar of this genre and is the film from this period that I will use to illustrate the way pregnancy melodramas mounted an explicit attack on 1950s morality. It is in this film that American puritanism is given its most perverse and demonic personification in the form of a frigid and tyrannical mother, Helen Jorgensen (played by Constance Ford), the mother of Molly (Sandra Dee). Helen and her husband Ken (Richard Egan) decide to vacation at Pine Island, a summer resort in Maine managed by Bart and Sylvia Hunter (Arthur Kennedy and Dorothy McGuire). It turns out that the Hunters have a very handsome and sensitive son, Johnny (Troy Donahue), just about Molly's age. But more to the point, we learn that Sylvia Hunter and Ken Jorgensen had had a passionate premarital affair on Pine Island twenty years earlier, and that each has regretted, ever since, leaving that relationship, in which sexual fulfillment and love were completely intertwined, for basically loveless and sexless marriages.

On the island, with the ocean pounding insistently all around them, Johnny and Molly begin courting, and Sylvia and Ken, meeting secretly at night in the boathouse, resume their affair. One day, Johnny takes Molly sailing, and they are shipwrecked overnight on a secluded beach. When they are rescued and return to the hotel, they assure their parents that "nothing happened," but Helen refuses to believe this story. She calls in a doctor and subjects Molly to a "complete physical" to confirm she is still a virgin, a procedure that makes Molly hysterical and Johnny furious. Helen also announces that she is aware of Ken and Sylvia's affair. The teenagers are shocked at their parents' infidelity, but remain deeply in love with each other. In the face of the scandal, Molly is sent to a finishing school in Boston and Johnny to a prep school in Virginia. Both the older couples divorce, so Ken and Sylvia can marry.

Ken and Sylvia then try to win back the love of their respective children, and finally convince Molly and Johnny to come visit — at the same time — their new ocean-front home. During this visit (also to the accompaniment of pounding waves), Molly locates a secluded shack where she and Johnny can be alone, and they make love. Not surprisingly, when Molly returns to school she discovers she is pregnant. But in this story, Johnny's instinct is not to leave her, and he certainly does not lose respect for her. He loves her and wants to marry her, and the prospect of having a baby makes him feel "warm all over." Unable to run away and get married because they are too young, they must turn for help to Sylvia and Ken, who, because of their own mistake twenty years earlier, are sympathetic and support the marriage. By the end of the film, Johnny's father has been hospitalized and Johnny and Molly take over the management of Pine Island as husband and wife to live in true wedded bliss.

Girls viewing the film are given two female points of identification, Molly (Sandra Dee) and Sylvia (Dorothy McGuire, always lovingly shot in soft focus). These are the beautiful, soft, to-be-looked-at women who are also compassionate, decent, and capable of true love. Their constant reward is that the men in the film always look at them lovingly, even gratefully. Both women straddle old and new definitions of womanhood: they are man-centered, nurturing, soft-spoken, and compliant, yet both have strong sexual urges that they regard as healthy and that they act upon.

Helen Jorgensen, on the other hand, is a witch no girl would want to emulate; she is identified, both by the dialogue and by the way she is shot, as coldhearted, twisted, and evil. She never says one thing in the entire film, or is photographed in any way, that is designed to invite identification by the spectator. She is a highly materialistic, status-obsessed monster who constantly equates sex with dirt: we know she is despicable because she refuses to share a bed with her husband. She is harshly lit, never bathed in the warm, rosy light that suffuses Sylvia's face. When we first meet her, it is not in the soft-focus close-up that introduces us to Sylvia; she's in a long shot, dressed mannishly and looking stern as she insists her husband wear a pretentious yachting outfit when they first arrive at Pine Island. Frequently, we also see her from unflattering low-angle shots (that also accentuate her authoritarian personality), and she constantly is spying on her daughter and her husband by watching them through windows or hiring the hotel staff to follow their movements. As spectators, girls know how to regard women in films who try to gain power by looking, and our rejection of Helen and her attitudes is firmly reinforced by the way her husband and Johnny look at her: with complete contempt. In Helen, sexual repression is personified as mean spirited and unnatural, as sick and retrograde. At one point Molly complains to her father of her mother, "She's anti-sex. She says all a boy wants out of a girl is that and that when a girl marries it's something she has to endure. I don't want to think like that. Poppa, she makes me feel ashamed of even having a body."

In this film, and others like it, the new relativism shows the destructiveness of the old morality in bold relief and maps it onto characters we care about. The female viewer can identify only with the two women who violated prevailing but clearly outdated sexual prohibitions against premarital and extramarital sex. Neither woman is branded for life, loses the respect of her man, or is punished in any way by the narrative. On the contrary, both women are amply rewarded: they get sexual fulfillment *and* their men and live happily ever after. In the person of Helen Jorgensen, the old sexual mores, embodied in an emotionally shriveled crone, must be exorcised, because they kill love and happiness.

But *A Summer Place* is also about the contemporary crisis in the patriarchal order, and it seeks to recuperate patriarchy in the face of the new relativism, increased sexual freedom for women, and the challenges of a rebellious youth culture. Sylvia's first husband, Bart, is constantly seen drinking (sometimes with his pinky in the air) and wearing an ascot; he cannot fix the leaky plumbing, manage the resort business, or, because he's too drunk and emasculated, make love to his wife. He is, simultaneously, emotionally crass and insensitive, mouthing old double-standard clichés to his son, urging him to regard girls as sex objects. By the end of the film, he has virtually drunk himself to death. Ken, on the other hand, is financially successful and virile, yet he strives to be compassionate and sensitive to Sylvia and Molly. If patriarchy is to survive, this character suggests, it must cultivate the feminine traits of nurturance and empathy while retaining economic and sexual power. But for the young female viewer it is in Johnny, the tender, loyal boy with his blond hair waving softly, even girlishly, over his forehead, that she sees her fantasy of a more humane and feminized patriarchy realized.[33]

Other pregnancy melodramas drive home the same message. In *Splendor in the Grass* it is repression that wins out, to the lifelong regret of two people obviously destined for each other, Deanie (Natalie Wood) and Bud (Warren Beatty). Set in Kansas in 1928, the film has built into it the message that American puritanism is an inhumane, thwarting ideology best left in the past. Again, the voice of repression comes from the mother, who constantly tells Deanie that "no nice girl" has sexual feelings for a boy, and that boys don't respect a girl they can go all the way with. The mother, when she's not spying on people through windows, is seen avidly following the stock market, and, as in *A Summer Place*, unnatural sexual repression is seen as a symptom of overweaning (and equally unnatural) materialism. Bud and Deanie constantly struggle against their sexual desires (often to the accompaniment of the pounding of the local waterfalls), repressing their urges as advised by their parents, until their love is destroyed. Deanie ends up in a sanatarium, and Bud is sent off to Yale by his wealthy, insensitive, money-grubbing father. Once the stock market crashes, Bud quits college and returns to Kansas married to a waitress he met, and leads the life of a struggling, unfulfilled farmer. Deanie and Bud's love was sacrificed to hypocritical, inflexible, and overly authoritarian sexual codes, a loss the narrative indicates was a completely unnecessary waste.

In another example, Connie Stevens, as the title character in *Susan Slade*, also falls in love and gets pregnant, only to have the father of the child killed in a mountain climbing accident before they can get married. Trying to conceal Susan's supposed shame, her family moves to Guatemala so she can have the baby in secrecy, and when they return to California two years later, Susan's mother (Dorothy McGuire) pretends the child is hers. Meanwhile, Susan is being courted by two boys, Hoyt Brecker (Troy Donahue), the sensitive, brooding local stable hand and aspiring novelist, and Wells Corbett (Bert Convy), the overconfident son of her parents' wealthy friends. After an accident nearly kills the baby, Susan refuses to live with her lie anymore, and acknowledges the child as her own. Once Wells hears her confession, he backs off from his earlier marriage proposal; Hoyt, however, affirms his love for Susan and they live happily ever after. Again, as in the other films, it is as if materialism and upper-class values and pretensions promote and nurture sexual hypocrisy. The truly attractive, decent, and lovable boy is the one who sees a girl for what she is and does not judge her by some outmoded, barbaric double standard. Again, the girl who indulges her passions (within the context of love, of course) is rewarded by the narrative and gets Troy Donahue. And Natalie Wood, in *Love with the Proper Stranger*, gains, through her illegitimate pregnancy, independence from her suffocating family and the love of Steve McQueen.

The Music of Girl Groups

It was in the popular music of the era, however, that the contradictory messages about female sexuality, agency, and rebelliousness received the widest array of expression. Tin Pan Alley, jolted out of complacency by the runaway success of rock and roll in the 1950s, began in the early 1960s to pursue the teen market much more aggressively.[34] Music publishers and producers hired teenage songwriters such as Carole King and Ellie Greenwich, cultivated many teen girl singers, and organized a host of new labels, all to produce records they hoped to sell to adolescent girls. As a result, pop music was the one area of popular culture in which the broadest range of adolescent female voices could be heard, producing what has come to be called "girl-talk" music. The main buyers of girl-talk records were, not surprisingly, young girls.[35]

While much has been written about the cultural significance of Elvis Presley, Bill Haley, and other male rockers to the baby-boom generation, the girl groups have received little serious scholarly attention.[36] Any music performed and favored by adolescent girls is routinely considered to be lightweight, formulaic, overly commercialized fluff of only fleeting import because female singers and their audiences are considered to have only a rudimentary understanding of what constitutes "real," authentic, artistically serious music.[37] In addition, the music of teenage girls is not thought to have any long-term influence, either on other music or on social change. When the music of girl groups has been considered by historians of popular music, it has been condemned for feminizing, and therefore ruining, rock and roll.

Yet, recent feminist analyses of girl music — most notably the work of Susan McClary and Barbara Bradby — challenge such interpretations, and urge us to consider how "girl-talk" music has functioned in shaping the identities of its listeners. Central to this process of identification, and to the success of such music, is the way these songs automatically assume, and give voice to, the ambivalent position of adolescent girls within patriarchal society. Both scholars focus on how such music provides multiple subject positions for the girl singers and their audiences, so that the listener can be, by turns, an active subject in pursuit of her man and a passive object, waiting and yearning to be noticed. Both women suggest that it can be empowering for young women to be able to try on such different personas, especially those that defy patriarchal norms and expectations. Then Bradby goes further. She suggests that such feminine discourses, filled with these kinds of contradictions, may have had some historical effectivity, since they are an integral part of the "historical process of conflict and change." She notes provocatively that "certainly it is striking that the name of the form 'girl groups' prefigures the main organizational form of the women's movement, the 'women's group,' which was also a form for the development of talk."[38]

One of the reasons popular music is so critical to women's history is that music is the cultural form most open to highly personalized readings and the form most closely tied to sexual expression and rebellion. As Susan McClary notes, because music is "often concerned with the arousing and channeling of desire," and because it "can cause listeners to experience their bodies in new ways," certain types of music can "influence and even constitute the way listeners experience and define some of their most intimate feelings." Thus, such music can and does "participate actively in the social organization of sexuality." As young people embraced rock and roll, McClary continues, "their notions of sexuality — their perceptions of their own most intimate dimensions of experience — split off irrevocably from those of their parents."[39] One key departure, and an important one, was the articulation of a position of active sexuality by schoolgirls.[40]

The question listeners were confronted with was this: Should she or shouldn't she? By extrapolation, of course, the question quickly became, Should I or shouldn't I? These questions were not only about sex, they were also about the degree to which girls should be assertive with boys, about how much agency it was proper for a girl to have in the world. They were also asking about whether girls should listen to their mothers, or rebel against them, especially when it came to obeying bourgeois codes of morality. Circumscribed within the confines of heterosexual love and marriage were images of rebellion, agency, defiance, and power, driven by an upbeat, usually danceable, and almost always euphoric music that seemed to promise transcendence and change.

Sexuality emerged, in these songs, as an eternal ache, a kind of irresistible, unquenchable state of constant tension. It involved "both desire and its prohibition."[41] The undeniable push for outlet clashed with the pull for containment; the need for expression collided with the need for sublimation; and the desire to seduce merged with a fear of seduction. The pleasures and pains of vulnerability comingled. The understanding that male-female relationships were necessarily masochistic, particularly for the girl, circulated with rejections of female victimization and passivity.

The discourse of girl group music was private, confidential, confessional, and knowing, and, either openly or furtively, it often was about sex. Through these songs, which were, by turns, boastful, rebellious, and self-abnegating, girls could assume a variety of female subject positions, some of them empowering and others masochistic. The songs were about escaping from yet acquiescing to the demands of American patriarchy. In them, girls enjoyed being looked at with desire; but they also enjoyed looking with desire themselves. They were surveyors, not just of themselves and their girlfriends, but of boys too. They were totally confident; they were abjectly insecure. Some songs said, "Do," and others said, "Don't." Sometimes the voices were those of an active subject out to get the guy or showing off her boyfriend to her friends. At other times, the voice was that of the passive object, yearning patiently to be discovered and loved. Most interesting, and most frequently, the girl played an active role in both her imaginary and real construction of herself as the object of the boy's desire.[42] As girls listened to their radios and record players, they could be martyrs to love, telling their former boyfriends to "walk on by," authorities who "know something about love," sexual aggressors, pursuing boys and urging them to call "any ole time," or, occasionally, prefeminists, as in such songs as "You Don't Own Me" and "Don't Make Me Over."

But it was not just that a song such as "I Wanna Be Bobby's Girl" offered a very different subject position from "You Don't Own Me." What is so interesting about so many girl-talk songs is the way contradiction is embedded within individual songs. As Barbara Bradby argues, girl-talk songs are different from male rock songs because "the female subject in the performance is divided against herself."[43] In the same song, a girl can be both passive and active, a victim and an agent, a duality encouraged by the structure of lead singer and chorus in most girl-group songs. By singing these songs to themselves, girls could imagine conforming and rebelling at the same time.

In all these songs, however, it was young girls who were speaking subjects, and, fanned by high sales, the proliferation of so much girl talk legitimated adolescent female subjectivity as having a rightful and necessary place in pop culture discourses. In these songs, girls were tied to each other by a special, exclusive knowledge of the pains and joys of narcissism and masochism. They knew things about boys and love that they shared with each other, and this shared knowledge — smarter, more deeply intuitive, more worldly wise than any locker-room talk — provided a powerful bonding between girls.

Female rebellion was expressed in a variety of ways. Most noteworthy were those songs that celebrated the rebel hero, the boy who rejected the moral codes of bourgeois society, the boy every girl's parents loved to hate. By allying herself romantically and morally with the rebel hero, the girl singer and listener proclaimed her independence from the safe, predictable expectations about being domesticated within a tame, respectable marriage.[44] He was the motorcyle rider the girl's parents were always putting down in "Leader of the Pack"; the social misfit who never did what he was supposed to do in "He's a Rebel"; the boy who cannot afford nice presents for his girlfriend because he is living on unemployment in "He's Sure the Boy I Love." But also of critical importance to these and other songs in which girls confided to each other about their boyfriends was the fact that the girls were knowing, active, speaking subjects while the rebel heroes and other boys were the objects of the girls' gaze and of their talk.

Because there is not space here to analyze all these personas or songs, I would like to discuss briefly how the contradictions between female agency and passivity were both managed and exacerbated in certain categories of songs. In "tell him" songs, such as "Wishin' and Hopin'," "Easier Said Than Done," and "Tell Him," the girl is advised to abandon the time-wasting and possibly boy-losing stance of passively waiting for *him* to make the first move. She is warned that passivity may cost her her man and is urged to act immediately and unequivocally. Yet the form of this action is to state her undying devotion to the boy, to do her hair exactly the way *he* likes it, to do what he wants to do, and to tell him she would die for him. The girl makes the first move, but only so she can quickly assume a more compliant and passive role. Nonetheless, In "Tell Him" and "Easier Said Than Done," the pulsing, exuberant dance rhythyms of the songs, with their euphoric feel, reinforce the liberating sense of transcendence from old gender restrictions, at least in the area of courting. In "Da Doo Run Run," the lead singer of the Crystals asserts that she will indeed make that boy hers, while the Chiffons in "He's So Fine" sing about picking out the right boy and going straight after him. Should a girl make the first move or not? The question was asked in girl-talk songs many times, and often the answer was yes.

In songs about teen desire, girls clearly responded with sexual pleasure to their boyfriends; for instance, in "And Then He Kissed

Me," the girl describes a new kind of kissing that she clearly wants more of. And in many advice songs, which warned about playboys, advised how to identify true love, and acknowledged that "you can't hurry love," the message that girls knew a thing or two, and that they would share that knowledge with each other to beat the odds in a man's world, circulated confidently from song to song. The fact that many of these songs explored the inner feelings of the girl singer herself provided easy and instant identification for the introspective female listener eager to latch onto any glamorized public representation of female subjectivity. Also key to this identification was something the already-fragmented teen subject recognized and took great comfort in: the division of the girl singer into two equally compelling voices — active and passive views of herself.[45]

Genies and Witches

On television, dealing with sex, and especially female sexuality, was a much more delicate matter. Network censors, prodded by nervous advertisers and FCC standards, imposed a host of now infamous taboos on the writers, producers, directors, and performers of television shows. But let's consider how such discourses worked their way even into television, and what young girls did begin to see on the tube. In the midst of the omnipresent westerns in the early and mid-1960s were new sitcoms, such as *Gidget* and *The Patty Duke Show*, designed specifically for teenage girls. What is much more fascinating, however, is the appearance of a new female mutant on TV, a hybrid of old and new, of negative and positive stereotypes. We saw the ghoulish Morticia in *The Addams Family* as a femme fatale; we saw a genie who was not a rotund, balding man but a shapely and beautiful young woman; and we saw a witch who was not a murderous old hag but an attractive young housewife. The potentially monstrous and grotesque was transformed and tamed; what we saw, in other words, was the metaphorical containment of the threat posed by unleashed female sexuality.

In *Bewitched, I Dream of Jeannie, Nanny and the Professor*, and *the Flying Nun*, a new version of the story of Pandora's box was acted out. Otherwise "normal"-looking female TV characters possessed magical powers, which men begged them not to use; if women did use them, their powers had to be confined to the private sphere. If women used these powers outside the home, in the public sphere, the male world was turned completely upside down. Business simply could not be conducted as usual, and logic and rationality were overthrown and rendered useless. Men were made impotent by these powers, and the husbands of such women were constantly stripped of their male authority and made to look foolish and incompetent in front of their male superiors. Although the men insisted (usually unsuccessfully) that their women not use these powers, there were two exceptions that the shows' narrative systems permitted: to complete domestic chores, and to compete over men.

Bewitched ran from 1964 to 1972, and for its first five seasons it was among the top twenty highest-rated shows; the year of its debut, it soared to number two, topped only by *Bonanza*. In *Bewitched* we have a woman's dream and a man's nightmare. Darrin was surrounded by an endearing yet constantly troublesome matriarchy, a domestic situation in which his wife, mother-in-law, daughter, and other relatives all were witches, endowed with magic powers that constantly threatened his professional status and his authority as head of the household. Samantha embodied important contradictions, for she was a happy, respectable suburban housewife who nonetheless exerted power beyond the domestic sphere. Samantha had magical powers, but she also excelled at the more mundane female duties of ensuring that social interactions ran smoothly. Often it was up to her to come up with an explanation for Darrin's boss or other outsiders to account for the bizarre goings on. Invariably, her explanation placated the irate or confused father figure, and often she succeeded in using the explanation to make Darrin or some other hapless man look good in the eyes of the older male authority figure.

What is especially interesting about the show is the way it offered, yet sought to diminish, a criticism of female confinement in the home. In the process, a fantasy about how the world might be better if men just listened to women once in a while was repeated week in and week out. It is hard to imagine a woman watching who did not identify with the fantasy of cleaning the kitchen or preparing dinner just by twitching her nose. But there were other telling fantasies as well, about having some agency in the public sphere. In an episode from the first season, Samantha and her mother, Endora, ate at Mario's Pizza and decided the food was so good that Mario deserved some publicity. Samantha, by twitching her nose, stopped the presses at the local paper and inserted a full-page ad that read "Eat at Mario's." When the ad came out, Darrin's client and Mario's competitor, the head of Perfect Pizza, was outraged and dropped Darrin's ad agency for letting Mario's get the upper hand. When Samantha learned that her husband's account was in jeopardy, she worked to repair the damage. She and Endora, using their magic, filled the town's billboards with ads, covered the sky with skywriting, and placed "Eat Perfect Pizza" placards on all the pedestrians in town. The delight they took in orchestrating this ad campaign was clear, as they each tackled a new medium, giggling and saying, "It's your turn" and "Now yours." At the end of the show, with the account saved, Darrin complained, "I'd appreciate your letting me handle my accounts by myself," to which Endora responded sarcastically, "Do you think you can?" Samantha insisted, "Of course he can—except under special circumstances."

In other episodes, Samantha used her magic to get the mayor to fix the town's traffic lights, to persuade a French fashion designer to design clothes that look good on "the average American woman" and not just on fashion models, and to expose political corruption and help get a reform candidate elected to city council. The repeated combination of magic, diplomacy (at which Samantha excels), and good, common sense made Samantha's solutions to problems the ones that were clearly the most viable and sensible. Here was an attractive suburban housewife with a great deal of influence, not just in her home, but in her immediate community. Her interventions in the public sphere were a mixed blessing, but often they expedited the solution to a particular problem. And despite his anger and frustration over the personal humiliations caused by Samantha's magic, Darrin always loved and admired her. The female point of identification here, Samantha—most frequently referred to by her masculine nickname, Sam—was passive and active, flouted her husband's authority yet complied with the role of suburban housewife, was both conforming and transgressive: she gave expression to traditional norms and prefeminist apsirations, all in one metaphorically fascinating character.

I Dream of Jeannie (1965–70, and a show enjoying one of the longest syndication records in television history) also featured a woman with magical powers, but this show was predicated on a more flagrant sexual display of Jeannie's body and her desires. And, of course, the narrative rested on a male fantasy of a regular, everyday guy discovering a beautiful, naive, unworldly woman at his beck and call who will do anything for him and calls him "master." But the implied powerfulness and availability of her sexuality were always a potential or actual threat to her master, Captain Tony Nelson, and sometimes he was most relieved and happiest when she was "in her bottle." Jeannie was always more amorous and sexualized than her master, and this, of course, is what got them into so much trouble. Captain Nelson tried in vain to contain Jeannie both physically and sexually. In those episodes where Jeannie's bottle was lost, there was considerable tension until it was found and Jeannie could get back inside it again. In *Bewitched*, Darrin's work in an advertising agency was compromised constantly by the inappropriate exercise of female power. In *I Dream of Jeannie*, the ante was upped: now, magic inspired by female desire, jealousy, and possessiveness constantly threatened to disrupt one of the crowning achievements of 1960s male technocracy, the U.S. space program. Even NASA was no match for female power and sexuality run amok.

Conclusion

All of the texts discussed here, while seemingly silly and inconsequential, together constituted an important and breakaway "on the one hand, on the other hand " discourse about girls taking action that not only revealed, but also accelerated, the dissolution of 1950s gender codes. In an attempt to cash in on the burgeoning teen girl market of the 1960s, a market that included conformists, rebels, and millions of girls who were both, the culture industry created a range of texts with many, often conflicting, points of identification for young girls. The films, songs, and TV shows of the period provided girls with different personas to inhabit, and while some were just as conforming, passive, and sexually restrained as any 1950s stereotype, others were not: they rejected mom's advice, they took up with the wrong kind of boy, they went all the way, and they had superhuman powers their husbands didn't.

No single film or TV show or book changed history. But the way their various representations overlapped, reinforced, and even contradicted each other had a cumulative effect on what young girls thought might be possible for them in the future. Instead of viewing the emergence of feminism in 1968 as a break with the past, we should see the women's liberation movement as, simultaneously, a reaction against and a product of this prefeminist pop culture imagery. Considering the way popular culture heightens our own internal contradictions, our fragmented subjectivity, is not interesting only theoretically; it helps us understand that at certain points in history, as young people wrestle with the implications of their increasingly ambivalent stances toward establishment culture, they can and do change history. And this is exactly what young girls in the 1960s did.

Many of these texts and the female personas they offered to young girls glamorized a new mind-set, a liberation from the rigid sexual dogmas of the past. We cannot know how young girls appropriated the meanings of all these texts, but it is clear that some of the positions offered to them were, in fact, prefeminist. Because teenage girls were invited to assume subject positions that were rebellious, that rejected the double standard, that provided girls with permission, even encouragement, to have some agency in the world, they gradually, over time, became more emboldened, more questioning of the status quo, and more desirous of liberation, first from minor constraints, and then from very large ones indeed. After nearly a decade of trying on the personas of the rebel, the sexual sophisticate, the knowing girl who was bonded to other girls in a group, and the witch with larger-than-life powers, some girls — certainly enough girls — decided they did not want to imagine, fantasize, or pretend anymore. By the early 1970s, they wanted this power for real.

Notes

1. See chart listings in Norm N. Nite, *Rock On Almanac* (New York: Harper & Row, 1989).

2. Charlotte Greig, *Will You Still Love Me Tomorrow?* (London: Virago, 1989), 38.

3. Landon Jones, *Great Expectations: America and the Baby Boom Generation* (New York: Coward, McCann & Geoghegan, 1980), 73.

4. Some scholars date the beginning of the boom at 1946, when the number of births exceeded three million and continued to rise, while others choose 1942, the first year births exceeded three million. Although these dates are somewhat arbitrary, I prefer 1942 because of the impact eighteen-year-olds were having on the culture in 1960.

5. Beth L. Bailey, *From Front Porch to Back Seat: Courtship in Twentieth Century America* (Baltimore: Johns Hopkins University Press, 1988), 9–10.

6. Jones, *Great Expectations*, 68.

7. Here I follow Stephen Heath and others who argue that sexuality is not something biologically fixed or immutable, but something that is constructed and constituted through our interactions with cultural representations of what sexuality supposedly is. See Stephen Heath, *The Sexual Fix* (New York: Schocken, 1982).

8. Accounts of the rise of radical feminism include Sara M. Evans, *Personal Politics: The Roots of Women's Liberation in the Civil Rights Movement and the New Left* (New York: Vintage, 1979); Alice Echols, *Daring to Be Bad* (Minneapolis: University of Minnesota Press, 1989).

9. See, for example, Judith Hole and Ellen Levine, *Rebirth of Feminism* (New York: New York Times Book Co., 1971), ch. 2; Maren Lockwood Carden, *The New*

Feminist Movement (New York: Russell Sage Foundation, 1974); Sara M. Evans, *Born for Liberty* (New York: Free Press, 1989), ch. 12.

10. Janice A. Radway, *Reading the Romance* (Chapel Hill: University of North Carolina Press, 1984); Linda Williams, " 'Something Else Besides a Mother': *Stella Dallas* and the Maternal Melodrama," in *Home Is Where the Heart Is*, ed. Christine Gledhill (London: British Film Institute, 1987); Judith Mayne, "The Woman at the Keyhole: Women's Cinema and Feminist Criticism," in *Re-Vision: Essays in Feminist Film Criticism*, ed. Mary Ann Doane et al. (Frederick, Md.: University Publications of America, 1984).

11. Williams, " 'Something Else Besides a Mother,' " 314.

12. Laura Mulvey, "Notes on Sirk and Melodrama," in *Home Is Where the Heart Is*, ed. Christine Gledhill (London: British Film Insitute, 1987), 75; John Fiske, "Television: Polysemy and Popularity," *Critical Studies in Mass Communication* 3 (December 1986).

13. Mulvey, "Notes on Sirk and Melodrama," 75; Fiske, "Television," 391–408.

14. For example, see Hole and Levine, *Rebirth of Feminism*, 218–22.

15. See John D'Emilio and Estelle Freedman, *Intimate Matters: A History of Sexuality in America* (New York: Harper & Row, 1988).

16. David Boroff, "Among the Fallen Idols: Virginity, Chastity and Repression," *Esquire*, July 1961, 98.

17. "Sex on Campus," *Newsweek*, August 12, 1963, 75.

18. Pearl S. Buck, "The Sexual Revolution," *Ladies' Home Journal*, September 1964, 43.

19. William I. Nichols, "Let's Not Panic at the 'New Morality,' " *Reader's Digest*, July 1966, 75.

20. Donald A. Eldridge, "More on Campus Mores," *Saturday Review*, June 20, 1964, 58.

21. Buck, "The Sexual Revolution," 44.

22. Virgil G. Damon and Isabella Taves, "My Daughter Is in Trouble," *Look*, August 14, 1962,

23. Boroff, "Among the Fallen Idols," 98.

24. Joan Beck, "The Big Question for Teens: Morality," *Today's Health*, May 1965, 27.

25. Eldridge, "More on Campus Mores," 58.

26. "The Second Sexual Revolution," *Time*, January 24, 1964, 55.

27. "If Only They Had Waited," *Reader's Digest*, January 1965, 87.

28. "Unstructured Relations," *Newsweek*, July 4, 1966, 78.

29. "The Second Sexual Revolution," 54.

30. Eldridge, "More on Campus Mores," 58.

31. A study done in 1964–65 by Mervin Freedman at Stanford established that three-fourths or more of America's unmarried college women were virgins, and that premarital intercourse among college women was usually restricted to their future husbands. A later study also established that the sexual revolution really began in the 1970s. See Mervin Freedman, "Sexual Behavior of College Girls," *School and Society*, April 3, 1965; Sandra L. Hofferth, Joan R. Kahn, and Wendy Baldwin, "Premarital Sexual Activity among U.S. Teenage Women over the Past Three Decades," *Family Planning Perspectives* 19 (March/April 1987).

32. I have chosen these films because they relied on teen idols and starlets—

Troy Donahue, Sandra Dee, Natalie Wood, Warren Beatty, Connie Stevens, and Connie Francis—who, it was hoped, could lure in young audiences. Three of these films were also among the twenty top-grossing films of the year: *Splendor in the Grass* (1961, ten; 1962, nineteen), *Where the Boys Are* (1961, twenty), and *Love With the Proper Stranger* (1964, eighteen).

33. I am grateful to Joan Braderman for this observation.

34. Greig, *Will You Still Love Me Tomorrow?* 38.

35. Barbara Bradby, "Do Talk and Don't Talk: The Division of the Subject in Girl Group Music," in *On Record,* ed. Simon Frith and Andrew Goodwin (New York: Pantheon, 1990), 343.

36. Exceptions include Greig, *Will You Still Love Me Tomorrow?*; Alan Betrock, *Girl Groups: The Story of a Sound* (New York: Delilah, 1982); Bradby, "Do Talk and Don't Talk."

37. For a discussion of the exclusion of women from music and the dismissal of female music, see Susan McClary, *Feminine Endings: Music, Gender and Sexuality* (Minneapolis: University of Minnesota Press, 1991).

38. Bradby, "Do Talk and Don't Talk," 344.

39. McClary, *Feminine Endings,* 8–9, 25.

40. Bradby, "Do Talk and Don't Talk," 345.

41. Jacques Lacan, quoted in ibid., 343.

42. Ibid., 358.

43. Ibid., 345.

44. Greig, *Will You Still Love Me Tomorrow?* 51.

45. Bradby, "Do Talk and Don't Talk," 356, 359.

CONTRIBUTORS

Holly Allen is a Ph.D. candidate in the American Studies Program at Yale University. Her main areas of interest include late nineteenth-through mid-twentieth-century social and cultural history, with a focus on gender, class, and nationalism. She is also interested in contemporary cultural studies and feminist theory. Her dissertation (in progress) is currently titled "Fallen Women and Forgotten Men: Gendered Anxieties about Community, Home, and Nation, 1929–1947."

Gerald J. Baldasty teaches in the School of Communications at the University of Washington. His research in the past five years has dealt primarily with the U.S. press in the nineteenth century and focuses on how business concerns shape the news. He is the author of *Commercialization of the News in the Nineteenth Century*.

Jon Bekken, former general secretary-treasurer of the Industrial Workers of the World (IWW), has published articles on the labor movement and related subjects in labor newspapers throughout the world. He has presented his research on labor and working-class newspapers, new communication technologies, book publishing and distribution, and community radio to the Association for Education in Journalism and Mass Communication, the American Journalism Historians Association, the International Communication Association, and other professional associations and labor conferences. His historical writings and book reviews have appeared in the *Journal of Communication Inquiry*, *American Journalism*, the *Journal of Communication*, and *Nature, Society, and Thought*, among other journals. He is an assistant professor in the Department of Communication Studies at the State University of New York at Cortland. He received his Ph.D. in communication from the University of Illinois.

Nancy E. Bernhard is a Henry Luce Fellow in Religion and Public Policy at Harvard Divinity School. She earned a doctorate in American history at the University of Pennsylvania.

Susan J. Douglas is professor of media and American studies at Hampshire College. She is the author of *Inventing American Broadcast-*

ing, 1899–1922 and is completing a book on feminism, antifeminism, and the mass media between 1960 and 1980. She has published both scholarly and journalistic articles on the history and impact of the media in the United States, and currently writes the "Pundit Watch" column for the *Progressive*.

Albert Kreiling is associate professor of communication arts at Johnson C. Smith University in Charlotte, North Carolina. He teaches communication history, communication research, and public relations. He is the author of articles in several journals and anthologies, as well as a current director of one professional communications association and a former officer of two others.

Robert W. McChesney is an assistant professor in the School of Journalism and Mass Communications at the University of Wisconsin — Madison. He is the author of *Telecommunications, Mass Media, and Democracy: The Battle for the Control of U.S. Broadcasting, 1928–1935* and has had more than a dozen scholarly articles published since 1987. He earned his Ph.D. in communications at the University of Washington. Before entering graduate school, he published a rock magazine, the *Rocket*, in Seattle, and worked as a free-lance sportswriter for the wire services.

Eileen R. Meehan is a political economist specializing in the culture industries and media arts. She has written on the history of the ratings industry, the blind-spot debate, commercial intertextuality, and the commodification of culture. She received her doctorate from the Institute of Communications Research at the University of Illinois, Champaign-Urbana, in 1983, and she currently teaches in the Department of Media Arts at the University of Arizona in Tucson.

John C. Nerone is research associate professor at the Institute of Communications Research of the University of Illinois. He is the author of *The Culture of the Press in the Early Republic* (1989) and *Violence against the Press in U.S. History* (in press).

Christopher Simpson teaches journalism at the American University in Washington, D.C. He has won the National Jewish Book Award for historical writing, the Joel H. Cavior/Present Tense Literary Prize, the Investigative Reporters and Editors Prize for investigative reporting, and other national prozes for history and journalism. He served as research director for Marcel Ophul's documentary *Hotel Terminus: The Life and Times of Klaus Barbie*, which won the 1989 Academy Award and the International Critics Prize at the Cannes Film Festival. His work has been translated into German, French, Japanese, and other languages.

William S. Solomon is assistant professor of journalism and mass media at Rutgers University. He has a Ph.D. in sociology from the University of California, Berkeley, and has worked as an editor at the *Providence Journal*, the *San Francisco Chronicle*, and the *Oakland Tribune*. He researches and writes on media history and sociology of news.

Lynn Spigel is an assistant professor in the School of Cinema-Television at the University of Southern California. She is author of *Make Room for TV* (1992) and coeditor of *Private Screenings* (1992) and *Close Encounters* (1991). She is also coeditor of *Camera Obscura: A Journal of Feminism and Film Theory*.

Linda Steiner teaches in the Department of Journalism and Mass Media at Rutgers University. Her research interests include feminist theory and ethics as well as mass media history, with particular attention to feminist and women's media. Her research has been published in *Critical Studies in Mass Communication*, *Journalism Quarterly*, *American Journalism*, and *Journalism History*.

Michael Warner is an associate professor in the English Department at Rutgers University. He is the author of *The Letters of the Republic: Publication and the Public Sphere* (Harvard University Press, 1990), on which his contribution to this volume is based. He has also edited *Fear of a Queer Planet: Queer Politics and Social Theory* (University of Minnesota Press, forthcoming) and, with Gerald Graff, *The Origins of Literary Studies in America* (Routledge, 1988). His articles on American culture and gay theory have appeared in such places as *Raritan*, *American Literature*, the *Village Voice*, and *Social Text*.

INDEX

379

Woman's Journal, 66, 70, 72–73, 84–87,
90–91, 93, 96 n. 72, 97 n. 81
Woman's Standard, 90
Woman's Tribune, 68, 73, 88–89
Women's Christian Temperance Union,
90
Women's Educational and Industrial
Union, 90
Women's Trade Union League, 164
Wood, Natalie, 361–62
Woodhull, Victoria, 83, 87

Woodhull & Claflin's Weekly, 83
Workingman's Advocate (Chicago), 160
World Briefing (TV show), 301
Wren, Jack, 293
Wright, Edward H., 190
Wythe, George, 29

Yale University, 320, 346 n. 34
You Asked for It (TV show), 269
Young, Donald, 346 n. 34
Young, Frank, 180